AF681114

Law and Local Society in Late Imperial China

MARK A. ALLEE

Law and Local Society in Late Imperial China

Northern Taiwan in the Nineteenth Century

STANFORD UNIVERSITY PRESS
STANFORD, CALIFORNIA 1994

Stanford University Press
Stanford, California
© 1994 by the Board of Trustees of the
Leland Stanford Junior University

Printed in the United States of America

CIP data are at the end of the book

Stanford University Press publications
are distributed exclusively by Stanford
University Press within the United States,
Canada, and Mexico; they are distributed
exclusively by Cambridge University Press
throughout the rest of the world.

Acknowledgments

SUSAN Naquin and Wallace Johnson as mentors and friends have been instrumental in guiding and nurturing my own intellectual and scholarly development. Sue in particular has been stern taskmaster and sympathetic advocate in just the right proportions as I wrestled with this work as dissertation and manuscript. I thank them for their support and encouragement over a number of years. I owe a less personal but not less important intellectual debt to the many earlier Chinese, Japanese, and Western scholars of Taiwan whose diligence and insights made this project possible.

While in Taiwan I was the beneficiary of assistance from researchers at the Academia Sinica, especially Chang Wejen of the Institute of History and Philology and Chang P'eng-yuan of the Institute of Modern History. The staffs of the Fu Sinian Library, the National Central Library–Taiwan branch, the Archives of the Taiwan Provincial Historical Commission, and the National Palace Museum Library were unfailingly helpful.

In the United States, my research in several East Asian collections—at the University of Pennsylvania, Princeton University, and the University of Chicago—has always been a pleasant and fruitful experience, and I thank curators, directors, and staff for their help.

Several readers and commentators have struggled to help make this a better book. I want to thank especially Jonathan Ocko, William Alford, Roger Thompson, and Philip C. C. Huang. Noriko Kamachi kindly brought some important recent Japanese studies to my attention.

My early research was supported by grants from the Social Science Research Council and the Pacific Cultural Foundation, and I thank them for their support. I am also indebted to Loyola University Chicago for financial support and time off to complete the manuscript.

At Stanford University Press, Muriel Bell has skillfully and tactfully shepherded the manuscript to publication.

At all stages of work, my wife, Ruth, has provided inspiration, encouragement, and assistance in too many ways to acknowledge fully. To her and my son, Spencer, I dedicate this book.

M.A.A.

Contents

Tables, Figure, and Maps

TABLES

FIGURE

MAPS

Note to the Reader

BELOW I list the Qing reign periods, describe my practice in the use of Chinese and Western dates, and provide a summary of common weights and other measures used frequently in the text.

REIGN PERIODS

Shunzhi (SZ 1–18), 1644–61	Daoguang (DG 1–30), 1821–50
Kangxi (KX 1–61), 1662–1722	Xianfeng (XF 1–11), 1851–61
Yongzheng (YZ 1–13), 1723–35	Tongzhi (TZ 1–13), 1862–74
Qianlong (QL 1–60), 1736–95	Guangxu (GX 1–33), 1875–1907
Jiaqing (JQ 1–25), 1796–1820	Xuantong (XT 1–4), 1908–11

CHINESE AND WESTERN DATES

In most instances in the text, lunar dates are rendered as they appear in the source documents in year, month, and day order and then are followed in parentheses by the corresponding Western dates: for example, GX 8/4/23 (8 June 1882). Intercalary months are indicated by an "i" before the month number: for example, GX 13/i4/5.

MEASURES OF WEIGHT AND DISTANCE

16 *liang* = 1 *jin* or catty
1 *jin* = 0.597 kg or 1.3 lb. (approximately)
100 *jin* = 1 *dan* or picul

1 *li* = 0.576 km or one-third mile (approximately)

CURRENCY EQUIVALENTS

1,000 cash = 1 tael (approximately)
1 tael = 1 *liang*, a Chinese ounce of silver

1 *yuan* = 0.7 *liang* (approximately)
10 *jiao* = 1 *yuan*
1 *yuan* = 1 dollar

Law and Local Society in Late Imperial China

1

Introduction: History and Law

SOCIETY THROUGH COURT RECORDS

"History from the bottom up" has been the rallying cry of more than one generation of historians. The struggle to shift the focus of writers and readers of history from the conspicuously obvious actions and attributes of elites, central governments, and (inter)-national politics to the finer detail of local society and government, ordinary people, and their everyday lives and concerns has achieved a significant degree of success. Such an approach reminds us that many of the political, economic, and social forces that engender historical change are generated by the interplay of social groups composed of common men and women. Having lived unremarkable lives as individuals, they have left relatively few traces of themselves or their activities to assist those who come after in understanding the past. Nevertheless the bottom-up approach to history, while a valuable corrective to a profession that once seemed to focus too much on governments and great men, often fails to live up to our or its own expectations.[1]

The failures of social history sometimes result from an excessive swing of the pendulum to a perspective that seems to portray societies and people for whom politics, government, and the state did not exist or were irrelevant. One of my objectives in this study of a nineteenth-century Chinese locality is to strike a balance between methodological approaches that describe at one extreme a polity without subjects or conversely autonomous social groups to which the state is almost irrelevant. In the field of Chinese history the former kind of distortion has been more common. The success and continuity of the traditional Chinese state long rendered it nearly impossible for historians of China to see much else but government. Still, there has been some tendency to view the ordinary Chinese peasant's existence as one in which the imperial state was merely an unpleasant but occasional intruder extracting wealth or compelling donations of labor and returning little of worth.

This disjunction between state and society is of course a distortion produced by our limited ability to perceive very clearly the loci of interaction between Chinese government and the Chinese people. In traditional times, these nodes of interaction were the lowest levels of government, the counties, departments, and subprefectures that formed the interface between the entire multilayered, hierarchical state structure and the peasants, artisans, shopkeepers, intellectuals, and other members of most social groups in the country. This study attempts to inch closer to these vital points of intersection by utilizing records of litigation filed at a local court toward the end of the imperial period.

These case records suggest the great significance of law in traditional Chinese society and the importance of understanding the relationship between the two if we wish to comprehend either. The relationship was dynamic, and each exerted a powerful influence stimulating change in the other. It is commonly accepted that laws and legal systems reflect in some general way the society that produced them and change, however imperfectly, in response to new social realities. It is no less true, in China as elsewhere, that powerful institutions such as legal systems shaped or even initiated social transformation. Each of these points—but especially the second—will be argued in greater detail through the rest of this study. The evidence from these cases will show how the decisions of a local court in inheritance disputes, charges of refusal to pay land rents, problems between different ethnic and subethnic groups, and other cases operated to encourage the evolution of local society in specific ways.

The local court that generated the case records on which this study relies was situated in a town just a short distance from the seacoast in the northwestern quadrant of the island of Taiwan. This town, first named Zhuqian and later rechristened Xinzhu,[2] was the seat of successive basic-level administrative units that were part of the Chinese state ruled by the Qing dynasty, whose demise in 1911 marked the end of two millennia of imperium. The officials in charge at the lowest level of the imperial government hierarchy administered counties (*xian*), subprefectures (*ting*), or departments (*zhou*). The subprefects[3] and county magistrates posted to Zhuqian and Xinzhu were responsible in ascending order to prefects, provincial-level officials (governor-general, governor, judicial commissioner, financial commissioner, circuit intendant), and the central government ministries. All were ultimately subservient to the emperor.

China's long imperial epoch terminated in early-twentieth-century revolution. Already by that time, however, Taiwan had been lost to China as a result of the Treaty of Shimonoseki ending the Sino-Japanese War of 1894–95. The island remained a Japanese colony until the end of World War II. For that reason, this study concludes in 1895, when the Chinese court system in Xinzhu ceased to function. The next chapter will set the scene and sketch the history of the political units and of the process of Chinese settlement in the area governed by local chief administrators headquartered in Zhuqian / Xinzhu.

Other historians of China have taught us that the interaction of state and society was most intense and thus most likely to have produced usable historical evidence when crimes were committed. When rebellion, first on the list of the ten most serious crimes, was successfully suppressed, the records and accounts of the government campaign and, sometimes, the testimony and confessions of those involved in the uprising have revealed in often intimate detail the lives of ordinary people, albeit in extraordinary circumstances.[4] Summaries of more ordinary cases appealed to the highest judicial organ, the Board of Punishment in the capital, have also been a productive resource in getting closer to Chinese society.[5] These somewhat more prosaic legal records, however, have been so severely compressed and shorn of detail that often only issues of legal technicalities remain clear, while the circumstances surrounding the original crimes or disputes that gave rise to the cases have nearly disappeared from view. Recently the availability of routine memorials on criminal cases (*xingke tiben*) in the First Historical Archives, Beijing, has begun to produce very interesting and important work on late imperial society and law.[6] These routine memorials, while extremely valuable, also suffer, although perhaps to a lesser degree, the defects of compression and abstraction characteristic of other central government documents.

The virtues of these sources and methods of exploiting them are manifest, but the realities they describe are to some degree illusions. Rebellions and those who hatched them, even when unsuccessful, were not part of everyday life in Qing China. Nor were bizarre crimes or ambiguous legal issues representative of the quotidian criminal trials and civil litigation handled by local courts. It is precisely the unremarkable nature of the disputes and minor offenses ordinarily dealt with by local courts that make such cases valuable for their insight into daily life.

To a lesser degree the approach adopted in this research cannot avoid the same criticism of atypicality. A criminal trial is a symptom of some breakdown of the social order. Assaults, armed affrays, robberies, murders, and kidnappings described in the cases were symptoms of social pathology. Civil cases, even though considered less serious, indicated that one or both parties to a transaction felt their relationship so out of kilter that only the courts could redress the balance. Rent payment disputes, arguments over land boundaries, and struggles within families over inherited property, while not of course unknown, were also not everyday occurrences.

Law case records have conspicuous imperfections as historical evidence. Certainly criminal suspects with life or liberty to lose and litigants hopeful of material gain had clear reasons to conceal the facts. But local officials hearing cases were well aware of this and usually tried to ferret out the truth. With careful, skeptical evaluation the petitions, statements, reports, testimony, and findings included in the legal cases prove to be extremely valuable and thus far underutilized sources for historical inquiry.

A less obvious analytic ambiguity is introduced by distinguishing between criminal and civil legal cases in traditional China. The sharp distinction drawn between the two categories in the Western tradition was not nearly so clear in China. Of course, even in the West, a single act may render one liable for both civil and criminal penalties. The possibility of dual liability postulated by Western legal philosophy is, however, not the same as the attitude of Chinese jurists that the analytical and procedural differences between what we now think of as criminal and civil cases were insignificant. What I will refer to throughout as civil cases were, to the Chinese courts, merely "minor matters" that were handled with procedures that differed only slightly from those used in criminal cases. A single legal system handled all cases (except those involving bureaucrats charged with administrative malfeasance). However, even though the procedures of "civil" adjudication were usually not significantly different from those of "criminal" trials, it will occasionally be convenient for the purposes of our discussion to make the distinction. I shall have more to say about the two kinds of cases later in this chapter in a discussion of the sources for this study. Here let me simply assert that for this locality the records of civil litigation in many ways are more useful than criminal cases in revealing fundamental socioeconomic institutions and processes.[7]

Such a statement is merely another way of pointing out that local court case records such as those I use are invaluable materials for anyone hoping to comprehend the lives and concerns of ordinary men and women who have otherwise disappeared from the record of the past. Law case records also take us a giant step closer to understanding the relationship between local courts and local society. Only after we have taken this step will we begin to be able to evaluate properly the role and significance of the legal system in the Chinese tradition. First, however, in order to understand both the possibilities and limitations of a study such as this one, it is imperative to understand the nature of the case records and their history.

SOURCES FOR THIS STUDY

The Dan-Xin Archives

Preserving the records of over 1,000 proceedings, the Dan-Xin archives (*Dan-Xin dang'an*) are a collection of case files that until

1895 were stored in the archives of the local government offices in Zhuqian and Xinzhu. These cases, although a substantial body of material, are only a small fraction of all the litigation handled by the local yamen during the years between 1789 (the date of the earliest case in the collection) and 1895. David C. Buxbaum has already described and characterized the Dan-Xin archives in a general way.[8] The preliminary observations and conclusions drawn by Buxbaum remain valid, although certain details require correction. In what follows, I shall draw on my own research in the cases as well as Buxbaum and other sources to sketch the history and nature of these cases.

When Japanese troops moved into Xinzhu in 1895, the yamen and its contents passed intact into the hands of the new colonial authorities. These documents included an extensive collection of records of all kinds, including those now known as the Dan-Xin archives, the only portion of the collection known to have survived to the present. The new Japanese administrators were able to draw up a quite useful and in the main accurate outline description of Xinzhu's former administrative system using the yamen materials.[9] During the first years of the colonial period, at least one Japanese researcher probably relied on the legal case records when formulating a description of the legal process under the former regime.[10] According to Dai Yanhui, after 1895, custody of the Dan-Xin cases, then prosaically denoted as the "Taiwan documents" (*Taiwan bunsho*), was assumed successively by the Xinzhu local court, the Court of Appeals, and eventually the Literature and Political Science Department of Taihoku (Taibei) Imperial University.[11] With the end of World War II, Taiwan reverted to Chinese control. The university, eventually to be renamed National Taiwan University, retained the Dan-Xin materials, which were nominally part of the law school collection.

Even before the end of Japanese rule, Dai, a Japanese-trained Taiwanese lawyer, had begun to utilize the cases for research purposes. Over the years Dai, with the help of others, sorted, put in order, and classified the cases into three broad categories: administrative, civil, and criminal (see below). Selections were published in 1955 (35 documents) and in 1971 (475 documents), in both instances taken from the administrative cases.[12] So far no further publication of any Dan-Xin cases has yet appeared.[13] Access to the documents has been limited, but fortunately the cases are available on microfilm at several institutions in the United States and abroad.[14]

The Dan-Xin cases have received relatively little scholarly attention. Dai himself has written several important articles, since collected and republished, that rely heavily on administrative cases from the archives.[15] Ke Fangzhi utilized several of the civil cases in an article on residential lease contracts, and recently Shi Tianfu has found deeds and other documents from several of the cases useful in illuminating the early settlement of the region just north of Xinzhu.[16] In English, so far as I am aware, there is only Chang Bin Liu's study of commercial law.[17] In Japanese, there is Shiga Shūzō's introduction to the types of documents found in the case files.[18]

Several reasons may help account for the archive's neglect. In the first place, for many years virtually the only resources available for the study of the traditional Chinese legal system were either legal codes and other prescriptive legislation issued by the imperial government or drastically compressed summaries of legal cases that had been appealed to the highest judicial authorities in the capital. Although some excellent work based on these sources has been done,[19] and much remains that could be accomplished in this area, legal history and sociological jurisprudence are underpopulated fields of sinological study. A new translation of the Qing Code has now been completed, although as of this writing it has not yet been published.[20] Of earlier dynasties, only codes of the Qin (221–207 B.C.), Tang (618–907), and Yuan (1264–1368) have been translated even in part.[21]

Others have used somewhat different approaches to the study of law in Chinese history with some success. William Alford, for example, was able to find many details on one particularly notorious murder case that became a center of national attention in the 1870s. Hugh Scogin has shown how Han period land documents can help us understand the legal treatment of contracts in early (and perhaps late) imperial China.[22] Brian McKnight has published useful studies of imperial amnesties and forensic medicine.[23] Japanese historians, particularly Niida Noboru, have been the most imaginative in sifting through literature, drama, and other nonlegal sources for material. In the People's Republic of

China the 1980s saw some renewed interest in the legal thought and legal system of the imperial period.[24] Still, it remains true that research on the social role of law has been meager.

We might expect social historians to evince more interest in the use of legal records. Even after the publication of Buxbaum's article, though, the Dan-Xin cases have remained largely unused. Thus we find that even the increasing popularity of social history over the past two decades or so has not created much interest in the cases, and that few scholars have been drawn to the archives because of an interest in the law itself.

Beyond these problems of sources, access, and academic fashion, there is also the fact of Taiwan's location on the periphery of the Chinese empire. The island's remoteness from the traditional centers of Chinese civilization and culture may raise questions in the reader's mind of the applicability of this case study to other parts of China. Such questioning, however, can be directed against research focused on any locality in China. In an empire constructed from a number of discrete macroregions, local histories come to represent the whole only as they are aggregated and synthesized in considering issues of empire-wide significance.[25]

Fortunately for practitioners of local social history, one positive consequence of changing fashions in historical research has been a growth in and acceptance of local and regional studies of areas outside Beijing and the lower Yangtze, which as the political, social, and economic centers of China had long drawn most scholarly attention. Numerous monographs focusing on regions, provinces, counties, cities, and even villages and individual families have appeared. In the field of Taiwan studies, a lonely but meritorious example of this genre is Meskill's excellent history of an important central Taiwan lineage. It has been the social scientists, though, who have shown the most initiative, since they have seen Taiwan as offering an unparalleled opportunity to do fieldwork. By supplementing fieldwork with sources from the imperial and Japanese colonial periods, anthropologists have produced most of the important work in English on Taiwan local history.[26] These promising beginnings have recently been augmented by studies that have started to reveal Taiwan's importance on China's maritime frontier during the late imperial period.[27] We may hope that such work may serve to kindle a new interest in the island's history as well as to suggest its place in macroregional and larger contexts.

The Dan-Xin Case Files

In spite of the natural deterioration of paper and ink in century-old documents, using the original Dan-Xin case materials would have been preferable to the microfilm. Unfortunately, this was not possible until after the bulk of the research for this study was completed, and thus my research has relied almost entirely on the microfilm version. This imperative introduced the usual problems and frustrations familiar to anyone who has worked with this medium. The nature of Chinese archival materials themselves added a few special hurdles. Although nearly all of the documents in the case files were written in very legible regular script (*kaishu*) calligraphy by professional clerks, most annotations or emendations were written in running (*xingshu*) or even cursive (*caoshu*) style. Deciphering the personal idiosyncrasies of the latter two writing styles was impeded by the obscurity inherent in microfilm and aggravated by errors or carelessness during the filming process. Some items that appear in contrasting colors of ink or paper and so are perfectly legible in the originals appear uniformly black (and often perfectly illegible) on the film. This is especially true of the seal impressions in red ink that were stamped over black-inked text and the labels written with black ink on red slips of paper such as were pasted on sketch maps. In general, however, the microfilmed Dan-Xin documents are reasonably clear and readable. Errors that appear in this study should not be attributed to physical damage or defects in the source materials.

As for the use of the Dan-Xin archives in historical research, Buxbaum has discussed the issues of the type of disputes, the time period of the archive cases, and the frequency and representativeness of the cases that have survived. The character of the Dan-Xin cases will become more apparent in the main body of this study, especially in Chapters 3 through 6. In those chapters I discuss five complex cases that display features typically found throughout the case files. An aspect of several of the longer cases, including three of the five core cases of this study,[28] is that a single case file often contains other distinct subcases that are in some way related.

Appendix 1 provides a translation of the table of contents of the

Dan-Xin archives as organized and classified by Dai Yanhui and published along with the selected documents mentioned earlier.[29] Of the 1,161 total cases in the archives, nearly half (574, or 49.4 percent) were classified as administrative.[30] As a glance at the case classifications in Appendix 1 will confirm, these cases arose out of the operations of the local yamen or its agents and for the most part do not typically reflect disputes between private individuals. For this reason I have not drawn on these "administrative cases" for this study except in Chapter 8, where a description of certain quasi-official personnel is necessary to understand the extent of the yamen's law enforcement capability. Consequently, the discussion here, as in the bulk of the text, will emphasize the civil and criminal cases that make up the remaining 50 percent of the collection. Of the 587 civil and criminal cases, 62.2 percent were criminal complaints and 37.8 civil.

Below the broad, tripartite grouping, the cases are placed in more specifically descriptive categories such as armed robbery, marriage, rent resistance, and the like. Dai derived these categories from labels on the original files, internal evidence, and traditional legal concepts. The three superordinate groupings are, however, based on analytic principles drawn mainly from Western legal traditions.[31] Qing legal authorities did not think of the cases in this way. Many writers have concluded that there was no explicit concept of civil as distinct from criminal law.[32] Shiga Shūzō, for example, speaking of the entire dynastic period, held that "no institutional distinction was made between civil and criminal judicial procedure, even under the Ch'ing."[33] In fact, as Buxbaum has already shown, even to Qing lawmakers there were some clear differences (notably in procedures governing the acceptance of complaints for adjudication) between criminal proceedings and certain other cases, that is, those we now conceive of as involving civil matters.[34]

Most of the cases that Dai Yanhui classified as "civil" (*minshi*; see Appendix 1, part B) in the Dan-Xin archives were, in the view of Qing legal officials, minor disputes over household matters, marriage, and real property (called in Chinese *huhun tiantu*). These categories are articulated clearly in a substatute contained in the legal code of the Qing dynasty.[35]

Each year from the first day of the fourth month through the thirtieth day of the seventh month, the time when farmers are busiest, no complaints from the people (*minci*)—except for serious matters of breaking the law such as plotting rebellion, sedition, or treason, robbery, homicide, corruption, or bribery and also cases of treacherous brokers or shopkeepers who swindle merchants of their goods in which investigation has shown there is definite proof, all of which are to be accepted and handled as usual—that involve minor matters of the household, marriage and real property (*huhun tiantu deng xishi*), are to be approved for adjudication.

Such disputes were "minor" in the sense that they were ideally to be resolved through mediation and compromise without recourse to the courts. As the Dan-Xin cases show, the preferred option for local judges faced with "minor" disputes was to refer the parties to a mediator, even if the complaint had been brought to court because mediation had already failed. When outside arbitrators were unable to resolve the issue, the local magistrate not uncommonly then took on the mediator's role himself.

In traditional Chinese law these *huhun tiantu* disputes were not regarded as seriously as crimes involving force, violence, or personal injury. In contrast, in the Qing legal code one entire section containing 82 statutes and hundreds of substatutes was devoted to such "minor" matters.[36] Procedurally, litigation stemming from disputes that the court had decided constituted "minor" matters of household, marriage, or real property could be filed on only six days of each month, would not be accepted at all during the busiest time of the year for agriculture (that is, the fourth through seventh lunar months), and could be appealed from local courts up through the prefecture and to the provincial financial commissioner—but no higher.[37] Once a lawsuit was accepted by local courts, however, there were few differences in the subsequent process of initial adjudication before appeal. The course of litigation at the local level will be explored in more detail in later chapters, where I will draw on the case file records of both "minor" or "civil" disputes and "serious" or "criminal" offenses as both were defined in the Code substatute cited above. As the preceding discussion has suggested, "minor" and "serious" complaints in traditional Chinese law can only be approximated by the labels "civil" and "criminal" as used in Western law. This qualification should be kept in mind in the following chapters when at certain points for the sake of convenience I will refer to cases as "civil" or "criminal."

The final point that must be addressed in this brief characterization of the cases is their dating, frequency, and representativeness. Buxbaum provides a useful table listing the number of cases per year.[38] My own count of the cases, on which the following discussion is based, yielded totals that are not significantly different. Only two of the 587 civil and criminal cases occurred before 1840. By the 1870s, the survival rate of case records increases greatly, with nearly two-thirds (384, or 65.4 percent) of the civil and criminal cases filed during a fourteen-year period, 1878–91.[39] Buxbaum, speaking of a slightly different time frame, 1879–95, notes that during this period the percentage of civil cases relative to all cases remained relatively constant at somewhere around 15 to 20 percent. He suggests that because the ratio was relatively constant, it gives a real indication of the proportion of different types of cases heard by the court.[40] If, however, we confine our comparison to civil and true criminal cases, the above conclusion becomes less certain. The administrative cases may be excluded because the documents in them are not directly connected to any type of litigation. The number of criminal cases is also misleading. Of the 236 criminal cases for the 1878–91 period, 37 percent (88 cases) fall into the "General Matters" category. The nine subcategories, which are listed in Appendix 1, contain files that were compiled because of administrative measures or problems that arose in connection with criminal cases. Consequently, these 88 files are not true case files and artificially inflate the criminal case total.

Once the administrative cases and the "General Matters" criminal cases are excluded, we find that the annual ratio of civil to true criminal cases varied widely from more than twice as many civil as criminal cases (14 versus 8) in 1888 to less than one-third as many civil cases (4 versus 13) in 1885. The variations even out over the course of the 1878–91 period. In fact, there are by my count exactly equal numbers of civil and true criminal cases—148 in each category. I infer from this not that Buxbaum was mistaken but that the numbers we have are not reliable enough to reach valid conclusions. We simply have no idea of the true number of cases, whether civil, criminal, or administrative, that were handled. Taiwan's subtropical climate, the method of storage in a premodern government office, and changes in policies on retention of archival materials must have resulted in a high and probably highly erratic rate of document loss. Even deliberate destruction of records during the transition to Japanese rule cannot be ruled out. Anyone who had previously received an unfavorable court ruling might well have seized the opportunity to destroy all records of the adverse decision.[41] Moreover, had the yamen in Zhuqian had storage responsibility for cases originating in the much larger commercial center at Mengjia (present-day Taibei), the incidence of commercial disputes in the Dan-Xin archives might have been quite different.[42] If we add to these considerations the murky history of the archives during the Japanese colonial period, it seems that any statistical manipulation of the numbers would be a frivolous exercise. The cases must be utilized in a different fashion.

The Core Cases

The amount of material in the 1,161 Dan-Xin cases is considerable. My intention in selecting a few complex cases for close analysis has been to choose case files that were generated by and thus capable of illuminating some of the most vexing social and economic issues during the period (1840–95) in northern Taiwan. In other words, I argue that the five cases chosen show both directly and indirectly many of the problems that led ordinary people in Danshui and Xinzhu to appeal to state power to resolve disputes. Each of the five cases was before the court for three or more years, one for over a quarter-century. In the relevant chapters the three civil and two criminal cases have been summarized, each prefaced with an analysis of the socioeconomic and cultural factors that combined to generate legal proceedings.

In range and sheer bulk these five core cases provide a representative sample of the whole while at the same time reducing the scope of this study to manageable size. Each of the five case files contains more than 100 documents. One has more than 200.

While these core case summaries provide concrete, narrative foci for this study, the later chapters, which describe and analyze litigants, certain court personnel, and the trial process at the local level, are based on evidence drawn from the Dan-Xin archives as a whole. In Chapters 7, 8, and 9, apart from the five summarized cases, I will cite data from numerous other civil, criminal, and (as noted above) even administrative case files as well.

Other Sources

The Dan-Xin cases by themselves would provide a peculiarly skewed and incomplete view of both society and local government in Taiwan. For background, context, and supplementary information I have relied heavily on more conventional sources: local gazetteers, memoirs, and government documents. Over 300 such works were reprinted between 1957 and 1972 in a series of publications by the Bank of Taiwan's Economic Research Office.[43] This undertaking has been a very great boon to those interested in Taiwan's past.

One of the late-ripening fruits of Japanese imperialism during the late-nineteenth and twentieth centuries has been publication of findings from survey and research programs carried out by colonial or occupation authorities in order to better understand and control their new possessions. In Taiwan after 1895, the Japanese Government-General (*Sōtokufu*) financed a massive research program on socioeconomic conditions and political arrangements under the former administration. Invaluable published materials have resulted, including reprints of many historical documents, records of interviews with local inhabitants, drawings, maps, and photographs, as well as numerous articles and book-length works. My debt to these sources will be evident in subsequent chapters.

Besides such published works, a large body of archival materials generated by the Government-General is held by the Taiwan Provincial Historical Commission (*Taiwan wenxian weiyuanhui*) at its headquarters in Taizhong. These documents are mostly records of the day-to-day administration of the colonial government, but the archive does include some material relevant to the pre-1895 era.[44] In addition to these "primary" materials, I have relied heavily on the large number of secondary works on the history of their locality by Chinese in Taiwan. A number of journals specializing in Taiwan local history have been extraordinarily rich sources.[45]

After a short introduction in Chapter 2 to the physical and historical environment of the locale on which this study is focused, I will move on in the following four chapters to an analysis of some of the areas of social and economic conflict that were the proximate causes of litigation and criminal behavior. I shall attempt to impart a fuller sense of immediacy and historical reality through summaries of five long cases, which, because of their complexity or simply because of their drawn-out nature, illustrate many of the facets of the relationship between society and the legal system. The three chapters (7–9) that follow will explore in more detail the roles that litigants and court personnel assumed or into which they were thrust. These chapters will also analyze some of the institutional and procedural constraints influencing the actions of litigants and the resolutions of the cases in which they were involved. Each of these chapters centers on successive stages of a typical legal proceeding. Finally, the concluding chapter attempts to characterize and assess the role played by the legal system in binding together the diverse social and ethnic groups within its jurisdiction. In nineteenth-century Taiwan and in traditional China generally, law and the courts reacted to changing social and economic circumstances. At the same time, the legal system influenced the nature of social change. Through this study of local court records we are able to examine in minute detail the intersection of state and society in late imperial China.

2

Danshui and Xinzhu During the Qing Dynasty

The Geographical and Historical Context

GEOGRAPHY

The farm villagers, market townsmen, aboriginal tribesmen, and city residents whose cases were tried by the Dan-Xin court made their homes on the northwestern coastal plains and hilly uplands of northwestern Taiwan. The Dan-Xin area is bounded on the west by the waters of the Taiwan Straits and on the east by the nearly impenetrable central mountains of the island.

Danshui subprefecture included all the land between the Dajia River, its southern boundary, and the port city of Jilong on the northern tip of the island. (The central mountains were inhabited by unpacified tribes and were not considered part of the subprefecture.)[1] The area is made up of several topographical regions, as indicated on Map 1.

Further administrative changes resulted from increases in population, areas of settlement, and numbers of villages and towns; the growth of commerce and trading networks; and foreign policy considerations. These reorganizations resulted in a more articu-

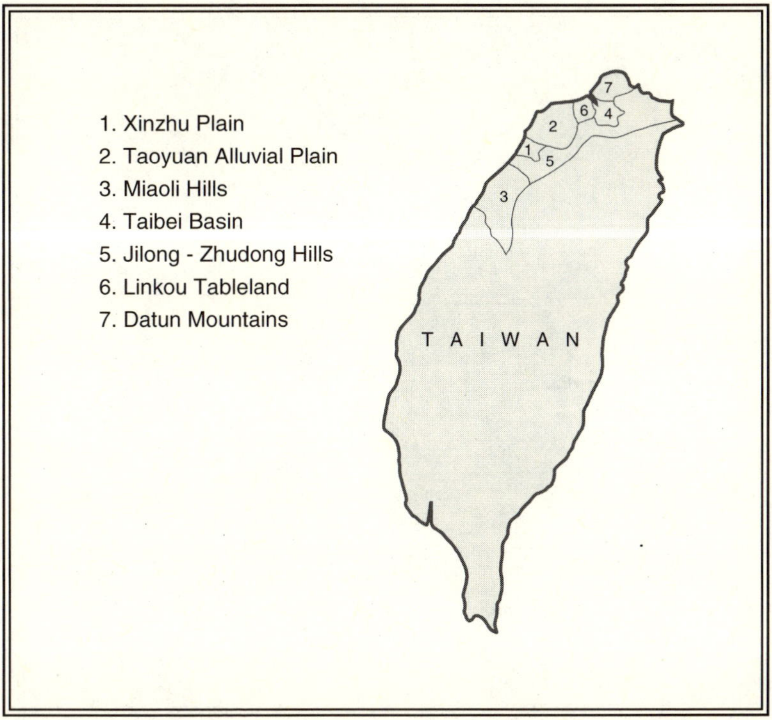

MAP 1. Taiwan and Danshui Subprefecture Before 1875. Adapted from Chen Zhengxiang, vol. II, 769, Map 313.

lated administrative structure and more intensive government control. First the subprefecture was abolished and Xinzhu county was created from a part of it. Then the southern half of Xinzhu county was split off to form Miaoli county. This process, over a fifteen-year period ending in 1889, halved and then quartered the area controlled by the local yamen that produced the records on which I have based this study.[2]

THE EVOLUTION OF ADMINISTRATIVE JURISDICTIONS[3]

After the collapse of the Ming dynasty in 1644, Zheng Chenggong (called Koxinga by Europeans) and his descendants engaged in an ultimately futile attempt first to dislodge the new Qing dynasty

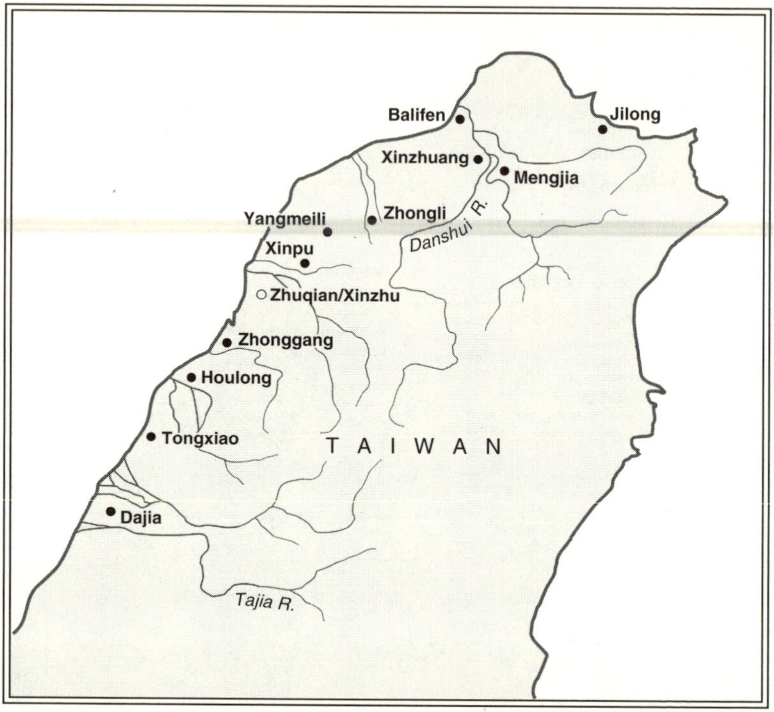

MAP 2. Danshui Subprefecture in the Nineteenth Century. Adapted from Taiwan sōtokufu kambō bunshoka, front matter; Chen Peigui, 2–6.

and then merely to maintain one last stronghold against it. First in southeast China and then, after 1662, on Taiwan, Zheng and his forces continued their resistance. In 1684, a year after the remnants of the Zheng regime finally surrendered to the Qing, Taiwan (or more accurately the part of it already settled by Han Chinese) was formally incorporated into the empire. Taiwan *fu*, a prefecture subordinate to Fujian province, was established (with its headquarters in modern Tainan), encompassing the entire island. At first, the new prefecture was divided into three subordinate counties. In 1723, in the wake of a major rebellion and some expansion of Chinese settlement into the island's north, the office of Danshui subprefect was created.

Along regional frontiers where defense and security were the major problems facing local government, the Chinese state tended to establish subprefectures or departments rather than counties.

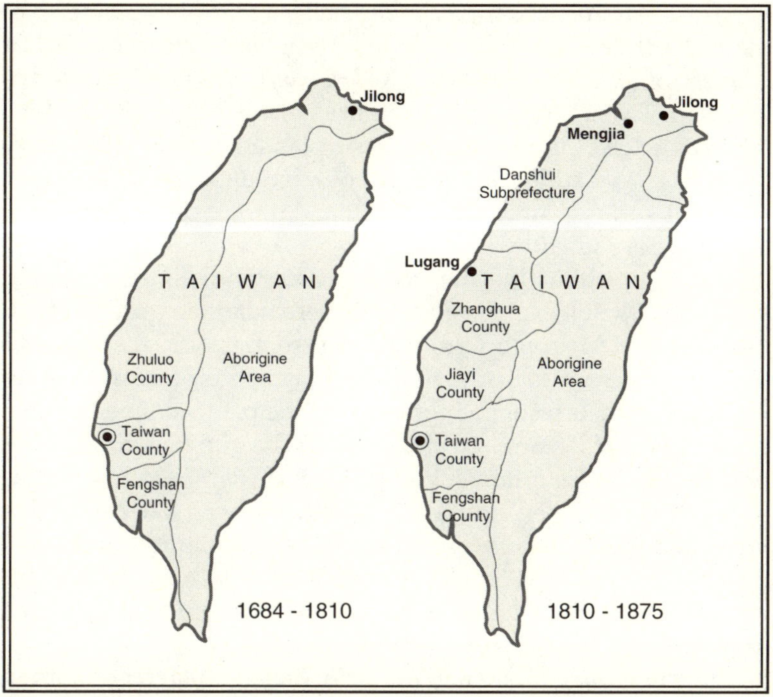

MAP 3. Pre-1875 Taiwan Administrative Units, 1684–1810 and 1810–75. Adapted from Yang Xi, 29–30.

Whereas a county magistracy could be assigned to neophyte officials, only men with previous administrative experience could receive appointments as subprefectural or departmental chief administrators. In this way the state ensured that strategic posts would be staffed by men with demonstrated competence.[4] The creation of Danshui subprefecture epitomized the policy.

The new subprefecture was to be responsible for maritime defense and apprehension of criminals for the entire area north of Zhanghua county in central Taiwan.[5] At the time, the Han population in the north was not felt to be sufficiently high for the institution of a new administrative center, although a location, Zhuqian, had already been selected. Therefore, for a 30-year period after the creation of the new administrative post, Danshui subprefects were still headquartered in the Zhanghua county seat. In the meantime, in 1731, subprefects were officially made responsible for judicial and fiscal administration (*xingming qianliang*) for the area north of the Dajia River (see Map 2). In the same year, the vanguard of Chinese officialdom, a police chief (*xunjian*), was finally posted in Zhuqian. Two years later, the site was fortified for the first time when a hedge of thorny bamboo was planted around it.[6] Military protection was added in the form of a battalion stationed there, and finally in 1756 offices were built and the subprefect moved to Zhuqian permanently.

Farther north, at the mouth of the Danshui River, a second police chief's office had been established at Balifen (near present-day Guanyin Mountain) in 1733.[7] In 1750, this official's post was moved farther up the river to Xinzhuang, the off-loading site for merchant vessels bringing goods to the incipient commercial center that would become greater Taibei. (The site of Xinzhuang is now in the southwestern suburbs of Taibei city.) In 1790, after the area had experienced continued growth, the post was elevated to vice subprefect (*xiancheng*) and moved again slightly down and across the river to Mengjia, the earliest settlement within the actual city limits of modern Taibei. The position was thereafter known as the Mengjia vice subprefect.[8]

The yamen in Xinzhuang and later Mengjia played an important role in the governance of the northern third of the subprefecture. Even before the end of the eighteenth century, Mengjia was a faster growing and more prosperous port town than Zhuqian. Two adjacent commercial towns, Dadaocheng and Dalongtong, both founded in the nineteenth century, eventually combined with Mengjia to form the most important commercial, marketing, and export center on the island. In addition to the yamen of the vice subprefect, a large concentration of military offices came to be located there. The subprefectural seat, however, remained in Zhuqian.

In reality, Danshui subprefects spent only half their time in the subprefectural seat. For a variety of reasons it became necessary and desirable for them to spend much of their time in Mengjia. Mengjia was one of four locations for official granaries where tax grain was delivered. Because of the granary and because of the locale's growing commercial importance and rise in population from at least the last quarter of the eighteenth century on, much official business (including litigation) was generated in the area.

Since no official subordinate to the subprefect was entitled to accept lawsuits, subprefects found it expedient to set up temporary headquarters in Mengjia, if only to prevent the vice subprefect from reaping all the licit and illicit rewards accruing to government officials who controlled wealthy areas. The affluence of Mengjia merchants and of the town in general made such temptations more difficult to resist for the vice subprefect and his staff, and made the subprefect's annual trek northward that much more pleasant.

Of greater implications for this study was the fact that, as a result of this system of dual subprefectural seats, the records of most legal cases handled by the subprefect while in Mengjia remained there and have not survived. Thus, out of necessity this study focuses only on Zhuqian / Xinzhu and its hinterland. Studies of the Taibei basin and its dependent areas whose law court was in Mengjia must be left to others.[9]

The subprefecture's southern half was not devoid of official presence. In 1816, a police chief previously stationed in Lugang in Zhanghua county was transferred to Dajia, a market town on Danshui's southern boundary.[10] With the establishment of the Dajia post, Danshui's administrative boundaries and centers remained stable until 1875 (see Map 3).

Internally the subprefecture was divided into twelve townships (*bao*). These townships were important units for quasi-official administrative and law enforcement organizations designed to extend yamen control outside the immediate vicinity of Zhuqian (see Map 4). I will have more to say about them in Chapter 8.

By the 1870s, and especially in the aftermath of an 1874 foreign policy crisis with Japan, the Qing government decided that the northern part of Taiwan had assumed such strategic and commercial importance that another administrative upgrading was warranted. There was, in fact, a complete reorganization of the administrative structure on the island. In the north, a new prefecture was created to control the upper third of the island. The site chosen for the prefectural seat was the outskirts of Mengjia on the Danshui River. Danshui subprefecture was abolished, and its former territory was split into two counties with the dividing line being essentially the Touchong, a stream rising near Yangmei (in modern Taoyuan county) and flowing west and slightly north to enter

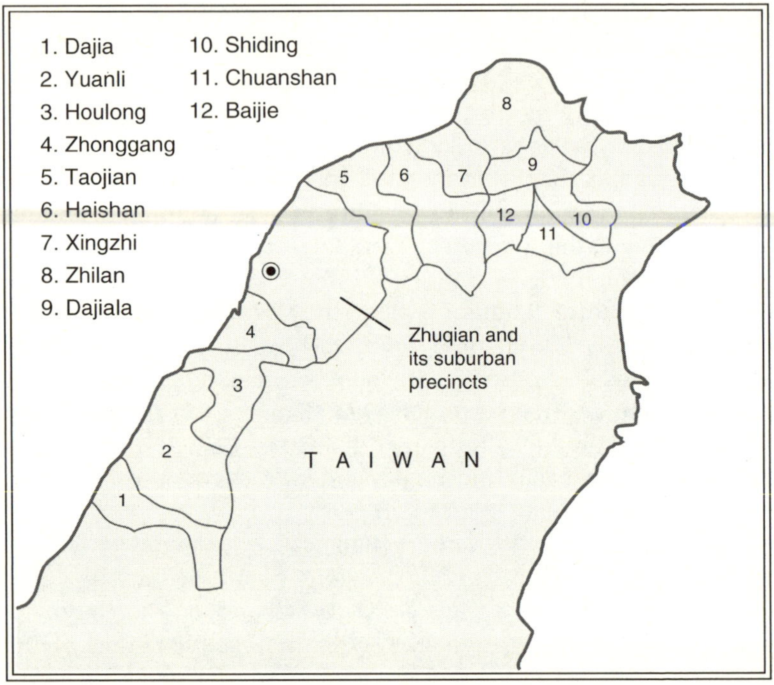

MAP 4. Townships in Danshui Subprefecture in 1840.

the Taiwan Straits about 25 kilometers north of Zhuqian. Land north of the Touchong stream fell within the jurisdiction of Danshui county (which eventually had its own yamen and court), and as such it passes out of the scope of this study.[11] Old Zhuqian, renamed Xinzhu, became the seat of a new county of the same name. The old yamen offices remained in use by the new local chief administrator and, fortunately, continued to store records of the former administration. Xinzhu's territory extended from the Touchong in the north to the Dajia River in the south. It retained the former township structure, except that Taojian *bao* and the other five northern townships were lost to Danshui county.

The above reorganization did not become a reality for five years after the decision was made. While awaiting construction of the new prefectural offices and walled compound that would include Danshui county's yamen as well, Taibei prefects made Xinzhu their headquarters. During this period when Xinzhu was the temporary prefectural seat, prefects acted as chief administrators for both new counties. By 1879, a new prefectural city had been completed, and the first Xinzhu county magistrate was appointed.

In the late 1880s, further changes again halved Xinzhu's territory. In 1887, the island was detached from Fujian and became a full-fledged province in its own right. Two years later, Xinzhu's three southern townships were placed within the jurisdiction of another new county, Miaoli. During the period after 1879 and again after 1889, a complex series of subdivisions and name and boundary changes took place in the townships. Some of these transformations were never fully implemented or even recognized by local inhabitants, so may be passed over in silence.

From their administrative seat in Xinzhu, county magistrates governed an area that by 1889 was only a fourth to a third the size of that administered by Danshui subprefects 25 years earlier. The decrease in the area from which law cases originated is lessened by one degree of magnitude if we exclude the northern third of the subprefecture, where litigation had been filed in Mengjia rather than Zhuqian. Obviously this decrease in the area of administrative jurisdiction was designed to maintain local government control in the face of population growth and the spread of settlement.[12]

The geographic focus of this study, dictated by the surviving documents, extends therefore from the Taoyuan alluvial plain southward to the Dajia River. For reasons already set forth, the Taibei basin and the rest of Danshui subprefecture's extreme northern dominion are excluded.

HAN SETTLEMENT: AN OVERVIEW

The administrative reorganizations of the nineteenth century were directly correlated with the expansion of Chinese settlement in Zhuqian's hinterland and dependent areas from the Miaoli hills to the Taoyuan alluvial plain.[13] This settlement had begun at least two centuries earlier. The earliest evidence of the migration and settlement of mainlanders on Taiwan dates from the 1590s.[14] These settlers, who dwelt along the southwest coast, remained few in number until the middle decades of the seventeenth century. In 1624, Dutch East Indies Company representatives claimed Taiwan, which occupied a strategic point off the Chinese coast between their main East Asian stronghold, Batavia (in Java), and their Japanese entrepôt, Deshima. Dried venison, deerskins, and rattan, all obtainable from Taiwan's aboriginal inhabitants, were valuable trade items for the company. The Dutch also realized that the island could produce cultivated crops such as sugar. For this reason the company initiated a policy of encouraging and even financing Chinese immigration, settlement, and land reclamation.

Chinese settlers came from southern Fujian province and were concentrated in the beginning around the Dutch fort and factory, which were situated within or near the site of the modern city of Tainan in southwestern Taiwan.[15] During the 39 years of Dutch control over the island,[16] the Chinese population may have grown to between 40,000 and 50,000. Settlement remained clustered in the small area around modern Tainan, stretching into the northern sector of modern Gaoxiong county.[17]

In 1662, the Dutch were ousted from Taiwan by Zheng Chenggong, a Chinese loyal to the fallen Ming dynasty. Zheng and his successors maintained control over Taiwan until 1683, when Qing naval and military forces finally seized the island. Chinese settlement continued to expand during the Zheng period. Population may have doubled to 100,000 during these two decades. As before, migration accounted for the bulk of population growth. Settlements could be found in a much wider area than before, but the great majority of the population remained concentrated in the southwest.[18]

During both the Dutch and the Zheng periods, several persistent patterns of migration and demography became evident. First, immigrants were predominantly male. Not only did population growth stem mainly from immigration, but also natural increase was less a factor than it might have been had more immigrants been accompanied by their families or been able to acquire wives on the island.[19] The gender imbalance in Taiwan's Han population was due not only to the difficulty of passage across the Taiwan Straits but also to the tendency of migration to be seasonal and temporary. Many farmers, in spite of the dangerous sea crossing, came to the island during the growing season and then returned to their southern Fujian homes after harvest.[20] Thus by the late seventeenth century, Chinese settlement was well under way in Taiwan but was still confined largely to the southwest. In the north, only one Chinese settlement near the Dajia River was established, and it was probably very short-lived. The future Danshui/Xinzhu area was still empty of Chinese inhabitants, but that soon changed.

The earliest attested settlers in our area were a group of more than 100 natives of Tong'an county, Quanzhou prefecture, Fujian. These Hokkienese speakers were led to the Zhuqian plain (*pu*) sometime in the first years of the eighteenth century by a relative and neighbor, Wang Shijie. Wang had first planned to settle there in 1682, but his scheme had to be put in abeyance for two decades from the fall of the Zheng regime until he received permission from Qing authorities.[21] The homesteads of Wang and his companions clustered in and around the site where Zhuqian city came to be located. The spot had long been occupied by the settlement (*she*) of an aboriginal group, the Zhuqian tribe, from which the name of the locale had been taken. Wang and his followers lived and traded with the Zhuqian tribe uneventfully.

By the early 1720s, other enterprising pioneers had begun to follow Wang Shijie. Another Quanzhou native, Wang Qichu, was the driving force behind reclamation and settlement of lands predominately on the northern edge of the Zhuqian plain and on the Taoyuan alluvial plain as well.[22] Wang Qichu and Wang Shijie as well had received reclamation permits from the government and so were known as reclamation or settler households (*kenhu*). Since the lands to which they and later *kenhu* held title were too extensive to be farmed by a single household, they recruited tenants, who rented land from them.[23] In this way Han settlers paying land rents to Wang Qichu under his corporate[24] or *kenhu* name, Wang Yangzhan, were already to be found as far north as Daqiqian (the northwestern section of modern Yangmei township, Taoyuan county).

The early settlers in the Zhuqian plain were Quanzhou natives. By the second decade of the eighteenth century, men from several Zhangzhou prefecture counties in Fujian may have come to the Taoyuan plain, especially in the areas of modern Yangmei and Zhongli cities. Immigrants from Guangdong's Chaozhou prefecture also began to reclaim land at the latter site (Zhongli). At the same time, slightly farther north, Hakkas, ethnically Han but with a culture and dialect sharply distinct from those of other mainland Chinese, made their way into the area after leaving their homes in Jiaying department, Guangdong. Hakkas, descendants of northern Chinese who had migrated to south China centuries earlier, were a minority group whose language and different customs made them the target of discrimination and violence from the Fujianese, who comprised the majority of immigrants to Taiwan.

South of the Zhuqian plain in present-day Miaoli county, Zhangzhou prefecture natives seem to have been the first to establish permanent settlements. After arriving in Taiwan at either Zhuqian or Lugang, an important mid-island port, these immigrants made their way to locations near the outlets of the Zhonggang and Houlong rivers.[25] In this way, by the 1720s Han settlers had made their presence felt throughout much of the coastal areas of what would become Danshui subprefecture.

The sequence and pattern of settlement exhibited during the first several decades of Han immigration and settlement in the Danshui area indicated the broad outlines of subsequent developments. One such pattern is discernible in the relations between migrating Chinese and the autochthonous tribal peoples.

In the seventeenth century, the Dutch had extended their dominance over a number of nearby plains-dwelling tribes, which became accustomed or resigned to coexistence with both the Europeans and the Chinese immigrants. As Han populations spread and became dominant, a process of assimilation began to blur outward distinctions between Han and pacified tribes. Chinese settlers termed peaceful tribes "cooked" aborigines (*shu fan*). Mountain-dwelling tribes that in large part remained hostile to the Chinese until the twentieth century were called "raw" aborigines (*sheng fan*).

In many cases relations between Han settlers and the "cooked" aborigines were initially harmonious. Eventually, however, the tribes were pressured into moving. The Zhuqian *she*, for example, moved from the site where the subprefectural seat was established to Jiushe outside the city in 1733. During the next thirty years, the members of the tribe that had not become completely sinified were pushed east and north to the Xinpu and Fangliao areas.[26] The government also attempted to ensure tranquil relations between Han settlers and hostile, upland "raw" aborigine tribes farther in the interior by establishing a boundary beyond which Chinese settlement could not legally spread.[27] The futility of such legislation is apparent when we observe that the official boundary was steadily forced into the interior. New lines were drawn four times during the Qianlong reign (1736–95) alone.[28]

Characteristic patterns of subethnic settlement also began to emerge in the early eighteenth century. Hokkienese speaking natives of Fujian's Quanzhou and Zhangzhou prefectures were usually the first to migrate to the new frontier. In some localities, however, Hakkas were the earliest settlers.[29] At times, even when Hakkas had already established villages in desirable coastal or river valley locations, they were pushed by the more numerous Hokkienese into less desirable locations in the foothills and uplands, usually during outbreaks of armed communal feuding (*xiedou*). In 1826, for example, clashes between Hokkienese and Hakkas in Zhanghua county spread northward into the Dajia area. Hakkas in Danshui subprefecture's southernmost township were driven away from the coast into the mountainous interior.[30] Such was usually the case. The extremely high proportion of Hakkas in the total population of the areas around Zhuqian / Xinzhu and to the south meant that Hakka villagers could often hold their own against the Hokkien tide as they were unable to do elsewhere. As we shall see, during the nineteenth century, the proximity of Hakka and Hokkienese villages required that the cadre of subcounty quasi-officials include appointees of both linguistic groups.[31]

During the eighteenth century, on balance the Qing government seems to have viewed Taiwan as a liability because the island's remote location made control of Han Chinese difficult. Moreover, growth in the Han population would inevitably lead to conflict between them and the native aborigine tribes. In hopes of avoiding both problems, the government instituted policies of forbidding or restricting immigration as well as establishing strict boundary lines between land held by Han migrants already on the island and lands inhabited by the aborigines.[32]

Several factors, however, interacted to promote the spread of settlement in spite of government efforts to restrict immigration and protect aborigine land. The relatively empty island was a magnet for both land-poor agriculturists and capital-rich merchant investors from the crowded southeast coast and Lingnan regions of the Chinese mainland. Local government's attempts to control either immigration or land reclamation were bound to be ineffective in a subprefecture where the chief administrative officer was nonresident until after midcentury. Aborigine settlements found it easier and more profitable to rent the land they controlled to Chinese settlers rather than cultivate it themselves or endeavor to block illegal settlement. The allocation of land to aborigine military colonists (*tun*) late in the century after a major rebellion was intended both to ensure the livelihood of the tribes who had helped the government put down the revolt and to help prevent future uprisings. Instead, the land grants merely afforded opportunistic Han settlers the chance to lease and reclaim lands belonging to the military colonies. By the turn of the nineteenth century, most of the plains, lowlands, and foothills had already been penetrated and opened to Chinese settlement.

By around 1800, the area north of Zhuqian, including the entire Taoyuan plain, had been fully opened. South of Zhuqian, most of the eastern section of the Miaoli hill region in addition to the low-lying coastal plain were spread, somewhat sparsely, with Han settlements.[33] At that time, the plain around Zhuqian was fully settled, but nearby mountains just to the southeast were still controlled by aborigines. Along the subprefecture's rather indeterminate eastern boundary, attempts to move into upland clearings were usually abortive because of attacks by hostile tribes.

During the first two decades of the nineteenth century, Han farmers gradually filled less desirable land previously unsettled in the lowland areas. Pressure from indigenous population growth and continuing immigration combined with the lack of open land at lower elevations to initiate a gradual extension of settlement into uplands. This movement continued and perhaps increased slightly during the Daoguang reign (1821–50). The most visible and successful expansion of settlement into formerly impenetrable aborigine land was in the nearby mountains southeast of Zhuqian. In the 1830s, a well-funded and tightly organized private settlement organization, the Jin-Guang-Fu Large Guardpost (*da'ai*), situated its headquarters in Beipu, an upland plateau about fifteen kilometers from Zhuqian, and began reclamation. By hiring a large number of guards and establishing numerous outposts at strategic defensive positions scattered through the mountainous area, Jin-Guang-Fu was able to successfully defend settlers from attacks by the some 34 unpacified tribes that had driven back earlier pioneers.[34]

After 1850, British merchants engaged in the China trade created an increased demand for Taiwan's camphor, for which they traded opium. As Chinese entrepreneurs filtered into the mountain forests to fell the huge camphor trees, which were hacked into chips to be distilled into the finished product, clearings were created where agricultural crops could be planted. Thus a steady, although not particularly rapid, expansion of open land and therefore settlement continued in the latter part of the century in the hills and mountains to the east.[35]

Although the subprefecture authorized and sometimes even subsidized individual instances of settlement in the upland areas, its support was tepid at best in the absence of a general policy initiative emanating from the central government. Qing policymakers were finally goaded into action after 1874, when Japan sent an expedition to punish aborigines who had killed a boatload of castaway Okinawan fishermen blown onto the southern Taiwan coast during a storm. Seeing this act as a harbinger of Japanese designs to seize control of the island, the Qing government approved a new activist policy intended to pacify the "raw" aborigines and open up the central mountains to Han settlement.[36] In this way the entire island could be legitimately claimed as Chinese soil. No longer would areas inhabited by "raw" aborigines be considered outside Chinese jurisdiction. Between the 1870s and the end of Chinese sovereignty in 1895, military attempts to subdue hostile tribes in the newly created Xinzhu county were considerably less than successful, however, and sometimes met with embarrassing defeats.

The commercial demand for two upland products late in this period had a much greater impact in opening the mountains. In the Xinzhu area the rise of relatively large-scale tea cultivation and greatly increased production of camphor impelled further intensification of settlement by tea planters in the hilly regions and deeper penetration of camphor distillers into the mountain forests of the county's eastern reaches.[37]

In spite of their efforts, the Chinese were never able to pacify or exterminate the mountain tribes completely, especially in the north. Even at the end of the period treated in this study, a trip into the inner mountains remained a hazardous undertaking, and permanent settlement there even more so. Still, the trend of ever-expanding Han settlement in remote and rugged regions was clearly apparent, even though its culmination would await a new century, when settlement policy would be determined by Taiwan's Japanese overlords.

In the following four chapters I will explore specific instances of crime and litigation engendered from and conditioned by the culturally and ethnically diverse society that flourished under the political, historical, and environmental conditions just outlined. I will begin by considering the effect of northern Taiwan's frontier heritage.

3

The Frontier Heritage

ROOTS OF ENDEMIC VIOLENCE

As of 1863 nominal Chinese control over Taiwan had lasted more than 200 years. During those two centuries, Han settlement had gradually spread throughout most of the coastal plains and foothills and even into the more dangerous uplands. The frontier heritage of lawlessness and violence was difficult to exorcise. Land-hungry Chinese continuously penetrated regions already populated, if only sparsely, by tribal peoples who violently resisted the intrusions. Such conflict produced frontiersmen accustomed to surviving among head-hunting aborigines by stealth, cunning, and, if necessary, response equal in degree of ferocity to the attack. Local strongmen who, independent of government control, recruited private armies for protection and aggrandizement of their power bases had not entirely disappeared. The island's rugged terrain further impeded the ability of any level of government to extend its power far into the countryside. Despite institutional innovations by the subprefectural and county government to increase the effectiveness of their police powers, violent crimes were common and often went unsolved and unpunished.[1]

Problems of integrating frontier areas into the empire or conversely of attempting to prevent or limit Chinese settlement were of course nothing new for the imperial state, especially during the Qing period. Differing objectives along northeastern and northwestern frontiers had taxed Qing policymakers since the foundation of the dynasty. In the northeast, attempts to seal the Manchurian frontier to Chinese immigration in order to preserve the ancestral home of the Manchus ultimately failed, and the imperial government finally in the nineteenth century faced the necessity of integrating the southern Manchurian region more completely into the empire. In the northwest and in Central Asia, conquest and annexation during the eighteenth century ended the age-old threat of nomadic incursion but left the imperial government groping for quick and effective methods to integrate these vast "New Dominions" (Xinjiang) into the Qing state.[2] Even in areas long considered integral parts of the empire, rebellion, war, and depopulation could create frontiers in areas previously settled. The Qing government faced such problems as encouraging (re)-settlement, handling disputes over land and water rights, and formulating the proper state policies to encourage settlers without prejudice to autochthonous peoples.[3]

Thus by the nineteenth century, the central authorities had an extensive body of experience and precedents to draw on in dealing with the problems of northern Taiwan. As in other areas of the island, however, two special characteristics of society in the Dan-Xin locality multiplied the chances for outbreaks of violence or for criminal activity and vitiated state efforts at local control. These two peculiarities, ethnic and subethnic rivalry and the disproportionately large male component of the population, are well known to students of Taiwan's past. As might be expected, the interaction of these factors in an area still close both physically and chronologically to the frontier kept the Xinzhu yamen court busy and its jails full.

Ethnicity

The most evident ethnic division in Taiwan was between aborigines and Han Chinese. Before the coming of the Chinese, the island's population consisted entirely of Malayo-Polynesian peoples who lived on the abundant deer of Taiwan's forests and plains and engaged in dry-land rice agriculture.[4] Continual encroachment onto tribal land was reason enough for enmity between Han Chinese and the tribes, and certainly the aborigines had no lack of other grievances against the Han as the demand for forest products, especially camphor, caused Chinese producers and traders to push ever deeper into land officially reserved for the native tribes.

Far more destructive and more significant was conflict within the Chinese settler population. These intraethnic disputes, which often became violent, were termed "armed affrays" (*xiedou*).[5] They troubled all of Taiwan, although the Dan-Xin area may have been marginally more fortunate in this regard than some other areas.

Hokkienese speakers from Fujian had been the earliest migrants to the area,[6] although by the late Qing, Hakkas descended from settlers from Jiaying department and other areas in Guangdong probably had come to make up a majority of the county's population.[7] Southern Fujian's commercial prosperity, the scarcity of agricultural land in that province combined with its availability in Taiwan, and the profits to be made in the sugar and rice trade had induced many natives of Quanzhou and Zhangzhou, adjacent prefectures in southern Fujian, to come to Taiwan to invest in land.[8] Later-arriving Hakka migrants from Guangdong tended to become tenants of Hokkienese landowners.[9] An example of a prosperous Hokkienese trading family from Quanzhou that had invested in land farmed by Hakka tenants, most of whom were from Guangdong, may be found in the rent resistance case summarized in Chapter 4.[10] I shall argue in the next chapter that in the nineteenth century, the ability of tenants to assume de facto control of land rights from investor-owners prompted the latter to initiate much rent arrears litigation regardless of the ethnic or cultural background of the parties. Nevertheless, in cases such as that involving the Wu lineage and its tenants, the differences in language, social arrangements, and customary practices between Hakka and Hokkienese inflamed both sides, sharpening the disagreement.[11]

Conflict between these two groups, as well as between aborigines and Han Chinese, was not an unfamiliar occurrence in this part of the island.[12] However, *xiedou* between Hokkienese-speaking Zhangzhou and Quanzhou natives of Fujian were also common. After 1840, at least four major outbreaks (in 1844, 1853, 1859, and 1860) between Zhang and Quanzhou men were reported in various locales in the Xinzhu area.[13]

Although not unknown in earlier periods, ethnic feuds and armed affrays became more generalized beginning in the 1780s, as the most accessible and best land in Taiwan began to fill up with Chinese settlements. After that, intensifying competition for land, water, and markets caused the affrays to become more frequent and widespread until they began to subside 80 years later in the 1860s.[14] The generally later-immigrating Hakkas were bound together by linguistic solidarity in the competition with Hokkienese. Distinctive cultural practices and similar economic circumstances also encouraged Hakka solidarity. Much wider income differences among the Hokkienese tended to foster disunity except when dissimilar Zhangzhou and Quanzhou groups were faced with a threat that compelled them to unite.

Both Hakka and Hokkienese tended to build and unify around community temples rather than ancestral halls, perhaps a reflection of the weakness of lineage organizations during the eighteenth and early nineteenth centuries.[15] Against this background, well-organized feuding groups might form alliances with neighboring fellow ethnics until large areas were involved in the fighting.

Government authority on all China's peripheries was weak. In southeast China, for example, the government was virtually powerless to prevent recurrent armed affrays similar to those in Taiwan. Nonetheless, as we might expect, numerous official measures were tried to reduce all kinds of conflict, including the feuding that plagued Taiwan.[16]

Nor were private initiatives lacking. In 1853, for example, Zhuqian's most prominent literatus and Taiwan's first *jinshi*, Zheng Yongxi, attempted to use his reputation to persuade the area's fractious citizens to settle disputes harmoniously rather than resort to armed affrays, but his essay "Exhortation to Harmony" (*Quanhe lun*)[17] was no more effective than official measures to control strife. No more than a year after Zheng's essay was published, a simmering, year-long series of armed affrays between Hakka and Hokkienese settlers broke out in the Fangli area near the subprefecture's southern boundary.[18]

Even though disputes always originated in specific wrongs—and land ownership and use by far outranked all other issues in their potential for creating perceived injustice—ethnic and cultural differences were important factors in intensifying disputes over land rights, boundaries, rent payment, debt repayment, and other issues. In the same way, when violent criminal acts occurred, passions were even more inflamed if criminal and victim were Hokkienese and Hakka. Ethnic diversity combined with subethnic solidarity more readily gave rise to organized confrontation. As we have seen, the armed affray was not confined to Taiwan, and fights between native place groups were a feature of the Zhangzhou and Quanzhou region even before large-scale emigration to Taiwan. There was, however, an eccentricity to Taiwanese society that, in an unquantifiable but very real way, created a predisposition toward violence and lawlessness. Ironically, this peculiar feature, gender imbalance, was, as we shall see, an unforeseen byproduct of deliberate government action.

Gender Balance in Taiwan's Frontier Society

Through the first century of Qing rule in Taiwan, the aim of central government policy was chiefly to dampen unrest in order to prevent uprisings against the authorities. To minimize unrest, principally between indigenous tribes and Han Chinese, Qing policymakers attempted to prevent Chinese settlement from spreading beyond arbitrarily and narrowly drawn boundaries into areas reserved for aborigines. As suggested above, the restrictions were a failure. The boundary was continually breached in the eighteenth century and repeatedly redefined to reflect new realities of settlement.

Moreover, a long ambivalence toward Taiwan as a Chinese colony resulted in restrictions on migration. The central government formulated a category of negative regulations designed to limit the growth of Han population by forbidding emigration from the mainland or restricting it to males only.[19] It was the latter policy that ended in contributing to the very lawlessness and rebellion that the restrictions were designed to prevent. By excluding family members of immigrants over long periods of the late seventeenth and eighteenth centuries, government regulations produced at first in Taiwan a population with a high proportion of "migrant laborers crossing for the spring planting and returning to their mainland homes after the fall harvest."[20] Time and the rigors of the crossing resulted in more and more of these men deciding to remain on the island permanently without their families. A population imbalance was apparent even in the early eighteenth century. In 1721, one central Taiwan village was reported to have a population of 256 men and one woman.[21] While the restriction on family migration was never wholly enforceable, and some single immigrants were able to obtain wives from among the aborigines, the large number of unmarried men remained a characteristic of Taiwanese society even in the nineteenth century.

The consequences of a large number of men without women were predictable. Without the restraint imposed by family and marital responsibilities, immigrants easily fell into habits leading to social deviance, at least as defined by the mores of traditional Chinese society. Gambling and the resulting indebtedness seem to have been particularly rampant. Poor men without home, land, or work were a constant feature of village life in Taiwan. In the eyes of government, these men were little more than wandering vagrants and were considered especially prone to criminal acts. Lacking family and lineage ties, these rovers created fictive kin organizations by uniting in sworn brotherhood with other men from many walks of life. Viewed with alarm and suppressed by the government, sworn brotherhoods were perforce transformed into secret societies that rightly have attracted much scholarly attention.[22] In Taiwan the most famous of the brotherhoods was the Heaven and Earth Society (*Tiandihui*), although others such as the Small Sword (*Xiaodaohui*), Father and Mother (*Fumuhui*), Thunder God (*Leikonghui*), and Eight Trigrams (*Baguahui*) existed as well. There were, in addition, many unnamed societies.[23]

Contrary to the fears of Qing officials and the patriotic fantasies of later Chinese, brotherhoods in Taiwan probably were organized primarily for the purpose of mutual help in sustaining a livelihood for their members and not in order to overthrow Manchu rule and restore the Ming dynasty.[24] Given official suspicion and consequent repression, however, the societies were forced into opposition to the government and—inevitably perhaps on a poorly policed frontier—into illegal activities. Occasionally opposing sides in disputes such as those over land or water rights utilized the organizing device of sworn brotherhoods to enhance group solidarity and strength.[25] It was perhaps inevitable that these brotherhoods and secret societies became an important source and sustaining force for the communal armed affrays discussed above. In short, these groups were transformed from an effect to a cause of social conflict. Often these sworn brotherhoods may have been no more than predatory bandit gangs. Close proximity to mountain sanctuaries and a lack of effective police organizations allowed such gangs to operate freely. In the following case summary we shall see one manifestation of the frontier heritage in rural Xinzhu.[26]

Case 33319: Armed Robbery (*qiangdao*)
GX 8/3/1–GX 12/6/7 (18 April 1882–8 July 1886)

The Xinzhu area was, for Taiwan, relatively pacific. The endemic low-level violence epitomized by the armed affray that was common in many other settled parts of the island did not seem as prevalent in this area. However, as this case, which began in 1882, shows, violent crime and perhaps even something of the frontier legacy were still significant problems even at the end of the third century of Taiwan's settlement.

On the initial date noted in the case heading above, Zhan Ajing and Lan Tong, joint owners of a store specializing in opium, filed a petition [33319:1] alleging they had been armed robbery victims.[27] Zhan, who was the primary complainant in this first petition, resided in Jiuxionglin village, Zhubei second township. He was a Hakka whose ancestors had immigrated from Guangdong province.

Zhan charged that on the night of GX 8/2/29 (16 April 1882) during the third watch of the night, that is, sometime between 11:00 P.M. and 1:00 A.M., 30 to 40 robbers had broken into his shop, the He-Xing firm (*hao*), by first opening a hole in the roof tiles and then breaking into the store's storage cases and stealing all the money and goods. The complainant had tried to run out and call for help, but the intruders knocked him down, injuring his ribs and back. After setting fire to a shed, the robbers escaped along the Sanchongpu and Zhongkeng roads (see Map 5). The

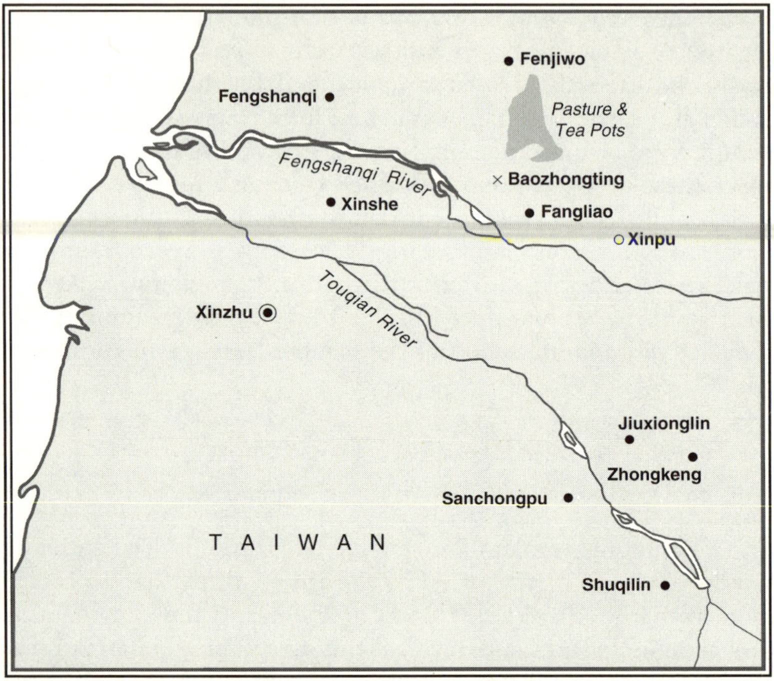

MAP 5. The Jiuqionglin, Xinpu, and Shuqilin Areas.

alarm was given, and the robbers were pursued, but without success. Only a few of the tools they used to break in were recovered. Zhan claimed that he recognized one or two of the robbers but did not know their names. The crime was reported to township chief (*baozhang*) Li Yuliang, village head (*zhuangzheng*) Xu Benli, *baojia* leader (*baozheng*) Ye Guoqin, and manager (*dongshi*) Zeng Dingyuan, who had investigated and could attest to the crime.[28] To conclude his petition, Zhan asked that he be examined to verify his injuries and requested that the robbers be captured.

In his endorsement, Magistrate Xu Xizhi was skeptical that Zhan did not know the names of the robbers that he recognized but ordered that Zhan's injuries be examined and that he be questioned. Zhan's ensuing testimony [33319:3] gave a more detailed description of his losses. The robbers had stolen 220 silver dollars, 150 strings of copper cash, more than 600 ounces of opium, and 4 shop bills (*dianqi*) from the He-Xing firm.[29] The store, which employed one worker, had been in business for fifteen years selling opium. Zhan was examined by the coroner (*wuzuo*), whose statement that he had a knife cut on his ribs on the right side and both his kneecaps had been injured by blows from a club was entered into the record of testimony. On the basis of Zhan's testimony and the coroner's findings, Magistrate Xu ordered runners to investigate and capture the robbers.

On GX 8/3/2 (19 April 1882), only a day after Zhan's testimony, his partner Lan Tong's son, Lan Huagun, joined the case by filing a petition [33319:4] supporting Zhan. Huagun, a government student (*shengyuan*) of 28, was also a Hakka with the same native place registration as Zhan. Earlier Huagun had been ordered by the governor to go to Miaoli with a deputed official to investigate and take care of some guardpost business.[30] For that reason he had not been at his father's shop when it was robbed. Huagun noted that Zhan had cooperated in an investigation by village head Xu Benli and two other local notables and had discovered that the two robbers he had seen and could identify were men called Liu Zaixing and Liu Haixing. These men were the sons of a neighbor, Liu Dongjin, who the petitioner claimed was a harborer (*wojia*) of criminals.[31] The Liu brothers were now not the only ones that Zhan recognized. Others were Fan Ahai, Zhan Ajian, Huang Azan, and Qiu Yuelai. Lan Huagun charged that Huang and Qiu were still being "harbored" by Liu Dongjin, and he asked that the magistrate quickly send a runner with a dispatch to the military battalion so soldiers could capture the criminals and recover the stolen goods. Magistrate Xu responded in his endorsement to Lan's petition by saying that runners should be sent to determine whether or not Liu Dongjin actually was a harborer and if the two alleged robbers were staying with him.

Lan Huagun followed up his first petition with a second [33319:6] a day later. He again named Zhan Ajian, Fan, Qiu, and Huang as robbers. Lan had accompanied runners, who had in fact been sent to Liu Dongjin's home in an attempt to capture Huang and Qiu. The latter two suspects (Lan claimed) had both still been at Liu's the morning of the previous day. Liu, however, had discovered that Lan and runners were coming to capture them and warned them to flee. Only Liu and his two sons had been apprehended and sent to the yamen. Some of the stolen goods, including a scale and weights and a seal ink box, had been recovered serving to prove, Lan's petition asserted, that the Liu brothers had been part of the robber gang.

Magistrate Xu endorsed Lan's petition with an order to interrogate Liu Dongjin and his sons. During his questioning two days later, Liu testified [33319:9] that he was an innkeeper and his sons porters. He admitted they had after the robbery carried goods from the opium shop, but only to save them from a fire burning there. All items had been returned. The magistrate, noting that several articles had been found in Liu's inn, ordered him and his sons jailed while runners searched for the other robbers. A few days later, the head of one section of lictors reported [33319:11] that he had succeeded in capturing Fan Ahai, another of the accused, with the help of village officials.

A day earlier, Mrs. Liu, née Chen had come to the defense of her husband, Liu Dongjin, and their sons. On GX 8/3/8 (25 April 1882), apparently acting on her own, she filed a counterplaint (*su*) [33319:10] claiming the charges against her husband and sons were false.[32] She stated that her husband and sons had been implicated because of the enmity of Zhan Pengcai, a cousin of Zhan Ajing. In the previous year Pengcai, whom she termed a "gentry bully" (*gunjin*), had assigned (*pai*) her sons to collect part of the subscription to pay for a work project in the area. They were assigned 80 "names." By this she apparently meant they were required to collect money contributions sufficient to pay for the hired labor of 80 men, which amounted to a total of 1,600 dollars in subscriptions for the people of their village. Moreover, Pengcai had ordered her sons to add 20 dollars of their own money so there would be no shortage. Liu Dongjin and Zhan Pengcai argued about the matter, creating ill feeling that was later exacerbated when her sons were not willing to take the names and amounts in the subscription register and turn them all in to settle accounts.[33] Zhan Pengcai was thus taking advantage of his cousin being robbed and wounded to incite him to accuse Liu Dongjin and his sons falsely of harboring the robbers and the stolen goods. Mrs. Liu closed her accusation by asking for their release, but the magistrate's endorsement instead ordered all three Liu men together with Zhan Ajing to be interrogated in the tribunal.

Fan Lianwang, Fan Ahai's father, related a variant of Mrs. Liu's story when he came to his son's defense. Lianwang, 69, a resident of Zhongkeng, a hamlet near Jiuqionglin, stated in a petition [33319:13] that he and his son made a living by farming and carpentry. His son's trouble was, he claimed, caused by a dispute with Zhan Pengcai over the latter's ordering him (Lianwang) to subscribe five dollars for construction of a bridge on the Dajia road.[34] Fan claimed this was improper because he was a tenant farmer.[35] His son went to remonstrate with Pengcai, and there was an argument. Later, when Zhan Ajing was robbed, Zhan Pengcai used it as an excuse to implicate Ahai in the robbery, which the complainant noted was a capital (*dabi*) crime.[36] Fan Lianwang also accused Pengcai of seizing Ahai when he was on the way to a carpentry job on the morning of the sixth and demanding 100 dollars for his release. Only when Lianwang was revealed to be too poor to pay did Zhan turn Ahai over to the yamen and have him accused of robbery. Fan's petition concluded by begging the magistrate to be benevolent and merciful in discovering the truth of the matter. Magistrate Xu, wondering why the son was accused if in reality he was law-abiding, ordered further investigation.

Fan Ahai himself was not queried about his version of events until eleven days later, on GX 8/3/20 (7 May 1882), when he and the three Liu men were interrogated [33319:21]. He claimed that on the night of the robbery he was in Shizhangli village at the home of a family named Tian, for whom he had been working as a carpenter. Fan testified that he had been falsely accused by Zhan Ajing because Fan had accused his relative, Zhan Pengcai, of embezzlement when he had demanded five dollars in commuted labor contribution for the Dajia road construction project. According to Fan, the official subscription quota had been only three dollars. Liu Haixing, the 32-*sui*-old son of Liu Dongjin, was also questioned. His explanation of the charges brought against them by Lan Huagun was that Lan owed him money for work he, Haixing, had done. They had argued, and Lan then accused them all of complicity when the store was robbed. In other words, the position of all the accused was that for various reasons Lan Huagun had used the robbery of his store as a pretext to get even with them.

Both the Lius and Fan Ahai received outside support in the form of reports attesting to their honesty [33319:22 and 23] filed by their neighbors on GX 8/3/23 (10 May 1882). Each report was signed by numerous local dignitaries, including three degree holders in the former case and several village elders and the head of the carpenter's guild in the latter. Both groups were to enter into bonds for the prisoners, but Magistrate Xu was not yet willing to allow their release. He seemed especially distrustful of Fan Ahai's statements.

Until this time, the case had been straightforward although unresolved. A complicating factor entered the equation when sometime on or before GX 8/3/26 (13 May 1882), a yamen runner reported [33319:17] the capture of Zhan Ajian, who had, according to Lan Huagun's petition [33319:4], been one of the robbers. Zhan Ajian was also a suspect in two other, different robberies. The runner report stated that Zhan Ajian had been implicated in the robberies of Zheng Shiyou, a Xinpu village man, and of Fan Asheng of Shuqilin village.[37] The magistrate interrogated Zhan on the same day he was reported captured, at which time the prisoner, who claimed Zhangzhou, Fujian ancestry, denied involvement in the robbery of Zheng Shiyou in Xinpu. He did, however, admit to being involved peripherally in robbing the He-Xing store belonging to Zhan Ajing (and Lan Huagun).

We might pause to note that in spite of his surname, which is usually associated with Hakkas, Zhan Ajian testified that he was of Zhangzhou prefecture ancestry; that is, he was Hokkienese. Many Hakkas were of necessity fluent in the Hokkienese dialect. Given his surname, however, it is extremely unlikely that Zhan could persuade yamen personnel that he was descended from a Zhangzhou family if it were not true. In the case, all others whose native place registration can be discovered were Hakkas. If Zhan Ajian actually was Hokkienese, we might assume that his criminality, whether real or perceived, was traceable in part to his status as a sociolinguistic outsider in an area largely populated by Hakkas.[38] As we return to events of the case, we shall eventually find that of all those accused in the case, the court could prove none guilty except Zhan.

When brought before the magistrate's bench, Zhan Ajian (not to be confused with robbery victim Zhan Ajing) testified [33319:19] that a group of ten men robbed the store. He himself had not taken part in the actual robbery but, as he admitted, had expected to receive a share of the loot. Zhan claimed to know by name only five of the ten robbers. He identified each of those five by naming their fathers; Zhan knew the names of only four of the five men he implicated. None of the men (Fan Ahai, Liu Dongjin and his sons) already jailed in connection with the case were named by Zhan Ajian, and his veracity concerning the others he did name soon came under suspicion.

On GX 8/4/7 (23 May 1882), the Shuqilin village overseer and others now came to the defense of the five men Zhan Ajian had implicated. In a joint report [33319:27] signed also by a number of local degree holders, functionaries, and shopowners, the overseer charged that the men Zhan Ajian named in his testimony were falsely accused because they had assisted either in capturing Zhan after he had stolen goods belonging to Fan Asheng or in delivering him to the authorities. The report of the overseer and the others arrived at the yamen on the same day as at least five documents [33319:28, 29, 30, 32, 34] filed by the fathers of four of the men implicated by Zhan and even by Fan Asheng, the Shuqilin robbery victim, to refute Zhan's charges. Late in the fourth month, two men plus the fathers of two others implicated by Zhan Ajian along with Lan Huagun and Tian Chengye had been summoned to the yamen. They were interrogated [33319:46] together with the five prisoners (Zhan Ajian, Liu Dongjin and his two sons, and Fan Ahai).

The interrogation covered not only the original robbery of the He-Xing store but also events surrounding the other two robberies that had eventuated in the capture of Zhan Ajian. The common thread tying all three together was the alleged involvement of Zhan Ajian. It was for this reason that the magistrate's interrogation and other developments in the course of these legal proceedings that are discussed in the following pages seem only indirectly related to the He-Xing store robbery. In a sense, the focus of the proceedings shifted from the victims of the three separate robberies to those in custody for alleged participation in the crimes. The main focus of the court from that point on was the five prisoners, Zhan Ajian, Fan Ahai, Liu Dongjin, Liu Haixing, and Liu Zaixing.

From responses to his questioning at the hearing convened late in the fourth month, the magistrate became convinced that Zhan Ajian had indeed falsely accused at least some of the Shuqilin villagers, who were said to have helped capture him. The record of testimony taken from the villagers and their earlier petitions and counterplaints revealed some of the circumstances of the Shuqilin robbery that had been tied to Zhan Ajian. It seems that Fan Chengye had stored or perhaps pawned several valuable items at a Shuqilin shop belonging to Cao Ayuan. During the night of GX 8/3/19 (6 May 1882), the store was broken into and a kidskin jacket and jade bracelet, some money, and other articles were stolen. When the robbery was discovered, the overseer, an irrigation canal manager (*jiashou*),[39] store owner Cao Ayuan's son, and other residents of Shuqilin and its neighboring villages, which were part of a linked-villages compact,[40] tracked down and captured Zhan Ajian. Zhan was wearing the kidskin jacket when seized. After Zhan was captured, the *jiashou* and another local functionary calling himself a *jieshou* collected money to pay for escorting the prisoner to the yamen.[41] A wealthy Shuqilin resident contributed money toward sending Zhan to court, and for this reason Chen Desheng and Gan Nanwang, sons of the *jieshou* and the wealthy contributor, respectively, were named along with the others by Zhan in retaliation. Three of the villagers charged that a "litigation meddler" (*andu*), who had been hired by Zhan Ajian's wife to try and have him released before he was taken to the yamen, instructed Zhan to implicate them all.

Unfortunately for Gan Nanwang and Chen Desheng, Lan Huagun also testified during the GX 8/4/24 (9 June 1882) hearing. Although Lan's interest would seem to have been only in the robbery of his He-Xing store in Jiuqionglin, he obviously felt that those implicated in the Shuqilin robbery were guilty of the earlier crime as well. Lan characterized Gan Nanwang and Chen Desheng's father as dishonest. He disputed their claim that the overseer would have called on them to collect or contribute funds. That duty was the *jiashou*'s responsibility. Lan was, however, willing to vouch for the honesty of the sons of the *jiashou* and the shopkeeper.

At the same session, the magistrate directed his attention toward Tian Chengye, at whose home Fan Ahai claimed to have been doing carpentry work on the night the store belonging to Zhan Ajing and Lan Huagun was robbed. Tian explained that Fan had been at his home during the period 8/2/15–8/3/3 (2 April to 20 April), and that Fan had never gone far away. Lan Huagun noted that this statement may have been in contradiction to an earlier petition [33319:40] in which Tian had said only that Fan had departed after GX 8/2/16 (3 April 1882). Lan's opinion seemed to weigh heavily with Magistrate Xu, who ordered that Gan Nanwang, Chen Desheng, and Tian Chengye be interrogated a second time. Tian was questioned [33319:51] again three days later. At this later session Tian changed his story slightly, admitting that Fan slept in an outer room and could have crept away on the night of 16 April without his knowledge. Surprisingly, Tian's latest version of events resulted in a mere verbal reprimand and then release under bond. He claimed that his age—73 *sui*—and lack of sophistication caused his confused testimony. Magistrate Xu, after a mild rebuke, approved his release.

Gan and Chen were not as fortunate, however. For the following five months they remained in detention along with the others as the magistrate was bombarded with petitions from relatives of the suspects asking for their release and offers from minor local notables to enter into bonds for the release of one or another of the prisoners (with the exception of those initially accused, Liu Dongjin and his sons, for whom no one came forward). Countering such efforts on behalf of the accused, Lan Huagun and Zhan Ajing kept up the pressure with several prompting petitions asking that the prisoners be forced to testify truthfully and then be punished. Magistrate Xu conducted two court interrogations [33319:60, 69] during the five-month period. On both 8/5/20 and 8/6/28 (5 July and 11 August), Lan and Zhan Ajing were questioned. At the earlier session Zhan Ajian and the still-imprisoned villagers he had implicated were again examined. At the later hearing the magistrate concentrated on Fan Ahai and the three Liu men. In addition, Zhan Pengcai, whom both Fan and the Lius blamed for maliciously dragging their names into the case, was summoned from Xinzhu county's school to court for questioning after the magistrate transmitted a request for his attendance to the subdirector of schools. At neither of these interrogation sessions was the magistrate able to gain much further insight into the situation. He did conclude that Zhan Pengcai, although related to storekeeper Zhan Ajing, was not involved in the case. The magistrate concluded that if Pengcai had assigned Fan a contribution, Fan would have been given a receipt. Schooled by legal procedures that relied heavily on written documentary evidence, the magistrate naturally decided that because Fan had no receipt, his story was false.

During the ninth month of GX 8 (1882), Gan Nanwang's extended detention in the Tea Section runners' office began to break down his health. On 8/9/26 (6 November), Tea Section runners reported [33319:82] that Gan had become ill with vomiting and diarrhea. Gan was only the first of the incarcerated suspects to fall sick. Late in the twelfth month, the head of a lictor section informed the magistrate that Fan Ahai, who was jailed in the outer room of the section's office, had become ill during the night of 8/12/20 (28 January). Several months later, Liu Dongjin was found to be suffering from a severe fever. Gan was eventually released under bond so he could receive medical treatment at home. Fan apparently recovered, since he was not released. On GX 9/7/15 (17 August 1883), Liu, who was older than the other two men, died from his illness in spite of receiving examination and treatment from a doctor on at least three occasions.[42] Both of Liu's sons and Zhan Ajian as well were later to fall prey to serious but nonterminal diseases.

Four months after his father's death, Liu Zaixing was released to a doctor's care on GX 9/11/24 (23 December 1883), the same day that his jailer reported him ill [33319:120, 121]. Zaixing's brother, Haixing, was made to remain in detention nearly two more years and had to suffer through two bouts with illness before he was released under bond [33319:140] on GX 11/5/1 (13 June 1885). Thirteen months later, Zhan Ajian, by then the only suspect still imprisoned, obtained release under bond [33319:149] after contracting a fever.

By the time of Zhan Ajian's release on GX 12/6/7 (8 July 1886), the case had dragged on inconclusively for over four years. Five different magistrates, including Xu Xizhi during two different periods of tenure, were unable to elicit an admission of guilt from anyone except Zhan Ajian. Liu Dongjin, who because of the discovery of some of the stolen goods in his possession was the most likely suspect other than Zhan, died without ever acknowledging involvement. All other suspects, including Fan Ahai, who had been in jail since a few days after the robbery, and Chen Desheng, who had been implicated by Zhan Ajian, were eventually freed.

Chen was released, apparently for lack of evidence, during the twelfth month of GX 8 (ca. January 1883) after his father made several applications to the yamen and a guarantor agreed to enter into a bond for the prisoner.

Fan, in contrast, was held for two years. His fellow villagers had come forward as character witnesses for him several times, but he was not released until Tian Chengye's grandson, Tian Songlai, submitted a prompting petition and offered testimony [33319:129, 131] corroborating Fan's alibi. He testified that in the past Fan had done carpenter work for the Tian family many times. Fan had come to the Tian household on GX 8/2/26 (13 April 1882) and remained there until 8/3/3 (20 April). While Fan was staying with the Tians, he and Tian Songlai slept on the same bed, and therefore Songlai could be certain that Fan had not gone out on the night of the robbery. Songlai explained that his grandfather had been intimidated by Lan Huagun and so had been afraid to confirm Fan's story. The grandson, after establishing Fan's innocence, albeit somewhat tardily, entered into a bond [33319:132] on GX 10/3/23 (18 April 1884) to secure the prisoner's release.[43]

Early during the course of this case, Lan Huagun, who had originally applied strong pressure on the yamen to convict Fan Ahai and the three Liu men, had abruptly lost his enthusiasm. In the eight months following the robbery of his store on GX 8/2/29 (16 April 1882), he had filed three prompting petitions [33319:61, 66, 85] that urged Magistrate Xu to take the view that Gan Nanwang should pay compensation for the stolen goods. Such a finding would have been premised upon an acceptance of Zhan Ajian's implication of Gan. The last of the three documents, which was dated GX 8/10/3 (13 November 1882), went so far as to assert that a court directive had been issued ordering compensation. No directive is now in the file that would support Lan's claim. In fact, the magistrate's endorsements on the earlier prompting petitions of GX 8/5/28 and 8/6/13 (13 July and 27 July 1882) rejected the implication that Gan Nanwang's guilt had been proven. Whether Lan would have continued to cling to an opinion counter to the magistrate's is unknown. Four days after the 13 November prompting petition, Lan himself was implicated in the killing of a heretofore unmentioned suspect in the original robbery and was apparently jailed.

In mid-1883, very soon after Magistrate Xu Xizhi's successor took office, Lan Huagun and his father filed two petitions for Lan's release that tell most of what little can be known of this part of the case.[44] Allegedly, on GX 8/10/7 (17 November 1882), several men, none of whom had earlier been mentioned in connection with this case, came to see Lan Huagun at the He-Xing store. The leader of this group was one Wen Fengyun. Wen and the others claimed that three brothers, Huang Wang, Huang Lian, and Huang Shan, were the actual robbers.[45] Wen and his companions had in their possession some of the stolen goods that they claimed to have recovered from the Huangs and offered to capture the robbers and turn them over to the court. After Lan accepted the offer, Wen and his group were able to effect the seizure of only Huang Wang, who suffered a serious knife wound in the process. The prisoner was taken to the yamen but died of his wound before the magistrate, who had gone "down to the countryside," could return. According to the Lans, a corrupt yamen gate keeper and a "rascal familiar with litigation" saw in Huang's death an opportunity to blackmail Lan Huagun by implicating him in the suspect's death. Because Lan refused their demands, the pettifogger, who was also surnamed Huang, incited someone to file a complaint against Lan charging him with Huang Wang's death. Lan claimed further that by the time Magistrate Xu had returned to Xinzhu and began to deal with the complaint, Huang Yun had persuaded Wen Fengyun to change his story and Zhan Pengcai, who was alleged to be Zhan Ajian's cousin, to take a leading role in pushing the case against Lan forward.

At this point, it will be helpful to turn to the only other document that is pertinent to the case. A GX 11/10/21 (27 November 1885) report [31808:3] inventorying prisoners held at that time in the Xinzhu yamen jail listed Wen Fengyun among them. A short summary of the case against Wen supplies additional details and perspective. According to the summary, Huang Yun, also known as Huang Ayun, had been the younger brother of Huang Wang (referred to as Awang). On GX 8/12/9 (17 January 1883), Huang Yun had filed a complaint that accused Wen of knifing and killing Huang Wang at the instigation of Lan Huagun. On the basis of this charge, Wen and Lan had both been arrested and interrogated by Magistrate Xu. Wen had testified that during a visit to Lan's store, Lan had asked him if Huang Wang had been one of the robbers.

Wen's statement seems to imply that he had responded in the negative to Lan's question or had denied any knowledge one way or the other of Huang's possible involvement. Wen added that he had no idea what Lan had done after their conversation.

Lan, in contrast, had testified that Wen had told him Huang Wang had been among the robbers. Lan, however, denied having harmed Huang in any way. According to Lan, the deceased Huang had fatally injured himself by falling down (*zixing pudie shensi*). The magistrate's reaction to Lan Huagun's explanation of Huang's death had been to send in a report impeaching Lan and depriving him of his degree holder's gown and button, that is, his *shengyuan* degree. In this way Lan had been reduced to commoner status and thus could have been tried for the crime. The prisoner inventory report went on to reveal that, fortunately for Lan, the crisis of the French invasion and blockade of northern Taiwan had caused most judicial proceedings to be suspended. Higher authorities had eventually ruled that Lan could be freed under bond, and he had been released.[46]

To return to the Lans' own accounts of the accusation made against Lan Huagun, Magistrate Xu was said to have summoned members of the Huang family, including Huang Xi, who was another of Huang Wang's brothers, and two of his sisters-in-law to testify. None of them could identify Lan as one of the men who captured and fatally wounded Huang Wang. (The Lans' three narratives, of course, make no mention of the fact that Huagun had once testified that Huang's fatal injury had been accidental and self-inflicted.) In spite of this failure to place Lan at the scene of the supposed crime, Magistrate Xu had had Lan arrested and kept under detention in the yamen's Tea Section runners' office. There he apparently remained until the new magistrate, Zhou Zhikan, arrived in Xinzhu early in the sixth month of GX 9, at which time Lan Tong and Lan Huagun began to petition for the latter's release. They were successful probably in part because Lan's father appealed to higher authority. Lan Tong's petition had appended to it a copy of an endorsement by the provincial governor to a report or petition, which unfortunately is not contained in the case file. The governor ordered Lan Huagun released because it had not been established that he had been at the scene when Huang Wang received his ultimately mortal wound.

Because of the scanty documentation of Lan Huagun's arrest,

impeachment, and release, it is difficult to assess the events leading to Lan Huagun's several months of detention or to place the entire episode in the context of the case as a whole. From the records that are available, it appears that once Huagun obtained his release, he made no further attempt personally to press for further action against Zhan Ajian or the other suspects. Indeed, when Lan Tong submitted a petition [33319:122] that tentatively attempted to interest Magistrate Zhu Chenglie[47] in making further inquiries into the guilt of Huang Wang and even Zhan Pengcai, the document was endorsed in such a way that may have convinced both father and son to let the case drop. Zhu replied that Huagun himself should file another petition if he wished the court to conduct a trial and pass sentence. The case file contains no further legal papers from the Lans, and as already noted the case was never definitively resolved. All the arrested suspects were released, one after another. Only Zhan Ajian ever admitted guilt. Only one magistrate, Fang Zuyin, seemed prepared to pass sentence.

On GX 12/4/27 (30 May 1886), Fang drafted a court directive on an interrogation notice [33319:143] concerning Zhan. Fang observed that Zhan's continuing attempts to incriminate others militated against leniency. The magistrate, however, also noted Zhan's long incarceration, apparent regret for his crime, and desire to reform. In view of these factors, Fang decided to request permission from higher authorities to place Zhan in shackles (*suodun*) on public display to inculcate respect for the law. Fang's threat seemed to have persuaded Zhan that his stubborn insistence that he should not be the only one punished for the robbery was no longer viable. On 30 May, Zhan was brought before the magistrate and begged to be allowed to search for a guarantor so he could be released [33319:144]. The task of finding a guarantor fell to the local constable (*dibao*) because Zhan had no relatives to do it for him. His wife had left him and returned to her parents, and his mother had just died. With no family to handle his affairs, the responsibility fell to the local community's representative, the *dibao*. The magistrate had begun the process of releasing Zhan perhaps because the prisoner's health had begun to fail. He was reported [33319:145] to be feverish and spitting up blood on the eighteenth of the fifth month. Finally, by GX 12/6/7 (8 July 1886), a shopowner, also surnamed Zhan, agreed to enter into a bond [33319:149] so Zhan Ajian could be released temporarily for medical treatment. If he survived or was returned to the yamen is unknown, because the case file contains nothing more.

In this case, whatever the truth of the specific charges and countercharges, the nature of the accusations is indicative of a society in which armed robbery, arson, assault, and private retaliation were everyday facts of life. If it did not seem remarkable that degree holders such as Lan Huagun and Zhan Pengcai could one day be engaged in official government business and virtually the next be accused of homicide or other very serious crimes and perhaps be stripped of rank and status,[48] how much more unexceptional must the presence of gangs of habitual robbers, harborers of criminals, and the like have seemed to the residents of Xinzhu county.

In a sense it was not surprising. The potential gains made theft and robbery very tempting. Even if the amount and value of the goods stolen from the He-Xing store were exaggerated by the owners, to assert in a public forum that hundreds of dollars in silver and copper currency and opium of similar worth were stored in the shop made it and other similar commercial establishments inviting targets. The widespread use of opium and the consequent (or perhaps precedent) existence of large amounts of the narcotic in Xinzhu could have only increased the crime rate. Frontier toughs, inter- and intra-ethnic feuds, weak or at least insufficiently strong government control, predatory foreign intervention, and drugs made a volatile and violent social mix. Add to this northern Taiwan's economic boom considered in Chapter 5, and the problems faced by local law enforcement and the courts become manifest.

4

Land Relations

MULTI-TIERED LAND RIGHTS

As might be expected in an agrarian society, agricultural land rights were at the root of most of the disputes that were brought before the Danshui subprefectural and Xinzhu county courts. The issues described in each of the core cases on which this study is based provide insight into several aspects of these land disputes, and these in turn are germane to understanding rural society in the area. I shall turn now to the nature of land holding and land rights existing in nineteenth-century northern Taiwan, topics particularly well illustrated by a so-called rent resistance case summarized in the latter part of the chapter. The attitudes and practices defining these land rights had been determined during the process of land reclamation and settlement in the hinterland of Zhuqian city beginning in the late seventeenth century and extending through the end of the period of this study.[1]

The reclamation and settlement process led to institutionalized land relations whose complexity in turn gave rise to a plethora of disagreements. By the nineteenth century, in Danshui subprefecture and later Xinzhu county as well as in some areas of central and northeast Taiwan, a three-tier system of landlord-tenant relations had evolved. In the immigrants' old home areas, especially Fujian, comparable systems had developed, and it was natural that the patterns of land tenure already familiar to immigrants coming from southeast China would be replicated on Taiwan's frontier.[2] The historical processes by which such similar systems developed in the long-settled mainland provinces and in eighteenth- and early-nineteenth-century Taiwan were, however, different, even though the outcomes looked remarkably similar.

On the island of Taiwan as a whole, three distinct modes of land settlement can be discerned.[3] Sometimes individuals obtained either land reclamation permits (*kenzhao*) from the government or deeds (*kenpi*) from aborigines and began to farm the land themselves. Such owner-cultivators seem to have been most common in southern Taiwan. Sometimes a reclamation permit holder would recruit tenants instead of opening the land himself. Wealthy individuals might provide tenants with oxen, tools, seed, and financing for irrigation projects. Often, however, tenants provided their own tools and supplies (as seems to have been true in the boundary dispute case). A partnership engaged in litigation over land boundaries notes in one of their prompting petitions [22510:18] that their tenants, who were growing tea and sweet potatoes, "themselves provided working capital" (*zibei gongben*).[4] At least one secondary source asserts that tenant self-capitalization was often the case in northern Taiwan.[5]

In Taiwan, land reclamation permit holders (*kenhu*) had a three-year grace period before their newly settled farmland had to be reported to the local yamen and rated for taxation. (After the land was rated and taxes assessed, the *kenhu* usually were referred to as *yehu*, "landlord.") Landlords were responsible for paying the combined land and poll tax, which in the Dan-Xin case files was always called "primary assessment" (*zhenggong* or *zhengke*). Naturally landlords used part of the rental revenues for this purpose. The rent paid to landlords was called "large rent" (*dazu*).

Tenancy rights to the land were defined contractually. Contracts might on occasion define the tenant's right as perpetual,[6] but permanent tenure was conditional on the tenant's continuing to live up to his contractual duties. Usually the tenancy period was not specified. From another perspective, given the highly commercialized agricultural economy and the long history of immigrants investing in land, tenancy rights became alienable, merely another commodity. In cases when a tenant prospered, he might acquire rental rights to land from another tenant who wished to move or had been forced to leave the land. Tenants who accumulated more land than they could work or who moved to other occupations thus often sublet some of their land to another, secondary stratum of tenants, who then became the land's primary cultivators and paid rent to the original tenant. Such rent was termed "small rent" (*xiaozu*). The original tenant was still responsible for payment of the large rent to the landlord, who, as before, remitted taxes to the government. The terminology that was used in discussing landlords and tenants reflected the different stages in the evolution of the three-tier system. The words *kenhu*, *yezhu* (or *yehu*), and *dazu hu* (household that receives large rent) all referred to a landlord holding the right to collect large rent. Those people who paid rent to this landlord were called tenant households (*dianhu*), or households that receive small rent (*xiaozu hu*). Although the lowest tier in the three-tier system is often referred to as the "primary cultivator," the middle-tier small-rent householders often farmed at least some of the land to which they held the rights. Primary cultivators paid small rent to *xiaozu hu*; small-rent householders paid large rent to *dazu hu*. In the usual case, small-rent householders did not personally deliver large rent payments but required their tenants (the primary cultivators) to do it for them.

The tax for which large-rent households were responsible was determined by the kind and quality of land. In Danshui and later Xinzhu, paddy and dry-land fields reported to the yamen to be rated for taxation were each surveyed and assessed by yamen personnel in one of three grades according to the quality of the land. In this locality (and throughout Taiwan) land was customarily measured in units called *jia*. A standard *jia* was approximately 11.3 times larger than the *mou*, the measure of land area standard throughout most of the rest of China.[7] In Western terms, a *jia* equaled about 0.970 hectares (2.396 acres).[8] An imperial edict of 1733 fixing the tax rates directed that for this purpose one *jia* would arbitrarily be considered to equal eleven *mou*.[9] The conversion was mandated apparently to facilitate yamen bookkeeping.

The imperial order commanded that Danshui tax rates were to be the same as those prevailing in Tong'an county, Fujian, where land taxes were levied in terms of *mou*. After Taiwan became a full-fledged province and its first governor, Liu Mingchuan, ordered the land in Taiwan entirely resurveyed in 1887, the tax was levied in terms of *jia*, the measure that still was the de facto standard among the populace, rather than *mou*.[10]

One mode of land settlement may be discerned in our rent resistance case. The tenants claimed in a petition [22202:92] that their ancestors had already been renting reclaimed land registered and rated for taxation during the early Qianlong period (1736–95). Land in the area of their village, Daqiqian, had been opened to settlement by the 1720s. The tenants' assertion that the large-rent rights to their land had first been owned by a reclamation permit holder named Jiang Shengben seems plausible. We know from other sources that Jiang obtained a permit to reclaim dry fields from an aborigine in 1735.[11] The large-rent collection right first held by Jiang Shengben eventually came into the possession of the complainants in the case, the Wu lineage.

The transfer of large-rent collection rights is partially described in a series of documents [22202:154–57] submitted in evidence by the Wu family. These four documents, two sale contracts (*jinmai qi*) and two agreements for supplemental payment (*zhaoxi qi*), illustrate the method by which such rights were commonly bought and sold.[12] One source claims it was customary throughout Taiwan in sale or mortgage for the seller or mortgager to be entitled to one request for supplemental payment.[13] As Ch'en Ch'iu-k'un notes, one basis for *zhaoxi* was rising land values, or in other words the difference between the original sale or mortgage price and later market value of the land.[14] By 1873, in Danshui subprefecture, however, this custom had been so abused that it was one of four evil practices explicitly denounced and outlawed on an inscribed stele erected by the city's north gate by Subprefect Xiang Dao.[15] The two sale contracts [22202:154, 156], both dated JQ 7 (1802), record a transaction between Wu-Shun-Ji and two families surnamed Lin and Pan to finalize the sale of the right to collect large rent. The Lins and Pans had jointly held rent collection rights for a parcel of land in the Daqiqian area. The Pan family had owned the right to two-thirds of the rent and the Lins to one-third.

Wu-Shun-Ji paid 1,240 taels of silver to the Pans and 620 taels to the Lins. The parcel of land is specified by a description of its boundaries. Neither the area nor the rental income is given.[16] The contracts state that the right to collect tenant/large rent was accompanied by the obligation to pay the land and poll tax, meltage fee,[17] and aboriginal rent.[18] The land tax for which the Pans had been liable was 25 *shi* of grain. The Lin contract did not mention a tax figure, but it presumably would have been half that of the Pans. Both contracts note that the original settler was Jiang Shengben.

The Lin contract includes an appendix explaining that the documents attesting to this family's purchase of the land-rent rights were destroyed during a rebellion in QL 51 (1786).[19] An appendix to the Pan contract merely states that the contract recording their purchase of the rent collection rights in QL 34 (1769) had been lost. Both the Lins and the Pans promised that they would not in the future take advantage of the absence of the original documentation and attempt to extort money from Wu-Shun-Ji. These promises both reflected and strengthened the importance of such documents in Chinese society.

The Lins had decided to sell because they needed the money for another enterprise. The Pans had accumulated arrears of public items—that is, they were behind in tax payments—and so decided to sell. Both contracts were for irrevocable sale (*juemai*), with the sellers agreeing that the contract precluded any future right to redeem the land rights or demand supplemental payments from the buyer.[20] The explicit repudiation of supplemental payment rights was, however, without force. In JQ 12 (1807) and 13 (1808) the Lins and Pans obtained extra payment of 100 and 200 dollars, respectively. We cannot tell why Wu-Shun-Ji agreed to the extra payments. As noted earlier, local custom sanctioned at least one supplemental payment; perhaps the lineage felt one further payment to each of the sellers was preferable to an expensive court battle, especially since some of the documents necessary to establish the ownership history of the land were missing.

Single lineages, such as Wu-Shun-Ji appeared to be, owned large-rent rights to much of our area's farmland.[21] The Lins and Pans also owned and sold the land-rent rights as a corporate entity. Two Lin brothers and two of their nephews, who undoubtedly had succeeded to their deceased father's share, were joint sellers. The Pan land sale was similar. The rights to rental income might have been parceled out among several branches of the family, but the lineage acted as a corporate body in adversarial proceedings with outsiders. We shall see the duty of acting for the entire lineage in litigation rotate among different lineage members in the case summary at the end of this chapter.[22]

The case involving another corporate body, the Jin-Liu-He partnership, illustrates a different reclamation process.[23] If an individual (or his lineage) was not sufficiently wealthy to underwrite the reclamation project alone, he might recruit investors to form a partnership. The Jin-Liu-He partners in the case claimed to have obtained their rights from two men who had also combined their assets in order to reclaim the land. Although their opponents in the case disputed the Jin-Liu-He partners' account of the history of the rights to the particular property in question, we must assume that such a procedure was common even if the facts were in dispute in this particular instance.

As described, in JQ 9 (1804), the two men had pooled their money and bought the rights to a dry upland clearing. The purchase was formalized by a land settlement deed (*kenpi*) that the original land holder, an aborigine, drew up and handed over to them in return for a monetary payment. More than 50 years later, in XF 7 (1857), the two equal shares held by the partners' descendants were split, three for one, and the newly created shares were then sold to new partners. The reclamation and settlement process just outlined shows that even in the absence of lineage connections and resources, small investors were able to pool their resources to enter the land market. We may also note that in this instance, the aborigine land owner by the sale of a *kenpi* permanently severed his connection to any use of or benefit from the land. In some instances aborigine tribes or individuals acting as representatives of the tribes, rather than selling reclamation permits to Han Chinese, rented land directly to tenants, thus becoming large-rent landlords themselves. It is clear that whatever the Taiwan aborigines' conception of their relationship to the land had been before Chinese immigration began, by the late eighteenth century pacified tribes at least were accustomed to the conception of owning and renting land.

GOVERNMENT AND QUASI-PUBLIC LARGE RENT

There were other types of corporate landowners, including the government, which could own large-rent collection rights in the same way as private individuals and corporate bodies. In the case of individual landlords, either Han Chinese or aborigines, whose income from the land was Han large rent (*Handazu*) and aborigine large rent (*fandazu*), rents accrued to a discrete person. Normally, however, aborigine large rent was paid to a tribe or settlement as a whole rather than to a single individual. There were three types of government lands on which large rent was paid to the yamen. Government estates (*guanzhuang*), army garrison lands (*longen zhuang*), and confiscated (*chaofeng*) lands all were leased to tenant farmers who were responsible for payment of large rent. Finally, certain organizations and institutions were supported at least in part by large rent. Among these were academies and two security forces in the area. We shall turn to these latter organizations first.

Military Settlement Rent

Local military settlements (*tun*) as well as government and civilian guards hired to protect against aborigine attacks were financed by rental income. Again, in these cases something resembling a three-tier system of land rights may have evolved, except that the payments corresponding to large rent went directly to the local government yamen or to guard leaders for distribution to the troops.

Both the military settlement system and the guard organizations came into existence in the aftermath of the Lin Shuangwen rebellion that wrested control of much of the island from the Qing government until the uprising was suppressed in 1788. After this challenge to imperial control, the government decided on measures designed to prevent future uprisings and to reward its local allies who had been useful in suppressing the rebellion.[24] Two groups had rallied to the government side and provided tangible military support. Aborigines, who had preferred the inconsistencies of government policy toward them to Han settler predations, and Hakka settlers, who for the most part had refused to support the Hokkienese-led rebellion, both raised military units to fight on the government side. In 1786, several thousand aborigine soldiers had joined government forces led by the Danshui subprefect in patrolling along the Dajia River at the subprefecture's southern boundary to prevent rebel soldiers from moving north. After the rebellion was ended by 9,000 Qing troops sent from the mainland under the command of the Manchu general Fukang'an, he memorialized the throne in 1788 proposing that the aborigine soldiers who had fought with him be rewarded by being hired permanently and being provided with a material base for their support.[25] Regularizing these aborigine troops would also provide added insurance against further uprisings on the turbulent island. The method chosen (here as elsewhere on Chinese frontiers) was to form "cooked" aborigine tribes or villages into military settlements or colonies (*tun*).[26]

Fukang'an's memorial suggested allocating both reclaimed and unreclaimed lands for support of the new military settlements. The largest proportion consisted of reclaimed land already cultivated by aborigines or rented by them to Han tenants. Unreclaimed lands outside the legal boundary of Chinese settlement made up a much smaller proportion of the total. In the area outside the aborigine boundary, mountain or upland fields suitable for cultivation but as yet unreclaimed would go directly to the members of the new military settlements. The memorial suggested that these as yet unreclaimed lands could provide "sustenance and support" (*yangshan*). It is not clear whether there was much *yangshan* land in Danshui subprefecture. There is no reference to this category as such in the local gazetteers.

"Military settlement fields" (*tuntian*) were also created by dispossessing Chinese landlords of large-rent rights to land that lay outside the boundary for legal Chinese settlement and for which they had already recruited tenants. The tenants were to retain their rights to the land so that primary cultivators paid land rent to secondary landlords corresponding to small-rent households. These secondary landlords, who had formerly paid large rent to reclamation permit holders, now paid the same rent, but it was categorized as military settlement rent (*tunzu*). Moreover, the land was now considered to be the same as government land, and the *tunzu* was paid to the local yamen, which then disbursed it to the settlements.[27] Thus as we shall see in the dispute over the boundary between pasture and tea fields, one of the accused protested that the armed men he had allegedly led in an attack on the tea cultivators actually were a passing detachment of military settlement soldiers who had been led by their sergeant to the yamen to receive their rations [22514:21].

As the foregoing discussion suggests, the military settlements themselves were able to grant reclamation rights, recruit tenants, collect rent, and even sell rights to the land. In this way the military settlements or their members were or could become landlords, and the rent they received differed from large rent in only one respect: they were not liable for government taxes.[28] The absence of tax liability was significant; it certainly removed one of the pressures that impelled Han landlords to ask the local court's help in enforcing large-rent payment. This pressure is clearly evident in Wu-Shun-Ji's suit against its tenants. Not only did the Wu lineage depend in some degree on large-rent income for its own maintenance, but also failure to receive these rents could lead to tax arrears and prosecution to force payment of back taxes. This was one threat that aborigine landlords did not need to fear.

In this arrangement, the nature of land relations at first glance might have seemed fundamentally different in principle, since the ultimate holder of rights to the land was the government. As contracts for sale of military settlement land small-rent rights show, however, there was no requirement to notify the government or obtain the yamen's permission for the sale. The contract needed only to note that the land carried a *tunzu* obligation.[29] Cases of resisting the payment of military settlement rent, while not unknown (see, for example, 17410), were relatively few. Tension resulting in appeal to the local court seemed largely absent.

Military settlement payments were budgeted as part of the subprefecture's annual expenses. Sometimes this item was not always paid in full by military settlement rent because the harvests were inadequate or land was even permanently ruined by natural disasters, especially flooding. One instance of this kind of mishap apparently happened sometime in the 1850s or 1860s. By 1871, flooded land near the villages of Jiuqionglin and Yangmeili had resulted in the permanent loss of 1,527 *shi* of military settlement rent.

One of the decisions [22202:147] handed down in the rent resistance case ordered the landlord Wu-Shun-Ji to provide supplementary military settlement rent. According to the subprefecture's gazetteer, Wu and another man named Chen Yucheng were required to pay 420 *shi* in supplementary military settlement payments.[30] The case documents are not forthcoming on the legal basis for the subprefecture's judgment, but we may conjecture that the large-rent landlord's liability for the regular land tax and meltage fee made him the logical candidate to bear any new surcharges.

Guardpost Rent

The spread of Chinese settlement into more mountainous areas in the eastern part of the subprefecture necessitated defensive measures against attacks by "raw" aborigines. In the absence of sufficient government military forces to ensure the settlers' safety, an institution called the guardpost (*ai*) began to prove its usefulness. These posts were established by the local government at strategic points and manned with armed guards (*aiding*), who were to be on the lookout for aborigine warrior bands and, in the event, were responsible for warning settlers and fending off attacks. The subprefecture's first six guardposts, with a total of 125 guards, were established under government auspices in 1788.[31] Most later guardpost organizations were formed and financed by settlers themselves with government permission. Pioneering entrepreneurs eager to claim virgin land modeled their civilian guardposts (*min'ai*) on the government guardpost (*guan'ai*) model when the local administration proved unable or unwilling to expand its network of frontier defense stations. By 1871, 25 of the 29 guardposts in the subprefecture were civilian guardposts. Although both types of posts had the same function, they differed in the way they were financed.

Some government guardposts were supported entirely by government revenues. Other posts, however, received 60 percent of their rations from rent paid by former tenants of people whose estates had been confiscated for any number of reasons by the government. The remaining 40 percent was supplied by the yamen.[32] In this latter case, the guardpost had taken the place of the former landlords without any alteration of the fundamental three-tier land rights system. The primary cultivators and the small-rent households stood in the same relationship to the guardpost as they had to the former large-rent households (*dazuhu / kenhu*).

Civilian guardposts were formed in two ways.[33] A single village or several villages sometimes organized guardposts, hired a guardpost head and guards, and drew financing from the income of village common properties and contributions made by large- and small-rent households. Such an arrangement amounted to a community endowment for public purposes. Guardposts organized by reclamation permit holders (*kenhu*), that is, landlords, were more common in Danshui subprefecture. The landlord was responsible for 40 percent of the guardpost rent (*aizu*), with 60 percent coming from his tenants.[34]

In the nineteenth century, guards were paid at an annual rate of 30 *shi* of rice commuted to silver at one dollar per *shi*. In 1871, there were 23 civilian guardposts ranging in size from 8 to 125 guards, with a total of 498 guards. By that time, at least one of the guardpost organizations, Jin-Guang-Fu (discussed below), which was the largest of them all, could not pay all its guards from rent. It required a 400-*shi*-per-year subsidy from the subprefectural government.[35] A determination of whether this failure to pay its own way reflected mismanagement, an inability to enforce rent collections, or simply that settlement in that particular area was not economically feasible without government support awaits further research.

As in the case of military settlement tenants and the military guardposts supported by tenant rents, the three-tier system evolved as tenants sublet their land and began to collect rent from new primary cultivators. The potential for conflict inherent in the arrangement was without doubt as great as in cases involving ordinary landlords and tenants, such as those that produced the litigation discussed in this chapter and Chapter 5. An even greater possibility for abuse existed because of the responsibilities and powers accruing to guardpost personnel.

When a new guardpost was authorized, a guardpost head (*ai-shou*) was appointed to command the guards and manage the post's activities. The guardpost head was responsible for collecting the guardpost rent and, in the case of government guardposts, receiving the disbursement of government subsidies. When to this consideration was added the remote locations of the guardposts, it is not surprising that in some instances the guardpost authorities came to assume a de facto governmental role in enforcing law and order. The yamen's cession of adjudicatory authority to the guardpost almost certainly meant that rent resistance cases were resolved at that level. Although the Dan-Xin archive contains 37 guardpost case files, some with references to rent resistance [17302:48, 17337:1], no case deals with protracted attempts by a guardpost head to force a tenant in arrears to pay guardpost rent. It is unknown if guardpost leaders as a matter of course were granted authority to settle serious criminal offenses without resort to the subprefectural or county yamen.

The Jin-Guang-Fu Large Guardpost (*Jin-Guang-Fu da'ai*), a classic case of a powerful, almost autonomous, guardpost, has been touched upon in several studies.[36] The organization was formed in 1832 by partners owning a commercial firm in Zhuqian city who decided to finance reclamation and settlement in the mountains east-southeast of the subprefectural capital.[37] Two years later the guardpost head commanded 32 separate subposts and 340 guards. Disputes among people living in areas under guardpost control were settled at the main guardpost office at Beipu. Reportedly, even capital criminal cases were tried and sentence passed without the necessity of review or possibility of appeal to the yamen in Zhuqian.

As with ordinary large rent, the amount of guardpost rent levied varied in different locations. A copy of an undated report [13212:1][38] that was almost certainly submitted to Liu Mingchuan in 1888, when the guardpost system was abolished, gave some approximate figures for eight Taiwan counties. In Xinzhu's northern townships, guardpost landlords received anywhere from eight to eighteen *shi* per *jia* of paddy fields per year.[39] In Xinzhu's southern townships, *aizu* ranged from two to ten *shi* annually per *jia*.[40]

Government Rents

A small proportion of the land in the region was farmed by tenants whose large rent went directly into the subprefecture's or county's treasury, not for redistribution, as in the case of military settlement rent, but instead to become part of the general operation funds for yamen use. The reclamation of government estates had originally been entirely underwritten by official funds with no tenant self-financing. There were government estate lands at only two places in the subprefecture, at Quantoumushan on the western edge of the Gemalan plain and at Heshangzhou, an island in the Danshui River. The total rent collected including miscellaneous fees was just under 2,500 *shi*.[41] Although from the perspectives of the land's primary cultivators and original tenants the government was in effect the same as a large-rent household, from the yamen's perspective these rent payments were tax revenue from which a landlord had not first taken a cut.

Government also was the effective landlord for what were called confiscated (*chaofeng*) lands. Confiscated land was described as either *panchan* or *shengxi*, but only the former existed in Danshui.[42] *Panchan* lands had come into existence only after the Lin Shuangwen rebellion of 1786–88, when rebel landlords had been dispossessed of their land rights. Most of these lands were in Jiayi and Zhanghua counties in central Taiwan; however, Danshui subprefecture contained just over 639 *jia*. After 1804, a head tenant (*dianshou*) appointed by the Taiwan prefect began to collect the rent, which amounted to more than 15,845 *shi*. From then on it seems that only "tax grain" totaling 657.5 *shi* commuted to silver at a rate of 1.3 dollars per *shi* continued to enter the subprefecture's coffers. The remaining rent grain, although first paid to the subprefecture, was shipped to granaries belonging to Taiwan prefecture to be disbursed as extra rations to the military. In 1864, fields in the subprefecture belonging to two men who fled after being implicated in the Dai Chaochun uprising (1862–64) were confiscated. The rent, which amounted to only 75 *shi*, was assigned to the water god shrine to pay for incense and other supplies.[43]

Although civil government enjoyed the supplementary income of government estate and confiscated land rents, in the latter case most of Danshui's *panchan* rent ended up as extra military rations. The needs of the military garrisons in the subprefecture were partially supplied by another kind of rental income as well. The Lin Shuangwen rebellion convinced Qing authorities of the need for a larger force of regular troops. New garrisons were manned with troops from mainland provinces, chiefly Fujian. These soldiers, who by virtue of a three-year tour of duty followed by rotation home were called "rotating forces" (*banbing*), were stationed mostly in Zhanghua county and Danshui subprefecture. To pay for them, *banbing* units were given the settlement rights to land that they in turn could rent to tenant farmers. As with privately held land, a three-tier system of land rights developed with the military post functioning as the landlord and small-rent households and primary cultivators sharing land rights.[44]

RENT RELATIONS AND ASSESSMENTS

Large Rent

In every case the amount of large rent paid was fixed by a contractual agreement between the large-rent landlord and his tenant. As Japanese survey teams discovered, however, customary practice seemed to dictate that rental rates not fluctuate too greatly. This relative stability allows us to arrive at some general conclusions about rent assessments. My discussion of this subject along with the customary basis that fixed the range of possible large-rent rates in landlord-tenant contract negotiations will rely on Japanese colonial government survey findings, which were conveniently summarized by Azuma Yoshio in his study of Taiwan's economy.[45] Whenever possible, large-rent data extracted from the Dan-Xin rent resistance cases will be cited to buttress Azuma's conclusions.

Tenants here as in other parts of the island paid large rent either as share rent—a percentage of the harvest—or in a fixed amount. It was often said that large rent normally was set at a rate of 10 to 20 percent of the harvested crop.[46] In Danshui subprefecture the most common share rent rate was 15 percent. In 1860 a landlord in a prompting petition [22202:128] explained, "Rent is levied according to the quality of the harvest. If a tenant gets ten *shi*, he keeps 8.5, and 1.5 goes to the landlord. This is termed levying the 1-9-5." This formula meant that of the entire harvest, the tenant paid 10 percent as rent and kept the remaining 90 percent minus a 5 percent deduction. The 5 percent was justified as a fee levied to meet administrative, clerical, and other expenses associated with the landlord's managerial agent and rent office (*zuguan*).[47] The formula seems to have been customary in north Taiwan's villages even during the initial phase of settlement. Leases dated as early as 1732 set the rent according to the 1-9-5 formula, saying that this method "is in accordance with village custom."[48]

The 1-9-5 rate was not the standard everywhere in the Danshui/Xinzhu area. Japanese investigating local customs for the new colonial administration found that in the three townships that comprised the newly created Taoyuan county between Xinzhu and Taibei, there were "a very few" instances of large rent being set at 20 percent of the crop.[49]

The other way of levying rent was to set it at a fixed amount no matter what the harvest. A lease drawn up in 1737 records the agreement between landlord and tenant that rent on a plot of land the latter intended to bring under cultivation would be four *shi* the first year, six *shi* the second, and eight *shi* per year beginning the third year of cultivation and continuing thereafter in perpetuity.[50]

Even in the event of contractually fixed rent, custom in northern Taiwan by the nineteenth century dictated that the amount paid be set at an estimated 10 percent of the normal harvest for the land in question.[51] Although there were no rigidly defined standards, a set of informally accepted large-rent proportions had developed by the third decade of the century. Rent that had originally been set in negotiations between reclamation permit holder (*kenhu*) and tenant on the basis of the land's quality, ease of reclamation and cultivation, and access to water later became informally defined by the type and grade of the agricultural land officially determined for taxation purposes.

The large-rent figures shown in Table 4.1 were commonly accepted in the Danshui/Xinzhu area. The large-rent lord's land tax (*zhenggong*) obligation is included to show the net after-tax income derived from large rent. The table applies to the period before 1843 (DG 23), the year in which the government mandated that tax payments were to be made entirely in silver. As Azuma notes, the grain measuring instrument (*dou*) used by large-rent lords was at least 10 percent larger than the standard or market *dou* that was used when grain was measured for payment of taxes. Consequently the putative net income figures are actually too low. The actual net income per *jia* of land has been calculated as shown.

After the conversion in 1843 to tax payments in silver dollars, the income to be gained from possessing large-rent collection rights was cut in half because the government set the commutation rate of payments in kind to monetary payments at double the market price of grain.[52] Table 4.1 illustrates the change.

TABLE 4.1

Estimates of Large Rent Amounts and Income in the Danshui/Xinzhu Area

	Paddy fields			Dry fields		
	U	M	L	U	M	L
Before 1843 in *shi* per *jia*[a]						
Large rent amount	8	6	4	6	4	2
Land tax quota	2.74	2.08	1.76	2.08	1.75	1.72
Nominal net income	5.26	3.92	2.25	3.92	2.25	0.29
Actual net income[b]	6.06	4.52	2.64	4.52	2.64	0.48
As of 1843[c]						
Large rent amount	8	6	4	6	4	2
Large rent amount measured in market *dou*	8.8	6.6	4.4	6.6	4.4	2.2
Land tax quota[d]	5.48	4.16	3.52	4.16	3.52	3.43
Nominal net income[e]	2.52	1.84	0.48	1.84	0.48	−1.43
Actual net income[f]	3.32	2.44	0.90	2.44	0.90	−1.23
Effects of inflation as of 1887[g]						
Large rent amount[h]	8	6	4	6	4	2
Market price[i]	14.72	11.04	7.36	11.04	7.36	3.68
Land tax quota[j]	5.48	4.16	3.52	4.16	3.51	3.43
Net income[j]	8.24	6.88	3.84	6.88	3.84	0.25

[a]Data from Azuma, 261–62, with his numbers rounded to two decimal points. Paddy fields were more productive than dry fields, and three grades ("upper," "middle," and "lower") were recognized for each.

[b]The container (*dou*) used in measuring the volume of large rent grain was at least 10 percent larger than the standard or market *dou*, and the figures in this row correct for that fact.

[c]Data from Azuma, 271, with his numbers rounded to two decimal points.

[d]Land tax quotas are the pre-1843 amounts doubled to reflect the conversion of the tax payment to silver dollars in 1843, at the rate of two silver dollars per *shi* of tax grain.

[e]The difference between the official large-rent amount and the land-tax quota.

[f]The difference between the large-rent amount measured in market *dou* and the land-tax quota.

[g]Data from Azuma, 280, with his numbers rounded to two decimal points.

[h]In *shi* per *jia* of cultivated land.

[i]In silver dollars computed at an assumed average price of 1.84 dollars per *shi*.

[j]In silver dollars.

Inflation caused the income of large-rent landlords to increase somewhat during the years between 1843 and 1887. Large-rent income during the period may have been close to the figures shown in Table 4.1.[53]

In 1885, Taiwan was granted full provincial status with Liu Mingchuan as its first governor. One of Liu's first objectives was to find a way to make the new province financially self-supporting. To achieve this goal, Liu proposed to increase land tax revenues first by conducting an island-wide cadastral survey so as to ensure that all cultivated land was on the tax registers and second by rationalizing and simplifying the land tenure system in order to clarify the relationship between land rights and tax obligations. In brief, land tenure was changed to transfer all land ownership rights and land tax obligations to small-rent landlords in exchange for a 40 percent reduction in their large-rent obligations. Although both the cadastral survey and the transformation of the land tenure system were only partially successful, and then only in the northern half of the island, the change was visible in Xinzhu and other northern counties.[54] After Governor Liu's reforms, large-rent obligations per *jia* would have been near the following silver dollar amounts: 8.83 for "upper" grade paddy, 6.62 for "middle" paddy, 4.42 for "lower" paddy; 6.62 for "upper" grade dry fields, 4.42 for "middle" dry fields, and 2.03 for "lower" dry fields.

When large rent was fixed, the potential rent payment problems were obvious, especially in years when the harvest was poor. When the rent was a percentage rather than being constant, there could be problems as well. The tenants' petition that will be cited below in the rent resistance case summary claimed that the original landlord took 15 percent, while Wu-Shun-Ji, the new large-rent household, demanded 18 of every 100 *shi* harvested. Moreover, the tenants complained that when they paid the rent, the Wu lineage representative used an oversize measure.

Problems and abuses such as those just mentioned generated the many landlord-tenant lawsuits in the Dan-Xin archives. Crop failures might prevent small-rent right holders from paying their large-rent obligations. Alternatively, small-rent right holders, who normally were cultivators as well as secondary landlords, might naturally be reluctant to pay large rent to *dazu hu*, who had no connection to the land. At the same time, large-rent landlords might feel they had no choice but to maximize rent collections because of their dependency on the rents for fulfilling land tax obligations. Maximizing large-rent income could mean demanding payment at a rate higher than that set by contract and custom, or the collection process could be manipulated. Wu-Shun-Ji is alleged to have tried both. As we shall see in the rent resistance case below, large-rent right holders might on their own attempt to intimidate or force tenants to pay. Some large-rent landlords faced with involuntary rent arrearages or active refusal to pay could appeal to the courts to enforce contracts even as the landlords simultaneously employed coercive self-help measures such as taking tenants hostage.

It would be a mistake, however, to conclude that these tenants were helpless in the face of large-rent landlord coercion. Tenants of large-rent landlords were not easily driven off the land when economic hardship caused them to fall into arrears. Ordinarily such tenants had invested their own capital to reclaim land and were reluctant to throw away what they had ventured.[55] When nonpayment was intentional, large-rent landlords might find that their tenants were men of substantial resourcefulness who could mount a formidable resistance.

Subethnic solidarity often enabled tenants to call on neighbors of the same native-place background for support against the large-rent landlord. It was difficult for urban or market town landlords such as Wu-Shun-Ji to enforce rent payment unless a scofflaw tenant was unwary enough to allow himself to be captured. Those farming the land were tough men. Northern Taiwan was, after all, still undergoing frontier expansion in the second half of the nineteenth century as settlers pushed eastward into the mountains. As Han pressure on "raw" aborigines continued, even residents of earlier settled areas had to be prepared to fight off raiding tribesmen. Subethnic discord and armed affrays were not yet historical curiosities even in relatively pacific northern Taiwan. These ever-present dangers plus the frontier ethos passed down from earlier days in Taiwan had created a society whose men and their families could be expected to resist coercive measures with violence. As we shall see in the account presented later in this chapter, even when Wu-Shun-Ji had persuaded the yamen to send its own police force to seize rent-resisting tenants, the yamen runners' attempt to make the arrests ended in a humiliating rout.

Nor were tenants economically powerless. Since, as we have seen, they often were able to supply at least part of their own working capital while reclamation permit holders frequently had to form partnerships because of limitations on their own resources, the economic gap between large- and small-rent households may often have been relatively small. Some indication of the size of tenant lands can be seen in three lists submitted in evidence by landlord Wu-Shun-Ji in the rent resistance case. Wu gave the yamen two different tenant registers [22202:138, 168], each giving the amount of land rented by each tenant. Although the lists are not identical and sometimes give different figures for the same tenant, when aggregated, the totals and averages are close enough to inspire confidence. The first register contains 87 entries, and the second, 88. Field areas in *jia* range from less than 1 on both lists to more than 26 on the former and more than 19 on the latter. The average amount of rented land per tenant is relatively close on both: 5.11 and 5.6 *jia* (3.99 and 4.37 hectares), respectively.

One of the tenant registers and a list of tenants in arrears [22202:138, 148] also record Wu's claims about the amount of rent owed. In spite of the fact that petitions filed by both Wu and the tenants stated that the rent was based on a percentage of the harvest, the figures listed are fixed yearly amounts. Rents given in the earlier document, which also specifies land holdings, are a constant five *shi* per *jia*. Total rents in both lists vary widely, since they are in proportion to the amount of land rented. In spite of the suspicion that the figures in the back-rent list must have been inflated, a calculation of the average amount of annual rent owed shows some difference but not a glaring discrepancy. According to the tenant register, Wu claimed an average rent of 25.55 *shi* per *jia* from his tenants in Daqiqian village. Tenants that he charged with rent arrearages owed an average of 30.75 *shi* per year. If these figures have any reliability at all, and assuming that even a fixed rent would have been no more than 20 percent of the crop, the average tenant's land realized an annual harvest of over 125 *shi* of grain.

Although a statistical average may blur reality to some extent,[56] this does not invalidate the point that there was a significant group of well-off tenant farmers with sufficient resources to support protracted litigation. Their prosperity can also be seen in the presence of degree holders among tenant farmers. In the boundary dispute case, two of the petition filers who described themselves as tenants included an imperial student through purchase (*ligongsheng*) and a military government student (*wusheng* [*yuan*]) [see 22510:14]. Jiang Lianshui and Jiang Aqing, two of the tenant farmers sued by Wu-Shun-Ji, were wealthy enough to make substantial contributions to the local charity granary.[57] The clearest indication of not just a modicum of prosperity but of rising levels of agricultural output was the contention of Wu-Shun-Ji's tenants that large rent was a fixed amount rather than a percentage of the harvest. Under conditions of increases in grain production over time, those tenants would naturally prefer that the amount of large rent that they had to pay be held to a constant, absolute figure. With fixed rather than percentage-share rents, tenants' incomes would increase each year, not merely in absolute terms but as a percentage of the total harvest. Moreover, in such circumstances a large-rent landlord such as Wu-Shun-Ji would have less incentive to keep close tabs on the actual productive capacity of the land. Were he able to demand a percentage share of the harvest, Wu and other large-rent households would naturally have attempted to monitor and supervise the grain production process much more closely. Their tenants, that is the small-rent households, clearly had a vital interest in consolidating and expanding their control of land rights while limiting as much as possible the ability of large-rent landlords to interfere or even have much knowledge of true conditions on the land.

Although this ascendant group of small-rent householders increasingly wrested control of the land from large-rent landlords during the course of the nineteenth century, the latter group managed to preserve some of the contractual privileges that had accrued to it during the early phase of land settlement. In theory at least, large-rent landlords retained some leverage over their tenants. The still-fluid nature of power relationships between primary and secondary landlords during the late Qing period became evident in a 1901 interview with five northern Taiwan farmers.[58] The question-and-answer session was one of the few instances in which informants were asked specifically to address some of the same issues under consideration in this study and therefore is discussed at some length in the following paragraphs.

In the informants' opinion, a large-rent householder had no power to prevent a small-rent householder from doing anything he pleased to the agricultural land on which the large rent was levied. The small-rent householder, however, was considered to be liable for the large-rent payment if he decreased or even completely destroyed the productive capacity of the land. The farmers felt that a small-rent householder was free to build a dwelling for himself or anyone else on his paddy or dry fields without notice to the large-rent householder. However, thus decreasing the amount of productive land did not lessen his rent obligation. Even if the small-rent householder "dug holes" in his land to the extent that it became valueless and incapable of producing a crop, the tenant still was liable for the large rent.

The informants felt that if a small-rent householder contemplated actions that might allow or result in damage to the land to such an extent that the large rent could not be paid,[59] he would be prudent to purchase the large-rent right if possible and so eliminate any continued liability. If such a unification of land rights had not occurred and the large rent could not be paid, the large-rent householder had several options. He could seize any other assets of the small-rent householder in arrears in lieu of large rent.

Alternatively, two of the informants felt the large-rent householder could expel the small-rent householder from the land (literally, "forbid him to carry on operations") and recruit another small-rent householder. The possibility of forbidding the tenant to continue operations on the land was a minority opinion, however. The other three informants being interviewed felt a large-rent householder would not have had the ability to get rid of his nonpaying tenant. Of course, as we have seen, the tenant could avoid any danger of being evicted by purchasing the large-rent rights, if possible.

The obverse of the small-rent householder's option to unify land rights was what was referred to as reversion to the large-rent householder. In short, this meant that the possibility existed for a large-rent landlord to consolidate the rights to the land held by buying out the small-rent householder.

The informants' testimony summarized above describes conditions during the period before Liu Mingchuan's 1888 reform of the land tax payment system. Liu, the Taiwan provincial governor, had decreed that the tax burden was to be shifted from the landlord / large-rent right holder to the small-rent households in return for a 40 percent reduction in the latter's large-rent obligation. Before 1888, the landlord's responsibility for government taxes may have provided him with some official sanction for the powers ascribed to him by the informants. Moreover, it made his large-rent claim superior to those of any other creditors who might have wished to move against a tenant's assets. Only after the large rent was paid could a tenant's assets be seized to satisfy other debts. After 1888 the large-rent obligation was not superior to creditors' claims. The informants felt, nonetheless, that even after the tax reform, a landlord, because of his continued ability to derive some income from the land, could intervene to prevent his tenant from damaging the land so as to decrease its value.

Beyond an understanding of the shifting power relationship between large-rent landlords and small-rent tenants, two other points emerge from the question-and-answer session. First, the primary cultivators of the land were never mentioned. Their ability to influence any disposition of land rights seems to have been nil. Small-rent householders were not entirely divorced from the land. Occasionally they "dug holes" in it. In fact, as case evidence has already shown, at midcentury a majority of the small-renters in the Daqiqian area were such small-holders that they could hardly have survived on rent collection alone. It may be that by the last decade or so of Qing rule during the period the informants would have remembered best, small-rent tenants who also cultivated some land themselves had largely, but not completely, disappeared.

Second, because it was not inconceivable that a large-rent landlord could, in certain circumstances, expel a small-rent householder from his lease, no notion that permanent tenancy was customary in this area can be maintained. In point of fact, the near universality of contractually established land relations shows that tenancy rights, whether of small-rent householder or primary cultivator, were limited to a period defined by contract or were ended by nonperformance of either of the contracting parties. Consequently, there are few instances of true permanent land tenure explicitly granted to tenants. As Shepherd notes, "The permanency of a farmer's tenure was a matter of degree and reflected the relative bargaining power of landlord and tenant at the creation of the relationship," that is, at the time contractual relations were created.[60]

The overall tone of the relationship between large- and small-rent householders described above conflicts somewhat with the characterization of the relationship presented by some authorities.[61] In their view, by the nineteenth century large-rent householders no longer possessed any right or power over land except a legal right, often unenforceable, to collect large rent. Small-rent landlords actually occupied the land, had an unrestricted ability to use it or dispose of it as they pleased, and usually possessed the official survey deeds (*zhangdan*). Large-rent landlords were, in this view, the same as tax farmers. As the 1871 Danshui subprefecture local history put it, large rent "is really the same as the mainland practice of contracting to collect and pay [taxes]."[62] As we have seen above, Taiwanese interviewed after the Japanese conquest were divided in their opinions concerning the rights of large-rent householders. Certainly in the 1850s, large-rent households such as Wu-Shun-Ji possessed the right and occasionally the ability to seize small-rent tenants for nonpayment and deliver them into yamen custody. We must also be careful to note that such seizures in the Wu-Shun-Ji case [22202] occurred only when the offending tenant came into the city or other population centers where the Wu family had agents stationed. Obviously such powers of arrest, even though legally recognized, did not extend much beyond urban boundaries.

In other words, even after the middle of the nineteenth century, a large-rent landlord might retain sufficient potency to be a significant danger to recalcitrant tenants. This danger obviously continued to decrease. But, by 1895, the transfer to small-rent tenants of absolute power to dispose of land was still not entirely complete.

Small Rent

Rent paid by the primary cultivators of the land was termed small rent. Unfortunately, the Dan-Xin cases seem seldom to mention this kind of payment explicitly. One of the very few instances of a small-rent dispute for which any kind of documentation remains in the case record arose during the armed robbery case summarized in Chapter 3. On GX 10/2/18 (15 March 1884), Mrs. Liu née Chen, widow of Liu Dongjin, complained [33319:127] that a tenant to whom her husband before his death had rented some paddy field land was squatting on the land past the term of the lease without paying rent.[63] Mrs. Liu's plaint was accompanied by a copy of the paddy field lease (*cheng bak shuitian zi*) [33319:128].[64]

Under terms of the lease, Liu Dongjin rented tenant Luo Qingyun irrigated paddy fields near Dadu village.[65] The combined large and small rent amounted to ten *shi*, with eight *shi* to be paid after the early harvest in the sixth month and the remaining two *shi* after the late harvest. The term of the lease was six years, from the winter of 1875–76 to the winter of 1881–82. The size of the plot was not specified, although its location was. Luo agreed to pay a non-interest-bearing security deposit of fourteen dollars. Luo also agreed to loan Liu ten dollars with annual interest of 0.26 *shi* on each dollar (that is, total annual interest of 2.6 *shi*). The interest would be used to offset part of the early harvest rent payment so that, in the end, Lo's annual rent would amount to a total of only 7.4 *shi*.

Mrs. Liu's plaint explained that after her husband had rented the land out, he used the lease as collateral to borrow 50 dollars from a third party, Fan Chenkang. This type of loan was called "title deposit" (*taijie*), meaning that the lender took possession of land deeds or, in this case, the paddy field lease paper until such time as the loan was repaid. During the last year of Luo Qingyun's tenure on the land, he refused (according to Mrs. Liu) to pay the rent. Luo contended that his fourteen-dollar deposit was to serve in lieu of the final year's rent grain payment. Mrs. Liu's husband had tried to expel (*qigeng*) Luo in order to get a new tenant, but Luo refused to vacate the land. Moreover, Luo not only was farming the paddy fields illegally but also had refused to pay rent since 1881. In the meantime, Mrs. Liu's husband had been arrested for his alleged involvement in the armed robbery case and subsequently, in 1882, died in jail. Mrs. Liu ended her complaint by begging the magistrate to arrest Luo, force him to pay the rent, and order him off the Liu family's land. The magistrate ordered runners to go and determine the truth of the matter, but whether or not any further action was taken is unknown.

Several characteristic features of the relations between small-rent landlords and their tenants may be seen in the paddy field lease entered into by Liu Dongjin and Luo Qingyun. This type of lease required a deposit that was non-interest-bearing but refundable. Rent, which included the allocations for both large- and small-rent landlords, was payable in two installments, one each following the early and late harvests. In this case, the lease specifically notes that the first payment would be during the sixth month. The late harvest payment was probably made in the tenth month. The location of the land is specified in the rental agreement but never, the size of the plot.

This rental arrangement exhibits certain atypical elements as well. The landlord or small-rent right holder probably farmed no land himself. In documents submitted to the court and during testimony given in the armed robbery case, Liu characterized himself as an innkeeper and seller of odds and ends, never as a farmer. Nor were either of his sons engaged in agriculture; they worked as porters. The Lius were quite different from the cultivator-renter small-rent landlords living and farming in the Daqiqian area who were involved in the dispute with large-rent landlord Wu-Shun-Ji. This difference is probably connected to the second atypicality of the Liu-Luo episode. Liu Dongjin's inability to expel Luo from the land was undoubtedly due to the fact that the landlord had only a tenuous connection to the land in question. The innkeeper lived in Jiuqionglin some distance from the Dadu village plot, thus reducing his ability to monitor Luo or force him to leave the land. In this way, too, Liu may be contrasted with the Daqiqian small-rent householders.

The rarity of litigation over small rent, at least as reflected in the Dan-Xin archives, may indicate that in most instances so-called primary cultivators, the bottom level of the three-tier land rights system, lacked easy access to the legal system because of disadvantaged economic circumstances, physical remoteness from the yamen, intimidation by landlords, or other reasons. From the opposite perspective, it may have been simpler and cheaper for small-rent landlords involved in disputes with renters to expel the tenants and recruit new ones. Unfortunately, data are almost nonexistent. So, too, is information on small-rent assessment rates. We again must refer to Azuma's study of Taiwan's economy.

As in the case of large-rent figures, Azuma tabulated estimated small-rent amounts for various periods.[66] Here we shall employ them to indicate the economic return realized from small-rent rights. The small-rent relationship and rent payments made to the small-rent householder by the primary cultivator of the land were also set by contract. Thus, they varied with the nature and fertility of the land, availability of irrigation, and size of the rent deposit (*qidiyin*) paid by the tenant-cultivator.[67] In general, though, the highest small-rent rate was 40 percent of the harvest. Table 4.2

TABLE 4.2

Estimates of Small Rent Amounts and Income in the Danshui/Xinzhu Area

	Paddy fields			Dry fields		
	U	M	L	U	M	L
Income before 1843 in *shi* per *jia*[a]						
Small rent amount	32	24	16	24	16	8
Large rent amount	8	6	4	6	4	2
Nominal net income	24	18	12	18	12	6
Actual net income	23.2	17.4	11.6	17.4	11.6	5.8
Income as of 1843 in dollars per *jia*[b]						
Small rent amount	40	30	20	30	20	10
Large rent amount	8.8	6.6	4.4	6.6	4.4	2.2
Net income	31.2	23.4	15.6	23.4	15.6	7.8
Income 1843–87 in dollars per *jia*[c]						
Small rent amount	80.15	60.12	40.08	50.10	33.40	16.70
Large rent amount	14.72	11.04	7.36	11.04	7.36	3.86
Net income	65.43	49.08	32.72	39.06	26.04	12.84
Income after 1887 in dollars per *jia*[d]						
Small rent amount	80.15	60.12	40.08	50.10	33.40	16.70
Large rent amount	8.83	6.62	4.42	6.62	4.42	2.03
Land tax	5.48	4.16	3.84	4.16	3.84	2.05
Net income	65.84	49.34	31.82	39.32	25.14	12.62

[a]Data from Azuma, 266, with actual net income calculated on the basis of the 10 percent oversize *dou* measure.

[b]Data from ibid., 273. Small rent payments were made in silver at a rate of one dollar per *shi*.

[c]Data from ibid., 280, Table 6. Amounts are given in silver dollars per *jia* based on an average market price of 1.67 dollars per *shi*.

[d]Data adapted from ibid., 285, Tables 7 and 8, with his figures rounded to two decimal points.

couples this presumption of a 40 percent rate with the rule of thumb that large rent was 10 percent of the crop.

The estimates of small-rent amounts and income indicate that the economic rewards of small-rent householders steadily became greater through the nineteenth century. Their net income remained virtually unaffected by the reforms of 1887 since their new tax burden was offset by an equal decline in their large-rent payments.

These estimates are valid only as approximations. Specific cases varied widely according to the factors of land quality and so on mentioned above. For example, in a dispute litigated in 1875–76 over succession to an estate, a description [21402:18] of the property owned by a lineage surnamed Zheng lists a one-*jia* parcel of land with a small-rent quota of 100 *shi* of grain, or three times the figure given by Azuma for the best grade paddy fields.

The grain prices used to calculate money incomes also fluctuated widely. In the same case just mentioned, court testimony [21402:11] places the value of ten *shi* of grain at 100 dollars, or more than five times the $1.67/*shi* grain price used by Azuma for his pre-1887 estimates. The possibility of wide oscillations in rents and prices emphasizes the need for caution when utilizing the above estimates.

Many of the aspects and dilemmas of landlord-tenant relations and the interest of the government in them are illustrated in one of the longest, if not the longest, case contained in the Dan-Xin archives. The remainder of this chapter is devoted to a summary of it.

Case 22202: Rent Resistance (*kangzu*)
XF 2/2/8–GX 4/10/24 (28 March 1852–18 November 1878)

Tension within Taiwan's multitier system of land relations generated many disputes that found their way into the legal system. It is impossible to quantify, but there seems little doubt that among the most bitterly contested lawsuits were those resulting from the increasing difficulty so-called large-rent (*dazu*) landlords experienced in collecting rent from their primary tenants. The case summarized here graphically illustrates several issues, including the interest of the state in large-rent land relations, the parameters of large-rent landlords' ability to compel rent payment, and the costs and benefits of an appeal to the courts for help in collecting such rent.

The extant records of this particular case cover a period of 26 years (1852–78), but evidence offered during the course of the litigation shows that the dispute had been before the yamen court for at least an additional nine-year period before 1852. The complainant was a large-rent right holder called Wu-Shun-Ji, the name of a corporate lineage that may have been one collateral line of a higher-order lineage.[68] During the course of the case several different lineage members took the lead in pressing their common complaint. Nearly every reference to a given case leader was in the form "Wu-Shun-Ji viz. (*ji*) [name of lineage member]."[69] The first document in the case file is a petition (*bing*) dated XF 2/2/8 (28 March 1852), filed by Wu-Shun-Ji viz. the *shengyuan* Wu Shifen. Wu Shifen continued to act for the Wu lineage through XF 7 (1857–58). A petition [22202:91] of XF 8/3/13 (26 April 1858) was filed by the *jiansheng* Wu Jiqing acting as the lineage representative. Two years later Wu Jiqing's uncle, Wu Guoying, took over the case until at least TZ 1/7/8 (3 August 1862), when he submitted his final petition [22202:178]. That petition was the penultimate filed by the Wu lineage. On TZ 3/3/7 (12 April 1864), the name of Wu Jiqing reappeared affixed to the last of his family's submissions [22202:197] to the court.[70]

This case file is a prime example of one in which the records of two or more analytically distinct actions at law were stored together because the original plaintiff brought suit or was otherwise significantly involved in each instance. Wu-Shun-Ji brought charges of rent resistance (*kangzu*) against many tenants over the years. During the second month of XF 7, at least 44 tenant farmers joined in filing a petition [22202:76] responding to Wu's accusations. Eighty tenants were parties to a settlement reached during a later stage.

An additional factor that tied the case together was geographical proximity. All the tenants involved in the litigation lived in or at least possessed the cultivation rights to land in the vicinity of Daqiqian village (*zhuang*) (see Map 6). Daqiqian, located between 20 and 25 kilometers northwest of the yamen, was actually a much larger area than its designation as a village implies.[71] A number of smaller villages or hamlets such as Sanhu *zhuang*, Shuitou *zhuang*, and Shuiwei *zhuang* that were named as places of residence by tenants were considered part of Daqiqian.

The Wu-Shun-Ji effort throughout the litigation was to prod the court to aid the lineage by forcing tenants to pay large-rent arrears. The Wu lineage was most successful when it took the initiative in bringing recalcitrant tenants to court, where they were, in effect, held for ransom until a settlement on payment was reached.[72]

Wu-Shun-Ji broached its case by petitioning [22202:1] the court on XF 2/2/8 (28 March 1852), charging that several Daqiqian

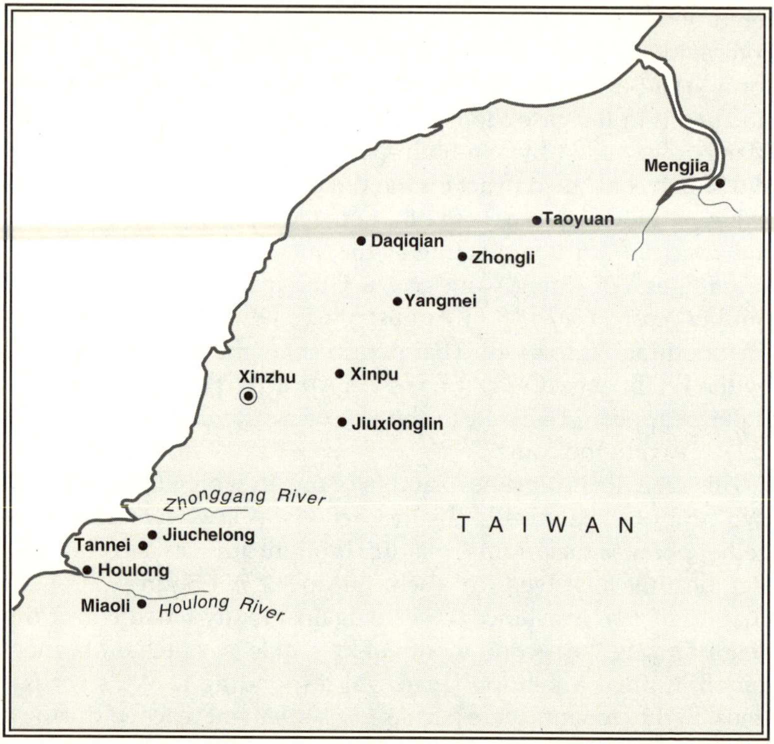

MAP 6. The Daqiqian, Zhonggang, Houlong, and Tannei Areas.

tenants had refused to pay tax rent (*kezu*) for ten years.[73] By using the term *kezu*, the lineage was not so subtly reminding the court that large-rent collections were the source of the government's land tax revenues. A subsequent warrant [22202:2] containing extracts from the Wu petition listed the tenants as Jiang Ashou viz. Jiang Aqing, Xu Aqian, and Fan Linxiang. In the warrant the subprefect, Zhang Qixuan, noted that Fan and the Wu lineage had brought charges against one another earlier. The court had passed judgment, although Zhang did not mention in whose favor. Sometime after that judgment, the tenant Xu Aqian successfully petitioned the Zhejiang / Fujian governor-general, Liu Yunke (in office 1843–50), accusing his landlord of concealing taxes (that is, taxable land) and levying excessive rent (*nike fouchou*). Under the Qing Code, concealing taxable land was punishable by confiscation of the unreported acreage, payment of all back taxes, and corporal punishment of up to 100 blows with the heavy stick, depending on the amount of land not reported.[74] The Wu lineage's charge and Xu's counteraccusation were the core issues in this case and remained unchanged through years of litigation.

As indicated above, the Wu lineage was successful several times in pursuing its claims. In the last month of XF 3 (30 December 1853–28 January 1854), Jiang Shuangnian, Jiang Shuangquan, and Luo Axi, three Wu tenants, were unwary enough to come to Zhuqian, where Wu Shifen had them seized and turned over to a yamen runner.[75] In an XF 3/12/22 (20 January 1854) petition with an appended list of tenants' rent arrears [22202:17, 18] and again in court testimony [22202:21] a day later, Wu Shifen claimed that the two Jiangs were sons of Jiang Ade, who had been in arrears since DG 24 (1844) and owed back rent grain amounting to 1,068.2 *shi*. Luo was also the son of a tenant, Luo Asi, whose refusal to pay rent extended back to DG 23 (1843) and who thus owed 748.66 *shi*, according to Wu.[76] Wu accused Jiang, Luo, and their sons of banding together to resist (*huikang*) paying rent. The term *huikang*, used by Wu, had serious connotations, especially in Taiwan. As noted in Chapter 3, the Qing government was very sensitive to the activities of secret societies (*hui*) and their supposedly generative role in rebellions against the state.[77] To characterize the tenants' refusal to pay as *huikang* clearly implied they were jointly acting for treasonous purposes.

Jiang Shuangnian, who at 20 *sui* was three years older than his brother Shuangquan, admitted the truth of Wu's charge. At the same court session that heard Wu Shifen's testimony, Jiang Shuangnian explained that he and his brother had been coming to ask Wu to allow them to pay the back rent in installments when they had been detained and handed over to the runner. Luo Axi also confirmed that his father had once had a large-rent obligation to Wu-Shun-Ji but that the actual liability had over the years through a complicated set of transactions been shifted. In DG 27 (1847), his father had sold the right to rent the land to one Guo Longming. Axi claimed that Guo had also accepted the obligation to pay the rent arrears as part of the terms of the agreement. But subsequently, Guo had resold the tenancy right to Luo Achun, a relative of Luo Asi. Luo Axi's contention was, therefore, that at that point,

Luo Achun was actually liable for the unpaid rent. The prisoner, Luo Axi, insisted that his father, Luo Asi, had asked the Wu lineage for an extension and was searching for their relative, Luo Achun, to persuade him to come forward and pay the back rent.

Subprefect Zhang's findings, drafted in the form of a directive (*yu*) copied at the end of the transcript of the testimony of Wu and the three captives, revealed him to be unimpressed with the explanations offered by Jiang Shuangnian and Luo Axi. He agreed with Wu Shifen that these tenants had banded together to refuse to pay rent but concluded that their refusal began only in DG 27 (1847), not the earlier dates claimed by Wu. The directive noted explicitly that Wu-Shun-Ji's large rent had to be paid so that this landlord could pay regular and supplemental taxes, which had been earmarked to provide for military salaries (*bingxu*). Zhang ordered the three captives to be detained in the yamen jail (*toumen guan*) until all the back rent had been paid. The three had, in effect, been taken hostage until their back rent was paid.

The Jiang brothers remained in detention for nearly eight months waiting for mediators to negotiate a settlement with Wu-Shun-Ji. Under terms of an agreement worked out by two mediators, Ye Songqing and Jiang Dianbang, the landlord ultimately was willing to settle for much less than he had initially demanded according to a petition [22202:23] the brothers submitted on XF 4/i7/29 (1 September 1854) to Ding Yuejian, subprefect Zhang's successor. The version of the case related in this document differed in several ways from Jiang Shuangnian's court testimony before subprefect Zhang. The petitioners continued to admit their liability but only for part of the back rent. They claimed that in DG 25 (1845) the family estate had been divided among themselves and their two uncles Jiang Lu and Jiang Jiu. Presumably their father, Jiang Ade, had died, and they were heirs to his share of the estate. The arrangement had apparently never been formalized, probably because the brothers were minors at the time.[78]

Refusal to pay rent began also in DG 25 (1845), when two other tenants, because of indebtedness to other creditors, stopped paying rent to Wu-Shun-Ji. The manager of Wu-Shun-Ji's rental income at the time had forcibly seized the rent, which so angered the financially strapped tenants that they persuaded other tenants to band together and refuse to pay rent. Shuangnian and Shuangquan's petition went on to say that at the time of their capture by Wu Shifen, their uncles were still managing the entire estate. The Jiang brothers (the petitioners) were still in the yamen jail because they were even now unable to persuade their uncles to pay the arrears.

The petition also explained the amount of rent the two brothers owed. Their father, they asserted, paid 15 of every 100 *shi* of grain harvest to Wu-Shun-Ji as large rent. At some point, however, the rent had become a fixed amount. The prisoners explained that they had now asked the two mediators to draw up an estate division agreement (*fencuan jiushu*) clearly delineating their own large-rent liability and separating it from that of their uncles. Under the formalized arrangements, the total large rent for the undivided estate would be 70 *shi* per year. For the years after DG 25 (1845), the younger Jiangs' share of the rent was 10.5 *shi* annually. The remainder was the responsibility of their uncles. Thus Jiang Shuangnian and Shuangquan owed unpaid rent totaling 105 *shi* for the years DG 25–XF 4 (1845–54). They claimed not only that Wu-Shun-Ji had now agreed to their lesser liability but also that the landlord had agreed to give them until the late harvest (three months away) to repay. Given these circumstances, the prisoners asked to be released.

Subprefect Ding expressed some skepticism in his endorsement (*pi*), wondering why the Wu lineage representative had not filed a release bond for the brothers if it had agreed to the arrangements. The brothers probably had been slightly premature in their claim to have reached an agreement: Wu Shifen's petition [22202:25] confirming the resolution of his lineage's dispute with the two was not submitted to the yamen until two months later. Nevertheless, at that point, the two were released.

As for the other prisoner, Luo Axi, it took him a year longer to resolve his dispute. His father, Luo Asi, first reported in a counterplaint (*su*) [22202:31] dated XF 5/3/8 (23 April 1855) that several months earlier, in XF 4/11 (20 December 1854–17 January 1855), he had paid over 100 *shi* of grain to Wu-Shun-Ji. He had taken this action in hopes of obtaining his son's release, even though he had long ago sold his rights to the land and thus was legally no longer obligated for large rent. Luo complained that his son was still being detained even though Wu had submitted a petition agreeing that he should be released.[79] Subprefect Ding's endorsement pointed out that Luo Axi[80] could not be released until the chief tax clerk (*liangzongshu*) obtained confirmation from Wu-Shun-Ji that Luo had paid the rent arrears in full. Another three months passed before, on XF 5/6/28 (28 July 1855), the chief tax clerk reported [22202:32] that Wu had confirmed receipt of full payment of rent grain. Luo Axi then had to wait several weeks longer before being released under bond from the yamen jail.

Men in the employ of Wu-Shun-Ji were at work in the villages outside the subprefectural seat as well as near the yamen. In the latter half of XF 5 (1855), two more tenants were seized when they ventured into towns near Daqiqian. On XF 5/7/18 (30 August 1855), Wu Changliu, Wu-Shun-Ji's manager, seized Li Sheng when Li was in Taoyuan market town (*jie*) and turned him over to a yamen runner. Wu Shifen charged (and Li admitted before the court) nonpayment of large rent (nineteen *shi* annually) for as long as ten years [22202:34, 36].

A second tenant was reported [22202:39] captured on XF 5/10/22 (1 December 1855). Wu's manager had offered a reward for information leading to the capture of nonpaying tenants. In this way the manager was able to discover that Fan Linxiang's[81] grandson, Fan Atian, was passing through Zhongli market town, had captured him, and turned him over to runners of the Third Fast Runner Section, who had an office in Taoyuan.[82]

Li Sheng had quickly confessed and in a relatively short time came to an agreement to pay the back rent to Wu-Shun-Ji. After only five months in detention Li filed a petition (*cheng*) [22202:49] explaining to the subprefect that he had agreed to pay Wu three years' back rent immediately and to clear the remainder of the debt in installments over a three-year period. Since a Taoyuan store owner (*puhu*) had agreed to enter into a bond guaranteeing that Li Sheng would pay, Li asked to be released. A Wu-Shun-Ji petition [22202:48] handed in the same day, XF 5/12/20 (27 January 1856), confirmed these arrangements, and Li was released under bond [22202:50] immediately.

The lineage's claim against Fan Linxiang was not settled so easily. The capture of Fan's grandson provoked the first active opposition not only against the landlord but also against the yamen itself. When Wu Shifen reported Fan Atian's capture, he noted that Fan's relatives were gathering and might pose a threat. A few days later, on XF 5/10/27 (6 December 1855), Lin Yong, the head of the runner section that had been holding Fan in Taoyuan, relayed more disturbing news to the subprefect [22202:42]. During the early morning of the twenty-second of the month, Fan Linxiang and a gang of rent-owing tenants armed with muskets had swarmed into Zhongli (where Fan Atian had been captured) and had taken captive a man they considered to be the informant. The next evening an even more alarming report that Fan was leading his gang from Xinpu to Taoyuan to free his grandson reached the runner office there. Wu Changliu, the Wu-Shun-Ji manager, had also heard the rumor and, fearful that Fan Atian would be forcibly liberated, had taken him back from the runners before moving him to another location. The runner section head asked the subprefect to send militia troops to take Fan and deliver him either to court or to Mengjia to await trial.

Subprefect Ding followed Lin Yong's suggestion. As Lin had mentioned in his report, two local leaders, one an overseer (*zongli*), the other a *baojia* head (*baozheng*), were in Zhuqian at the time.[83] On XF 5/11/16 (24 December 1855), Ding ordered [22202:43] them to muster a large number of militia to help Lin Yong take Fan Atian to Mengjia. There he was to be held until Ding arrived and could question him.[84] By XF 5/12/9 (16 January 1856), runner Lin reported [22202:45] that Fan Atian had been delivered. Fan was interrogated [22202:47] by the subprefect the same day and readily admitted that there were rent arrears. The 20-*sui*-old prisoner denied any detailed knowledge of the debt, however, because his father and grandfather were still alive and managing the family's leased property. At the same court hearing, Wu Shifen claimed that Fan Linxiang had not paid large rent for fourteen years and owed over 1,000 *shi*. The subprefect accepted this figure as accurate and, realizing Atian's importance as Linxiang's heir, ordered him jailed until the back rent was paid, despite his probable lack of personal responsibility for nonpayment.

Subprefect Ding rationalized the court's unswerving support of Wu-Shun-Ji and its severity toward Fan and the other tenants in a directive [22202:52] issued during the second month of XF 6 (1856). After summarizing the developments in the case, Ding explained again that nonpayment of large rent was a serious matter, since it affected the state's revenue and military supplies (*guoke bingxu*). Moreover, the tenants, he declared, by banding together to refuse to pay rent, showed they had no respect for the law. The subprefect ordered Jiang Guohua, the overseer of the Daqiqian area, to induce or direct the tenants to pay in full.

By XF 6/4 (4 May–2 June 1856), Ding Yuejian had been transferred to Jiayi county and replaced as subprefect by Tang Jun. On XF 6/7/6 (6 August 1856), Tang responded to Fan Linxiang's inability or refusal to make good his large rent arrearage by bringing Fan's grandson before the court to be "called to account" (*tibi*). Atian maintained that his family was preparing to pay the "public items"[85] (*gongxiang*) and begged for five more days to gather the back rent. Subprefect Tang was not convinced that the Fan family was moving as quickly as it could and in a directive appended to Fan Atian's testimony [22202:56] ordered him beaten with the heavy stick (*zhangze*). The prisoner was threatened with another flogging if there were further delays.

Although Tang Jun's tenure as Danshui chief administrator was only slightly more than a year, he was energetic in applying pressure to the recalcitrant tenants. Tang's energy, however, may not have been an unmitigated blessing for Wu-Shun-Ji. The subprefect's endorsement to a Wu petition [22202:57] dated just two days after Fan Atian was beaten noted that the chief tax clerk's account books showed not inconsiderable amounts of unpaid regular and supplemental grain tax (*zhenggong bugu qianliang*) under Wu-Shun-Ji's name. Attached to the petition itself was a long and detailed list [22202:58] of tenants and their arrearages totaling 15,888 *shi*. Rather than ordering the tenants to pay Wu, the endorsement declared that the arrearages should be collected and stored to await a court hearing. Shortly thereafter, on XF 6/7/18, 22, and 27 (18, 22, and 27 August 1856), Tang amplified the endorsement by issuing a flurry of orders with detailed instructions to yamen personnel, local notables and village leaders, and tenants.

The subprefect commanded runners and tax clerks to work with Jiang Dianbang, who was head of Jin-Guang-Fu Large Guardpost, the area's largest settlement organization, plus Zhongli overseer Wang Zuolin and Dahukou overseer Dai Shuisheng and other functionaries to gather the rent grain owed by Daqiqian tenants.[86]

The yamen issued a book of stamped tax slips (*yinchuan*), each with name and amount of arrearage written in, that the three were to give to tenants to serve as certificates of payment (*zhizhao*) once the arrearages were cleared. By XF 6/8/6 (4 September 1856), Tang had indicated his intention to go to Daqiqian personally and hold hearings if the tenants did not pay. To make further resistance impossible, the subprefect authorized Jiang, Wang, and Dai to lead a force of 100 musketeers (*niaoqiangshou*) and 50 commoner guards (*zhuangding*) to the area and await his arrival [22202:65].

The backing of such a large armed force allowed Jiang, Wang, and Dai to succeed in collecting some of the back rent without the presence of the subprefect. A group of tenants, bowing to the inevitable, reached an accord with Jiang and his two colleagues in which 500 *shi* of back tax grain would be turned over, with the remaining arrearages to be paid in later installments. The three men reported in two petitions [22202:69, 74] dated 9/14 and 10/25 of that same year (12 October and 22 November 1856), that nineteen tenants had turned over 489.1 *shi* of grain, nearly the full amount agreed upon.[87] The two overseers and Jiang had arranged to transport the grain to a grain-dealer-cum-miller (*longpu*) in Sihu village who bought the grain. They reported that the sale at 0.65 dollars per *shi* realized a net of 300.798 dollars after transport costs of 0.035 dollars per *shi* were deducted.[88]

The name of Xu Aqian headed the list [22202:71] of tenants who agreed to the 500-*shi* payment. Xu, who according to Wu-Shun-Ji's reckoning owed 1,051 *shi*, had been unwilling to turn over more than 40 *shi*. As he had done earlier, Xu again contested Wu's rent claims in court. During XF 7/2 (24 February–25 March 1857), Xu, joined by at least 43 other tenants, filed a joint complaint (*jiancheng*) [22202:77] accusing Wu-Shun-Ji of levying excessive rent, of illegally using an oversize grain measure when collecting large rent, and of concealing or not reporting land under cultivation to be rated for taxation.[89]

According to Xu and his fellow complainants, during the early Qianlong period (1736–95), when their ancestors had settled the land to which the original reclamation permit holder (*kenhu*), Jiang Shengben, held title, 25 *jia* of land were reported for taxation.[90] The annual large-rent levy had been 600 *shi*, of which 25 *shi* went to cover the regular tax (*zhenggong*) and 100 *shi* the supplementary grain tax (*bugu*). Over the years more fields had been reclaimed and put into cultivation. There had been a survey that found their fields under cultivation had increased to 440 *jia*. These fields had even been provisionally rated by a tax clerk, with the tax fixed at four *shi* per *jia*. Xu was not explicit but implied that the survey results and proposed tax rating were never officially reported to the yamen. In any case, the current rent levied by Wu-Shun-Ji had gone up to over 3,000 *shi*, but the lineage had managed to conceal the existence of this new land, thus avoiding increased tax liability. The tenants pointed out that in XF 6 (1856), they had paid 500 *shi* of back rent under court supervision. Moreover, the tenants made the claim that in 1847, they had, at the direction of former subprefects Huang Kaiji and Cao Shigui, paid 445 dollars from the sale of back rent grain to Wu.

The charge of excessive rent levies also led Xu and the others to an important related issue. They explained that rent levied by Wu-Shun-Ji was excessive because Wu used the "1-9-8" method to determine the amount owed. The "1-9-8" method was a shorthand way of referring to rent levied as a percentage of the harvest. In this scheme the landlord collected one-tenth of the crop in large rent. In addition, a fee of 8 percent was tacked on for administrative expenses.[91] Thus, as Xu explained in a complaint [22202:92] submitted to a subsequent subprefect on XF 8/4/8 (20 May 1858), of every 100 *shi* harvested, Wu took 18 in large rent. Jiang Shengben, the original landlord, had taken only 15. The method of determining rent that Xu Aqian and the other tenants were pushing for was fixed rent of so many *shi* per *jia* of cultivable land. Thus, they asked the court to carry out a new survey and rate the land for taxation based on the number of *jia*. The tenants won a momentous victory on this point as Subprefect Tang endorsed their complaint with a note that a survey should be carried out and the land rated for taxation according to its quality (*zhaoze shengke*).

Continued litigation by the landlord delayed the implementation of Tang's decision. Indeed, the Wu lineage persuaded later subprefects to continue to bring pressure on the tenants to pay back rent. Late in XF 8 (1858), En Yu gave runners a warrant [22202:104] with orders to bring in Xu and seven other tenants. This act provoked Xu and others to resort to forcible resistance. Runners reported [22202:105] that when they attempted to approach Xu in his house, he and his family first barricaded themselves inside and then rushed outside and assaulted at least one of the yamen agents. Subprefect En began to realize that Xu and the other resisting tenants could only be made to pay if confronted with a more imposing force than a few yamen runners. On XF 9/3/18 (20 April 1859), En decided to send runners to clean and put in order a public hall (*gongguan*) in Dakengqian village near Daqiqian. En intended to proceed to that village with a force of commoner guards to surround and arrest Xu and the others [22202:112, 113, 114].

The runners, however, were unable even to enter the village. On XF 9/4/13 (15 May 1859), they reported [22202:115] that Xu and an armed mob of tenants had set up a barricade of barrels filled with night soil and prevented the runners from moving into the village. The tenants, armed with muskets, had concealed themselves behind the barricade ready to fire on the runners. En Yu was prepared to request the assistance of local garrison troops in carrying through with his plan to arrest Xu Aqian. At that point unrelated disturbances arising from the celebration of a rite of cosmic renewal (*jiao*) in Mengjia diverted the yamen's attention. To maintain firm control over the situation there, Subprefect En decided he had no choice but to set aside his plans for Xu Aqian and travel to Mengjia. Overseer Dai Chaoqing and other local leaders were directed [22202:116] to wait for En to return to do their part in the arrest of Xu Aqian and his fellow tenants.

In fact, no further action was taken for nearly a year until the tenure of a new subprefect, Ning Changjing. The Wu-Shun-Ji lineage earlier had elected to ignore the issue of fixed versus variable rent, in effect seeming to concede the point, preferring to recover some back rent whether or not its claims against the tenants had been excessive. Then, on XF 9/11/20 (13 December 1859), Wu Jiqing, acting for the lineage, petitioned the new subprefect to act against Xu Aqian. During the first months of XF 10 (1860), Ning took less drastic action than the Wu lineage demanded, attempting to persuade the tenants to cooperate in a new survey to settle the dispute [22202:120–26]. It was at this juncture that, from the perspective of Wu-Shun-Ji, the case took a disastrous turn. The Wu representative filed an XF 10/i3/17 (27 April 1860) petition [22202:127] asserting that rent had been levied using the "1-9-5" method (i.e., rent levied at a rate of 15 percent of the harvest) on land not yet rated for taxation. Inexplicably, the petition admitted that the levy had been on fields newly reclaimed during the Daoguang period (1821–50), and that the new fields totaled over 1,000 *jia* in area. Not unexpectedly, Ning in his endorsement wondered if Wu was paying taxes on the 1,000 *jia* from which it collected large rent. The subprefect also ordered a survey and rent collection by a reliable man selected by the yamen.

A directive was apparently issued to that effect, although no copy is preserved in the case file. The directive provoked a panicky response [22202:128] from Wu Guoying and other lineage leaders. Guoying protested against the yamen directive's apparent order that a fixed rent rate was to be assigned to the land. The petitioners argued that the "1-9-5" system, which had been used for over a century in the area and was the method employed by more than ten other landlords in the area, was appropriate for the Daqiqian locale. According to Wu Guoying,

> The land we inherited consists of dry fields dependent on irrigation from ponds built to store rain water. When rain does not fall in time, the land is often blasted by drought for more than ten *li*. Sometimes there are several seasons when no seed can be sown and no crop harvested. . . . Rent is levied according to the quality of the harvest. If a tenant gets ten *shi*, he retains 8.5 *shi* and 1.5 *shi* goes to the landlord. This is termed the 1-9-5 levy. Since it harms neither taxes nor agriculture, it is an excellent rule with good intentions. Landlord and tenant are mutually dependent.

Subprefect Ning, while conceding that Xu and the tenants should be made to pay back rent, was unimpressed with Wu's line of argument, which, after all, could have been convincing only if propounded by the tenants.[92] After reminding Wu that a landlord should not levy rent on tenants in an exploitative way (*canbo kulei dianren*), Ning concluded his endorsement by indicating his intention to supervise a land survey personally and reach a decision in the case based on it.

At a hearing on XF 10/i3/24 (14 May 1860), Ning interrogated [22202:131] Wu Jiqing and Xu Aqian, who, putting aside his previous resistance, had now voluntarily responded to a court summons. His confidence was well founded. Ning accepted Xu's contention that there were 440 *jia* of cultivated paddy fields (*tian*) farmed by Wu-Shun-Ji tenants. In a proclamation [22202:132] published the same day, he decreed that the fields were to be rated as of the lowest grade (*xiaze*), large rent paid to Wu was to be fixed at five *shi* per *jia*, rent grain was to be measured with the standard market measure (*shi dou*), and Wu was required to pay taxes on all 440 *jia*.

Despite the favorable ruling, the tenants continued to fall behind in large-rent payment. In the fall of XF 11 (1861), Wu Guoying filed a series of petitions complaining that Xu and the others were ignoring the court order. Qiu Yuejin, who was back for a second term as subprefect, had Xu and three other tenants arrested and brought in for a hearing. Wu Guoying and Jiqing were called as well. On XF 11/9/25 (28 October 1861), after hearing the testimony [22202:151] of the six men, the subprefect reached a decision that was something of a compromise. Just as Wu Guoying had charged in his testimony, each of the four tenants admitted that they had resisted large-rent payment since DG 20 (1840), or for more than 20 years. Qiu's decision forgave all but four years' back rent.[93] In addition, the subprefect arbitrarily decided that additional reclamation since the Daoguang survey had increased the amount of cultivated fields to 500 *jia*. All of the 80 tenants renting land from Wu-Shun-Ji were to reach agreement among themselves on allocating responsibility for future large-rent payments on the newly registered 500 *jia*. Large rent was increased to six *shi* per *jia* payable after the early harvest. As for the Wu family, their tax burden was increased substantially. Qiu ended their liability for the 100-*shi* supplementary grain tax item but added a new collection of 500 *shi* of military settlement rent (*tunzu*), also payable annually at the early harvest.[94]

Qiu's directive did not tell the whole story, however. Four days before, on XF 11/9/21 (24 October 1861), one of Wu's petitions [22202:146] complaining about Xu Aqian had prompted Qiu to note in his endorsement that, while the tenants certainly were in arrears, Wu-Shun-Ji had been collecting 2,000 *shi* yearly that should have gone to the government in taxes. The landlord had fallen several years behind in taxes and deserved to be heavily punished. So, paradoxically, Wu-Shun-Ji's continuing litigation against its tenants was successful in recovering some of the debt at a cost to the lineage of finding itself dunned for back taxes and liable for increased charges in the future. The lineage either had not foreseen or, more likely, had been confident of avoiding the net increase in tax liability it would logically incur when the court had agreed to try and update the amount of cultivated land (and thus taxes) on the books under Wu's name.

Xu Aqian and the three other tenants arrested and brought to court still had a substantial debt to clear. Their four years' back rent amounted to 2,800 *shi* of grain. Because they were being held in detention, Xu and the others submitted a petition [22202:152] on XF 11/10/7 (9 November 1861) requesting that an overseer and reclamation permit holder (*kenhu*) from the Daqiqian area collect the grain, sell it, and turn it over to the court. By the end of XF 11 (1861–62), overseer Dai Chaoqing and settler head (*zong kenhu*) Jiang Ronghua reported in the last of four petitions [22202:160, 162, 164, 166] on the subject that they had collected a total of 2,590 silver dollars from the tenants. This sum was the equivalent of slightly more than 2,800 *shi* at the current market price of 9 *jiao* (0.9 dollars) per *shi*.

In the months after Qiu handed down his decision, Wu Guoying and another lineage member, Wu Zhixiang, petitioned again [22202:161, 165] protesting the judgment but were harshly rebuffed. The subprefect's endorsement to the latter petition threatened that further "recklessly troubling the court" would leave the yamen no alternative but to send a report to higher authorities recommending that the landlord be impeached (*xiangge*) to deprive him of his degree.[95] Then he could be punished for the crime of concealing taxable land. For this crime the lineage's land would be confiscated to be used by the government as a source for military supplies for the mainland.[96] No more protests were filed by Wu-Shun-Ji. A few days later, on XF 11/12/29 (28 January 1862), after testimony [22202:170] at another court hearing, Wu Guoying submitted a compliance bond (*zunyi jiezhuang*) demonstrating Wu-Shun-Ji's acceptance of the terms of the court decision and a money receipt document (*lingyin zhuang*) acknowledging he had received the back rent. At the same time the 80 tenants also signed a compliance bond [22202:172] agreeing to the settlement, and Xu Aqian and the other three prisoners were finally released under a bond [22202:174] guaranteeing their good behavior signed by Jiang Ronghua and Dai Chaoqing.

Even with the release of the last four tenants the case did not end.[97] On TZ 3/3/7 (12 April 1864), Wu Jiqing filed one last petition [22202:197] charging Xu Aqian and Li Afan with organizing a large group of tenants that refused to pay rent (*huizhong kangna*). Xu and Li, Wu charged, formed an armed gang, blocked the road, and seized rent grain being transported, thus preventing other tenants from paying.[98] From the first year of the Tongzhi period (1862–74) until the end of the case, however, subprefects confined their efforts to attempting to carry out an accurate survey of fields leased by tenants.[99] Wu-Shun-Ji initiatives against its tenants may have been stifled in large part because previous litigation had been so costly. Indeed, a number of times the yamen had to dun the Wu lineage because it had fallen behind in paying the *tunzu* tax.[100] The reversal of fortunes experienced by Wu-Shun-Ji was dramatically illustrated in the last two documents [22202:222, 223] in the case file. In the tenth month of both GX 3 and 4 (1877 and 1878), Taibei prefect Chen Xingju ordered runners to compel Wu to remit the military settlement rent tax.[101] If it were not paid, runners were authorized to arrest the lineage representative and bring him to court in chains.

The Wu lineage's continuing tax problems meant that documents continued to be added to the case file long after the major disputes over rent payment had been resolved. It is quite possible that Wu-Shun-Ji's legal problems continued after 1878, the date of the last item in the file. Beginning in 1879, however, the Daqiqian area became part of Danshui county. Records of any further litigation would have been stored in that county's yamen archives, which unfortunately are not extant.[102]

This case is a demonstration in microcosm of some aspects of the gradual transfer of control over land from large-rent to small-rent landlords carried out in the various locales of central and northern Taiwan during the eighteenth and nineteenth centuries. Large urban-dwelling lineages such as Wu-Shun-Ji were heavily dependent on their right to collect large rent. One of the lineage's representatives explained [22202:153] with some hyperbole that the rent supported not only himself and his immediate family but also 400–500 lineage members in both Taiwan and the mainland. Beyond satisfying tax obligations, the rent was necessary to meet expenses for geomancy, worship in and sweeping of tombs, and festivals. The ability of lineage members to obtain degrees, whether by examination or by purchase, undoubtedly depended on their rental income. Other financial ventures such as moneylending by Wu Jiqing may have been funded from large-rent collections.[103]

Such a lineage may have possessed the legal right to large rent but was increasingly bereft of the ability to collect it, even with yamen backing. As we have seen, lineage managers and agents were effective only in Zhuqian and the larger market towns in the Daqiqian area. The Wu tenants, who were also secondary (small-rent) landlords, were able to defy the lineage and even in some cases yamen runners by virtue of several factors. Their somewhat remote location midway between Zhuqian and Mengjia insulated them from government control to some degree. The tenants lived in close proximity to the land to which they held rights, farming some themselves and subleasing the rest. Their ties to the land were stronger and more immediate than those of the city-dwelling lineage. Finally, in this particular case, most or perhaps all of the tenants were also bound together by the sociocultural and linguistic ties of their Hakka subethnic origins. The bonds of language and tradition cemented even more firmly the solidarity of economic interest.

5

The Export Economy

UNTIL the 1870s, Taiwan was on the margins of the Qing world. Although its economic importance as a rice supplier to Fujian was undeniable, it was considered a social and political backwater. After 1683 and the final consolidation of Manchu rule, the central government soon shifted its attention to inner Asia, traditionally the area of foreign policy concern, while relegating its maritime frontier to a back burner.[1] The island and its inhabitants became a focus of attention to policymakers in the capital only when major rebellions such as those of Zhu Yigui (1721) and Lin Shuangwen (1786) threatened the state's sovereignty. Decisive steps in policy formulation concerning the island took place only rarely. The government's stance toward the major problem of migration to the island was not settled until 1790, when emigration from the mainland was finally legalized after over a century of ambivalence and vacillation. However, even before the shock of the Japanese expeditionary force in the early 1870s prodded the central government seriously to consider the island's importance in formulating foreign policy for the first time since the seventeenth century, the power of foreign market demand for several Taiwan products had begun to link this remote frontier firmly into a network of global trade. Although rice had become first or second (to sugar) in Taiwan's exports soon after Chinese immigration became significant in the seventeenth century,[2] three products—sugar, tea, and camphor—made up the bulk of Taiwan's exports after 1860. Sugar, grown mainly in the southern half of Taiwan, was relatively unimportant to the Dan-Xin region's economy. In contrast, the foothills and upland plains of northern Taiwan were nearly ideal for tea cultivation. By 1895, tea was a vital cash crop and export commodity.[3] As James Davidson, writing just after the turn of the century, noted:

> [T]he district under Tea cultivation is a comparatively small one in the north. Although occupying about one-sixth of the territory utilized by sugar, and only a fraction of that given up to rice, or the area covered with the vast camphor forests, the production brings to the island nearly five times the receipts obtained from sugar, over five times the receipts obtained from camphor, and more than one half of the total value of the whole export trade of Formosa.[4]

As for the second most important export commodity for Xinzhu and northern Taiwan, the camphor tree was native to deep forests blanketing the island's mountain ranges. As the above quotation makes clear, by the 1890s for the island as a whole, camphor began to approach sugar in export returns. Although a distant runner-up to tea, camphor was nevertheless a key part of the northern economy.[5] The only obstacles to production of either commodity were the rugged environment and the presence of those with previous claims to the area.

In some cases, early Chinese settlers had already claimed rights to areas suitable for growing the tea bush. The Hakka farmers of Fenjiwo, Fangliao, Fanzibei, and Xinshe villages, whose claims to an upland clearing in its entirety led to the boundary dispute case [22510/22514] to be discussed below, were one instance of this phenomenon. Of course, aborigine settlements were most likely to possess rights to such otherwise undesirable land. Indeed, both parties to the just-mentioned dispute professed to have obtained valid deeds from aborigine headmen. So, in this way increasing outside demand generated strife among the hill folk of northern Taiwan and created work for the local court.

Even more than tea cultivation, camphor distillation was usually possible only with the forbearance of local tribal settlements. Since the largest trees were in the deepest parts of the mountain forests, those seeking the greatest profit ran the most danger of encountering hostile "raw" aborigines and losing their heads for their trouble.[6] Even pacified tribes such as the Shilixing settlement, which controlled the area east of Miaoli where Chen Zhenxiang obtained his camphor, were capable of launching attacks on Chinese settlements because of friction with camphor distillers over obtaining permission to set up distilleries and rights to profits from the trade.[7] Government efforts to regulate and tax trade in both camphor and tea gave rise to smuggling and *lijin*[8] evasion and increased the difficulty of preventing disputes and criminal activities. Understanding the size and foreign connections of production and marketing of each commodity may enable us to comprehend its place in the local economy.

Tea

The earliest mention in the sources of tea production seems to date from the late Kangxi period. The Zhuluo county gazetteer of 1717 mentions that a variety apparently native to Taiwan was being grown in the mountains of what is modern Nantou county. A few years later, Huang Shujing mentioned that in the same area tea was being fire dried.[9]

A Fujianese processed variety, *wuyi* or Bohea tea, was first produced in Taiwan in the Jiaqing era (1796–1820). This newly introduced variety was first produced in northern Danshui subprefecture.[10] There is some limited evidence that tea was exported from Taiwan in the early nineteenth century, but little is known of this early trade.[11] By the Daoguang period (1821–50) many of the inhabitants of two northern Danshui townships, Shiding *bao* and Quanshan *bao*, depended on tea for their livelihood. The government allowed it to be marketed by guild merchants only after the tea was shipped to Fuzhou, the provincial capital, where a duty of two dollars per picul was levied.[12] It would appear that most of this tea was domestically consumed.

Tea production and export began to mushroom after 1865, when Western merchants became aware of the tea-producing potential of the island. In that year the Englishman John Dodd came to Taiwan to examine the state of tea growth and production. In the following year Dodd's firm began to buy Taiwanese tea for export, and the first shipments were recorded.[13] The stimulus provided by larger, foreign markets spurred rapid growth, as indicated by Tables 1 and 2 in Appendix 3.

The growth of the tea industry in Taiwan before 1895 can be divided into three periods. From the first year of significant tea exports in 1866 until 1873, trade increased at a fairly rapid pace, with total exports reaching over 2.6 million pounds in 1872 and then declining to only a little over 2 million pounds in 1873. In these years (1866–73) John Dodd began to advance funds to cultivators around what is now the city of Taibei to plant tea. In 1869 direct shipment to the United States, soon to become the major consumer of Taiwan tea, was initiated. Previously tea had been transported to Amoy and then transshipped for delivery to foreign markets.[14] Oolong (*wulong*) tea was the only type processed during these years.

During the second period, from around 1875 until 1885, tea output increased dramatically until overproduction led to a drastic fall in the price of Oolong tea in 1885. The growth of exports to the United States, government encouragement of tea planting, and competition among growers to expand the amount of land under cultivation all contributed to the temporary glut.[15]

Changes in the nature and structure of trade became observable in the years before Taiwan became a province in 1885. A second type of tea, *Baozhong*, began to be marketed. At first it was shipped in bulk to Fuzhou for processing, and its low price in relation to Oolong tea made it popular among consumers.[16] In 1881 exports of Baozhong tea from Danshui were recorded for the first time after the Quanzhou tea firm Wu-Fu-Lao began processing the tea in Taiwan. At about the same time Wang Anding and Zhang Zhankui, merchants from Anqi county in Guangdong, entered the export trade by establishing the Jiancheng firm in Taiwan. Both developments spurred the growth of Baozhong exports from Taiwan.

In spite of the entry of Chinese firms into the domestic sector of the tea trade, foreign firms such as Dodd, Tait, Elles, Brown, and Boyd controlled the trade because of their monopoly over international shipping and their ability to control prices offered to producers. Price control was possible not only because of the shipping monopoly but also because tea production continued to be financed, although indirectly by that time, by the foreign firms. In a familiar pattern, Chinese brokers and firms became dependent on advances from British and American firms. It has been argued that the subordinate position of Chinese merchants in the tea trade caused them to be unconcerned about accurate measures and quality control, which in turn eventually led to a decrease in the price of Baozhong tea.[17] Fragmentary data primarily for 1892–95 that show a sharp rise in Baozhong prices cast doubt on this argument, however.[18]

Continuing strong exports to the United States allowed Oolong production to weather both a natural drop in trade with Europe during the Sino-French War (1883–85) and stagnation in exports to Europe after the war. Except for a temporary jump in 1893, however, the days of rapid growth in the Oolong market were over. Baozhong exports showed continuous growth, albeit at a much lower level, from 1881 to the Sino-Japanese War (1894–95) that marks the end of the third period in the tea trade.

Part of the package of reforms and improvements sponsored by Governor Liu Mingchuan after 1885 was designed to ensure the health of Taiwan's tea export trade. Beginning in 1887, Liu encouraged local merchants in Dadaocheng, the market and commercial center on the Danshui River, to form a tea guild (called Yung-He-Xing) with responsibility for rectifying the problems of measurement and quality control that had kept the price of Taiwan tea down. Competition from the new guild also helped to moderate the control over prices foreign firms exerted through their intermediaries, native firms headquartered in Canton and Amoy. To encourage tea production, tax rates were reduced. The land tax on tea plantations was now levied at two dollars per every 10,000 tea bushes. Lijin was kept down to four *jiao* (0.4 dollars) per picul.

In the Zhuqian / Xinzhu area, tea cultivation was first seen in the late 1860s or early 1870s in three areas forming a convex arc stretching from Dahukou (present-day Hukou) 13 kilometers almost directly north of the city, to Xinpu 9 kilometers northeast, and finally to Xiancaiweng (present-day Guanxi) 20 kilometers straight east.[19] Oolong as well as many other tea varieties were tried, with one called *qingxin* eventually proving the most popular. Four years after the tea shrubs were propagated by transplanted seedlings or slips cut from mature plants, they were ready for the leaves to be harvested. The leaves could be harvested as often as four times a year: spring tea around the beginning of the third lunar month, summer tea beginning in the middle of the fifth month, autumn tea starting in the seventh month, and winter tea after the middle of the eleventh month.

Some of the structural aspects of tea cultivation in rural Xinzhu may be glimpsed in the tea plot boundary dispute case summarized following this section.[20] The land was put into production at the initiative of a partnership, Jin-Liu-He, formed for that purpose. The land, a sloping, upland clearing, had originally been obtained from a member of the Zhuqian tribe. The terms of this transaction seem to have been unconditional sale. According to a contract [22510:8] submitted in evidence, adjacent pasture land obtained from the same tribe by nearby villages was granted to the villagers in perpetuity for the price of 1,000 dollars with no residual rights retained by the tribal owner. The land eventually used for tea cultivation was described as "sold to" forebears of some of the members of the partnership. There is no indication that Jin-Liu-He was obliged to pay rent to the tribe or that the partnership's right to the land was otherwise encumbered in any way.

The partnership recruited tenants to plant tea and sweet potatoes. Tenants provided their own capital and managed their plots themselves. At least one member of the partnership may have himself been cultivating or managing the cultivation of a significant proportion of the total number of shrubs. Liu Bukui testified [22514:89] that there were a total of 1,000,000 tea bushes planted in the clearing. Tenants had 600,000, and he cultivated 200,000. Liu's testimony did not account for the rest of the shrubs. Perhaps the remainder were accounted for by the other partners, by another separate partnership involved peripherally in the litigation, or by exaggeration.

The tenant families, as suggested by their self-capitalization ability, were relatively well off. Several of the tenants whose homes were attacked by neighboring villagers during the course of the dispute submitted complaints to the yamen to which were appended lists of their losses. One man claimed [22514:8] that among his property and possessions that were burned or stolen were his thatched hut dwelling, six red oxen, four pigs, 50 *shi* of grain, 4,000 catties of sweet potatoes, 60,000 tea shrubs, and sundry clothing and household goods. The thatched hut had been erected near the tea plots, suggesting that it was designed mainly for temporary use during the peak times of the tea cultivation cycle.[21] The owner and his family certainly had a more permanent home elsewhere to which they returned during part of the year. At least one of the partnership's tenants had sublet half his land. The man and his family had planted 30,000 tea shrubs and their sublessee a similar number [22514:19, 20]. Unfortunately, neither the terms of primary or secondary tenants' leases were disclosed.

Probably their contracts called for annual cash rents based on units of 10,000 bushes. An 1886 tea land lease from an area just to the east called for a four-year period to get the land into production followed by a ten-year contract period. During the first four years of production, the tenant was to pay ten dollars per 10,000 bushes. For the last six years the rent doubled. The tenant was required to pay a rent deposit of two dollars.[22]

Different arrangements were possible. In another case [22421] from about the same period (1882–83), the county court received a complaint from a resident of Tongluowan market town south of Xinzhu charging a tenant with refusing to pay rent on tea land. According to the complainant, the lease contract's terms stipulated that no rent was to be paid for six years. After that time the owner (*yezhu*), that is, the complainant, was to receive 40 percent and the tea cultivator 60 percent of the income from the crop.

The potential for conflict between tea landlords and their tenants was as great as in the case of ordinary land rent relationships. As continued population increase and immigration began to exert pressure on land even on this last frontier, the possibility of serious and sometimes violent disputes grew. The following case summary may serve to reveal some of these frictions.

Case 22510/22514: Boundary Dispute (*zhengjie*)
GX 8/7/28–GX 14/5/28 (10 September 1882–7 July 1888)

In 1882, when the record of this case began, Qing rule of Taiwan was near the end of its second century. Although the frontier was still a reality along the edges of the rugged mountainous core of the island, the coastal plains had already long been settled. As this case demonstrates, Han villagers could claim tenure of a century's duration even over many of the upland clearings in the foothills at the base of the central massif. With the explosive growth of tea exports beginning in the 1860s, the search for upland clearings and slopes suitable for tea cultivation began to engender conflict between earlier settlers and newcomers who viewed these lands as economically underutilized. In this case, the expansion of tea farming into a plateau contiguous to land occupied by a pasture and a cemetery both jointly held by four villages since QL 41 (1776) led to boundary disputes, crop destruction, and a homicide.

The antagonists were, on the one hand, a partnership claiming title to an upland clearing and the partnership's sublessor tea farmers and, on the other, residents acting collectively of Fanzibei, Fangliao, Fenjiwo, and Xinshe, four villages near Xinpu market town located some 20 *li* (about ten kilometers) northeast of the county seat. The partners and their tenants seem all to have been Hakkas. Most of the villagers were Hakka also, although a few were Hokkienese. The villagers asserted joint title to the same upland clearing claimed by the partners. The partnership, calling itself Jin-Liu-He, had first recruited tenants as early as XF 7 (1857), but tea bushes were not planted until GX 5 (1879). Sporadic disputes probably began soon after that. The problem apparently was not serious enough to enter the judicial system until GX 8/7/28 (10 September 1882), but even then the confrontation did not assume crisis proportions for another two years. A final resolution came four years after that.

As the second character in the Jin-Liu-He corporate name (*gonghao*) indicated, there were six partnership shares. According to the first petition [22510:1] and a contract [22510:5] submitted by its representative, title to the land claimed by Jin-Liu-He had been obtained from an aborigine by two men, Liu and Lan, in JQ 9 (1803). In 1857, the two "yielded" (*tuirang*) (that is, handed over without compensation) their reclamation and settlement rights to two of their descendants, Lan Bin and Liu Weiyan. These men then split their two equal shares of the property into six shares and sold four of them for 200 dollars each. At least three of the six shares were owned jointly by brothers or relatives.[23] Several of the partners possessed examination degrees. Liu Shangda held the *lingsheng* degree. Lan Bin and Liu Weiyan were *jiansheng*. All the partners seemed to be residents of Xinpu.

The tenants who leased tea land from Jin-Liu-He had already planted a large number of tea shrubs. Sweet potatoes were also being grown, indicating that the tenants were probably continuing to clear and prepare more land for planting new bushes.[24] Jin-Liu-He's first complaint charged that on the night of GX 8/7/22 (4 September 1882), unknown thugs had stolen or destroyed a large number of tea shrubs as well as a great quantity of sweet potatoes belonging to the partnership's tenants. A runner dispatched by the magistrate, Xu Xizhi, reported [22510:3] that theft and destruction of crops had occurred but was unable to discover the perpetrators. The report did list the boundaries of the tea land and also owners of land contiguous to the tea gardens. There were no further developments for almost exactly two years.

On GX 10/8/28 (16 October 1884), Liu Shangda and Lan Bin handed in a petition [22510:4] on behalf of the partnership charging several men with gathering a band of over 100 toughs armed with firearms and swords. On the 25th of the month, the toughs "swarmed onto our tenants' plots, destroyed several thousand tea shrubs, and dug up more than 5,000 catties of sweet potatoes." Significantly, three of the accused leaders, Luo Ayuan, Luo Asi, and Luo Axie, were among those found to own land neighboring the tea fields by the runner's investigation two years earlier. Naming names brought a quick response.

On the fifth of the following month, Luo Ayuan of Fenjiwo and eight other men filed a joint petition [22510:7] that, although not replying directly to the crop theft charge, made a counteraccusation against Liu and the others. According to Luo, the land in question had been purchased from the Zhuqian tribe over a century before by ancestors of the nine complainants. Liu Shangda and others had "colluded" with an aborigine to create a false contract and, on the strength of the forgery, had encroached on the villagers' land. Luo and the others submitted a copy of their deed [22510:8] dated QL 41 (1776), which indicated that for 1,000 dollars the Zhuqian tribe's interpreter (*tongshi*), Dinglaowen, and chief (*tumu*), Shiban, had granted an upland clearing to tenant farmers of four villages[25] in perpetuity for pasturing cattle.

Reports [22510:9, 10] from subcounty officials and a runner

confirmed that more crop damage had occurred, and a warrant [22510:12] ordered runners to summon all involved to court. Both the partnership and the villagers filed several more complaints, but, as far as can be determined from the case file, neither Magistrate Xu nor his successor, Peng Dasun, took any real action.[26] As seen in the armed robbery case in Chapter 3, French military activities in northern Taiwan disrupted the judicial system's functioning in 1884–85. Serious trouble flared anew in the second month of GX 11. On the third of the month (19 March 1885), *baozheng* Luo Rongguang warned in a report [22510:19] that the two sides in the dispute were not going to wait for a court hearing but were gathering their forces. Luo feared an armed clash was about to ensue. Magistrate Peng's comment written at the end of the report indicated his intention to send a runner with a court order intended to abort the clash and disperse the antagonists. The runner arrived too late. On GX 11/2/7 (23 March 1885), he returned with a report that Fan Jisheng, one of the tenant tea cultivators, had gone to his plot to prevent Luo Ayuan from damaging or stealing his crops and had been shot. Fan had expired on the night of GX 11/2/5 (21 March 1885), and his body had been turned over to a local constable.

At this point there is a puzzling discontinuity in the case or at least in the record of it still available. In spite of the death of Fan Jisheng, there was no further apparent action on the part of the county government for six months.[27] On GX 11/8/24 (2 October 1885), after receiving a complaint [22514:2] from Jin-Liu-He that was partially confirmed by a report [22514:3] from Zhuqian settlement interpreter Qian Yulai, Magistrate Peng drew up an order [22514:1] directing runners to go and suppress a new dispute. Because Liu Shangda was away taking the provincial examinations (*xiangshi*), the partnership's Liu Bukui filed the complaint. According to his allegations, early in the morning of the 24th, Luo Ayuan and "several hundred" of his cohorts had made another raid on the tenants' tea plots with much heavier destruction of crops. In the attack, which occurred between the autumn and winter tea harvests, more than 600,000 tea shrubs were said to have been uprooted and destroyed and seven houses belonging to tenants were looted and then burned. To the magistrate, the most serious charge made by Liu was that the intruders, who had been armed with spears, swords, and muskets, had displayed military emblems, had worn armor, and had claimed to have received an official directive authorizing their actions.[28]

The new accusation provoked a blizzard of petitions supporting and denying the allegations. The next day, Liu Bukui filed a prompting petition to which was appended a list of goods and property stolen or destroyed from the back rooms of a public hall (*gongguan*) that was owned by the partnership and was located near the tea plots [22514:6, 7]. On that and the following days [11/8/25–26 (3–4 October)], five tenants, Zhong Fanwu, Liu Afa, Tian Afan, Liu Awu, and Mrs. Fan née Yang, filed complaints with lists of burned and stolen property appended [22514:7–12, 17–20].[29] The tenants' accusations included the additional details that the marauders wore military settlement soldiers' armor (*tunding jia*) and that the instigator of the gang was a man named Liao Qionglin. Mrs. Fan, Fan Jisheng's widow, complained that her husband's killer had never been caught.

The villagers were not slow to respond. Four petitions [22514: 24–27] from men named in Jin-Liu-He and tenant accusations were accepted at the yamen two days later on 11/8/27–28 (5–6 October). Each of the four documents was signed by three or more men, and each group of petitioners was from one of the four villages. The villagers accused the partnership of encroaching upon pasture land and a cemetery, where the intruders destroyed graves. The villagers laid the blame for the incident on the 24th squarely upon the tea farmers who had tried to lead away cattle grazing in the villages' common pasture. Zhou Sunwei and four other men from Xinshe village admitted that there had been some destruction of tea shrubs when tempers flared. They denied burning any of the buildings, however, insisting that Liu Chunlian, described as one of the Jin-Liu-He partners who was present at the time, had seized the opportunity presented by the conflict and burned down some of the partnership's own tea sheds. By so doing he furnished the partnership and its tenants with a pretext to file false charges against the villagers and Liao Qionglin.

Liao himself had quickly responded to the accusations. In a GX 11/8/26 (4 October 1885) petition [22514:21], Liao described himself as an aborigine government student (*fan shengyuan*) and a teacher at a charity school.[30] Liao claimed that he had become involved in the affair in the previous year, when he was asked, apparently by the villagers, to attempt to mediate the dispute. Liao had no success in arbitrating the quarrel, but Liu Chunlian's attempt to encroach on the pasture and cemetery had been frustrated by the villagers' subsequent destruction of the tea shrubs. At the time of the latest dispute, Liu had known that a detachment of the Zhuqian tribe's military settlement troops were in the vicinity on their return trip from picking up rations in Xinzhu. Their presence gave Liu the notion to accuse Liao of leading aborigine soldiers in an attack.

But the case against the villagers and Liao was supported by Zhou Sunwei and his companions' admission to destroying tea shrubs and by a report [22514:16] from the Xinpu local constable. The constable included new intelligence that more tea shrubs were destroyed on the 25th near the location of the previous day's clash. This further outbreak of violence seems to have prompted another tea-growing corporate entity to file its own complaint [22514:28] against Liao Qionglin and Luo Ayuan.

This second partnership called itself Jin-Jian-Mao and was made up of Luo Fuzhen and two other men. The magistrate had already heard testimony [22514:14] from four of the Jin-Liu-He partners and three of their tenants on GX 11/8/25 (3 October 1885). At that time the magistrate commented that Luo Ayuan should be arrested. In his endorsement to Jin-Jian-Mao viz. Luo Fuzhen's petition, Magistrate Peng, although not commenting on the merits of the complainant's case, had come to the conclusion that Luo Ayuan and his followers were definitely guilty and should be prosecuted for illegally wearing military uniforms and destroying Jin-Liu-He's property. A warrant was issued on GX 11/8/28 (6 October 1885), and the next day runners reported fourteen individuals representing Jin-Liu-He and its tenants and eighteen residents of the four villages had been summoned to court for a hearing [22514:30, 33–34].

Testimony [22514:35] from both parties led the magistrate to conclude that title to the land was not clear. Lu Zhangquan, speaking for Jin-Liu-He, said Liao Qionglin became involved in the case two years earlier, when Luo Ayuan asked Liao to represent him in a dispute over a reclamation permit (*kendan*). Liao testified that he became involved when villagers asked him to evaluate (*ping*) a cattle pasture deed (*niupu qi*). He found that the deed dated from the Qianlong period (1736–95), while Jin-Liu-He's grant had a later Jiaqing (1796–1820) period date. For that reason, the partnership had a grudge against him. This testimony and the documentary claims of rights to the land held by both parties indicated to the magistrate that only an official investigation could clear up the dispute.[31] In view of the necessity of an official inquiry, it was very clear, so said the magistrate, that the villagers should not have tried to rectify the situation by destroying the tea shrubs.

Several villagers, including Zhou Sunwei, testified that on GX 11/8/24 (2 October 1885) some cattle belonging to a Fangliao man had strayed into a tea plot. The tea growers refused to return the animals, thus enraging the villagers and provoking them into the attack. This admission and the refusal of the magistrate to place much credence in the villagers' claim that Jin-Liu-He or its tenants had incinerated their own buildings caused eight men, two from each of the four villages, to be detained pending the outcome of an investigation. Magistrate Peng was especially incensed that the aborigine *shengyuan* had violated the imperial injunction against *shengyuan* involving themselves in litigation.[32] Even if there had been no pretense of acting under authorization of a court order to survey the fields, Liao, the magistrate asserted, had behaved so as to incite both parties.[33] Peng ordered Liao to be placed in custody of the yamen's Tax Department for the time being.

For the next three weeks, individuals on both sides of the dispute filed prompting petitions but gained no satisfaction from the magistrate. With no movement at the county level, Liu Shangda and the other partners submitted an appeal [22514:46] to the Taibei prefect, Liu Xun, on GX 11/9/21 (28 October 1885). The partnership advanced the theory that their case against the villagers had been sidetracked in Xinzhu because of collusion between Luo Ayuan, Liao Qionglin, two prominent Xinzhu residents, and two yamen clerks. Liu Shangda charged that Zheng Yongcheng and Lin Hengmao, whom he labeled "city tigers" (*chenghu*), had taken over the case (*baoan*) because they coveted Jin-Liu-He's land and saw this as a way to seize it. Zheng Yongcheng and Lin Hengmao were probably the corporate or legal names of record of two prominent landlord-gentry lineages. Each is mentioned several times in the local history for having made large contributions to public works such as the city's charity granary and bridge construction and renovation.[34] Once Liao and the villagers had been summoned and detained, Zheng and Lin allegedly bribed one clerk to delay processing the paperwork and another not to draft prompting documents.

The jailed villagers, too, accused the partnership of using yamen connections in the case. In an appeal to the prefect and in a prompting petition [22514:59, 61] filed early in GX 11/10 by Zhou Sunwei, the prisoner charged that Jin-Liu-He had been in a conspiracy with two yamen clerks and a Xinpu local constable who was a nephew to one of them to incite trouble between the villagers and tea growers.

Prefectural appeals [22514:50, 52] from the widow Mrs. Fan and Zhong Fanwu had followed by two days Jin-Liu-He's submission to the higher court. In spite of the prefect's indignation at the slow pace of judicial action and his energetic directions to press forward, the county moved no closer to apprehending Luo Ayuan. This lag was not the fault of Jin-Liu-He, which had not been idle. On 9/28 (4 November), the partnership moved on two fronts by filing prompting petitions [22514:54, 57] simultaneously at the prefectural and county yamens as it continued to press for satisfaction.

Finally on 10/17 (23 November), Magistrate Peng responded to the prodding from the Taibei prefect by drafting a report [22514:62] attempting to excuse his failure to adjudicate the case. Peng explained that even though he had brought the parties up for hearings three times, he had been unable to reach a decision because both sides held to their stories. He had confiscated the land deed held by the villagers but could make no decision on the boundaries without personally inspecting the site. Such scrutiny had so far been impossible because he had been working with the circuit intendant in handling another case and therefore had had no opportunity to get away. Since this latter case had been settled, Peng promised to take the necessary action in the case at hand.

Five days later, Peng issued a warrant [22514:64] ordering the arrest or summons of 51 persons, virtually everyone whose name had been raised during the case up to that point. Perhaps the most interesting feature of this document, which may have been intended merely as a temporizing measure, was its summons of

Zheng Yongcheng and Lin Hengmao. A month earlier, late in GX 11/9, the yamen had been pressured by the prefect to summon the two to court for "representing someone else in litigation and being leaders of an illicit society" (*bachi baolan baihui mengzhu*) [22514:48]. No such warrant was issued, however. By the time the later summons [22514:64] was drawn up, it is clear that Zheng and Lin had moved to protect themselves, because they were described as having brought charges of illicit sale against one Qian Wenjian. Qian, an aborigine, had also been named as part of a collusion to encroach on their pasture in a GX 11/10/1 (7 November 1885) prompting petition [22514:59] from four villagers. Charges, countercharges, and new warrants notwithstanding, no arrests were made. Nor was there any headway against Liao Qionglin. Another interrogation [22514:68] saw the detained aborigine *shengyuan* continuing to insist on his innocence.

About this time, Peng may have learned of his impending transfer. Prompting petitions [22514:69, 71] dated GX 11/11/13 (18 December 1885) were endorsed with advice that the filers wait for their case to be handed over to the new magistrate. On GX 11/11/18 (23 December 1885), Peng, in a notice of transfer [22514:72], informed his replacement, Fang Zuyin (who was to be one of Xinzhu's more energetic magistrates), that the eight villagers plus Liao Qionglin were being held and that the court was in possession of a reclamation permit and a contract submitted in evidence by Zhou Sunwei.[35]

The presence of a new magistrate inspired a by now familiar series of prompting petitions from both parties during the last part of GX 11 and early GX 12. The case even came to the attention of Governor Liu Mingchuan when a sublieutenant in charge of aborigine military settlement troops in northern Taiwan filed a report [22514:80] suggesting that the land in dispute simply be confiscated by the government. The governor, however, merely sent a copy of the report to Xinzhu with a comment expressing his hope that Fang could review the case and make a decision. Magistrate Fang quickly drafted a response [22514:82] that was dispatched on GX 11/12/13 (17 January 1886). He noted both parties had documentary evidence of their claims. He described Jin-Liu-He's proof as having a tax stamp. Fang repeated his predecessor's conclusion that only a personal, on-the-spot investigation could reveal the truth. At the time, however, the new magistrate was busy prompting payment from those wishing to purchase official rank (*juanshu*). Once this task was completed he intended to take both parties, inspect the land boundaries and the damage, if any, done by the villagers, and render a decision.

Before Fang could act, Liu Bukui and Lu Zhangquan, representing Jin-Liu-He and their tenant Zhong Haigu, reported yet another raid on the tea planters. Their petition [22514:85], filed on GX 12/1/4 (7 February 1886), charged that two days earlier a gang of 20 thugs dug up and destroyed tea shrubs that had been replanted and burned down rebuilt huts. Some huts were dismantled and the materials stolen. The tenants reported the crime to the local constable, who responded so quickly that a laggard gang member still engaged in tearing down one of the buildings was captured. The complainants accused gang leaders by name and claimed some of the thugs had been overheard saying they had been sent by Liao Qionglin's wife and Luo Ayuan. The petition was bolstered by a report [22514:86] submitted the same day by the Xinpu local constable. One day later, the runner on duty informed [22514:87] the magistrate that the captured gang member, Pengxu Huoyan, and the three complainants were on hand and ready for a hearing.[36]

On the fourteenth of the month (17 February 1886), the court brought the four men up for questioning. Liu testified [22514:89] that there had been over 1,000,000 tea shrubs planted in the clearing. The tenants had 600,000, he was cultivating 200,000 shrubs himself, and the remainder presumably belonged to the other partners, although he did not address this last point. The 28-*sui*-old Pengxu Huoyan made his living as a laborer. Because he had not yet repaid a loan of 300 cash made by Liao Qionglin's wife, she had prevailed on him to join five other men in cutting down the tea shrubs and pulling down three new huts. In spite of his prisoner's confessed guilt, the magistrate suspected his testimony was not completely true and ordered him held while further investigation was made [22514:88].

On GX 12/2/6 (11 March 1886), Fang ordered [22514:95] runners to summon Liu Bukui and Lu Zhangquan of the partnership and seven of those they accused to wait for him at the site of the boundary dispute, where he intended to inspect the situation personally. It appears that the magistrate examined the scene on 2/9 (14 March).[37] Sometime after his return to the yamen, he endorsed prompting petitions [22514:96, 99] filed earlier on 2/7 (12 March) by the partnership and by the villagers. His inspection had convinced him not only that there was a clear boundary between the villages' cattle pasture and Jin-Liu-He's land but also that the partnership's tenants had not encroached on the pasture land. In fact, in scathing comments in response to a prompting petition [22514:110] from the villagers filed on 12/3/11 (14 April 1886), Fang dismissed their reclamation deed as a forgery. Although the document was supposedly over a century old, "the inking is fresh and clear; the seal has all its lines. It is a fake."[38] By the end of the month, Fang had replaced the original runner in the case for a lack of forcefulness in searching out the accused. On GX 12/3/4 (7 April 1886), the magistrate issued a prompting warrant [22514:109] to a new runner, and by the end of the month Luo Ayuan and several others were apparently in custody.

Besides his own discoveries in the dispute, the magistrate may have been given added stimulus to act by the continuing involvement of two urban-dwelling landlords of Xinzhu, Zheng Yongcheng and Lin Hengmao, in the litigation. A warrant [22514:107] from late in the second month that had not resulted in arrests notes that Zheng and Lin had collaborated in a petition [not on file] charging that Liu Chunlian had colluded with the aborigine Qian Wenjian to encroach on land they owned in the upland clearing.[39] Whatever the reasons, a lengthy hearing list [22514:118] dated GX 12/4/9 (12 May 1886) to which was appended a draft of Magistrate Fang's findings based on testimony [22514:119] of those summoned or arrested marked a significant point in reaching a settlement.

In their responses to Fang's questioning, the partnership and its tenants on one side and the villagers on the other still held to their original stories. The only new information came from Lin Hengmao's manager (*guanshi*), but it exposes what may have been the real roots of the problem. The manager, whose name was not put in the record, testified that rights to all the land comprising the upland clearing were possessed by wealthy gentry (*yinshen*). The paddy fields of the villagers, who were the gentry's tenants, were so close together that there was constant fear of the cattle damaging crops. They had no place to graze their cattle, according to Lin's manager.

The magistrate's findings also made clear that the boundaries of Jin-Liu-He tea plots had been encroached upon along their western edge by villagers attempting to enlarge their pasture.[40] Luo Ayuan and others from Fenjiwo village had encroached on the northern edge of the partnership's holdings, but for a different reason. Luo and his accomplices had, according to Magistrate Fang, taken over land belonging to Jin-Liu-He for their own use, perhaps to plant tea shrubs themselves, as suggested by Liu Bukui. The dispute over its northern property line between the partnership and the Fenjiwo group, consisting principally of Luo Ayuan and his brothers, was logically separate from the conflict involving the pasture–tea plot boundary confusion. Moreover, the guilt for Fan Jisheng's killing was laid firmly on Luo, severing the issues even more cleanly. To his chagrin, however, the magistrate discovered that his runner had apprehended not Luo Ayuan but a man professing to be his brother, Luo Tingxiu, whose name had never before been raised in the case. Tingxiu claimed Ayuan was ill and would come to court for a hearing when he recovered. Magistrate Fang would have none of it. He accused the Luo family of hiring a substitute for Ayuan in order to obstruct the investigation. Fang declared his intention to issue a court order to the family head, Luo Chaosheng, to force him to turn over Ayuan and two of his brothers. The widow, Mrs. Fan, was instructed to wait for them to be arrested and tried.

As for the others, Fang had already determined that Liao Qionglin had been hired by the villagers to manage their litigation. He was to be returned to the custody of the county director of schools for supervision.[41] Zhou Sunwei and the other villagers were ordered to compensate Jin-Liu-He for the loss of 30,000 tea shrubs, about 5 percent of the 600,000 shrubs originally claimed to have been destroyed. Since the villagers had indeed asked the gentry Zheng Yongcheng and Lin Hengmao to help, the two managers were to take the court's decision, publicize it in the villages, and mark the boundary line between the pasture land and the tea plots as decided by the court. The boundary was clear-cut—the old official road running north from Xinzhu toward Mengjia. As it turned out, this was in accordance with Jin-Liu-He's original assertions as backed up by its land deed.

The boundary dispute was thus essentially settled, although it took several more months for the boundary to be marked, compensation paid, and Jin-Liu-He and the villagers to acknowledge a settlement. During this time, numerous prompting petitions were filed at the yamen in an attempt to hasten the process. There were some other loose ends apart from the homicide charge against Luo Ayuan that continued to trouble the court.

To take the latter issue first, in an endorsement to a GX 12/5/13 (14 June 1886) prompting petition [22514:135] from Jin-Liu-He, Fang noted that the murder of Mrs. Fan's husband had been made a separate case and was being handled independently. Later, in a report [22514:168] to the prefect and the governor summarizing the case, Fang briefly alluded to his finding that the military government student (*wusheng*) Luo Chaosheng, who was earlier identified as the family head, had ordered the killing of Fan Jisheng. Fang intended to request (or perhaps had already requested) his impeachment in a separate report so he could be arrested and tried.

The loose ends, which had not been dealt with at the GX 12/4/9 (12 May 1886) hearing, were Liao Qionglin, Pengxu Huoyan, and the villagers still in detention. Fang had decided not to release the villagers until all the details in the boundary case were finalized. Liao had been turned over to the county's director of schools, but no final disposition had been made. Pengxu Huoyan's crime had not been further adjudicated after his hearing earlier in the first month. Unfortunately, prisoners here as elsewhere were extremely susceptible to disease. Liao, who had already needed medical attention once before the hearing while confined at the school, died of illness within two months [22514:137].

Liao's death from disease at age 47 was mentioned only in passing with no report of the details in the case file. In contrast, Pengxu Huoyan's illness and death were fully documented [22514:122–28]. On GX 12/5/3 (4 June 1886), Pengxu was reported to have become ill during the fifth watch of the night. Fang ordered a physician summoned, but the prisoner died at noon. The magistrate immediately convened an inquest, during which, assisted by a coroner, he examined the corpse and questioned Pengxu's jailer. The jailer, who was actually the head of the runner section in whose detention room the prisoner had been confined, testified that Pengxu had not been mistreated. He had suddenly fallen ill with serious respiratory problems and did not respond to medicine administered by the doctor. Fang's entries in an inquest booklet showed no indication of wounds or injuries on the corpse, and he therefore concluded that the sole cause of death was "illness" (*huanbing*). The coroner entered into a willing guarantee bond (*ganjie zhuang*) signifying his agreement. Fang ordered the corpse to be placed in a coffin immediately and buried in a shallow, marked grave. Runners were to find and summon family members to come to the city and take the coffin away for permanent burial. Eight days later, the deceased prisoner's wife signed a receipt [22514:134] acknowledging that she had taken her husband's body to be permanently interred.

Several of the detained villagers also fell ill at different times. One who was treated for illness two days before the end of the previous year eventually obtained guarantees from three storekeepers and was released under bond on GX 12/6/5 (6 July 1886) [22514:92, 136]. At least two other prisoners and perhaps more were released to be treated for disease between the sixth and eighth months [22514:139, 141, 143, 147, 148, 151].

Finally, the mother of Lin Ahong, one of the incarcerated villagers, successfully appealed to magistrate Fang to release her son. The woman, Mrs. Lin, petitioned [22514:130] to tell Fang that since she was a widow, over 70 (actually 77) *sui*, feeble and bedridden, and with no other sons or grandsons to care for her, her son was legally entitled to be released. "Even in death and robbery cases where the circumstances are serious, a sole surviving son still is allowed to support his parents." Fang reluctantly agreed that the legal code contained a substatute with such a provision.[42] The code provision was not prescriptive but merely permissive, and Fang made a show of reluctance. "The woman's son, Lin Ahong, is a criminal in a case involving a killing. The crime would result in a sentence of military exile. How can I agree to a request for release under bond by analogy to the substatute on supporting parents?" He did, however, give credence to her illness and allowed her son to be released under bond to care for her. The magistrate ordered that once she had recovered, Ahong was to be returned to court. On GX 12/5/9 (10 June 1886), four days after his mother's petition, Lin Ahong, on the strength of a bond entered into by a shopkeeper, was set free. The case was settled without Lin or any of the other detainees being forced to return to jail.

One other unsettled matter was the claim of Luo Fuzhen, representing the Jin-Jian-Mao corporation, against Luo Ayuan and the others. Luo Fuzhen continued to file prompting petitions periodically but without favorable reaction from the magistrate. Even after the settlement between Jin-Liu-He and the villagers had been finalized, Luo continued to press for satisfaction. At last, more than eighteen months after settlement, Magistrate Fang peevishly commented that the petitioner had not come forward to advance his claims when the other parties and mediators had appeared before the court to announce the settlement. Even though Fang accused Luo of intentionally trying to entangle the court in litigation, he did offer to order mediators to take up Luo's claim [22514: 177]. Subsequent developments, if any, are unknown, since the file contains no further records.

As indicated above, outside mediators negotiated the settlement that was finally agreed to by the Jin-Liu-He partnership and the villagers. There may have been some foot-dragging by the villagers if we are to believe complaints in prompting petitions [22514:137, 150] that Liu Shangda submitted for Jin-Liu-He in the sixth and seventh months of GX 12 (1886). Ultimately, however, both parties agreed to comply with the basic terms that fixed the boundary dictated by the court. The partnership and the farmers of the four villages achieved this accord as well as an understanding on compensation for tea shrubs through the efforts of six mediators (*gongqin*), whose intervention had been solicited by Lin Hengmao and Zheng Yongcheng.

Notice of the resolution came to the yamen on GX 12/10/5 (31 October 1886) in a petition of reconciliation (*hexi cheng*) [22514:157] drawn up by the six mediators, who apparently were locally prominent men, since among them were a supplementary imperial student (*fugongsheng*) and a "dignitary" (*zhiyuan*). The petition reported that mediators and both parties had gathered at the disputed boundary. The dividing line between the two properties was clearly indicated to all, and a stone mound (*shidui*) was erected as a permanent marker. In addition, the mediators helped determine reimbursement—the amount was never revealed—for the destroyed tea plants and other goods. The petitioners requested, in view of the settlement, that the magistrate cancel the case and issue a proclamation publicizing the outcome. Accompanying the petition were yamen file copies of two "conciliation" bonds (*hexi ganjie zhuang*) [22514:158, 159] entered into by the parties and a document [22514:160] describing the Jin-Liu-He and the pasture boundaries, respectively. Magistrate Fang's endorsement ordered them to wait for an immediate hearing, reinterrogation, and court decision to conclude the case.

As good as his word, Fang called the accusers, accused, and mediators before him for a hearing the next day.[43] Liu Shangda, Yang Chun, and Zhang Dexuan all testified [22514:162] that the boundary dispute had been resolved, although Liu made another complaint concerning encroachment on the northern boundary. Liu acknowledged that compensation had been paid, and all asked that the case be closed. Fang's court order, drafted on the hearing name list [22514:161], summarized the case up to that point and agreed to cancel the litigation. Certain conditions were imposed. Although Jin-Liu-He's deed, which had been submitted in evidence, was returned immediately, the villagers' deed was not. Fang noted that the document lacked an official seal impression that would have indicated the fee on land transactions had been paid. The villagers were directed to pay the fee immediately in order to reclaim the deed. Yang Chun and his fellow villagers, moreover, were not free to return to their homes until a guarantor for their good conduct was found. All this had been prearranged, however, for on the day of the hearing, Zhang and the rest of the mediators entered into a bond for the villagers' release. At the same time, both property deeds were returned. Thus, except for Luo Fuzhen's continued importuning noted earlier, by GX 12/10/6 (1 November 1886) the dispute was effectively terminated.

This case demonstrates how the spread of tea cultivation in Taiwan could lead to acrimonious disputes and even violence and death. Even though tea grew best on normally marginal land, many such areas already had been claimed or at least used by earlier settlers for decades. The case is also notable for its demonstration of the importance of the court in prompting, maintaining, and validating a mediation process that technically took place outside the court system. I shall elaborate on this theme in the conclusion. At this point, however, let us turn to a discussion of the second of the major northern Taiwan export crops.

Camphor

The demand for this fragrant crystalline distillate of the wood and bark of the camphor tree was never as large as that for tea. Until chemists learned to utilize crystalline camphor in the manufacture of celluloid and smokeless gunpowder in the late 1880s, the substance was used chiefly in medicinal preparations. Some small amount was also exported to India for use in religious rituals,[44] but to the Chinese the most useful product of the camphor tree was the lumber. As early as 1725, when a factory to construct naval vessels using camphor wood was established in Taiwan, the government began trying to control the harvest of Taiwan camphor trees for lumber. In 1825, another such establishment was placed in Mengjia, and a military construction supplies office was charged with supervising camphor affairs. Officially, only workers supplying the government with camphor lumber for naval construction were allowed to distill camphor for private sale.

A real impetus for unauthorized trade became evident around the time of the Opium War (1839–42), however, after a British ship put into Jilong and offered opium in trade for crystalline camphor.[45] In 1855, foreign merchants received permission from the intendant of the Taiwan circuit to purchase camphor from the government.[46] Both British and American traders began to increase their purchases to the point that in 1862, two years after Danshui was officially opened as a treaty port, a new camphor bureau no longer concerned with lumber took over management of the government monopoly. The bureau's main office was in Mengjia, with branch offices in Zhuqian, Houlong, and Dajia. According to one source, 12,000 to 13,000 piculs annually passed through both the Mengjia and Dajia offices, with 1,000 to 2,000 piculs being monitored at Zhuqian and Houlong.[47]

As always, foreign merchants chafed at the trade restrictions and monopoly prices.[48] Friction increased as both Chinese producers and foreign purchasers tried to circumvent the monopoly.[49] In 1868, after authorities in Taiwan confiscated camphor in the possession of Elles & Co., the British consul (in a classic instance of gunboat diplomacy) ordered marines from two British men-of-war to land and occupy Fort Zeelandia, near modern Tainan. As a result the Chinese were compelled to end the government monopoly and allow foreign merchants to trade freely.[50]

Camphor prices responded to market forces, but foreign merchants probably reaped most of the benefit. Their purchase price fell from $16 to $7.80 per picul.[51] The latter figure was somewhat above the old $6 price obtained by producers, and Danshui did record a slight increase in exports (see Table 3, Appendix 3). Producers had to bear a previously unknown expense, however. To offset the revenue loss accompanying the end of its monopoly, the government instituted lijin on camphor. By shifting revenue extraction from foreign merchants to camphor producers, the new policy induced protest and lijin evasion by Chinese producers and even by some aborigine tribes who benefited from the trade. In the kidnapping case to be summarized presently, we shall see one manifestation of the protest and resentment occasioned by shifting the burden of revenue extraction from foreign to local entrepreneurs.

Trade was not seriously disrupted at first. The levels of demand and shipment were relatively constant (with some rise after 1868, as noted above) from 1864, the first year of recorded exports from Danshui, until 1881. The constant demand indicated by the export figures recorded in Table 3 in Appendix 3, though relatively low, prodded Chinese distillers to move ever deeper into the forested interior in search of suitable trees. This slow expansion into wild aborigine areas ultimately provoked widespread attacks that depressed production for a number of years after 1882. In 1885, less than 400 pounds were exported. The attacks by the tribal peoples were the primary cause of trade disruption. The French blockade of northern Taiwan in 1884–85 merely hastened the decline already evident.

The unrest in the camphor-producing areas, the expenses incurred in hostilities against the French, and his modernization efforts prompted Governor Liu Mingchuan to reestablish the monopoly in 1887 to increase revenues from the trade.[52] This second monopoly did not long endure. Merchant protests prompted the British ambassador in Beijing to intervene, and after prompting from the Zongli Yamen, the agency charged with foreign relations, the Revenue Ministry (*hubu*) recommended in an 1891 memorial approved by the emperor that the monopoly be abolished. In the meantime government pacification campaigns against the aborigines gradually allowed production to recover, and by 1893–95, demand created by new uses for camphor spurred exports to levels 400 to 500 percent higher than those in the 1860s and 1870s.

In the 1880s, however, the outcome was still in doubt. In the absence of effective government control, independent operators had to depend on their own skills in negotiating with tribes who controlled the camphor forests. At the same time such distillers had to deal with government revenue collection efforts. In looking ahead to the case summary, two aspects of the criminal incident and its aftermath deserve mention.

First, Chinese settlement in Xinzhu was pushed deeper into the mountains by frontiersmen such as Chen Zhenxiang, the defendant in the case. The dealings with the tribes of Chen and men like him in distilling and marketing camphor and perhaps opening new land for settlement were countenanced, even authorized, by the state. At the same time, men like Chen were among those most likely to create a great deal of trouble for local government. Such men could be expected to enter into irregular relationships with the aborigines, which easily led to crises. Chen and those like him inclined toward impolitic action in disputes with petty officials who attempted to regulate and tax the trade in camphor, a perishable commodity not easily stored except in facilities designed for the task. Once local strongmen like Chen got into trouble with the law, they often had military experience and connections that presented a ticklish problem to yamen authorities charged with prosecuting them.

Second, this case suggests how important the court system was perceived to be in reconciling frontier minority peoples to the Chinese social and political order. In this case, aborigine tribal leaders allied with Chen brought complaints against the kidnapping victim, Wei Qisheng. In this particular instance the aborigines' charges may have been groundless. Had there been a real grievance, however, the Xinzhu court would have been expected to resolve it equitably. Military authorities in northern Taiwan with justification were less than totally confident of their ability to campaign successfully against the aborigines. If aborigines could be persuaded that disputes submitted to the civil courts would be fairly decided, the danger of an uprising could be deflected. In an ironic fashion, civil government was the first line of defense for military forces on Xinzhu's frontier.

Case 32611: Kidnapping (*lujin*)

GX 13/8/16–GX 21/3/30 (2 October 1887–24 April 1895)

This case file opens with a petition charging Chen Zhenxiang with kidnapping a man in order to hold him for ransom. It required fourteen months (until 14/10/29 [2 December 1888]) for Chen to be found in Danshui county, arrested, and returned to the Xinzhu yamen. Although apparently considered guilty of the charge, he was eventually released under bond because of advanced age and illness, but not until after more than six years of imprisonment.

The motive for Chen's crime grew from a dispute with a former lijin station duty collector, Wei Qisheng, who earlier in GX 9 (1883) had confiscated smuggled camphor from Chen.[53] Chen had filed a complaint charging that Wei and others had stolen camphor from him. At about the same time as Chen's complaint, Wei at the Houlong lijin station submitted a report to the county yamen saying that acting on a tip he had seized nineteen piculs (*dan*) of camphor on a boat at the mouth of the Zhonggang river. Wei charged Chen with attempting to smuggle the camphor without paying the transit duty. An investigation backed Wei's version, and the magistrate at the time ordered Chen arrested. At this juncture Chen fled to avoid arrest, and so, as legally prescribed, his own complaint was voided and his case canceled.[54] Four years later, in GX 13/4 (ca. April–May 1887), Chen resubmitted his complaint to a higher official, probably the Taibei prefect, but his case was again dismissed. Just four months after that Wei Qingdao, Wei Qisheng's son, filed the kidnapping charge against Chen.

Chen's captive, Wei Qisheng, had already been freed before the yamen received the complaint [32611:1]. The day of the incident, GX 13/8/15 (1 October 1887), Wei, the former lijin collector, was returning to Houlong from a visit to Xinzhu. At the Zhonggang River, Wei took the ferry across the stream and, on reaching the south bank, was taken prisoner by Chen, who apparently was aided by an armed gang consisting at least in part of "raw" aborigines [32611:5]. On the same day a clerk employed in a store owned by Wei reported his abduction to the commander of a military detachment in Houlong. A nephew of Wei Qisheng also reported the crime to the locality's civil authorities, the overseer and the duty runner (*duibao*) for the township [32611:33, 37]. The overseer and runner, accompanied by soldiers, set out in pursuit. Luckily for Wei, he did not have to depend on the pursuers for rescue. As Chen and his followers with Wei in tow were passing through Tannei, a village about five kilometers northeast of Houlong, on their way toward the mountains, they aroused the suspicion of the village head (*zhuangzheng*), Zhou Adeng, who stopped them. Wei was released, and Chen and his men dispersed and fled. Chen himself reportedly [32611:25] resided in the village of Jiuchelong only half a kilometer past Tannei and so probably had headed for home.

Chen appears to have been a combination of local strongman and entrepreneur.[55] It is likely that he had recruited local troops to assist in military operations during various crises. He had been awarded a fifth rank military badge of merit (*wupin jungong*)[56] for his achievements in aiding government troops suppress one or more uprisings or possibly for helping government forces reoccupy Jilong during the French withdrawal from the area in 1884 [32611:161]. Chen had been involved in the pacification of the mountain tribes that was designed to end their opposition to expansion of settlement into upland areas.

During the course of his activities in earlier years, Chen and a partner applied for and received a license from the Taiwan arsenal to distill camphor in an area controlled by the Shilixing aborigine settlement.[57] One secondary source even asserts that Chen carried out reclamation and settlement in the same area.[58] He seemed to have established friendly relations with the settlement leaders, for two of them, Riaguai and Siyoumei, came to his defense in petitions [32611:6, 12] submitted to First Captain Zheng Youqin, the military officer in charge of guardpost braves and responsible for the military aspects of pacification and reclamation affairs for northern Taiwan, and to the Taibei prefect.[59] The two aborigine headmen (*tumu*) claimed that in GX 9 (1883) they had asked Chen to take camphor for them to Taibei for sale. When Wei had confiscated camphor from Chen, it was really a pretext for stealing it for himself. According to the headmen, they had heard that on GX 13/8/15 (1 October 1887), the day Chen was alleged to have kidnapped Wei, Wei and a fellow conspirator were going to divvy up the stolen camphor. When the headmen and some other aborigines went to try and get it back from Wei, he persuaded them that if they accompanied him to Tannei village he would pay them compensation for the stolen camphor. In this way they were tricked into going to the village and the home of Zhou Adeng. At that point Wei offered only partial compensation, which was refused. The aborigines' rejection of Wei's offer precipitated an argument that ended with Wei's men taking two of the aborigines prisoner.

The version of events offered by Riaguai and Siyoumei stopped short of denying that Chen had kidnapped Wei. Even so, it was regarded seriously by the authorities all the way up to the governor's office. At this time, in GX 13 (1887), when the two kidnapping charges were working their way through the legal system, Governor Liu was going to great lengths to solve the problem of conflict between Han Chinese and aborigines. Offenses against already partially sinicized tribes like those living in Shilixing settlement had to be quickly dealt with in order to avoid alienating or even driving them into a state of hostility against the government.[60] From his governor's office in Taibei, Liu Mingchuan himself replied to the settlement headmen's complaint. He ordered Xinzhu county to determine if Wei and his people had seized the two aborigines and, if so, to release them [32611:15].

During this period, Xinzhu county was administered by the energetic magistrate Fang Zuyin. First Captain Zheng had forwarded the headmen's original petition to the county yamen, causing Fang to order their complaint checked even before the governor's directive arrived. Runners dispatched to Tannei reported [32611:14] that none of the villagers knew of any kidnapped aborigines. So by GX 13/11/1 (15 December 1887), when Magistrate Fang drafted a report [32611:16] to his superiors summarizing the case, the facts as he saw them had been firmly established and supported Wei Qingdao's original accusation. Magistrate Fang was able to point to his runners' findings in Tannei and to cite a contradiction between the aborigine report and statements made by Chen Zhenxiang in GX 9 (1883), when Wei Qisheng had confiscated the camphor. At that earlier time, Chen had claimed he himself had financed the camphor distillation. The aborigine headmen, however, had asserted that the camphor belonged to the settlement, and Chen had merely been acting as its agent when he undertook to transport and sell the camphor.

The case might have presented the Xinzhu magistrate little difficulty except for Chen Zhenxiang's relationships with the aborigines and with the military. The involvement of aborigines, as noted above, caused intense anxiety among the civil bureaucracy from the governor on down. The army officer in charge of local military arrangements for the pacification and settlement program naturally also showed great concern. Should the Shilixing aborigines be provoked, his troops would be charged with suppressing them. As a result there was unusual pressure on the county both from higher-level government offices and from First Captain Zheng. The county yamen received at least seven orders and informal requests to make sure that no aborigines had been taken prisoner by the Wei family. Besides Governor Liu's demands transmitted through Taibei prefecture [see for example 32611:15] for a thorough investigation, First Captain Zheng prodded Magistrate Fang in both formal dispatches [32611:7, 19, 34, 39] and personal letters [32611:20, 26]. Zheng had campaigned against "raw" aborigines in the Wuzhi Mountain region east of Xinzhu in late GX 12 (1886–87).[61] Being responsible for quelling any unrest among peaceful tribes such as the Shilixing should the necessity arise, Zheng naturally had a more compelling interest in preventing a grievance from festering. His dispatches noted that unless the matter was cleared up, "it will cause an outbreak, and the lingering effects of error will cause loss of life in the future." Later, probably during GX 13/11 (ca. December 1886–January 1887), after it began to appear that Chen Zhenxiang rather than Wei Qisheng was at the root of the difficulties, Zheng warned that "the aborigines have been cheated often. If he [Chen] is not captured and severely punished, there will certainly be no peace between Chinese and aborigines."

Magistrate Fang had been inclined to believe that Wei had not taken any aborigine captives. On GX 13/9/29 (14 November 1887), Zhou Adeng, the village head who had released Wei Qisheng from his kidnappers, petitioned [32611:13] saying the charge against Wei was baseless. Four days later, runners from the First Lictor section reported [32611:14] that villagers knew nothing of the alleged crime. On GX 13/11/16 (30 December 1887), Fang wrote [32611:27] to Zheng saying that there was reason to believe that the headmen's complaint was not factual. Before long, however, a directive (*zha*) [32611:30] dated GX 13/11/24 (7 January 1888) from the Taibei prefect transmitted Governor Liu's order to Xinzhu county to make a thorough investigation of the possible capture of two aborigines. The magistrate was ordered to have Wei Qisheng (or Wei Yu, as he was referred to in the headmen's complaint) arrested and interrogated. If orders from the governor were not compelling enough, Fang continued to be prodded by First Captain Zheng. Also, by GX 13/12/15 (27 January 1888), the aborigine headmen, Riaguai and Siyoumei, had filed three petitions [32611:35, 40, 42] at the yamen reiterating their complaint against Wei. So, in spite of reports [32611:33, 38] from heads of the Second Lictor and First Fast runner sections, a report [32611:37] from the overseer who helped lead the pursuit of the kidnappers, and a dispatch [32611:25] from the commanding officer of the Houlong military detachment affirming that Wei had not taken anyone captive, Fang issued warrants [32611:36, 41] for Wei to be brought to court.

On GX 13/12/23 (4 February 1888), Magistrate Fang drafted a dispatch [32611:46] to First Captain Zheng reporting the results of a hearing four days earlier. Wei Qingdao, representing his father, who was ill, Overseer Chen Qingqi, and a local constable had been questioned. In their testimony [32611:45] all denied that the two members of the Shilixing tribe had been taken captive by Wei Qisheng. Fang's directive [32611:44] concluded that Chen Zhenxiang had probably fabricated the appearance of a crime by concealing the two missing tribesmen himself. Fang had wished to question the two headmen, but they had already returned to the Shilixing settlement before the runners could summon them to court. Even had yamen runners agreed to travel into the remote mountain area and to attempt to bring the aborigine headmen to court, the risk of an incident leading to a tribal uprising was too great for the magistrate to give such an order. The magistrate had to be satisfied with ordering not only the overseer but also Wei

Qingdao to help runners find and capture Chen. Fang's dispatch to Zheng requested that the first captain send braves to help capture Chen, who, the magistrate believed, had fled into the mountains.

During the early months of GX 14 (1888), Fang pressed the search for Chen Zhenxiang. Moreover, he attempted to establish beyond all doubt that no Shilixing tribesmen had been taken captive. A GX 14/4/6 (16 May 1888) warrant [32611:51] ordered the original First Lictor section runners to make a village-to-village search for the supposedly captive aborigines. As Fang reported [32611:52] to the governor eight days later, no sign of any captive aborigines had been found, and village heads had signed a joint surety bond (*lianhuan qiejiebing*) to that effect.[62] Fang asked the governor to issue a general order to all military battalions and counties to be on the lookout for Chen. Liu Mingchuan's endorsement [32611:54], written on GX 14/4/24 (3 June 1888), denied the request and directed Fang to arrange the hunt for Chen directly with First Captain Zheng.

At about the same time both Wei Qingdao and the aborigine headmen appealed to higher authorities. But as runners reported [32611:59] in the seventh month, no captive aborigines had been located, and Chen was reported to have fled north to near the Taibei prefectural seat.

Following a two-month hiatus, the search finally began to bear fruit. Early in the ninth month, the Xinzhu magistrate sent a dispatch [32611:64] to Danshui county magistrate Wang requesting that he arrest Chen and send him to Xinzhu. This dispatch or one similar to it apparently alerted First Captain Zheng that Chen was in the area. On GX 14/10/29 (2 December 1888), Zheng informed [32611:65] Fang that one of his subordinate officers had managed to obtain information that led to the capture of Chen Zhenxiang. A report with the same date from a Danshui county runner informed the Xinzhu magistrate that Chen had been brought to court there and requested Fang to take custody of him.

Another six-week delay ensued before the other major parties and witnesses in the case could be summoned. By GX 14/12/18 (19 January 1889), however, Wei Qisheng, Wei Qingdao, the overseer Chen Qingqi, and the Houlong local constable appeared before the magistrate, where, along with the prisoner, they offered their testimony [32611:74]. The testimony of the two Wei men and of the local constable offered nothing new. The overseer in his testimony, seemingly in reference to the earlier episode when Wei Qisheng confiscated Chen Zhenxiang's camphor, claimed that he had met Chen and told him to go to the Mazu Temple in Houlong for arbitration (*pinglun*).[63] Instead the camphor smuggler went to runners and falsely accused Wei Qisheng.

As for Chen Zhenxiang, the 56-*sui*-old prisoner revealed that he had become involved in the camphor business after Fujian Governor Cen Yuying had issued an edict, probably on GX 7/12/18 (6 February 1882), promoting the policy of opening mountainous areas for settlement while at the same time maintaining harmonious relations with the aborigines.[64] Chen rejected the allegations that he had kidnapped Wei, that he knew anything about the supposedly kidnapped tribesmen, or that he had any responsibility for the complaints filed by Riaguai and Siyoumei. These denials notwithstanding, however, the court concluded that Chen's grudge against Wei Qisheng for confiscating smuggled camphor led to collusion with aborigines to kidnap Wei. When the abduction proved unsuccessful, Chen fabricated the charge against Wei of kidnapping two tribesmen.[65]

Although Magistrate Fang had determined that Chen was guilty, the criminal act apparently was not kidnapping for ransom (*naren leshu*),[66] for which the least penalty would have been 100 blows with the heavy stick followed by three years' penal servitude. Characterizing the kidnapping as "unsuccessful" seems to have moved the crime into a less serious category. As for the fabrication of charges against Wei Qisheng, Chen never admitted guilt. Without testimony to the contrary from the Shilixing headmen who actually made the complaint against Wei, no definitive determination was possible. Thus, Xinzhu's magistrate was in somewhat of a quandary when it came to deciding on an appropriate punishment. Adding to the uncertainty in matching crime and sentence was Chen's honorary military rank, which had to be surrendered and canceled before any punishment could be inflicted. When first interrogated, Chen agreed to submit his badge of merit (*gongpai*) to the court.[67] As compliance bonds (*zunyi jiezhuang*) [32611:75–76] filed after the hearing by Wei Qingdao and Wei Qisheng show, the magistrate had the prisoner beaten with the light stick and placed in detention (*chize guanya*), presumably to make sure Chen carried through with his promise to the court.

Magistrate Fang seemed to have proceeded little further with the case during the first three months of GX 15 (1889). However, in a GX 15/4/12 (11 May 1889) report (*xiang*) [32611:79] sent to Governor Liu Mingchuan, Financial Commissioner Shen Yingkui, Judicial Commissioner Tang Jingsong, and Taibei Prefect Lei Qida, Fang suggested a possible disposition of the case: sentencing Chen by analogy to the substatute on confining insane persons who committed homicide.[68] Fang's idea was to impeach Chen of his honorary military rank and lock him up in confinement indefinitely, or at least until the prisoner could no longer interfere in aborigine settlement or land reclamation matters. When the latter state of affairs had been achieved, Chen's case could be reviewed and his release possibly recommended. If Chen was merely sentenced to a period of wearing the cangue, a beating, and then release, the magistrate feared that Chen would return to the tribal settlements and again stir up trouble.

Governor Liu saw no need to resort to sentencing by analogy. He immediately replied with an endorsement [32611:83] written on a summary (*jianwen*) [32611:82] of Fang's report that the substatute in question could not be applied to one who was not insane. Two months later, Liu's endorsement, received in Xinzhu on GX 15/5/1 (30 May 1889), was amplified in a directive [32611:91] transmitted through the prefecture. The governor ordered the magistrate to deprive Chen of his honorary rank by impeaching (*chige*) it, to send in for cancellation (*chuanxiao*) the medal of merit, and then to incarcerate and handle Chen according to accepted procedure.

As far as we can tell from the case file, Fang had been fairly active in trying to compel Chen to turn in his medal. Twice during the fifth month, and once in both the ninth and tenth months, Fang had Chen brought before the court for a hearing to press him to submit the medal. Each time Chen was unable or unwilling to comply, contending that a friend, Chen Jixun, who had been holding it for safekeeping, was unwilling to return it.[69] As it turned out, the prisoner remained in jail for just under two years before his son, Chen Zaisheng, submitted a petition [32611:104] along with the medal to the yamen. By that time [GX 16/11/1 (12 December

1890)], Fang Zuyin had been succeeded by Zhang Tinggan, and he by Shen Maoyin, as county magistrate.

Chen Zaisheng petitioned [32611:105] for his father's release on GX 17/1/23 (3 March 1891), but was told that the medal of merit, which had been sent to higher authorities, had to be canceled before any determination could be made. Chen Zhenxiang was still imprisoned three months later, when, in a report [32611:108] sent to higher echelons all the way up to the governor-general,[70] Magistrate Shen described the problems incumbent with holding prisoners in the Xinzhu jail over a long term. Besides Chen, one other prisoner, Peng Ying, a former yamen clerk impeached and jailed for constantly involving himself in litigation before the court, had been incarcerated for at least a year.[71]

According to Shen, the impeached yamen clerk had been sentenced to permanent imprisonment (*yongyuan jianjin*). Chen, characterized as an evil type who incited aborigines, had been sentenced to imprisonment with subsequent review (*jianjin chakan*) to determine his eligibility for release. Shen argued that even though their crimes and therefore their sentences were different, their natures or characters were the same. Thus, the way the two cases had been resolved was inconsistent. Having two prisoners incarcerated for long terms caused two problems for the county. Simply being responsible for their welfare or at least survival was burdensome. Disease, as we have seen, was a constant threat. Once already Chen had needed a doctor's care after contracting influenza early in the month [32611:106–7]. Moreover, Chen and Peng stirred up trouble by inciting newly arrested suspects who were put in jail with them to change or deny testimony already given. The magistrate pointed out that former Prefect Cheng Qi'e of Taiwan prefecture had received approval for a petition to send convicted criminals from that jurisdiction to the Penghu Islands. Shen suggested a similar resolution for both Chen Zhenxiang and Peng Ying. They could be sent to Penghu subprefecture, where they would be jailed for several years. When their terms were completed, they could be placed under the control of fishing port village headmen on different islands. In effect, they would be permanently exiled.

The magistrate in due course received a directive [32611:112] approving his proposed sentence from the judicial commissioner,

Cheng Qi'e, the former Taiwan prefect cited in Shen's report. On GX 17/7/6 (10 August 1891), a flurry of paperwork [32611:113–18] concerning the prisoner transfer issued from the Xinzhu yamen. Shen requested the prefect's permission to send the prisoners guarded by runners and soldiers to Danshui county, where they could be put on a ship for the islands. The transfer to Danshui was to take place on the 21st of the month. Shen sent a dispatch to the Danshui county magistrate asking him to assign Chen and Peng to a ship sailing for Penghu. Each criminal was described, and an impression of their fingerprints accompanied the dispatch. The prisoners would be transported in a wooden cage and would be clad in the red clothing of banishment (*qiu zuo mulong zhe yiku*).[72]

On the appointed day, Chen and Peng were brought before the magistrate for a last hearing, given a small amount of money for travel expenses, and handed over to runners to take the road north to Danshui. They never reached the Penghu Islands. On GX 17/10/12 (13 November 1891), a new Xinzhu magistrate, Shen Jiceng, sent in a request [32611:124] to his superiors that he be allowed to release Chen. It seems that while the prisoners were still in Danshui awaiting a ship, a general order from provincial authorities prohibiting any further transfer of prisoners to Penghu subprefecture was circulated. A jail under construction there had not been completed, so the transfer of prisoners from other jurisdictions had to be halted. For that reason Chen was sent back to Xinzhu.[73]

The motive for advocating release of the convicted kidnapper lay in the magistrate's fear of administrative sanctions if the prisoner died of disease. Shen requested approval for Chen to be released under bond and the case canceled in order to avoid discipline for death from disease in prison (*shoubi lingyu zhi chu*). In support of his contention that Chen could be released, the magistrate noted that the convict was old. The implication was that such an elderly man, now 59 *sui*, was naturally more vulnerable to disease. His crime had been evil, but Wei Qisheng had been rescued before being mistreated. Moreover, Chen had made no ransom demands. In the other matter of inciting aborigine headmen, Riaguai and Siyoumei, to make false accusations, not only had Chen denied the charges but also no endorsement of his guilt was on record. The lijin case was not relevant, since it had long ago been concluded.

The request was denied. A GX 17/12/26 (25 January 1892) directive [32611:128] from the Taibei prefect transmitted to Xinzhu county the governor's ruling. It stated that according to the original sentence proposed by Fang Zuyin and approved, Chen's release could be considered only after all matters related to aborigines and land settlement had been concluded. This was not the case; thus, as the magistrate noted in a petition [32611:129] for release submitted six months later by another of the prisoner's sons, he was unable to consider the request.

Magistrate Shen Jiceng's denial of a petition for release set a pattern for the next two and one-half years. Chen Zaixin, son of the prisoner, filed prompting petitions at roughly six-month intervals or sooner if a new magistrate had assumed office in Xinzhu. Each petition for his father's release was denied.

Finally, however, early in GX 21 (1895), Chen's luck took a turn for the better. On GX 21/2/2 (26 February 1895), Chen Zhenxiang himself submitted an informal petition [32611:159] begging to be released. The magistrate at the time, Wang Guorui, agreed that Chen's case could be reexamined and approval sought from higher authorities for his release from jail because an imperial "gracious proclamation" (*enzhao*) or amnesty had been received.[74] Two days later a summary of Chen's case record [32611:160] was submitted for review. It is unclear whether approval was ever formally given by upper echelons. As mentioned in a GX 21/3/9 (3 April 1895) petition [32611:161] handed in by Chen's wife, née Ke, China and Japan were at that moment embroiled in war. Indeed, Japanese forces already held the Penghu Islands. Chinese troops defending the islands had surrendered on March 26.[75] It is not improbable that the ordinary processes of higher level judicial review were suspended. Even if that were the case, however, Chen finally did go free. On the eighteenth of the month, as had happened numerous times during his incarceration, Chen's jailer reported [32611:162] that the prisoner was ill. On GX 21/3/30 (24 April 1895), a Xinzhu store proprietor entered into a bond [32611:163] that allowed Chen Zhenxiang, after six years of incarceration, to be released for medical treatment.

In closing, a look back at the earlier brief summary of the

institutional and market environment in which camphor distillers and traders such as Chen Zhenxiang operated may help us understand some aspects of his case. When Chen's smuggled camphor was confiscated in 1883 (GX 9), the market was depressed and falling fast. Kidnapping Wei Qisheng, the drastic measure Chen took four years later in an attempt to recover his losses, may have been motivated by a desire for revenge and recovery when it became apparent that the market for camphor was beginning to climb again. At the same time, when the Shilixing headmen, Riaguai and Siyoumei, added their own complaints in support of Chen, they were certainly aware of the desire of the government and especially the military to avoid provocations against peaceful settlements at a time when the success of Liu Mingchuan's pacification campaigns was still in doubt. Unfortunately for Chen and the aborigine headmen, their complaints did not receive enough substantiation to arouse a sympathetic hearing, particularly in the wake of Chen's failed assay at kidnapping and ransom.

In the preceding chapters we have seen that northern Taiwan afforded great opportunities for amassing wealth through agriculture, export trade, and commerce. Those who managed to become well-to-do were then faced with the challenge of retaining their hard-won position. In particular, wealthy lineages, which lacked the mechanism of primogeniture and were confronted with the natural fissiparous tendencies of complex social units, often generated bitter disputes over division of assets held in common. In the following chapter we will observe one common form that such conflicts took.

6

Lineage Division and Inheritance Disputes

As even a cursory scan of the Dan-Xin cases will reveal, familial conflict was a powerful generator of litigation in nineteenth-century Danshui and Xinzhu.[1] This section explores some of the ways that family or lineage members became involved in property rights disputes so serious that conflicts normally confined to the household spilled into the public area. In the Wu-Shun-Ji litigation against its tenants discussed in Chapter 4, we see lineage unity as successive lineage representatives sustained rent resistance accusations over many years. Extended lineages were prone, however, to divide or segment into collateral lines that were often competitive or even antagonistic. Moreover, by virtue of the Chinese mode of partible inheritance, each collateral line had a claim to a share of common lineage property. Therein lay the seeds of discord.

Although lineages exhibited distinct regional variation,[2] the type of organization that concerns us here is the "typical" southeast Chinese lineage, that is, "a corporate group which celebrates ritual unity and is based on demonstrated descent from a common ancestor."[3] An additional and crucial criterion, especially for the discussion here, posits that such corporate groups "derive benefits from jointly-owned property and shared resources."[4]

The Chinese in Taiwan had brought with them from the mainland and perhaps further developed customary procedures devised to improve the chances that lineage segmentation and property division would be harmonious. Nevertheless, even such customary practices as confirming the division of a lineage's common property by drawing up a valid legal instrument, such as a contract, not infrequently failed to prevent discord. When property and wealth accumulated through the efforts of a lineage elder were divided posthumously among his sons, disputes over the equivalency of shares were predictable, indeed nearly inevitable. If one heir himself was already deceased at the time of estate division, the potential for disagreement was even greater. The most difficult situation of all, and one capable of inciting extended litigation, was the case of the heir to a deceased collateral line head (one of the sons of the original lineage elder) being a minor or adopted son. Property nominally accruing to a minor heir was necessarily managed by an adult, normally one of the minor's uncles, who as claimants to shares of the estate themselves might be understandably ambivalent about their managerial responsibilities. As for adopted sons, the complexity and variety of Chinese adoption practices could easily open to challenge the adoptee's status as heir. The litigation (summarized later in this chapter) between Mrs. Zhou and her son on the one hand and her deceased husband's brothers on the other arose from such ambiguities of eligibility to succeed to property and is illustrative of lineage rancor more typical, perhaps, than long-term lineage solidarity.

In Taiwan as elsewhere in China, the general rule for succession to property gave equal rights to all male heirs. Property might be divided during a family head's lifetime, but more usually an estate division took place after the head of a household had died. Customary practice dictated that the eldest son receive a larger share of the estate to provide for the expense of ancestral sacrifices. In Taiwan an extra share was customarily created for the eldest grandson of the deceased head of household.[5] In the dispute over inherited wealth summarized below, Zhou Wuniang and his brothers seemed to respect the spirit of this custom in the property division contract that they had made with their deceased elder brother, Zhou Dongfu, by agreeing to remit a sum of "eldest grandson money" (*zhangsun yin*). In the case of a wealthy family, a portion of the estate was often put aside to provide for the support of any surviving wives. This share of the inheritance was termed a *yangshan* fund, and was seen in Zhou Wuniang's agreement to provide Mrs. Zhou with *yangshan yin*. If a lineage could possibly do so, another portion called common property (*gongye*) was set aside to finance the education of males and matrimonial expenses of females. Common property could be managed by the eldest surviving heir, or management could be rotated among heads of collateral lines.[6]

Managing rental income from real estate or income from other investments led to numerous disputes, especially when the heirs of one or more collateral lines were still minors. Lawsuits alleging misappropriation of rental income or illegal sale of common property were initiated by male heirs who had been minors at the time of the alleged wrongful management or by widows of deceased collateral line heads with minor children.[7]

When, after the death of a lineage head, division of lineage property became necessary, the mechanics of estate division involved making an inventory of the estate and calculating the value of each piece of movable property or real estate. After gathering to make offerings to the deceased, the heirs then drew lots (*jiu*) to decide which shares of the property would go to each. "[T]he farms and houses are marked or numbered previously, and the successors draw lots one by one to settle each one's portion. . . . The proper way was to write the designation of the property on pieces of white paper and throw these into water, letting each successor pick out one."[8]

Division by drawing lots was termed *jiufen*. Once the division was effected, a "lot agreement" (*jiushu*) or estate division agreement was drawn up by the heirs, with one copy going to each collateral line. These agreements described the property acquired by each collateral line and also the arrangements decided upon for managing common property.[9] *Jiushu* were very common, and a number of these documents can be found in the Dan-Xin cases or have been reproduced elsewhere.[10] Given the respect accorded by the courts to contractual evidence such as estate division agreements, the existence of an unimpeachable *jiushu* must have forestalled many allegations of inequitable property division. Mrs. Zhou's petitions in the litigation against her brothers-in-law continually insisted that a division of inherited property must be accompanied by a *jiushu*. Since the agreement entered into by her deceased husband Zhou Dongfu and his brothers dividing their father's estate was merely a contract (*heyue*), it could not, she argued, be considered a legal estate division agreement. This argument, however, left the court unmoved. Other documents could serve equally as well.

While the local court took familial rights and responsibilities as values to be maintained, the magistrate recognized that changing circumstances altered the extent to which claims could be justified by lineage ties. Mrs. Zhou sued in part to gain a share of a prosperous store founded by her deceased husband. It seems clear that her claim was weakened by the fact that the firm became prosperous only after her husband had stopped managing it.

To return to estate division, inheritance, as noted earlier, could be further complicated by the presence of adopted sons among the heirs. The head of a collateral line without a natural heir often adopted one of his patrilineal nephews or other agnatic relatives to carry on his line. Such an adopted heir was called a "crossing-collateral-line son" (*guofangzi*). An adopted son of this type was entitled to a full share in the estate even if natural children were subsequently born.[11] A more problematic situation arose when the adopted son was a nonagnate. In such cases the adopted son was usually obtained by purchase and was called a "caterpillar son" (*minglingzi*).[12] Okamatsu believed that a *minglingzi* could be denied a share of the estate by his adoptive father, but that if the latter did not make such an intention known, the *minglingzi* had the same rights as natural sons.[13] The record of Mrs. Zhou's lawsuit suggests that a "caterpillar son" was at a disadvantage in disputes over succession. Zhou Wuniang made certain to refer to Zhou Chuncao, Mrs. Zhou's son, as a *ming*-[*ling*]-*zi*. The magistrate, who effectively concluded the case by deciding on only a minimal award to Mrs. Zhou, also used the same term to designate her son.

Tacitly observed legal distinctions between adopted and natural sons also take us a step closer to understanding the role of the state in descent group formation. We see in another legal struggle over inherited wealth [22601] one of the techniques utilized by the legal system specifically to promote formation of the familiar southeast China type of corporate lineage. The subprefect's court directive [22601:25] in this 1847 case shows how the system supported orthodox descent group ritual practices and lineage longevity.

The case involved the descendants of a lineage founder named Zheng Kun who had had five sons.[14] The eldest (Xizhe) and the fourth (Qingzhao) sons were adopted. The second (Xijie), third (Maofang), and fifth (Chunjiang) sons were his natural children. A Miss Xu, who seems to have been Zheng Kun's primary wife, had raised Qingzhao. Maofang and Chunjiang were both sons of a concubine, Miss Huang, who along with her two sons was already deceased at the time of the lawsuit. After his death, Zheng Kun's estate had, in accordance with an estate division agreement (*jiu-shu*), been divided into seven equal shares (that is, one for each son and one for each of the two women) except for a certain amount that was to be put aside for funerary and sacrificial purposes after Kun's death. The deaths of Miss Huang and her sons Maofang and Chunjiang led the survivors to litigation over the disposition of the shares of Kun's estate that had previously gone to the three now deceased heirs. The court directive deciding the case ordered that the three shares were to revert to the trust established for financing sacrifices to Zheng Kun. However, in the event that Xijie, Zheng Kun's oldest natural son, fathered children himself, the second and third sons (should they be born) were to inherit the shares of Kun's estate that had originally been allotted to Maofang and Chunjiang. Xijie's putative eldest son would, of course, get Xijie's share eventually.

This bare outline suggests that the subprefect seems to have had at least two considerations in mind. First, rather than dividing the money equally among the survivors or giving it all to the surviving natural son (Xijie) at the expense of the adopted (Xizhe and Qingzhao) sons and Miss Xu, the subprefect decided that the three shares in dispute were to be used to support sacrifices (and perhaps other ritual observances) for Zheng Kun. In other words, the court's decision attempted to secure the future for this particular descent group of an ancestral estate, one of the characteristic attributes of a lineage. Second, at the same time, the court edict explicitly encouraged the sole surviving natural son to father children—thus stimulating the continued survival of the lineage through the natural son, Xijie, rather than his adopted siblings.

Before concluding this discussion of problems of inheritance, it should be added that the Chinese in Taiwan adopted children by purchase even when there were already natural heirs. Competition over estate shares was therefore inevitable. Pasternak explains this by suggesting that the impetus for such adoptions came from childless co-wives. A woman in this situation would "press her husband to adopt a son for her to guarantee her rights of access to the family estate in the face of competing claims from her co-wife, as well as from her husband's brothers and their wives."[15] Such a consideration might well have been one of the root causes of the dispute that follows.

Case 22609: Disputes over Wealth (*zhengcai*)
GX 8/10/23–GX 19/2/3 (3 December 1882–20 March 1893)

On GX 8/10/23 (3 December 1882), Mrs. Zhou née Xu, a widow of 57 *sui* living in Xinzhu, and her son Zhou Chuncao, then 35, began a protracted legal struggle to obtain what they considered their rightful share of the family estate. With a seemingly weak case from the beginning, the two showed extraordinary persistence and ingenuity in prolonging the case for nearly eleven years. Although their attempts to gain a more equitable (in their eyes) share of the family property were continually frustrated, mother and son displayed a remarkable ability to persuade higher authorities that further investigation and court hearings were warranted.

Mrs. Zhou's complaint was lodged against her deceased husband's three brothers. One of the three had also died by the time the lawsuit was instituted, so in actuality the defendants were the families of her three brothers-in-law. In effect, one collateral line (*fang*) of the Zhou lineage was suing the other three. Because the quarrel was considered to be an internal family matter, the woman and her son initially had to overcome the county court's reluctance to allow the dispute to be thrust into the public arena. Their first two submissions to the court [22609:1–2], a petition followed by a prompting petition ten days later, were both rejected by the county's chief administrator, Xu Xizhi. Although most of the magistrate's endorsement on the first petition is missing, some indication of the reasons for his refusal to accept the petitions can be discerned. Family disputes once aired for public consumption became "injurious to tranquility" (*shang heqi*). Such family strife should have been settled by lineage relatives. Even after Mrs. Zhou's second petition explained that the only relatives who could mediate the disagreement (that is, who were not parties to the litigation) were living on the mainland, the magistrate still refused to accept her complaint for adjudication. Her description of the property in contention was too confused and not sufficiently factual. Only after Mrs. Zhou and Chuncao had filed a second prompting petition [22609:3] with more specific information did Magistrate Xu order action taken. Moreover, not until the issuance of a summons [22609:4] signaled the court's willingness to become involved did those accused by Mrs. Zhou finally feel a necessity to respond. On GX 8/12/8 (16 January 1883), a countercomplaint [22609:5] rejecting Mrs. Zhou's charges was filed by a proxy on behalf of a *jiansheng*, Zhou Qichang, also known as Zhou Wuniang.[16]

The contentions of the parties laid out in these first filings remained essentially unchanged throughout the case. The basic issue was whether the estate had been formally divided in a way that was both legally binding and congruent with customary practice. Mrs. Zhou and son claimed it had not; her brother-in-law insisted it had. Ultimately, the documentary evidence submitted early on by Zhou Wuniang proved to be too strong for Mrs. Zhou and son Zhou Chuncao to overcome in spite of several reviews and rehearings by different magistrates.

The first stage of the case ended on GX 9/4/8 (14 May 1883) after both parties had submitted several petitions, a court hearing had taken place, and a decision had been rendered by the magistrate. In appraising this phase of the litigation, we find that both parties in the case were in agreement about some of the facts.[17] Sometime in the latter part of the Daoguang period (1820–50), Zhou Dongfu, Mrs. Zhou's husband, accompanied his father from their Fujian home in Anqi county, Quanzhou prefecture, to Taiwan, where they opened a dried fruit store (*ganguo dian*) called the Cha-Tai firm in Zhuqian city. Zhou Dongfu's three younger brothers, Yuhang, Yushu, and Wuniang, remained behind on the mainland. (Indeed, at that time the youngest, Wuniang, must have been a child under ten.)[18] By XF 9 (1859), the three brothers had come to Zhuqian to join Zhou Dongfu, who had inherited the store's management after their father's death seven years earlier. In that year Zhou Dongfu turned over management of the Cha-Tai firm to his younger brothers, and he, his wife, and his sons[19] moved out of the store (or buildings connected to it) into a separate residence. At some point, Dongfu had also opened a second store called the Cha-Yuan firm that had eventually gone bankrupt under his management.

In TZ 13 (1874), a year or two after her husband's death, Mrs. Zhou went to make a complaint against her brothers-in-law to a military officer named Huang, the commander of the military battalion stationed in Zhuqian.[20] Mediators (*gongqin*) were called in, and the collateral lines[21] of Zhou Wuniang and his two brothers agreed to remit 550 dollars to Mrs. Zhou.

There were, however, numerous points of disagreement, both of fact and of interpretation, that emerged from petitions submitted and testimony given by the two parties. In the first place, Mrs. Zhou insisted that her husband had turned over the store's management to his brothers because he had become ill, but the younger brothers had then expelled Zhou Dongfu and his nuclear family from their living quarters in the store. Zhou Wuniang, in contrast, claimed that his brother voluntarily handed over the running of the Cha-Tai firm because it was in financial difficulty. The three younger brothers had paid Dongfu 150 dollars plus a sum of 30 dollars referred to as "eldest grandson money" (*dasun* or *zhangsun yin*). In return for this consideration Dongfu had renounced all rights to the store and the rest of the estate inherited from their father, and these rights as well as responsibility for its debts passed to the three. In support of his contention, Wuniang offered as evidence a contract (*heyuezi*) signed by each of the four brothers. This document [22609:6], dated sometime in GX 9/6 (ca. July 1883), was copied into the case record and the original returned. Apparently in an attempt to cast doubt on Zhou Chuncao's status and thus, perhaps, his right to share in the estate, Zhou Wuniang's petitions referred to Chuncao as adopted (*mingzi*), a description later accepted by the court.[22]

Concerning the payment of 550 dollars, Mrs. Zhou contended that after her husband's death, she had had no money to pay debts incurred for funeral expenses. To pay these debts, her brothers-in-law had advanced her the money. She and the others had agreed that a like sum would be deducted from her share when a division of the estate took place.[23] Opposing this view, Wuniang's statements and testimony maintained that the 550 dollars was paid simply out of family feeling. His position was that the contract of XF 9 (1859) stood as proof that Dongfu's family had no claim to a share in the estate after that time. Later, after the oldest brother's death, his son, Zhou Chuncao, had through mismanagement and profligacy bankrupted the Cha-Yuan firm, thus leaving his mother destitute. When mediators interceded, Wuniang and the others had agreed to give her the 550 dollars even though they were under no legal obligation to do so. This contention, also, was supported by a document [22609:7] called a "monetary assistance acceptance" (*shishou bangzhu yin zi*). The copy of this acceptance document in the case file was dated TZ 13/11 (ca. December 1874) and was signed by Mrs. Zhou and her two sons.[24]

Mrs. Zhou attempted to strengthen her position by casting Yushu and Wuniang in a position of special obligation to her. She charged that when her husband Dongfu and his father left their home in Fujian to make the crossing to Taiwan, she cared for and raised the two youngest brothers, Yushu and Wuniang, who had been left behind. Thus, their unfamilial behavior in arrogating her collateral branch's share of the estate came very near to a violation of filial piety as well—or so she undoubtedly hoped it would be perceived.

Zhou Wuniang had submitted both the contract and the acceptance as evidence when he filed his first plaint on GX 8/12/8 (16 January 1883). On GX 9/2/25 (2 April 1883), the same day that the parties faced the magistrate's questions for the first time, Mrs. Zhou filed a prompting petition [22609:14] that called both pieces of evidence forged. She agreed that she and her brothers-in-law had indeed drawn up an agreement when she received the 550 dollars, but that this document provided for the money to be deducted later from her share of the estate. Mrs. Zhou failed, however, to submit any such document to substantiate her assertion.

On the 25th of the second month, the day of the first court hearing, Mrs. Zhou had made known to the court in some detail her estimation of the size of the Cha-Tai firm's assets.[25] She stated the firm owned agricultural land worth over 30,000 dollars that brought in over 2,600 *shi* of grain annually in rent. The store's merchandise and debts (that is, inventory and accounts receivable) were worth over 20,000 dollars. The value of the firm's buildings when the worth of repairs and improvements were taken into account was over 6,000 dollars in her estimation. Although she made the inference explicit only later in the case, the suggestion was that she would hardly have agreed to accept 550 dollars as her collateral line's share of a 60,000-dollar estate. In the mind of Magistrate Xu, however, Zhou Wuniang's documentary evidence was too compelling. After interrogating Mrs. Zhou, Chuncao, Wuniang, and Zhou Liang, the representative of Zhou Guoxiang who was away at the prefectural examinations, the magistrate was of the opinion that the contract and the acceptance were reliable proof, especially because the signatures of the mediators had been affixed. Mrs. Zhou continued to deny the validity of the acceptance not only because it was allegedly forged but also because only a particular kind of document, a *jiushu* or "estate division agreement," was proof that the collateral lines of a lineage had formally divided the lineage's assets. Magistrate Xu decided to summon the mediators listed in the assistance agreement for questioning.

Of the four men who had mediated the TZ 13 (1874) payment of 550 dollars, only two were available for questioning. One had died; a second, who was also a member of the Zhou lineage, had not yet returned from taking the prefectural examinations. Runners were successful in locating and summoning Chen Qianfu and Guo Tiansi, the other two mediators. Chen and Guo, city residents with native place registration in the same Fujian prefecture, although not the same county, as the Zhou family, offered sketchy testimony [22609:23] that tended to corroborate Zhou Wuniang's version of the 550-dollar payment. They also confirmed the validity of the assistance acceptance document and Mrs. Zhou's acquiescence in the transaction. The mediators' affirmation of the genuineness of the acceptance agreement moved the magistrate to accuse Mrs. Zhou and her son in his court directive [22609:23] of lying in her accusations. He stopped short of using the term "false accusation," which would have forced him to bring criminal charges against her and Chuncao.[26] In fact, in spite of the reprimand, he attempted to give Mrs. Zhou some satisfaction by displaying what he called "extralegal mercy" (*fawai zhi en*). The court's decision ordered Wuniang to pay 100 dollars for Mrs. Zhou's old age support. Even this limited victory for her was diminished, however, when Magistrate Xu added the proviso that she was to receive only 80 dollars of the award. The remaining 20 dollars was to be donated to the Mingzhi Academy,[27] a school in Xinzhu, to help defray student expenses, even though her son was not a student.

After the directive was handed down, both parties plus the mediators entered into compliance bonds (*zunyi jiezhuang*) [22609: 24–27] on GX 9/3/10 (16 April 1883). Three days later Zhou Wuniang filed a notice of remittance (*jiaoyin zhuang*) [22609:29], which was received the same day as Mrs. Zhou and Chuncao's notice of receipt (*lingyin zhuang*) [22609:31].

Although the case had seemingly been concluded, Mrs. Zhou and son, after a three-month hiatus, moved the focus of their legal effort to the prefect in Taibei. Their appeal had the positive consequence of keeping their case alive but at a cost they may not have anticipated when, as we shall see, the magistrate instituted legal proceedings against them. These proceedings resulted in the incarceration and corporal punishment of Zhou Chuncao.

On GX 9/6/28 (31 July 1883), Mrs. Zhou had handed in a petition [22609:32] to Prefect Chen Xingju charging her suit against her brothers-in-law had been unsuccessful because they had bribed the mediators and a yamen gatekeeper. The latter allegation prompted the prefect to endorse her petition with an order to the Xinzhu magistrate to reexamine the documents and reinterrogate those involved.

The newly posted magistrate, Zhou Zhikan, was not sympathetic. In fact, he was apparently so annoyed by the extreme language of one of her prompting petitions [22609:34] that he decided to send a report [22609:35] to the prefect with a copy going to Liu Ao, the Taiwan circuit intendant, requesting charges be filed against the woman and her son. The magistrate's report proposed that, should Mrs. Zhou again appeal to a higher court, her proxy filer, Chuncao, be arrested and sent to the county court for investigation. The prompting petition had also contained a passage attempting to justify their suit by citing a purported substatute (*li*) to the Qing Code that supposedly legitimated an eldest grandson disputing with relatives to obtain his share of an estate. Because there was no such provision in the Code, Magistrate Zhou became suspicious that Zhou Chuncao had hired a pettifogger who had composed the complaint and filled out the petition form. Magistrate Zhou's report to his superiors also suggested that the pettifogger be traced and apprehended.

Both proposals were approved by Intendant Liu, and after Zhou Chuncao on behalf of his mother once again filed an appeal with the prefect, Chuncao was arrested and sent under guard to Xinzhu.[28] Prefect Chen also ordered a scrivener to find the pettifogger and take him into custody, but without result.[29] On GX 9/10/19 (18 November 1883), Chuncao was questioned by the magistrate. While still maintaining that the estate had been improperly divided, Chuncao admitted in his testimony [22609:41] that he had been wrong in filing appeals. He also conceded that after he went to the prefectural yamen, he had hired a man in Mengjia to write up the appeal that resulted in his arrest.[30]

Even with her son in jail, Mrs. Zhou refused to concede defeat. On GX 9/10/28 (27 November 1883), she appealed [22609:42] directly to the circuit intendant, who, in surprising contrast to his earlier approval to punish Zhou Chuncao for continuing to press the lawsuit, endorsed her petition with an order to Xinzhu county to reexamine the case. The plaintiffs gained nothing but pain from a rehearing, even though, or perhaps because, a new magistrate presided. After questioning the opposing parties and two of the mediators, Magistrate Zhu Chenglie came to the conclusion that Mrs. Zhou was a "shiftless character" (*wulai zhi tu*). The magistrate considered himself to be lenient toward Chuncao when he ordered a mere beating with the light stick to admonish the prisoner.[31]

So the situation stood at the end of GX 9 (early 1884). Zhou Chuncao remained in detention through most of the first three months of GX 10. On GX 10/2/6 (3 March 1884), five men surnamed Zhou filed a joint petition [22609:56] supporting Mrs. Zhou's version of the dispute, but Magistrate Zhu was not swayed. Finally, late in the third month, after Chuncao's jailer reported [22609:58] that the prisoner was ill and spitting blood, Magistrate Xu Xizhi, who had just taken office, ordered his release.

No further developments are evident in the record until late in the following year, when an extraordinary order [22609:64] from Taibei Prefect Liu Xun to Xinzhu Magistrate Fang Zuyin revealed that the persistent Mrs. Zhou had been successful in reopening the case by appealing to an even higher level of officialdom than before.[32] She had taken advantage of a tour of inspection by two imperially deputed officials, Minister of Justice (*xingbu zhengtang*) Xizhen and Jiangsu Governor Wei Rongguang, to "stop their sedan chair" (*lanyu*) and submit, by proxy, an account of her grievances.[33] Subsequently they communicated with the provincial judicial commissioner, who in turn relayed their order down to Taibei prefecture and ultimately Xinzhu county. Within a month of receiving the order on GX 11/11/13 (18 December 1885), Magistrate Fang questioned the parties twice. He reached the same conclusions as earlier magistrates and again jailed Chuncao. The prisoner was to be detained by runners until a guarantor for his release could be found. Such a guarantor would have been required to certify that Chuncao would not reopen the case again. But, as the head lictor reported [22609:73], in view of the history of the case, it was difficult to find anyone willing to take the risk. Furthermore, the magistrate's appraisal of Zhou Chuncao undoubtedly gave any potential guarantors pause.

> Zhou Chuncao did not care [to wait with the patience] of the standing crane. In scheming to make a living, he presumptuously hoped to get his fingers greasy dipping them into someone else's turtle stew. Because he saw his uncles prospering, he induced his mother to make false accusations. Mrs. Zhou née Xu dotes on him blindly and can be manipulated as easily as cotton earflaps. Zhou Chuncao is insatiably greedy. Time after time he has shown his intention to implicate others falsely [22609:71].

Later, however, Fang did manage to muster some charity. In the first month of the following year, the court, after receiving a petition [22609:76] from Chuncao's wife explaining that he was the sole support of their family and, moreover, that his mother had become ill, agreed to his release if a guarantor could be found. Before Mrs. Zhou's brother finally agreed on GX 12/4/29 (1 June

1886) to enter into a bond for his release, Mrs. Zhou filed another prompting petition [22609:80] at the county yamen. Even though she could adduce no new evidence or arguments, rather than dismissing her petition out of hand, Fang ordered her to ask lineage relatives to mediate.

In the meantime, the magistrate had reported his findings to the prefect, the circuit intendant, and the provincial surveillance commissioner. His report [22609:78], dated GX 12/2/5 (10 March 1886), reviewed the case in detail and concluded that earlier magistrates' decisions in the case had been correct. By GX 12/5/2 (3 June 1886), all three superior offices had received the report and approved cancellation of the case.

Mrs. Zhou and son were not finished yet. Two months later, on 2 August 1886, Chuncao, acting as his mother's proxy, handed in a prompting petition [22609:88] charging that Wuniang had refused to comply with a settlement reached by lineage relatives. Because her son had contracted an eye disease and could no longer work as a hired laborer to support her, Mrs. Zhou had gone to the residence of her brothers-in-law to ask for clothing and food. They not only refused but also reviled and beat her. Her petition was accepted, but the magistrate was by this time completely exasperated. Mrs. Zhou was examined by a coroner, who found the only signs of injury were some light red weals on her hands.[34] His endorsement accused her of attempting to extort money from Wuniang and Yushu, of fabricating the accusation of being beaten and injured, and in this way of attempting to reopen the already canceled case. He concluded that her son, who incited her to this latest action, deserved to be punished again but instead would merely be reprimanded (*shenchi*). Finally, he threatened him with trial and heavy punishment should they cause any further trouble.

Mrs. Zhou and Zhou Chuncao made no further attempts to reopen the case during the exceptionally long tenure in office of Fang Zuyin. They did, however, hand in petitions to four subsequent magistrates within a month or two of each one's arrival in Xinzhu. Mrs. Zhou tried again as late as GX 19/2/3 (20 March 1893), by which time she had reached the age of 67 *sui*. It was a fruitless effort. One by one new magistrates endorsed the petitions with references to earlier chief administrators' findings and censured Mrs. Zhou and son with various degrees of severity. The two were careful, however, to avoid irritating any of the magistrates enough to provoke concrete proceedings against them, and no evidence of further action in the case can be found after the above date.

Before leaving this case, it may be useful to reflect on the common idea that has been passed down that Chinese were reluctant to go to court because of the danger, difficulty, and expense that legal proceedings entailed. Certainly some idea of the sort was one of the assumptions circulated in the realm of traditional Chinese lore. Numerous folk proverbs support this view.[35] Once we begin to examine some case evidence, however, a much different impression is formed.

Mrs. Zhou and her son were not reluctant to go to court even though their case was weak and the dispute of a type that the courts were loath to accept for adjudication. Rough treatment (jail and flogging) experienced by Zhou Chuncao and the expense associated with prolonged litigation did not prevent the two from numerous attempts to reinstitute the case. Although there is little direct testimony in the case files bearing on the cost to litigants of court trials, it was often felt prudent to hire legal specialists. In addition, various yamen personnel demanded fees for their services.[36] If, as in this instance, a litigant continued to push her case for several years, the expenses must have been considerable. The case materials leave us unenlightened concerning the source of Mrs. Zhou's financial ability to push the case in the face of so many setbacks. Perhaps she and her son received legal aid from a pettifogger on a "contingency fee" basis. Even so, as will be discussed in the next chapter, there would have been other costs, and Mrs. Zhou was obviously willing to carry the proceedings forward.

Hostility toward and fear of the law and legal proceedings as expressed through folklore are hardly indications of an aversion to using the judicial system. They rather are hints that enmeshment, voluntary or otherwise, in the system was not an unusual occurrence. Contrary to the traditional assumptions, Chinese proverbs decrying the cost and danger of litigation mean not that Chinese avoided going to court but instead are clear indications that litigation was extremely common.[37]

Nor is this case in which a woman played a leading role an isolated instance. Men readily and women occasionally turned to the courts for redress when they felt there was no other recourse or when other options seemed less likely to bear fruit. As the following chapter will demonstrate, petitions from female complainants were a regular, if not common, feature of the court docket.

Chapters 3 through 6 have explored several aspects of the social context of law and litigation and have reviewed several actual cases that embody the issues and conflicts agitating northern Taiwan in the nineteenth century. In the next three chapters I will turn to a consideration of the patterns discernible in the interaction between the legal system and its clients. In stages that roughly correspond to the major phases of the litigation process, the three chapters that follow will discuss some of the more important requirements of the legal process. I will seek to characterize litigants on the one hand and the bureaucratic machinery with which they had to deal on the other. In addition, I will trace out the implications and consequences faced by petitioners who appealed to the yamen for dispensation of legal remedies for wrongs suffered.

7

The Petition

FILING PROCEDURE AND REQUIREMENTS

The first hurdle facing a person seeking the help of the legal system for redress of a wrong suffered was proper and effective use of the petition that would put the legal machinery into motion. Petitioners were required to adhere to a series of procedural steps and rules while compiling and submitting their petitions. Some of these guidelines were enforced laxly or not at all. Violation or omission of other required steps could result in the subprefect or magistrate refusing to accept the complaint for adjudication. Certain violations could, in theory, even lead to punishment for the petitioner. For these reasons this chapter opens with a description and discussion of petition forms and their contents illustrated with a translation of a petition from one of the cases.

The Petition Form

The petition document with its standardized format enabled the subprefect or magistrate and his assistants to place a case within its proper context at a glance by requiring petitioners to provide certain basic data.[1] Because local government in China was notoriously underfunded, it could not provide the forms free of charge.

Moreover, charging a fee for both the form and for processing may have been viewed as a way to help reduce the number of frivolous lawsuits. During the nineteenth century, petition forms, which had to be submitted in duplicate, are said to have cost 400–500 cash each to purchase from the yamen.[2] In addition, a petitioner paid 80 cash as a registration fee to the Receipt and Distribution Office (*chengfa fang*) when submitting.[3]

Petitions were classified after receipt into several categories depending on the type and seriousness of the complaint, but identical forms were employed for all varieties of petitions. Only the content or time of submission differentiated the forms. When the complaint involved what were considered minor matters, the petition was referred to as a fixed date petition (*qicheng*). This kind of petition concerned such matters as disputes over property (real or movable), marriage, divorce, or commercial dealings— in other words, what Westerners might be inclined to call civil law disputes. Such petitions could be submitted only on certain appointed days. A complaint alleging that a serious crime such as homicide or robbery had been committed was assigned to another category called a summoning petition (*chuancheng*). A summoning petition could be submitted at any time. Petitioners sometimes attempted to present their complaints directly to the local chief administrator when he was outside the yamen traveling through his jurisdiction. This practice was called "stopping the sedan chair" (*lanyu*). A petition so presented was referred to as a sedan-chair petition (*yucheng*) or "kneeling-on-the-road petition" (*guilu cheng*).[4] Suzuki Sōgen notes a fourth type of petition termed a crying-out petition (*hancheng*).[5] When homicide or other loss of life had occurred, a witness or other aggrieved party could hasten to the yamen and make a verbal report. Later a formal, written complaint could be drawn up and submitted.

As the case summaries show, after litigation was initiated, defendants regularly submitted their own petitions in response to the charges against them. These documents were called counterplaints (*su*) to signify that they had been filed in rebuttal. Once accuser and accused had each submitted a first petition, one or both often filed numerous follow-ups pressing the court to take action. These prompting petitions (*cuicheng*) were by far the most common petition seen in the Dan-Xin archives.

Only a difference in content determined whether a petition was considered a fixed-date or a summoning petition. Sedan-chair and crying-out petitions were distinguished by their peculiar method of submission. In the case files, there are occasional petitions simply marked with the notation "crying out." Early in 1879, for example, several men were killed or wounded in attacks by mountain tribesmen on guard posts in the hills east and south of present-day Miaoli city. Relatives of some of the dead and wounded made their way to the yamen and filed *hancheng* [32101:2, 3] calling for redress. Contrary to Suzuki's contention that crying-out petitions could be used only when a suspected homicide had occurred, *hancheng* were submitted even in civil litigation. When Mrs. Zhou née Xu began to go to Zhou Wuniang's store and harass him, Wuniang filed a crying-out petition [22609:77] asking the magistrate to force her to stop.[6]

Sedan-chair petitions, in contrast, although not completely unknown in the Dan-Xin jurisdiction,[7] were exceptional because there was a formal prohibition against them (see below). Prompting petitions and counterplaints are clearly marked with the word *cui* or *su* but otherwise appear exactly like the other forms. Thus a short discussion of the format of the single translated example will suffice for all.

On such forms we first[8] find a space with entries for names and some limited personal data of the two parties, as well as of court or other related personnel.[9] Following these entries came a grid of 16 columns and 20 rows making a total of 320 squares where the petition itself was written. Above the grid, a warning against writing more than one word per square was printed in large, bold characters. The grid was followed by a preprinted entry detailing the chief administrative officer's posting, rank, honors, and surname and ending with the word "endorsement" (*pi*). A substantial blank space following the "endorsement" entry was left available for the comments, questions, or orders with which the subprefect or magistrate responded to the petition. The date the petition was accepted at the yamen followed. Then came a succession of more year-month-day entries that could be filled in with dates of earlier action or submissions in the case. (The translated example lists the date that the original petition received an endorsement.) In most instances, immediately below these date entries, the endorsement from the petitioner's preceding complaint was copied. Finally, a number of procedural rules to be followed in submitting the petition were printed at the very end of the form.

The following petition [22514:2] was the first submitted to the Xinzhu yamen by Jin-Liu-He after the dispute over the boundary between the partnership's tea plots and the four villages' pasture flared anew in 1885. The petition was written on a preprinted form. Words written entirely in uppercase in the translation below correspond to printed entries on the original form. Petition forms were folded together accordion-style with six equal sections.

Petition of Jin-Liu-He

ACCUSED (*beigao*): ________ RESIDENCE: ________

WITNESS (*ganzheng*): ________ RESIDENCE: ________

INNKEEPER (*xiejia*): ________

LOCAL CONSTABLE (*dibao*): ________ RESIDENCE: ________

SEAL VERIFIER (*renchuo*): ________

PETITIONER (*jucheng ren*): Jin-Liu-He viz. Liu Bukui; RESIDENCE: Zhubei second TOWNSHIP Xinpu *jie* VILLAGE; NATIVE PLACE REGISTRATION: Raoping [county, Chaozhou prefecture, Guangdong]; DISTANCE FROM CITY: 25 *LI*

HANDLING CLERK (*jingcheng*): Yu Sheng

SCRIVENER (*daishu*): [seal impression illegible]

ORIGINAL RUNNERS (*yuanchai*): Wang Zuo, Lin Jia

FORM COMPILATION (*zuozhuang*): Self-drafted

PETITION FILER (*chengzhuang ren*): Jin-Liu-He viz. Liu Bukui; AGE: 42 *SUI*; RESIDENCE: Xinpu *jie* VILLAGE; PROXY FILER (*baogao*): ________; AGE: ________ *SUI*; RELATIONSHIP TO ACCUSER: ________; RESIDENCE: ________

Zhubei; a case has already been initiated.[10]

IN NO CASE WILL THIS [petition] BE ACCEPTED AND READ IF IT CONTAINS ANY COLUMNS WITH TWO LINES OF WRITING[11]

In the matter of a bandit gang that tied up [their victims] and robbed or completely destroyed [property], we beg for [the court's] benevolence in personally joining with military officials, in issuing a cease and desist order, and in capturing and trying the criminals in order to save human lives.

I, [Liu Bu] kui, repeatedly have made accusations and pressed for action in a case in which the vicious hooligan Luo Ayuan formed a gang consisting of Luo Asi, Luo Aye, Luo Ashan, Luo Ayan, Luo Linxing, Yang Chun, Yu Chunfu, Yu Chunlai, and others who destroyed property and illegally occupied land. Our grievances are all in the original case file. Who would have expected that the hooligans, who had learned that Liu Shangda had not yet returned from the provincial examinations, relied on the influence of someone holding official rank (*shifu*) to band together a large gang of wealthy and powerful local bullies in sworn alliance? Early in the morning of the 24th of this month, Luo and the others came leading a gang consisting of Lin Awei, Lin Agang, Lin Ahong, Lü Guanniang, Luo Rongguang, Luo Axie, Luo Yunyue, and others. They were in command of several hundred ruffians, each of whom was armed with a rifle, sword, musket, or other weapon; each wore a uniform and some type of armor. Under pretext of an official directive, they swarmed onto our land and dug up or destroyed houses and tea plots belonging to Jin-Liu-He tenants. At present, all the men, women, old, young, and family members among the tenants have been surrounded and are under attack by the gang. Their fates have not yet been determined. Cattle, grain, household goods, clothing—everything has been stolen.

In this manner, without [our] previous grievances having yet been redressed, they become more perverse with each accusation. Moreover, they dared to form a sworn alliance to attack and plunder everything. The village people all know about it. It was immediately reported to the local constable, but a cease and desist order was not obeyed. If you do not personally join with military officials, issue a directive ordering them to cease and desist, and arrest and try them so as to save human life, not merely will household articles have been completely plundered, but I fear that it will be difficult to preserve the lives of the tenants and their families.

As for our losses, more than 600,000 tea shrubs planted by Jin-Liu-He tenants, seven tenants' dwellings, and household articles were plundered or utterly destroyed, leaving nothing. If [the tenants] were to die under such circumstances, how could they rest easily? Finally, lists of stolen goods and tenants' injuries will each be elucidated with additional reports in separate petitions.

Compelled by circumstances, we have set forth the details with utmost sincerity. I cry out to your intelligent honor to take responsibility for the enfeebled, with benevolence and promptitude personally to take action in concert with the military authorities, to issue a cease and desist order, to be rigorous in arresting Luo Ayuan and all other ruffians in the gang, and to investigate and settle the case. Accordingly, in unity with our tenants, we urgently implore your benevolence.

ENDORSEMENT OF EXPECTANT MILITARY PREFECT, ACTING XINZHU COUNTY MAGISTRATE, GRANTED ONE STEP OF MERIT

PENG: I find that previously in this case the court received a report filed by the interpreter Qian Yubing. It is on record that runners have already been issued a warrant with a directive to gentry to suppress violence. If Luo Ayuan and the others dared to wear military armor and plunder your Jin-Liu-He tenants' dwellings, tea plots, and household goods, it was extremely unlawful. Wait for an immediate order to runners to cooperate with military officials, to deliver a cease and desist order, and at the same time to arrest suspects and gather witnesses. A hearing with both parties present can be then held and the stolen goods recovered through prosecution.
One document containing the prefect's endorsement attached.
GUANGXU 11th YEAR 8th MONTH 24th DAY.
PETITIONER: Jin-Liu-He viz. Liu Bukui.
ENDORSEMENT OF ORIGINAL ACCUSATION SUBMITTED IN current YEAR 6th MONTH 27th DAY: [omitted]

[Instructions for Completing the Petition Form]

[1.] In homicide or robbery cases where the year, month, and day when the incident occurred are not entered [in the petition]; in cases of loss of life where the most serious wound is not entered; in cases of robbery where a list of the stolen articles is not entered; or [in cases of] receiving stolen goods where evidence [for the charge] is not entered, [the petitions] will not be accepted.

[2.] In cases of suicide or other loss of life where the circumstances are falsified and false accusation made, the scrivener will be brought up for a hearing and witness and accuser will be reciprocally punished.[12]

[3.] Anyone who does not wait until the days appointed for litigation but dares immediately to stop the magistrate's sedan chair to submit a stamped petition will not only have his petition refused but will be examined with severity. Moreover, the person handing in the petition will be harshly punished.

[4.] Petitions that do not have previous endorsements and judgments in the case copied and attached and those that do not completely record this yamen's successive endorsements will not be accepted.

[5.] Petitions that lack the names of the scrivener and the person drawing up the document and that do not clearly note the complainant's permanent residence and the inn where he is temporarily residing [while in the city] will not be accepted.

[6.] Anyone taking an old affair and bringing it up as something new in hopes of provoking a hearing or using baseless language to fabricate charges and false accusations will be harshly punished; the scrivener together with the person making the false accusation will have their degree of punishment increased.

[7.] Anyone not observing the issued petition forms, writing in double columns, or not submitting a duplicate of the petition will be refused.

[8.] Petitions from degree holders, women, the aged, the young, or the physically or mentally incompetent that are not submitted by a proxy filer will not be accepted; women's petitions that seek to involve many people will not be accepted.

[9.] Anyone who makes an accusation of an amnestied crime, aside from having his petition refused, will be punished.

[10.] Commoners, clerks, runners and the like as well as anyone not aged, a youth, or physically or mentally incompetent who submit a petition by proxy will not only have their petitions refused but accusers and proxies will be punished.

[11.] *Sheng* [*yuan*], *jian* [*sheng*], or gentry may not because of close relationship or harbored enmity file an accusation in cases that do not involve them personally; moreover, if they act as a witness for the accuser or accused, the case will not be accepted.[13]

With this description in mind, it will be worthwhile to consider briefly the requirements thus imposed on those drawing up a petition and the significance of the entries included on the printed forms.

Petition forms contained a printed list of procedural rules for the explicit guidance of petitioners, proxy filers, scriveners, and yamen personnel. These rules were couched in negative terms that set forth reasons for refusing to accept petitions or for punishing those who made improper submissions. The rules fell into two general categories: first, rules concerning the proper procedure that litigants were made to observe in submitting their complaints, and second, rules concerning attempts by litigants to deceive the court in their submissions.

The first category is the largest, with seven (1, 4–5, 7–8, 10–11) of the eleven prescriptive guidelines. Violation of these seven rules so flawed the petitioner's case that it would not be accepted for adjudication. Such flaws were merely technical, however, and did not result in penalty to the filer. They were sins of omission rather than commission. Thus, a petition would be refused when an accusation pointed to serious, violent crimes where victims were robbed of life or property and the petitioner had not specified the cause of death or the stolen goods. Incomplete, vague, or unsubstantiated charges were regarded at best as difficult or impossible to investigate. It was necessary that it be clear from the petition whether the petitioner himself drafted his complaint and if, as was required (see below), a scrivener had filled out the form. The rules also directed that a petition be submitted in duplicate, that official printed forms be used, and that the body of the complaint contain no more than 320 words (that is, one character per square) in the petition grid. If the petition had been preceded by earlier filings, previous endorsements were to be copied on or attached to it. Certain classes of persons were excused from personally handing in a litigation petition. They were entitled to use representatives called proxy filers (see below) in their stead. The most important group so exempt were the degree-holding gentry elite. This gentry privilege was accompanied by a positive obligation to remain uninvolved in legal cases. All degree-holding gentry were therefore forbidden to intervene in cases in which they were not personally concerned. Even testifying as a witness was banned unless a degree holder was personally involved in the case.

Under any of the just-described conditions, the court in theory merely declined to handle the case, and petitioners suffered no further consequences. Certain actions taken by litigants in this first stage of the legal process could, however, expose them to prosecution. When a lawsuit did not involve a criminal act, local yamens would normally accept petitions in the case on only six days each month.[14] Except on the 3d, 8th, 13th, 18th, 23d, and 28th of the month, civil complaints were not accepted. A survey of the dates on which petitioners in the three civil suits summarized in the preceding chapter submitted documents to the court shows that there were only occasional exceptions to the rule limiting civil petitions to six days per month. Litigants who sought to circumvent this restriction by attempting to "stop the magistrate's sedan chair to submit a stamped plea" could be punished, especially if the person presenting the document did so on behalf of another.[15] False accusation, as noted above, rebounded upon the author of the deceptive charges. Finally, no one could be accused of crimes that had been forgiven through imperial amnesty. Such an accusation would be refused and its originator punished. As we shall see after some further observations on the petition form, certain of these regulations seem to have had much greater authority than others.

As in the translated example, on most petition forms found in the Dan-Xin archives the first few entries before the name of the petitioner have been left blank. Of the five items, entries for accused, witness, and local constable are seldom found on petitions in the Dan-Xin archives. In occasional petitions the names of the innkeeper and the seal verifier were entered, but even those entries were rare.

People from outside the city who came or were summoned to court stayed at inns near the yamen.[16] Such establishments ostensibly catered to litigants' needs. The proprietors of such inns, however, were widely considered to prey on the ignorance of those not well versed in the workings of the legal system by overcharging for room and board, colluding with yamen clerks and runners in fraud and extortion, and manipulating lawsuits. Although Huang Liuhong, an early Qing magistrate, had written a handbook that among much else advised local officials to open publicly run litigants' shelters in order to provide an alternative to private inns, the latter continued to flourish.[17] The innkeeper entry on the petition form probably was designed for the convenience of runners sent to fetch litigants required by the magistrate for a hearing, but it is possible that making the innkeeper's name part of the case record was intended to check some of the more flagrant abuses.

As for the seal verifier entry, according to Chang Wejen it recorded the yamen staff member who had checked the scrivener's seal impression on the petition form against impressions of authorized seals kept on file.[18] This task was probably delegated to one of the junior clerks in the section handling the petition, although in at least one instance [31104:1] the Palanquin Office (*jiaosuo*), which was principally charged with maintaining a sedan chair for the magistrate's use, was listed as seal verifier.

Most of the individual entries on petition forms in the Dan-Xin cases contained the requisite information. It is not clear why the other three entries—accused, witness, and local constable—were seldom completed. The text of the petition itself, of course, made clear against whom the complainant was laying charges as well as the identity of any witnesses. Perhaps there was an implicit understanding among scriveners and yamen staff that those two items could be ignored. That "accused" and "witness" entries were routinely ignored suggests that properly identifying defendants and witnesses was felt to be the responsibility of the magistrate and his assistants. A complainant used his petition to make allegations. No one named therein became formally involved or implicated until the yamen so decided. A warrant with a list of those to be summoned or arrested signified that allegations contained in a petition had become formal charges.

The consistent failure to name the local constable might be more puzzling at first glance. The commonly held view of local law enforcement in late traditional China has conceived of the *dibao* as a crucial link between yamen and populace in matters of local control.[19] While this conception may be correct for other localities, as we shall see a different subcounty official, the overseer (*zongli*), played a more important role in Danshui and Xinzhu. Local constables existed in at least some townships but usually took a back seat to overseers in town and village administration.[20] Still, this begs the question. If another yamen agent or local representative was indeed a key factor in the legal process, why had an entry for it not replaced that of the local constable on petition forms? As subsequent discussion will show, overseers were men of greater respect and higher socioeconomic status than local constables. Subprefects and magistrates were rather more dependent on them than on local constables. It might have been awkward to number them among other low-status yamen servants even on petition forms.

Skipping the entries under the petitioner rubric for the moment, we come to items listing the handling clerk, scrivener, original runners, and method of form compilation. The clerk and runner or runners that were initially assigned to the case normally stayed with it until some resolution was reached.[21] The scrivener never wrote his name below the entry. Instead he impressed the entire area covered by these four entries with his seal of office. We will return to these seals later. Here I wish to note only that a seal identified the scrivener's ethnic background, that is, whether he was of Zhangzhou, Quanzhou, or Hakka stock. The last of the four entries under consideration here, the form-compilation item, explained how large a part the scrivener had played in drawing up the petition. Sometimes petitioners filled out the form themselves; sometimes they had written a draft that was copied on the form by a scrivener. Illiterate petitioners could relate their complaint to a scrivener, who would then reformulate their accusation in acceptable legalese. In all instances a scrivener was required to inspect and affix his seal to petitions.

Two separate columns with several entries were given over to information about the petitioner. The first of these columns called for data concerning the actual complainant. The entries are unremarkable except for the native place item. Even though by the earliest period (circa 1840) considered in this study settlement in Taiwan's north had a history of nearly one and a half centuries, society there still had not completely lost its sojourner, frontier character. The ethnic dimension of social interaction, including criminality, was still an important consideration for legal officials. Petitioners were required to enter their "native" mainland county even if they themselves were third- or fourth-generation descendants of immigrants.[22] The native place entry may also have been useful in determining that the petition had been accurately recorded. Given the linguistic variation between Hakka and Hokkienese or even between Zhangzhou and Quanzhou natives, ensuring that a petitioner's complaint had been recorded accurately by a scrivener speaking the same dialect may have been prudent on the yamen's part. One source asserts that this was a procedural requirement when filing.[23] Various petitions [for example, 32104:1, 32202:5] in which ethnicity of complainant and scrivener did not correspond, however, show that by 1870 at the latest, such a requirement was no longer necessary or enforced, probably because of linguistic convergence.

The second column containing entries with information on the petitioner was designed to indicate the person actually handing in the document at the yamen. If it was the petitioner himself, the information was redundant. However, certain groups were allowed to file by proxy. When this occurred, the form required entry of some minimal information identifying the proxy filer.[24]

Bypassing for the moment the spaces for the body of the petition and the subprefect's or magistrate's endorsement, the final entries on the form were several columns where the dates of previous petition filings could be noted. Normally only the date of the immediately antecedent petition was entered. Below that date were copied the endorsement or comments written by the chief local administrator on that preceding petition. Copying only a single endorsement rather than all previous comments as required by one of the procedural regulations seems to have been a compromise dictated by space limitations on the form.

Petitions and Endorsements: Form and Content

The petition translated to begin this chapter exhibits the three-part structure common to all such documents. The total space allotted for the complaint was small in order to force the petitioner to stick to the main points, to prevent persons not involved from being implicated, and to save time for court personnel. In a line or two the petitioner first summarized, formulaically and often rather cryptically, his accusation or plea and indicated the action he desired the court to take. The core of the petition opened with a short account of events leading up to the incident that provided that impetus for the complaint. If, as in the translated example, there had been previous filings, the complainant made the point that there was a record of the case that could be consulted for more details. Then the petitioner described the event that had impelled him to appeal to the court. If the petition was pursuant to a case already initiated, new developments that gave reason for a follow-up submission were explained. Often the reason for follow-up petitions was not a new development but instead no developments at all. Many petitions were handed in complaining that even though the yamen had accepted the case, issued a warrant, or even made arrests, no action had been taken to advance the case to the next step in the legal process. The petition ended with a brief, stylized recitation of the suffering undergone by the complainant and a call for the judicial officer to help. The appeal to the court was sometimes merely a general plea for justice, protection of the innocent, or punishment of the guilty. Often, however, the petitioner pointed out specific persons who should be summoned for a hearing to redress a wrong or should be arrested and tried for a crime. Occasionally, petitioners even specified the statutory basis for the action they suggested to the court.

Subprefects and magistrates used the space following the petition grid to indicate how the complaint was to be handled. It has been said that the endorsement on each initiatory petition was to be copied and posted for public viewing.[25] Few petitions with obvious procedural flaws were even accepted for inspection by the yamen. In circumstances where litigation was undesirable or a better alternative such as outside mediation existed, this opinion was noted and the petition rejected. Mrs. Zhou's first petition [22609:1] was not accepted for this reason.[26] To accept her lawsuit against her husband's brothers would be "injurious to tranquility." The court felt that lineage relatives not directly involved should mediate.

Apparent inconsistencies or contradictions in the petition might not result in its rejection, but the court's suspicions could focus upon the petitioner. As we have seen, when Wu Jiqing, representing the Wu-Shun-Ji lineage, carelessly admitted in a petition [22202:127] that it was claiming rent collection rights to as much as 1,000 *jia* of land, the case was transformed from mere rent delinquency or refusal to pay rent on the part of tenants to include probable tax evasion by Wu-Shun-Ji.

The most common reaction seen in endorsements was a cautious agreement that if that situation described in the petition was factual, then the wrong committed was truly lawless. Such endorsements ended by ordering the petitioner to wait until runners had been sent to investigate the charges. Even, or perhaps especially, when the allegation was of one of the most serious crimes such as armed robbery, magistrates proceeded cautiously. Zhan Ajing and Lan Tong claimed their store had been broken into and robbed by armed intruders who attacked and wounded Zhan. No arrest order was given until both men had been formally questioned and Zhan examined by a coroner.[27]

There is little direct evidence that indicates whether it was subprefects and magistrates or their legal secretaries who authored the endorsements. Ch'ü T'ung-tsu may be correct in saying that legal secretaries played the major role, even if hidden from public view, in adjudication.[28] In this regard, if the remuneration for Danshui and Xinzhu yamen private secretaries is any indication, those jurisdictions conformed to the norm described by Ch'ü. In 1869, the British vice-consul stationed in northern Taiwan remarked apropos of the importance of the subprefect's private secretaries, "The two highest secretaries of the Tamsuy Ting [Danshui subprefecture] (a neighboring mandarin), are said to receive from him respectively £510 (i.e. $2400) and £425 (i.e. $2000), or thereabouts, as yearly salary, besides some further allowances for mess, etc."[29] Even the lower of the two salaries was princely compared to the amount needed to support an entire family among the ordinary population.[30] If the vice-consul's figures were anywhere close to the truth, they are a measure of how much their employer, the subprefect, depended upon these men and how highly regarded they were. He, after all, had to pay them from his own pocket.

No matter how legal opinions were reached, it is possible to discern relative levels of sophistication and diligence in handling litigation. The best magistrates and subprefects were thorough and analytical in evaluating petitions and energetic in carrying out investigations. Fang Zuyin (in office ca. December 1885–May 1889) may have been the best of the local chief administrators posted to the jurisdiction during the late nineteenth century. As noted in the discussion of rural petitions in this chapter, he did not hesitate to go into the countryside to conduct his own on the spot investigations. He, or at least his secretary, subjected petitions to extremely minute inspection and comparison to other documents in the relevant case files. In 1884, when Mrs. Zhou filed yet another prompting petition [22609:88], numerous interlinear comments noting problems, inconsistencies, and errors attest to the care and attention devoted to handling the case. At the other end of the scale might have been Subprefect Zheng Yuanjie, who was accused of being so ineffectual or lackadaisical in apprehending criminals that he was impeached and removed from office.[31]

Other Petition Types

When petitioners brought their complaints or criminal accusations before the yamen court, often the objects of their charges responded with legal petitions of their own. These responses were termed counterplaints (*su*). After it was clear the yamen had agreed to act on a complaint, a respondent would normally file a *su* denying the original petitioner's contentions and often bringing countercharges of his own. In the boundary dispute case, when the Jin-Liu-He partners accused the villagers of destroying crops and robbing their tenants, the residents of the four villages countered by accusing the partnership of encroaching on common pasture land. Counterplaints were normally written on the same printed forms described above but with the word *su* written above the first petitioner entry. The same procedural rules governed their submission.

Complaints were not always drawn up using the printed forms sold by the yamen. Many of the petitions found in all types of Dan-Xin cases were written on blank paper. Such petitions, called *bing*, contained only the text of the complaint. Petitioners normally identified themselves in the first line only by giving name, rank (if any), and residence. The absence of scriveners' seal impressions show that such petitions seemed exempt from the normal requirement that these scribes scrutinize and approve them before submission. Petitioners who held an examination or purchased degree were entitled to this privilege. The yamen did not rigidly exclude non–degree holders, however. Mrs. Zhou, for example, filed at least two *bing* petitions [22609:42, 97] that were accepted and included in her case file.

When the magistrate was away from the yamen investigating a case, litigants involved in that case could submit petitions written on plain paper directly to him. These documents were the rural petitions (*xiangcheng*) that have already been mentioned. In 1886 during the boundary dispute case, Magistrate Fang Zuyin went into the countryside to inspect the area in contention personally. While he was there, the Jin-Liu-He partnership, its tenant tea farmers, and the villagers opposing them in the suit all delivered rural petitions [22514:97, 98, 99] to Fang. In this way we can see that the formalities governing petitioning procedures at the yamen were relaxed when the subprefect or magistrate was in the field. Of course, when petitioners gained such extraordinarily free access to the magistrate, it was probably little to his liking.

Acceptance of a petition did not mean a complainant's case automatically moved forward. It was necessary both practically and legally for litigants to press or prompt the court to take action. Local administration entailed a heavy workload with many items competing for a magistrate's attention. A litigant who was not persistent might find his case continually shuffled to the bottom of the court's agenda. In his pioneering study of the Dan-Xin archives, Buxbaum showed that complainants filed one or more prompting petitions in 79.6 percent of the 152 "civil" cases where any petitions are found.[32] In the three such noncriminal cases summarized in the earlier chapters, nearly all litigants submitted numerous prompting or follow-up petitions.

The Wu-Shun-Ji lineage, in its suit to force rent arrears payment, handed in 40 petitions during the 26 years covered in the case file. In the Jin-Liu-He partnership's four-year-long boundary dispute with the villagers, the partnership filed five petitions, sixteen prompting petitions, two rural petitions, and a petition appealing to the prefect. The villagers as a whole handed in six petitions, ten prompting petitions, one counterplaint, one rural petition, and one report. The partnership's tenants filed four petitions and nine prompting petitions, including one petition and five prompts from Mrs. Fan née Yang alone. The most persistent filer of prompting petitions in the case was Luo Fuzhen, who submitted eighteen of them without ever receiving any satisfaction.

The greatest variety of litigation documents submitted to various authorities is to be seen in the dispute within the Zhou family over lineage property.[33] Mrs. Zhou, by proxy, filed nine form petitions plus two others not on forms. In addition, she had her proxy filer hand in ten prompting petitions. These 21 filings do not count two appeals—one to the Taibei prefect and another to touring imperial officials—conveyed under her name. Zhou Wuniang, also known as Zhou Qichang, who was the main respondent in the suit brought by Mrs. Zhou, had been diligent in replying to Mrs. Zhou's charges early in the case. Besides an initial counterplaint, four prompting petitions, and three reporting petitions (*bing*), Wuniang also entreated the court's intercession with the crying-out petition mentioned earlier.

Litigants in cases such as those summarized stood to gain or lose a great deal and were therefore tenacious in pressing local courts to intervene in and expeditiously adjudicate the disputes. This conclusion is apparent from the kidnapping and armed robbery cases summarized in the previous chapters as well as from the more detailed information on petitions, prompting petitions, and other responding litigation documents recounted above. There is some evidence that prompting the yamen was not only expedient but also legally required in certain circumstances. In 1871, Wang Kunshou accused Chen Axing, with whom he had been in a dispute over land, of robbing and using a knife to slash Wang's son. The case [32201] continued desultorily until 1873, when the subprefect canceled it because Wang had failed to file a prompting plea in time. The subprefect adduced no statutory rationale for this decision, although it may have been based on a substatute requiring dismissal if the complainant did not come to court within two months for a hearing of the charges he had brought.[34] Such an outcome was unusual, indeed, unique among the cases contained in the Dan-Xin archives. Once a case was accepted for handling, many judges were quite tolerant of numerous promptings by litigants, sometimes, as the examples of Mrs. Zhou and Luo Fuzhen demonstrate, even after a decision had been handed down.

It is true that prompting petitions were often submitted when a new magistrate took office in an attempt to reopen an already concluded case. In such instances, the petitioner usually escaped with no more than a reprimand. Prompting petitions aimed at reopening a case were almost never refused outright. Instead, the usual course taken was to endorse them with a notation that no action could be taken until the case record had been examined.

It is difficult to agree with the view that the danger and expense of litigation were so great that Chinese sought to avoid legal entanglement at nearly all cost. In the first place, as I shall suggest later in this chapter, people of even moderate means could obtain legal advice, although sometimes the quality of the advice varied directly with its price. The danger to litigants, which the decline of the Wu-Shun-Ji lineage shows to have been real, has nonetheless been overrated in my opinion. Mrs. Zhou's son, Zhou Chuncao, was finally jailed and beaten, but only after violating a court decision. Later attempts to reopen the case brought no retaliation. Luo Fuzhen's eighteen prompting petitions gained him nothing, but neither did they bring down the court's wrath. The willingness of even ordinary people to utilize the state's legal apparatus should no longer be surprising to us.

LITIGANTS

Status

Almost all legal procedures, including criminal cases as well as civil litigation, were initiated by private citizens. Only occasionally did a sitting official bring charges.[35] Although the Qing state had an interest in minimizing the frequency of litigation in any given jurisdiction, it did not do so by limiting access to the courts or keeping its citizens ignorant of the statutes.[36] On the contrary, local officials had a positive duty to disseminate knowledge of the law to the common people through lectures on the *Sacred Edict*, an imperially promulgated set of hortatory maxims summarizing orthodox Confucian ideology. In the eighteenth century, abridged legal codes were among the materials issued to lecturers on the *Sacred Edict*.[37]

With the exception of the primary complainant in one case (discussed later in this chapter), in four of the core cases summarized earlier, the initial complainants were from the local elite or at least monied stratum of society. A lineage dependent on land rents, a partnership subleasing its tea plots, and two store proprietors clearly do not make a cross-section of northern Taiwan's society. It is not difficult, however, to find numerous examples of middling- and even low-status litigants bringing civil suit.

In 1874, Ke Shu, a porter (*jiantiao*), brought suit [23701] against his neighbor Tang Shuiyin. Ke had acted as a go-between to help Tang borrow money from a man named Chen. Later Tang had approached Ke on behalf of a man named Zheng, who wanted to borrow a jade bracelet from Ke. Ke complained that Tang refused to repay the loan to Chen who was therefore bringing pressure to bear on Ke. Moreover Tang was refusing to press Zheng to return the bracelet. Unfortunately, the outcome of the case is unknown.

Two years later, another porter was successful in litigating [23404] against two men named Xie, one of whom was a *shengyuan*. The porter, Du Zhong, made a living by collecting coal in the hills and carrying it into the city to sell. Du charged that the *shengyuan* and the other man along with their gang had stopped him outside the city's east gate and taken his load of coal, claiming as justification a debt owed them by yet another man named Zhan. Du claimed Zhan was completely unknown to him. A hearing was convened, and the *shengyuan* was ordered to produce Zhan in court within two days or return the coal to Du.

By way of contrast, in 1878, Zheng Liang, a peddler (*tiaofan*), was unsuccessful in his attempt to enlist the yamen's aid in a dispute over an inheritance that his uncle had supposedly swindled from him [21501]. The subprefect ordered Zheng to submit the estate division agreement to the lineage head, who could decide. Although the latter case was rejected, the cases of the porters were accepted for litigation, with at least one of them gaining a sympathetic hearing.

Most of those who initiated lawsuits were, not surprisingly, individuals of some means who could afford the financial drain that extended litigation entailed. With remarkable frequency, however, litigants who appeared before the bench did so not in an individual capacity but as representatives of corporate groups and collectivities. The legal standing of "corporate complainants" is one of the interesting issues raised by the Dan-Xin cases.

Collective Bodies as Litigants

The high incidence of collective or corporate legal personae that acted as litigants lends new credence to the old cliche about the subsumption of individual to group identity in Chinese society.[38] At the same time, the culturally specific emphasis on the collectivity was in this context a perfectly rational method of sharing costs and risks and unifying in order to offset a powerful opponent in litigation.[39] The Dan-Xin case materials illustrate with striking clarity a society in which individuals organized themselves into collectivities easily and rapidly for activities of all kinds, both legal and illegal. Some of these groups are quite familiar. Corporate lineages exemplified by Wu-Shun-Ji figure prominently in many of the Dan-Xin cases. The specific lineage member representing the family might change several times over the course of a given case. The identity of the individual was, however, immaterial. The lineage as a corporate body was the significant party.

In the same way, other, perhaps less familiar, legal persons that were represented by different individuals at different times appear in the cases repeatedly. Although it is not explicit in the case record, Lan Huagun seems to have been acting as the spokesman for his plundered retail business, the He-Xing firm, rather than as an individual in the armed robbery case summarized in Chapter 3. Huagun was not even present at the time of the crime. Indeed, Lan's father, who filed the first complaint, rather than Lan himself was one of the joint proprietors of the shop.

Another corporate commercial entity, the Jin-Liu-He tea-growing partnership, furnishes us with a much clearer example of a collective legal person involved in litigation. Lan Zhang, Liu Shangda, and Liu Bukui all at one time or another acted for the partnership in petitioning the court. Indeed, in some instances the partnership's agent himself operated through a proxy, as when the *lingsheng* degree holder Liu Shangda delegated his son to submit a petition [22514:73] to the court on behalf of Jin-Liu-He.

In the same case, we find that the partnership's opponents in the litigation acted not as isolated individuals but joined together as members of a "linked villages" (*lianzhuang*) corporate body. In this incident, the *lianzhuang* served to unify and solidify the villagers in the contest against Jin-Liu-He. A somewhat analogous development occurred in the rent resistance case involving Wu-Shun-Ji. The lineage several times accused certain of its tenants of illicitly banding together in order to resist paying rent [22202:95]. Whatever the truth of these allegations, it is a fact that the tenants en masse submitted a number of complaints [22202:77, 92, 98, 119, 133], with one signed by as many as 44 petitioners, to the yamen. Moreover, in at least one instance we have seen that Xu Aqian and three other men arrested for rent arrears had been seized and were made subject to a court order as representatives of a much larger body of tenants [22202:160].

Numerous similar examples of high-order lineages, multiplex village organizations, and corporate commercial bodies are scattered through the Dan-Xin archives. The de facto recognition by the court of legal as well as natural persons suggests that in the politico-legal realm as well as the social and economic spheres, the individual's ability to act or react to changed conditions was perceived to be strongly conditioned by parameters that included the identity and solidarity provided by participation in a larger collective or corporate structure. The legal system's acceptance and legitimation of such legal persons has certain implications that will be examined in the concluding chapter.

As the foregoing discussion implies, wealthy litigants or collective legal personae that could pool resources were most often willing to undergo the economic burden imposed by litigation. Nevertheless, the examples of Ke Shu and Du Zhong show that the supposedly fearsome traditional Chinese legal system was seen as an option for dispute resolution even by men of menial occupations and status. To the extent that this is an unexpected finding, the high incidence of women as petitioners may be even more startling. Mrs. Zhou, the widow of a bankrupt storekeeper, was, with the help of her son, able to sustain a lengthy suit against Zhou Wuniang and his brothers. Her case may serve as background to a more extensive consideration of this group of litigants.

The Legal Standing of Female Petitioners

The Dan-Xin cases take us a step closer to an understanding of the standing of women in litigation. Bodde and Morris have shown that women who were convicted of crimes were seldom allowed to exercise the privilege of monetary redemption even though the Qing Code permitted it.[40] How much latitude did the courts allow women to initiate or respond to legal proceedings? As the eighth procedure rule from the translated petition shows, women could not submit petitions themselves but were to employ proxy filers. Of course, because a woman's reputation could suffer great damage if she were forced to come before the court,[41] this provision might have been rationalized as a privilege accorded women.[42] Interestingly, the procedural regulation that women be represented by agents was not drawn from Qing legal statutes.[43]

Petitions filed by women are the first documents in 20 of the 224 so-called civil case files. Two other files [22225, 23303] open respectively with a warrant issued by the magistrate and an order from the prefect, both in response to complaints submitted by women. In another instance [22405], two women joined their husbands in filing an accusation. Several of these cases and others contain petitions or counterplaints filed by women in litigation initiated by others. In some other cases male petitioners traced the origins of marriage, family, or economic disputes to accusations by women. In 1882, a Xinzhu man who had borrowed money through title deposit[44] to pay for his kinsmen's defense when a Mrs. Deng accused them of murder sued his relatives because they refused to help him repay the loan [23308].

Apart from two marriage lawsuits [21203, 21207] and one adoption case [21401], the great majority (17 of 20) of lawsuits in which women petitioners took the lead stemmed from quarrels over property or income from property: one concerning tenant loans [22102], one concerning expropriation of rent [22303], three concerning encroachment on land [22403, 22408, 22433], seven concerning disputes over property [22603, 22604, 22609, 22610, 22612, 22614, 22615], one concerning disputes over common estates [22703], two concerning title deposit loans [22306, 22310], one concerning loans [23418], and one concerning resisting expropriation [23705]. The attempt by Mrs. Zhou née Xu to gain a share of the assets held by her deceased husband's brothers is typical in many ways.[45] This case [22609] falls within the largest discrete category of lawsuits—disputes over wealth—in which women played a leading role. All of these seven, including the case of Mrs. Zhou, were disputes over lineage property. But this category seems analytically little different from the subsequent type of case, disputes over common estates (*gongye*). Actually, besides the single case in that latter group, we may include two other lawsuits [22303, 22403] that were brought by women against their husband's relatives. The first was an accusation of illegally collecting agricultural land rent and the other a charge of illicitly taking over a parcel of land. In both these cases the land in question had been part of a common estate. Such quarrels total half of the 20 cases initiated by women.

I selected the case of Mrs. Zhou and her son for special scrutiny because it displays many features that are typical in instances of women involved in legal disputes. Mrs. Zhou was a widow, as were nearly all female litigants in these cases. If a woman's husband was living, he would have taken the lead in such litigation. Since women had no ability to own real (as opposed to personal) property, only their husbands as household heads had standing in court. None of the women complainants in the 10 common estate cases had living husbands. Of all 20 cases, there is only one in which it is clear that the initial complainant's husband was alive.

In 1883, a Xinzhu woman, Mrs. Xu née Chen, filed a petition [21203:1] asking that a slave girl she had purchased to serve as a cook be prosecuted for supplanting the complainant in her husband's affections. Even though Mrs. Xu's brother, a *jiansheng*, submitted two statements (*bing*) [21203:2, 3] supporting her charges, the magistrate refused to adjudicate the case. Instead he ordered the woman and her brother to ask relatives to settle the quarrel. In reality no case, in the sense of active court action or a formal response from Mrs. Xu's husband, ever developed. In any event, given the nature of the charge, her husband was hardly in a position to act on Mrs. Xu's behalf.

In another case [23418], a widow, Mrs. Zheng née Zhuang, through her seventeen-*sui*-old son, submitted petitions suing for the return of 100 dollars she had invested in a revolving loan society. The current manager had refused to repay the money, claiming the previous manager had mishandled the society's subscriptions and had left insufficient funds. The magistrate accepted the case and eventually ordered runners to mediate the dispute. Here it is evident that the object of dispute was Mrs. Zheng's personal assets. She sued to regain her money rather than a son's share of an inheritance or of a common estate.

If we move beyond disputes stemming from marriage, the family, or money and property to criminal cases, we find numerous examples of women filing petitions. When a man had become incapable of bringing charges himself, his wife obviously could petition the yamen. In late 1883, for example, a Miaoli woman came to the yamen to file an accusation [32605] that her husband had been kidnapped and robbed. Conversely, when a woman's husband was a detained suspect or imprisoned convict, she was allowed to petition on his behalf. When Liu Dongjin was jailed on suspicion of harboring robbers, his wife immediately filed a counterplaint in his defense.[46] After the kidnapper and camphor smuggler Chen Zhenxiang was imprisoned and repeated pleas for his release from his sons had been ineffective, his wife petitioned the Xinzhu magistrate for his release.[47]

The regulation necessitating that a woman's petition be submitted by proxy seemed to have been carefully observed. It is not clear to me that this regulation benefited either the state or female litigants. It seems merely an artifact of cultural norms that called for the seclusion of women, at least ideally. In any case, the rule was quite strictly applied. In some instances, although damage to a petition leaves us in doubt, usually other documents in the same file confirm that a proxy had been used. In some cases the file is so small or the documents are in such poor condition that it is impossible to be certain. (The loan society dispute mentioned above is one such example.) Proxy filers were legally required to be the petitioner's male, coresident relatives. This requirement could be waived if the woman had no male relatives. After robbery suspect

Zhan Ajian had been in the Xinzhu jail for three years, his mother, Mrs. Zhan née Huang, sent her only living relative, her daughter-in-law, to the yamen with a counterplaint [33319:126] begging for her son's release. Two other instances of possible waiver of the proxy filer rule occurred in the case of counterplaints [33319:10, 96] filed by Mrs. Liu née Chen, Liu Dongjin's wife, during the course of the armed robbery case summarized in Chapter 3. Not only Mrs. Liu's husband but also both her sons were in jail at the time and so were unavailable to serve as proxy for her. A later counterplaint [33319:119] filed after one son had been released listed him as proxy filer.

Zhou Chuncao consistently acted as his mother's proxy in her suit against her brothers-in-law. In fact, the magistrate gradually became convinced that he as much as she was the driving force behind the litigation. Asking why Chuncao might have wanted to persuade his mother to take the lead in the lawsuit affords us some understanding of the relatively high incidence of female litigants in suits over common or inherited property. Mrs. Zhou's brothers-in-law characterized Chuncao as an adopted son through purchase (*mingzi*) of their deceased brother. By so doing, they apparently hoped to weaken the adoptee's claim. It was not an unreasonable expectation. Other courts had already admitted that such adoptees were ineligible to inherit.[48] In the Taiwan case, by establishing his mother as the interested party, Chuncao may have hoped to neutralize any challenge to his standing as heir. In the final analysis, of course, Chuncao's claim did not succeed because Mrs. Zhou's husband before his death had already entered into an agreement that extinguished his and his descendants' rights to the property in question. Zhou Chuncao's adoptive status was not a factor in the decision.

However, in another case [21402] from 1874–75, a woman, Mrs. Zheng née Chen, was the defendant and her deceased husband's adopted son the plaintiff. The adopted son, Zheng Yi, accused Mrs. Zheng, who had borne her husband a natural son, of appropriating his (Zheng Yi's) share of the estate. The subprefect concluded that, according to precedent, an adopted son was entitled to a share of the estate, but his claim was inferior to that of the man's natural son. Accordingly, of the annual rental income of 33 *shi* of grain that was the father's estate, Zheng Yi, the adopted son, was awarded 10 *shi* and the natural son 23 *shi*. With the decision of the 1874–75 case on record, it was not surprising that his uncles made sure to reveal the origins of Zhou Chuncao.

In the case of Zheng Yi versus Mrs. Zheng née Chen, the woman was at a disadvantage because her son was only five *sui* old. Zheng Yi may have been encouraged to move against Mrs. Zheng because her son was not yet an adult. The tactic failed when other lineage relatives supported Mrs. Zheng's position. Attempting to protect minor sons' rights to common estate income brought other women to court. In 1884, a different Mrs. Zheng joined litigation [22706] already in progress with an accusation that one of her own adult sons was illegally taking estate income that should go to her minor sons. In this case, Mrs. Zheng was successful. After the magistrate concluded that the woman's adult son should be punished for unrighteous behavior toward his mother, he agreed to abide by the findings of lineage mediation.

I suggested in an earlier chapter that disagreements over succession, inheritance, and the rightful sharing in common lineage property were at the root of many lawsuits filed at the yamen. Men and women alike appealed to the court to restore to them their shares of common property or income from it. When Mrs. Zhou attempted for a second time to persuade the court to accept her case, she explained that her other lineage relatives resided in the mainland and could not arbitrate the dispute [22609:2]. I have already pointed out the consequent implication that one of the reasons the magistrate had refused to accept her first petition [22609:1], from which the endorsement is unfortunately missing, was his view that such disagreements should be within the lineage. Mediation was the alternative preferred by Danshui and Xinzhu judges in all litigation, whether initiated by men or women. The court was loath to accept Mrs. Zhou's case, but its reluctance stemmed more from the nature of the dispute than from her gender.

This is not to say that women were not seriously disadvantaged in legal proceedings. Mrs. Xu's attempt to bring charges against her philandering husband and his slave girl paramour got nowhere, even when the plaintiff's brother submitted a statement charging that his sister had been beaten, locked up, and denied food and water by her husband. The magistrate noted [21203:3] that it was not appropriate for "trifling" family matters to be litigated.

The Dan-Xin civil cases do, though, seem to show that if a woman's petition was directed against persons—even lineage relatives—outside her immediate household, if it was submitted in a procedurally correct way, and if mediation was not possible or not successful, then her case would be handled in ordinary fashion with judgment based on examination, testimony, and documentary evidence. Of course the documents reveal only a small part of historical reality. The browbeating, intimidation, coercion, and contempt with which women had to deal in court proceedings can be glimpsed in statements and petitions filed by men that characterized female litigants opposing them as prostitutes or procuresses. I would argue, however, that in spite of their social and legal disadvantages, many more times than we might suppose women (especially widows) turned to the legal system for aid in disputes of the kind mentioned in the above discussion. The number of cases with female litigants and the favorable decisions that are discernible in the record indicate that women went to court not in hopeless desperation but with real expectations of some degree of impartiality and even justice.

This discussion of women litigants has so far been confined to cases that originated from disputes over property, marriage, or the family. Criminal complaints in which women played a role add little to the picture already revealed. One simple reason for the paucity of new information is that criminal case files were on average much shorter and less detailed than records of civil litigation. Nevertheless, we should not pass to the next topic without a brief survey of women's criminal complaints. Among the cases in the Dan-Xin archives there are by coincidence an equal number (20) of criminal and "civil" cases in which the initial charges were filed by women.[49] These criminal cases concerned the following: one concerning homicide [32105], three concerning assault [32202, 32205, 32207], five concerning abduction through enticement [32401, 32402, 32407, 32408, 32410], one concerning kidnapping for ransom [32605], two concerning banditry [33309, 33330], one concerning fraud [33702], one concerning illegal sale [33802], one concerning brigandage [34108], four concerning unfiliality [35101–35104], and one concerning kidnapping and illicit sexual intercourse [35405]. One case file [35405] has only a cover sheet with no other documents.

Twelve of these cases were never resolved, but that was a common occurrence in all criminal complaints. Only one of the criminal charges [33802] was not accepted by the court. In that 1871 case, Mrs. Zeng née Xie complained that Zhang Liang and his nephew Zhang Jiu forced her to sell (*dian*) her land to them conditionally. She contended that that amounted to an illegal purchase, but her petition was rejected. Another case [33309], in which the accusation was armed robbery, was investigated but the charges dismissed. In two cases [32408, 32410] women charged that their daughters-in-law had been enticed into running away, and eventually the younger women were located by runners. In the former case the complainant was a Danshui county woman, so her daughter-in-law and the abductor were sent to the Danshui court for prosecution. The second case was mediated. Three cases [35102, 35103, 35104] of unfilial behavior were apparently not resolved by the court. The other instance [35101] of the same kind of case did find the court granting the petitioner satisfaction. In that case, Mrs. Chen née Liao complained that her daughter-in-law habitually had sexual relations with other men when the complainant's son was away working at his job as a porter. The magistrate ordered the daughter-in-law sent back to her family and compensation paid. Conversely, the three complaints by mothers against their gambler sons went unresolved even when one woman charged that her son had assaulted and knocked her down.

The cases are not remarkable except for the relatively high number of what might be called domestic disputes—women bringing charges against sons and their wives—that appear. In the five cases that might be so characterized it seems the court was not inclined to act unless the major focus of the complaint was another woman, that is, the petitioner's daughter-in-law. To judge from the limited evidence available, in criminal cases women complainants were not conspicuously ill handled by the legal system except in family disputes. In those instances, female complainants might have gained legal redress, but only at the expense of other women, their daughters-in-law.

PROXY FILERS (*BAOGAO*)

Proxy filers were a consistent feature of litigation. Although by law four classes of persons were required or entitled to employ proxy filers, only three groups, officials, women, and the elderly, are represented in the Dan-Xin cases.[50] There appear to be no instances in the Dan-Xin archives of incapacitated persons filing suit. The group most often seen employing proxy filers were degree holders, who are commonly held to have fallen within the category of "officials" as far as the law was concerned.[51] The Wu-Shun-Ji members representing the lineage in litigation were all lower degree holders. Proxy filers may have taken their petitions to court from the time the case was first initiated, but the first indication of it was not until 1858, when the *jiansheng* Wu Jiqing sent Lin Ruan to court with a petition [22202:96]. Here we see that just as in the case of the term "officials," the term "family members" (*jiaren*) was not interpreted in a literal sense. Proxy filers for degree holders were not required to be one of the petitioner's family or even lineage members. Several other instances of men with different surnames representing degree holders support this conclusion. When a hearing was held in the dispute between Jin-Liu-He and the villagers, the gentry Zheng Yongcheng was summoned [22514:118] but instead sent a surrogate, his manager, Xiao De. Thus, the requirement that officials and gentry be represented by family members seems to have been interpreted somewhat more loosely in practice to mean a member of the household, which included servants or employees as well as true relatives. Of course, as the case summaries have shown, it was far more common for family members in the literal sense of close relatives of the same surname to act as proxy filers. Sons and brothers of degree-holding complainants or respondents are listed time and again under the "proxy filer" rubric.

Women, who invariably filed by proxy, also—except in the one instance already mentioned—utilized sons or nephews to go to the yamen. According to one edition of the legal code, until 1873, a women could initiate a legal case as the complainant filing by proxy. After that date, a new procedural rule stated that a woman with an adult son could no longer file litigation. The son was thenceforth required to take the lead in any lawsuit or other legal proceeding.[52] Presumably a woman without an adult son was still allowed to use a proxy filer as long as the latter met the coresidence and kinship requirements. The cases, however, show that this new regulation was not observed in practice: perhaps an instance of long-established local conventions taking precedence over new guidelines issued by central authorities. Mrs. Zhou's proxy in her case that began in 1882 was her 35-*sui*-old son. The fact that Zhou Chuncao was an adult man eventually led the court to consider him the de facto chief litigant, and as a consequence he was jailed when the Xinzhu magistrate had charges brought against his mother. The 1873 change in the regulations concerning women petitioners may have been the basis for his incarceration.

SCRIVENERS (*DAISHU*)

A scrivener wrote accusations or petitions based on oral description or on the basis of a draft written by the complainant. During the Qing at least, scriveners were selected by the yamen on the basis of an examination. Unlike clerks, they did not work in the yamen for government officials, nor did they receive a salary. They were, however, issued a seal signifying quasi-official status. If a scrivener falsified details, he could be punished for false accusation (*wugao*).[53] Because making the scriveners liable for inaccuracies in documents they drafted was a way of decreasing the incidence of false accusation, some department and county yamens seem to have had a regulation that any self-drafted petition had to be examined and stamped by a scrivener before it would be accepted for adjudication.[54] The Dan-Xin cases bear out the contention that scriveners sometimes merely examined and affixed their seals to accusation forms drafted by complainants and did not recopy them.[55] On GX 20/3/3 (8 April 1893), for example, Chen Zaixin's self-drafted and self-copied (*zigao zishan*) petition [32611:146] requesting that his father be released from the Xinzhu yamen jail had been stamped with a scrivener's seal and was accepted by the magistrate.

Scriveners could be made responsible for more than just inspecting and stamping petitions. In 1858, several of Wu-Shun-Ji's tenants continued to resist the court's order to pay large-rent arrears. The subprefect issued a warrant [22202:104] that included an order to the scrivener who had handled the still-resisting tenants' petitions to trace and hand the tenants over to the court. As noted earlier, when during Mrs. Zhou's suit against her brothers-in-law her son Chuncao was suspected of hiring a pettifogger, a scrivener was ordered to take the latter into custody. In this area at least, scriveners sometimes acted as guarantors or even yamen underlings.[56]

During the jurisdictional periods of both the subprefecture and the county, there were said to have been five scriveners accredited by the yamen at any given time: two Quanzhou registrants, two Zhangzhou registrants, and one Yueh (that is, Guangdong or Hakka) registrant.[57] Each of them would be issued a rectangular wooden seal with truncated upper corners onto which the name of the issuing authority (the subprefect or magistrate) and the scrivener's native place registration and name were carved around the borders. In the center the paraph, or stylized signature (*huaya*), of the issuing authority was carved. The signature presumably allowed the seal to be verified as authorized.

PETTIFOGGERS (*SONGSHI; SUNGGUN*)

The antipathy of the state toward legal specialists has been well documented. The Qing Code prescribed administrative punishment for a local official who unknowingly allowed pettifoggers to operate in his jurisdiction. If it were discovered that the local official knew that such litigation specialists were active and had failed to report the fact to his superiors, he could be turned over to the Board of Punishment for his punishment to be decided.[58] Huang Liuhong advised his fellow magistrates to take pains to suppress pettifoggers.[59]

Given the people's need for legal specialists, the problem for local officials was that knowledge of the Code and the legal process was relatively widespread. It was not illegal to lecture on or study the legal code. In fact, officials who could be expected to preside over trials in the course of their duties were encouraged to study and improve their legal knowledge. The Qing Code provided even ordinary commoners a positive sanction to be familiar with the law.

> Common people and artisans of every sort who are able to read, explain, and thoroughly comprehend the law's meaning and who commit a crime through mistake or negligence or are drawn into a criminal act by another

person will on the first occurrence escape prosecution whether the crime is minor or serious. If the affair concerns rebellion, treason, or sedition, this statute does not apply.[60]

Published copies of the Qing Code were not difficult to buy, although they must have been expensive. There were, however, several publications apparently compiled to be used by pettifoggers that were specifically prohibited by law. Four titles—*Jingtianlei* (Thunder that startles heaven), *Xiangjiao* (Disputation), *Fajia xinshu* (New book for legal specialists), and *Xingtai Qinjing* (The mirror of Qin for going to law)—were listed in the substatute as examples of prohibited works used by legal specialists. However, even if printed books and their printing blocks could be confiscated and destroyed, nothing could be done about handwritten manuscripts and oral teachings.[61] The door was opened wider for legal specialists by a provision in the legal code allowing explanation of the law to an ignorant person who was involved in a case. The law code also permitted one person to write out an accusation for another (presumably illiterate) person. Thus, Qing legislation seems to have been designed to control legal specialists as much as possible rather than futilely to try and drive them out of business altogether.[62] There was perhaps a tacit acceptance of the need for such men.

Chinese legal historians generally assume that most legal specialists came from three groups. There were classically educated men, perhaps with low degrees, who had given up hope of being successful enough in the examinations to obtain an official post. Former yamen private secretaries (*muyou*), who had gained experience prosecuting legal cases, sometimes moved into what might be called the private sector. Another group that possessed a modicum of knowledge about legal matters was former yamen clerks.[63] The Dan-Xin cases yield a rather more interesting view of a range of persons who proffered aid and advice to litigants. Such "pettifoggers" could be found not only near the yamen court but also circulating in the market towns and villages of the area. They possessed varying degrees of knowledge, expertise, and experience. Presumably their fees varied in like degree so that legal expertise, at a diminished level of competence to be sure, was available to people of middling or even small means.

Legal experts probably congregated in the inns near the yamen where a person contemplating the prospect of or confronted with defending against litigation could most easily find them. In 1883, after his mother's lawsuit against her brothers-in-law had failed to progress satisfactorily, Zhou Chuncao went to Mengjia to file an appeal at the Taibei prefectural court. After his subsequent arrest and transfer back to Xinzhu, he explained in testimony [22609:41] how he had paid a specialist to draw up his appeal.[64]

> This petition was done by Mr. Lai whom I hired in a Mengjia inn (*kedian*). I gave him 200 cash (*wen*). Now I do not know where he has gone. When I went to Mengjia, I also stayed in that inn, the Yixing House.

The 200-cash fee charged by Mr. Lai seems quite low. As mentioned earlier, even at the county court merely buying the petition form (400–500 cash) and paying the registration fee (80 cash) could amount to nearly 600 cash. These yamen fees may well have been even higher at the prefectural level. If Chuncao told the truth about Mr. Lai, perhaps the *songshi*'s strategy was to buy into the case for a low initial fee, hoping for more lucrative compensation later as litigation continued.

Unfortunately, Zhou Chuncao's sketchy testimony seems to be the most complete account in the Dan-Xin archives of finding and hiring a litigation specialist. A number of scattered remarks or allegations about the use of *songshi* are, however, revealing.

In the years 1874–79, Huang Junxiang, formerly a yamen tax clerk, sued [22302] the *gongsheng* Huang Tingzhen, one of his kinsmen. Junxiang charged that he had agreed to loan Tingzhen money to finance the construction of irrigation canals in return for one-third of the rental income from the newly irrigated fields. Junxiang received a favorable ruling but later reopened the case with a new complaint. He charged that Tingzhen had employed a litigation specialist (*songshi*), named Huang Ronghua, who was also the yamen muster roll clerk (*maoshu*) and therefore familiar with ways to avoid compliance with the judgment in the case. While there is no sign in the case record that the magistrate acted on or accepted the truth of this allegation, it is safe to assume that it was a plausible accusation, whether or not a factual one in this instance. Yamen clerks, with their day-to-day familiarity with the flow of paper in the offices, were well placed to influence litigation under ordinary circumstances.

Huang Junxiang's case may have been especially open to meddling because it was adjudicated during the break-up of Danshui subprefecture and the creation of Xinzhu county. During the transition the newly created prefectural offices were in Xinzhu, and the Taibei prefect was concurrently acting Xinzhu county magistrate. The confusion engendered by dual responsibilities, travel between Xinzhu and the site of the new prefectural seat, and supervision of new administrative units such as Danshui county may have left the prefect-magistrate particularly vulnerable to manipulation by his staff.

The Dan-Xin cases contain numerous other accusations that one party or another was using yamen clerks or runners to influence litigation. In the case of Jin-Liu-He versus the residents of the four villages,[65] an appeal [22514:46] to the prefect filed by Liu Shangda suggested exactly how it could happen. Liu was complaining that jailed villagers had not been prosecuted because county yamen personnel had been bribed to take charge of the case improperly. Liu's first accusations had been handled by the clerk Yu Sheng. Yu, however, had been bribed (the appellant claimed) to put the case aside and delay processing it. Later, when the case finally had been pushed forward, another clerk, Lü Hsiang, who was responsible for drafting prompting warrants, did not do so. Litigants might avail themselves of yamen connections as well as the services of a litigation specialist. In one seventeen-year-long case [22403] that began in 1868, one collateral line of the Xinzhu Lü family accused another line of employing a litigation specialist in tandem with Tea Section runners in an effort to take sole possession of a plot of land.

Such behavior was expected from clerks and runners. Diligence on the magistrate's part could prevent the worst excesses. Aspiring members of the bureaucratic elite represented a potentially greater danger to the state. Their education, family connections, and ties to local society made lower degree holders a perennial worry. The state had been concerned enough about lower degree holders putting their education to use in litigious pursuits that, as mentioned earlier, a special imperial order had been given prohibiting *shengyuan* to enter court even as witnesses. Liao Qionglin, the *shengyuan* who had attempted to bolster the villagers' case against Jin-Liu-He, earned the magistrate's ire for "violating the horizontal tablet."[66] This Dan-Xin case thus seems to confirm the traditional view of legal specialists.

Liao Qionglin was certainly a lower degree holder identified and punished for interfering in litigation in the Dan-Xin cases. In that light he was by definition a pettifogger. It is less certain, however, that he was a litigation specialist in the sense that his livelihood was derived from advising litigants in the most advantageous methods to pursue in their cases. Liao described himself as a teacher. He also claimed that he had first become involved in the dispute when he had been asked to evaluate the deed to the villagers' pasture land. Liao was probably a good example of that entire group of *shengyuan* who had little or no prospect of a bureaucratic career but were able to support themselves by providing a range of services of higher literacy to an illiterate or only functionally literate population.

The examples cited so far seem to show that legal services or representation were available to rather unexceptional people of ordinary means. Zhou Chuncao, a petty tradesman, hired Mr. Lai to frame his appeal for 200 cash. The villagers who asked Liao Qionglin to help them against Jin-Liu-He were tenant (*dian*) farmers. The Dan-Xin cases, however, also bring to light evidence of another, even less exalted stratum of legal practitioners. Two homicide cases [32103, 32104] from 1883 show that complainants without yamen connections or without the means to hire lower degree holders to handle their cases sometimes became the clientele of itinerant *songshi*.

In the first case, the Dajia police chief reported that Chen Yu, a bandit operating in the area encompassing northern Zhanghua and southern Xinzhu counties, had been killed by residents of Tucheng village. Two months later, Mrs. Chen née Du petitioned by proxy, saying that the dead man had been her husband. Mrs. Chen claimed that her husband had been the victim of a lineage feud. He had been killed by members of the Zhang lineage who were suspicious of his ties to the rivals, the Huang family. The Chen Yu who had been shot and killed had not been the bandit at all. Mrs. Chen soon filed a continuation petition (*xucheng*) charging that the Dajia police chief and various local subcounty officials had been bribed to cover up the crime by identifying the corpse as that of the bandit. Mrs. Chen was quickly summoned to court and questioned concerning her charges. She made no apparent attempt to stick to the story related in her petitions, quickly admitting the truth of the police chief's original report. Mrs. Chen told the magistrate that when she finally learned of her husband's death, two months after the fact, she was vexed (*xinzhong bugan*) and decided to go to court. She testified that she asked a fortune teller (*suanming*) whose name she did not know to draw up the petitions for her.

In the second case, Zhu Guangbao, a resident of Luliaokeng village in the mountains northeast of Xinzhu, filed a petition complaining that his cousin, Zhu Jiechang, had disappeared while attempting to collect a debt. Guangbao had gone looking for his cousin and had discovered his corpse in a field belonging to Gan Afang.[67] Guangbao had gone to the *baozhang* to report the crime, and in the meantime Gan and others had buried the body in a hidden grave. The magistrate was suspicious because the petition had not been filed until several days after the alleged killing. Zhu was summoned for questioning, where he claimed that he had first reported the murder to the local constable (*dibao*), who had been unwilling to investigate. Guangbao testified that subsequently the *baozhang* had informed him that Gan had hidden his cousin's body. At that time Guangbao got help from a "fortune teller from the interior" (*neilai suanming xiansheng*) in drawing up a petition. Guangbao had not known (he said) that a complainant was required to hire a scrivener to draw up petitions.

Litigation specialists in a sense offered their services on an open market, illegal though it may have been. Corporate entities such as Wu-Shun-Ji and Jin-Liu-He, which often numbered more than a few degree holders among their members, were usually able to draw upon the talents of one or more of them to take charge of lawsuits. In certain circumstances the legal expertise of such men might be available to outsiders. Jin-Liu-He complained that the city gentry Zheng Yongcheng and Lin Hengmao had taken over the case (*baoan*) of the partnership's opponents in the suit. At the other end of the scale, fortune tellers provided services at the lower end of the market. It was one service among others that was available from these peddlers as they roamed the market towns and villages of the rural areas. Lower degree holders—such as Liao Qionglin—who resided away from the major urban centers can be placed somewhere in the middle range of litigation specialists. The guidance and counsel proffered by the two latter groups may often have been of questionable value. However, seeking assistance from specialists who set up shop in the vicinity of county or prefectural yamens was no guarantee of good advice. One could not assume their competence to be of a higher degree than that of the traveling fortune tellers. Mrs. Zhou and her son Chuncao were persuaded to submit a prompting petition [22609: 34] that not only endeavored to legitimate an interfamily lawsuit by citing a nonexistent substatute but also characterized the magistrate's endorsement to a previous petition as "excessively absurd" (*huangmiu taishen*).

There was a demand from nearly all social strata in nineteenth-century Taiwan for legal advice and service. Whatever the putative risks of litigation, the Chinese people went to court in sufficient numbers to generate and support a wide range of proto-advocates. Whether the establishment would ever have reached a modus vivendi can never be known. In the Code and the cases, the level of rhetoric in which such men are described as "litigation sticks" (*songgun*) or "lawsuit vermin" (*du'an*) remained the same. On the other side of the coin, at least one magistrate apparently acquiesced when men like Zheng Yongcheng and Lin Hengmao, who strictly speaking were not party to the dispute being litigated, took over direction of the case (*baoan*) for one side and effected a settlement.

Perhaps the key to the puzzle is that last phrase. Of paramount importance to a local subprefect or magistrate was effecting a settlement. His job performance was rated in large part on his ability to apprehend and convict in criminal cases and adjudicate and clear civil litigation. A practicing local judge quickly learned to tolerate a certain level of formally illicit legal advocacy so long as such practices allowed him to settle cases as quickly as possible. But before there could be any thought of adjudicating a case and closing the file, a magistrate had to address the difficult and frustrating task of reaching out beyond the yamen wall to summon witnesses, gather evidence, and arrest suspects. It is to these topics that we shall turn next.

8

Search and Arrest: The Warrant

WARRANTS AND SUMMONS

Once a subprefect or magistrate had accepted the litigant's plea, he began the process of discovering the facts of the case by ordering complainants to submit further evidence or by directing yamen runners to take one of several actions. Runners might be required merely to investigate to determine the truth or falsity of a complainant's petition. Normally the need for this kind of information gathering was simply noted in the endorsement to the petition and presumably orders were given verbally. In some situations, however, an actual document was drafted and a formal copy issued to runners. Such a document was usually called a warrant (*piao*). On rare occasions, instructions to runners were labeled "bamboo tallies" (*qian*), actually a kind of warrant used for the specific purpose of summoning persons to appear in court immediately. Runners may have carried special slips of bamboo to signify the urgency of the summons.[1] Once drafted and corrected, warrants were copied on official printed forms that were headed by the words *xinpiao*.[2] *Xinpiao* were stamped with the magistrate's official seal of office before being issued to runners. After being served by runners, official warrants were seldom stored in the case files, since draft copies were already on file. The five cases summarized in earlier chapters contain only a single *xinpiao* specimen [22514:109].

Official warrants were ornate and imposing documents. Inherently authoritative in China because of a culturally generated reverence for the written word, the warrant with its official seal signified the legitimate authority over the populace granted to the subprefect or magistrate by the government. Once issued, warrants in turn were transformed into concrete and undeniable symbols of the delegated authority granted to yamen runners.

Orders issued to runners directing them to follow up an earlier warrant were called notices (*dan*). It seems likely that notices were simply internal yamen memoranda never intended to be seen by the public. Most often follow-up warrants were called prompting warrants (*piaocui*). Prompting warrants would have been redrafted to be carried by runners. Occasionally prompting notices (*dancui*) also were issued.

The logic of bureaucratic routine dictated that warrants be quite formulaic. Almost invariably a warrant opened with a summary of the charges or complaints brought by the parties involved. Of course, when a warrant was issued by the subprefecture or county at the direction of the prefect or other higher authority, the order from the higher echelon was quoted at the beginning of the warrant. For example, in Mrs. Zhou's suit against her brothers-in-law she had managed to appeal to provincial (and perhaps even higher) officials, who then, relaying their orders through the Taibei prefect, directed the Xinzhu magistrate to issue a warrant [22609:66] summoning the parties for a new hearing. This warrant began with a summary reference to the prefect's order. Ordinarily, however, the first few lines of a warrant offered a precis of the charges. Usually the drafter, who was either the magistrate or one of his private secretaries, merely quoted from the complaints or petitions of the parties.

Following this synopsis of the charges, the warrant normally would continue with the selection of and directions to runners by the subprefect or magistrate. If it was the initial warrant or if new runners were being assigned to the case, the runners' names were given in full. As numerous examples in the Dan-Xin case files show, a 1779 Fujian provincial regulation ordering that only one runner be named to serve each warrant had quickly become a dead letter. When a follow-up warrant or notice was issued, runners were referred to as "the original runners" (*benyi*).

The orders and directions given to runners naturally depended on the circumstances of the case. If an ongoing criminal action or breach of the peace was feared, a warrant was immediately issued ordering runners to put a halt to the illegal acts. In GX 10 (1884), when reports reached the yamen that a dispute between villagers and tea producers over an upland clearing had again flared up, Magistrate Xu Xizhi issued a warrant [22510:6] ordering the head of the First Fast Runner section to ascertain if armed villagers were actually destroying tea bushes.[3] If they were, the runner was to post a cease-and-desist directive (*yuzhi*). In GX 13–14 (1887–88), Magistrate Fang Zuyin responded to an allegation that two members of the Shilixing tribe had been kidnapped by issuing several warrants [for example, 32611:51] ordering First Lictor section runners to search for and release the supposed captives if they could be found. Most commonly, runners were directed to search out and summon witnesses or arrest those accused of crimes. Accordingly, when Mrs. Zhou accused her brothers-in-law of cheating her of her share of the family estate, a warrant [22609:4] was given to a runner ordering him to summon both parties to court for a hearing. Occasionally during the course of litigation warrants were issued that simply directed runners to convey the commands of the subprefect or magistrate to the litigants.

Runners were usually given a set period of time in which to carry out duties outlined in the warrant.[4] The time limit was specified at or near the end of the warrant. Typically runners were allowed three days to serve a warrant. In pressing circumstances or when runners did not have far to travel, a warrant might specify that they had to return to court the same or the next day with their mission accomplished. Such time limits were more honored in the breach than in the observance, as the presence in the case files of numerous prompting warrants and notices testifies.

Arrest warrants and summons concluded with a name list of those persons required to come to court. When a collective legal person was named in the warrant, the name of the individual representing it at that point in the case was also given. Each person or group of persons enumerated were often categorized with a word or phrase describing their position in the case. The descriptive labels might be as straightforward as "original accuser" and "accused," or as long-winded as "accused by Zhou Sunwei et al. of perverse and illegal occupation [of land]" [22514:64]. Although the general locale where those listed in the warrant could be found was sometimes mentioned in the summary of the charges, warrants seldom gave runners specific locations to search. As explained in more detail below, warrants were assigned to runners generally familiar with the location in question. Moreover, runners were always directed to work with an overseer or local constable who would be even more knowledgeable about the inhabitants in his area of responsibility. For these reasons, runners would be expected to locate the persons named in warrants, assuming they had not fled to escape prosecution.

After attempting to carry out their orders, runners assigned to the case by the warrant filed a report describing the actions they had taken.[5] If ordered to summon persons to court, the runners had to attest that each person listed in the warrant had been delivered to the yamen or, if unsuccessful, explain their failure to do so. Once a warrant had been served, runners were required to turn it in for "cancellation" (*xiao*), since an uncanceled warrant could be reused as a tool for extortion.[6]

From the material already presented, it is apparent that an essential step toward comprehension of the interaction between government and society in Danshui subprefecture and Xinzhu county is a more thorough exploration of the nature of yamen runner organization and methods of operation. Following the translated warrant that concludes the initial section of this chapter, we shall turn to a consideration of these yamen police. The draft warrant [22202:16] translated below will illustrate part of the processes of summons and arrest already described. The warrant was issued during Wu-Shun-Ji's attempt to force tenants to pay large-rent arrears.[7]

Warrant and Summons

Acting Danshui Subprefect Zhang: A matter of contempt of a court judgment and obstinate resistance.

In this case, the court received a report filed by Daqiqian village landlord Wu-Shun-Ji saying that Jiang Ashou viz. Jiang Aqing and others disobeyed a court judgment and formed a society consisting of the defiant tenants Xu Aqian, Fan Linxiang, and others to resist payment of tax rent. Individual tenants respected the judgment and had prepared to pay but were stopped and robbed [of the rent grain] while on the road by Jiang Aqing and the others who had assembled their gang.

I find that in this case the court previously had received mutual accusations from the tenant householder Fan Linxiang and the landlord Wu-Shun-Ji. A former subprefect brought the parties up for a hearing and judgment, which is on record. Afterwards this subprefecture received a communication from Prefect Tong saying:

I have received the following endorsement from Governor-General Liu:

I have received a petition from Xu Aqian, a resident of the subprefecture, charging landlord Wu-Shun-Ji viz. Wu Gongyu and the tigerous manager Wen Dui with concealing taxable [land] and making excessive [rent] levies. I am handing down this endorsement and hope the Taiwan prefect will speedily send a dispatch to the Danshui subprefect ordering him to gather the witnesses, interrogate them carefully, pass judgment to conclude the case, and report on the proceedings.

At the time, runners were replaced and ordered to summon the parties. Subsequently petitions prompting action were received from the *shengyuan* Wu Shifen as well as from Jiang Shoucheng. Again the court ordered runners to press the summons of the parties, but they did not come to court. Their obstinacy was already extreme.

At this juncture, a report from landlord Wu-Shun-Ji viz. *shengyuan* Wu Shifen has been received saying the defiant tenants Xu Zhaoyuan viz. Xu Chuancheng and Xu Awu have refused to pay and owe more than 900 *shi* of rent grain. He requested that Xu Awu, who is already at court, be made to trace and turn in Xu Chuancheng to the court so [back rent] can be recovered through prosecution.

Apart from bringing him [Xu Awu] up for a hearing so he will turn in [Xu Chuancheng], it is proper once again to issue an order prompting action. This warrant has been made out in the hopes that the original runners Yu Gui, Lin Yong, and Gao Sheng will speedily cooperate with the area's overseer and local constable and immediately summon those persons listed below. Within three days, each of the individuals is to be reported as having been brought to these offices in order that they may offer evidence for a hearing and judgment. If the said runners further delay, they will be brought up for prosecution with no mercy. Act with great dispatch.

List:
Defiant Tenants: Jiang Ashou viz. Jiang Aqing, Xu Aqian, Fan Linxiang, Lü Axia, Jiang Lianshui, Li Afan, Chen Xinxi.
Manager: Wen Dui.
Petitioners: Jiang Shoucheng, Jiang Shouli.
Tenant Householders Named in Wu Shifen's Prompting Report: Xu Zhaoyuan viz. Xu Chuancheng, Xu Awu—already at court and called to account to track criminals.
Petitioning Landlord: Wu-Shun-Ji viz. *shengyuan* Wu Shifen.

Prompting Warrant.
Xianfeng 2nd year 10th month 6th day handled by chief tax clerk.
Draft.

STRUCTURAL COMPONENTS OF LOCAL LAW ENFORCEMENT

Notwithstanding their degraded "mean people" (*jianmin*) status[8] and their well-deserved reputation for corruption, yamen runners were the primary instruments by which subprefects and magistrates attempted to carry out the Dan-Xin area government's two most important tasks, tax collection and law enforcement. Runners were necessary but not sufficient to achieve these ends. They were assisted and supported by a variety of local functionaries with intimate links to the townships, market towns, farm villages, and aborigine settlements within the Dan-Xin jurisdiction. The focus of our attention in this section will be on the structures and their personnel that carried out the next step in the legal process: serving a warrant.

Yamen Runners

As in all local administrations in China at the time, each of the yamen offices had several of its own runners. Some of these office runners played a part in our cases when suspects were detained in one of the yamen offices. In Xinzhu, for example, the Tea Office, which served as a place of detention for several suspects in the cases summarized earlier, was assigned four runners.[9] By far the largest number of runners, however, were assigned to two independent runner forces that were each divided into sections.[10] There was also a much larger force of commoner guards (*minzhuang*) that acted as escorts for the subprefects and magistrates of

Danshui and Xinzhu. These guards could be called upon to assist runners in their police duties when circumstances demanded a show of force. If runners backed by commoner guards were insufficient to their task, the civil yamen could request help from the local military detachment.

The number of runners officially on the yamen payroll during the subprefectural period (that is, before 1875) seems to have been quite small. There were supposedly only 12 lictors (*zaoli*) and eight fast runners (*bukuai*). Of course, as noted, these runners could rely on 40 commoner guards for assistance, if necessary. These numbers, however, constitute only half the total police personnel in the entire subprefecture. In Zhuqian city itself, the police chief (*xunjian*) counted among his subordinates two lictors, four horsemen (*makuai*), four commoner guards, and eighteen archers (*gongbing*). When, in 1816, Zhanghua county's Lugang police chief was moved to Dajia, in the southern part of Danshui subprefecture, this official controlled two lictors, four guards, and eighteen archers.[11]

After Xinzhu county was formed from the southern half of the old subprefecture, the county magistrate could call on runner forces that were somewhat larger than those of the subprefecture had been. Fifteen ordinary lictors were subordinate to a lictor captain (*zaoli zong*) after 1875. The fast runners had been transformed into an element with much greater speed and force, if their redesignation as horsemen under a captain (*makuai zong*) is any indication.[12] The sources disagree on the number of commoner guards available to the new county magistrate. Japanese colonial period sources place the number as high as 44.[13] In 1888, however, Magistrate Fang Zuyin reported [11407:1] a total of only 28 guards on the payroll. There seems to be no information on the runners assigned to the county police chief (*xunjian*), the successor to the former Zhuqian police chief. The Dajia police chief had the same complement of police forces at least until 1888.[14] Beginning in 1889, the Dajia area became part of Miaoli county. The area around the new prefectural seat of Taibei that had formerly been the responsibility of the Mengjia vice subprefect (*xiancheng*) became part of Danshui county. Consequently, as the area administered from the city of Xinzhu (old Zhuqian) shrank, the total of all runner forces was cut by 50 percent or more, even though there may have been an increase of those based in the city itself.

This discussion has so far ignored any but runners formally on the yamen payroll. It is certain, however, that Danshui and Xinzhu were similar to other administrations in having a large number of irregulars, that is, men working with or assisting the formally appointed runners but not listed on the yamen books and not receiving an official salary. Such men were denoted as "extra" (*ewai*) or "unlisted" (*baiyi*) runners. In some other local administrative districts in Qing China, such extra runners numbered in the hundreds or even thousands, several times the quotas of authorized runners.[15] Unfortunately, there seems to be no information in the cases or elsewhere on the number of "extra" runners in the Dan-Xin area.

Runner Organization

Lictors and fast runners or horsemen were organized in sections (*ban*).[16] There were one section under the control of the lictor captain and three other ordinary lictor sections. Four sections of fast runners exactly corresponded to the lictor sections. Some of the runners had specialized duties, but when it came to law enforcement, each of the six ordinary sections of lictors and fast runners was assigned responsibility for any yamen dealings with specific areas in the subprefecture's or county's jurisdiction. During the existence of Danshui subprefecture, for example, three of the six ordinary runner sections were the duty runners for townships south of Zhuqian, while the remaining three lictor and fast runner sections were assigned to northern townships. Even though the area and number of townships administered from the yamen were halved and then quartered during the administrative reorganizations in the years after 1875, the same principle of territorial responsibility for runner sections was maintained.

Runners assigned responsibility for a township were called "township duty runners" (*duibaoyi*). Communication between the yamen and the rural areas arising from any criminal cases, civil litigation, or other affairs was the responsibility of the appropriate township duty runners. They remained with any case involving a person living in their particular township until it was resolved or until they were removed by the subprefect. Assignment to a single township area of operations allowed runners to gain more familiarity with the locale's physical and human topography. Such intimacy undoubtedly resulted in more efficient law enforcement.

At the same time, long assignment to a single area increased the opportunities and temptations for corruption among runners as they established working relationships and linkages of mutual benefit and dependency with a township's populace.

To strike a balance between the benefits and costs of the runner section–township ties, township assignments were not permanent. No runner sections operated exclusively either north or south of Zhuqian/Xinzhu.[17] The clearest statement of a runner section's area of responsibility dates from GX 3/6/20 (30 July 1877). Two weeks earlier all six ordinary runner sections had been ordered [21101:2] to conduct a careful search of the townships in order to ascertain the whereabouts of a minor functionary from the governor's staff who had been reported missing while on an inspection trip. Reports from five of the six section leaders are in the file. Unfortunately, only the report [21101:3] of the section leader of the Third Lictors, which searched Zhunan third and fourth townships, was explicit about the area that section covered. Several years later, in GX 11 (1885), the Third Lictor section was involved in handling a case from Zhubei second township. Even during the course of a single year, GX 9 (1883), this same section took part in investigations of cases in townships both north and south of Xinzhu.[18] The other five ordinary runner sections had similar assignment changes.

Such changes in areas of operation probably were due partly to the system of rotating yamen duty among the sections. Each section was on duty for a five-day period each month, according to the following schedule.

SECTION	DATES ON DUTY DURING MONTH
First Lictors	1–5
First Fast Runners	6–10
Second Lictors	11–15
Second Fast Runners	16–20
Third Lictors	21–25
Third Fast Runners	26–30

Runners in a section were called *zhiyi* during their five-day shift, and that section became responsible for any criminal case or civil litigation that came to the yamen during its shift. Thus each section's runners were for five days a month both township duty runners (*duibaoyi*) and shift duty runners (*zhiyi*). When the section on shift duty was not the township duty section for a given case, at least one township duty runner from the appropriate section was supposedly assigned to it.[19]

Each runner section had an office and quarters (*guan*) in the yamen. These offices apparently had holding rooms or cells where both suspects and convicted prisoners were detained. Often runner sections established branch offices (*waiguan*) in one of the market towns in their territory. The branch offices could be used to detain prisoners temporarily before transporting them to the yamen. In XF 5 (1855), the Third Fast Runner section maintained a branch office in Taoyuan market town. Fan Atian, who had been seized for resisting payment of large rent, was detained in the runner section's branch office while awaiting transfer to the vice subprefectural yamen in Mengjia, where he would be held awaiting trial [22202:39, 40].[20]

These branch offices may have originally had other legitimate purposes as well. In GX 18 (1892), at least two sections had branch offices. The First Fast Runner section had a Zhonggang market town branch office that had been in existence since the Danshui subprefecture era. It was set up as a location for persons buying land rights to pay the tax on this type of transaction and have their contract stamped, signifying its legality. Like the First Fast Runner section, the Second Fast Runner section too was using a branch office in its assigned township on the northern edge of the county. The office in Xucuogang had apparently been first established by a Danshui subprefect to report news of foreign shipwrecks in the area. By 1892, however, the Taibei prefect had received complaints that both runner sections were, in fact, using their branch offices to accept and adjudicate lawsuits, an activity reserved for the county magistrate.[21]

Runner Income

Most sources record that a runner's nominal annual salary was 6.2 taels or ounces of silver (six *liang* two *qian*) with a supplement of several *qian* to as much as one or two *liang* in years with an intercalary month.[22] In Xinzhu county, at least, runners were paid slightly more, 6.3 taels.[23] A runner's base pay provided only a bare subsistence livelihood for himself and certainly was insufficient to provide food for a family. If we consider only the average person's consumption of rice and ignore other foods necessary to sustain life, this conclusion becomes apparent. The earliest accurate determination of per capita rice consumption in Taiwan comes from the Japanese colonial period.[24] In 1920, the average annual per capita consumption of rice among Taiwanese farmers was 302.55 liters. If we can use this as a rough standard for extrapolating grain consumption during the mid-nineteenth century, then during the three decades after 1840, a runner's annual wage could buy rice equivalent to 1.99, 1.77, and 1.31 times the average per capita consumption. Rice prices rose steadily from the 1840s to the 1870s, with prices in dollars per *shi* as follows: unhusked: 0.62 in 1856, 0.9 in 1861, 1.0 in 1867 and 1878; polished: 1.5 in DG period (1821–50), 1.7 in XF period (1851–61), 2.3 in TZ period (1862–74). During the Daoguang period a runner's salary, which was equivalent to 8.74 dollars, could purchase 5.8 *shi* (609.91 liters) of polished rice.[25] As prices rose, the same income could buy only 5.14 *shi* (534.30 liters) and 3.8 *shi* (393.49 liters) during the Xianfeng and Tongzhi periods, respectively. Thus the 53 percent increase in polished rice prices over those three decades resulted in a 34 percent decrease in the amount of polished rice a runner could buy with his annual pay. Even before mid-century, a runner's salary was at best barely sufficient to feed two people. By around 1870, his buying power had eroded to such an extent that, depending on his salary alone, he could have done little more than keep himself alive.

Other estimates of living expenses for Chinese families suggest a runner's salary was much farther below the level of subsistence even than the above discussion indicates. George MacKay, a Canadian Presbyterian missionary in northern Taiwan during the years 1872–95, calculated that the average monthly expenses of a Chinese preacher and his family were "nine dollars and eighty-three cents in Mexican money."[26] Of this total, three dollars were required to purchase rice. Thus, slightly more than two-thirds of a family's expenditures went toward the purchase of nongrain foods and other necessities. But this figure for expenses was only a monthly total. Annual expenditures would have been reckoned at nearly 118 dollars. Even when rice and other commodities were still relatively inexpensive, a runner's $8.61 official annual wage could have been sufficient to support a family for no more than two months at best.

Given their inability to support themselves and their families from their official remuneration, runners and other yamen employees as well developed an irregular but officially tolerated system of fees.[27] Yamen servants customarily extracted a gratuity for their services from litigants or other persons involved in a civil or criminal case. It is difficult to determine at what point these fees crossed the line that differentiated expected litigation costs from corrupt and extortionate demands for bribes. Local chief administrators, however, had to make an effort to strike a balance between unreasonable stringency and excessive laxity when regulating runner fees. In 1846, Subprefect Cao Shigui established a regulation that Danshui runners could demand no more than two dollars in fees in any given case. Twenty years later, however, when another subprefect, Yan Jinqing, prohibited litigation fees for runners and clerks altogether rather than decreasing them, corruption multiplied vastly. Runners reportedly had begun inducing captured criminal suspects to threaten to implicate innocent people, who then could avoid being dragged into court only by bribing runners. The experience of the Shuqilin villagers who were falsely implicated in armed robbery by Zhan Ajian indicates that this phenomenon persisted, even though in 1873 it too was specifically forbidden.[28]

Illicit Runner Income: Evidence from the Cases

The varieties of runner corruption have been extensively, if not exhaustively, discussed in the literature.[29] Of the many customary fees (*lougui*) and other illegal and extortionate demands made by runners, it seems that only one violation was serious enough for local yamen heads to warn against specifically in any of the cases examined for this study. During the course of the bitter large-rent payment dispute between the Wu-Shun-Ji lineage and its tenants, on at least two occasions subprefects concluded that the best course was to go into the countryside and personally direct a survey and assessment of the fields leased by the tenants. In each instance, when the subprefect ordered [22202:78, 214] village leaders to make preparations for the party from the yamen, he stated clearly that he himself would pay the expenses of his attendants, clerks, and runners. Neither landlord, tenants, nor villagers were to be liable. In each case, the subprefect went on to say that if any "lawless rascal" from the yamen relied on his position to extort money (*xusuo*) from the local people, the offending runner or clerk would be arrested and punished.

Certainly local chief administrators were well aware that there were many opportunities for runners to demand customary fees. Land surveys and assessment for rent (and taxation) were particularly lucrative opportunities for runners. The occasion of survey and assessment was a crucial juncture for the large-rent and small-rent right holders as well as the actual cultivators, since the livelihoods of all three groups were a function of the amount of rent the two higher level groups could demand from the lowest. Runners might expect to be offered lavish fees by the owners of large- and small-rent rights to make sure the surveyed fields were recorded as larger and of higher quality than they in actuality were. At the same time, runners had a golden opportunity to demand payment from actual cultivators, who were, of course, anxious to avoid such an eventuality.

Their association with the yamen, backed with warrants as a tangible symbol of authority, often enabled runners to make their demands for customary fees with impunity. It should not be supposed, however, that these yamen police were always able to carry on their activities, legal or not, without resistance from litigants or suspects. As we shall see, runners were occasionally assaulted and even held prisoner by suspects not content to submit tamely to the magistrate's agents.

EXTENDING THE REACH OF YAMEN POWER

As described above, yamen runner forces were unreliable, inadequate, and malfeasant. In addition, their numbers were insufficient to enable the runner sections to carry out searches, summons, and arrests expeditiously in a jurisdiction where much of the terrain was remote and barely accessible. Nor could defendants or suspects be expected to obey runners docilely, even when these yamen agents' activities were lawfully authorized. The rent resistance case summarized earlier offers a prime example.

Toward the end of XF 8 (1858), the Danshui subprefect ordered four runners, including the yamen's head runners, Zhong Hong and Zhong Gui, to go to Daqiqian village and arrest several villagers who were refusing to pay large rent. One of these rent resisters, Xu Aqian, barricaded his entire family inside his house and refused the runners' demands to enter. When the yamen personnel persisted, the women of the Xu household threw a barrage of refuse and excrement at them. Subsequently Xu Aqian compounded insult with injury as he and perhaps ten other men wielding clubs swarmed out of the house and battered the runners into unconsciousness. Zhong Gui, if we are to believe a report [22202:105] filed by his fellows, was even taken captive.

The limited effectiveness of yamen runners as police prompted local administrators in Danshui and Xinzhu to search for ways to augment and supplement their runner cadre. In so doing, subprefecture and county heads aimed to create more intimate linkages to the people in their jurisdiction and to extend the reach of local government beyond the yamen wall into the countryside. The remainder of this chapter will discuss the mechanism created for this task.

Overseers

One of the often-cited problems of Chinese local government in the nineteenth century was its failure to grow and articulate so as to cope with the enormously large population that is one of the more notable features of Chinese society after the seventeenth century. A corollary to this thesis is that, especially after the devolution of power from the central to provincial governments during and after the Taiping Rebellion, 1850–65, many of the functions and services formerly provided by local yamen were arrogated by the local gentry.[30]

In Danshui and Xinzhu a different picture emerges in which, beginning in the 1830s, northern Taiwan subprefects and county magistrates tried to incorporate or co-opt rural elites into a formal and regulated quasi-bureaucratic structure extending below the yamen and into market towns and farming villages. This structure was not the same as the famous system of mutual surveillance and security known as the *baojia*, which was not implemented in Danshui, except on paper, until 1872.[31] Even then the *baojia*, supposedly so important for government control of rural areas in other parts of China, was merely employed for census purposes in northern Taiwan. In fact, the *baojia* was subordinate to and run by the quasi-bureaucratic network to which I shall now turn.

Even before Taiwan became part of the Qing empire in 1683, immigration to the island frontier had begun. Natural increase and continued migration caused Taiwan's population to grow in a fashion similar to but on a smaller scale than that of the rest of China.

The structural problems bedeviling local government control were intensified by lawlessness and violence endemic to the frontier areas that continued to exist in parts of Taiwan well into the nineteenth century. The continuing process of land reclamation and settlement led to clashes between immigrants, who were mainly Hokkienese from Fujian province and Hakkas from Guangdong, and between the tribal peoples native to the island and Han Chinese of both Hakka and Hokkienese extraction. The peculiar history of immigration of Chinese to the island from Fujian and Guangdong resulted in a variegated pattern of settlement with pockets of Hakka villages interspersed among the dominant Hokkienese population. Even in the areas north and south of the immediate environs of Zhuqian/Xinzhu city where the Hakka concentration was higher than elsewhere in Taiwan, Hokkienese speakers were well represented.[32] The imperial government's on-again, off-again attempts to prevent Han settlers from encroaching into land reserved for the tribal natives added even more variety to the ethnic and cultural mosaic.[33] It was a volatile mixture made even more potent by the competition for land and water among Han settlers and by the instability of a still predominantly male frontier society produced by a long government ban on family members accompanying immigrants. One of the resulting phenomena was frequent feuding or armed affrays (*xiedou*), often between Hakka and Hokkienese but sometimes even between Hokkienese villages whose inhabitants traced the roots of their antagonism to their origins in different prefectures in Fujian.[34] The consequent burdens on the thinly stretched fabric of local government authority were a source of constant anxiety for local administrators.

This disorder became so troubling to one Danshui subprefect,

Lou Yun, that in 1836 he directed towns and villages to begin to take more responsibility for law enforcement and policing. A leadership hierarchy in market towns and farm villages was to be created. Lou ordered that in the market towns (*jie*, a place with at least a few stores and other permanent commercial establishments) and villages (*zhuang*, a settlement of mainly farming households) of the subprefecture, four leadership positions were to be established.[35] Men were to be selected to fill the posts of overseer (*zongli*), manager (*dongshi*), village head (*zhuangzheng*), and assistant village head (*zhuangfu*).

The subprefect's conception of the responsibilities and duties of these local officers was expressed both in general terms and in specific measures they were to implement. "In essence," he wrote, "the responsibility of each overseer, manager, village head, and assistant is to restrain the village people and bring amity to the countryside." Lou Yun was explicit about the kinds of activities villagers were prone to that had to be restrained.[36] He seemed most concerned about villages reacting to outside events or giving shelter to suspicious individuals not native to them. Min and Yue (Hokkienese and Hakka) villages were not to start trouble when violence broke out in neighboring areas, nor were they to allow vagrants from outside to stay. Lou was concerned to prevent two kinds of undesirable behavior that had been common throughout the history of settlement not only of his subprefecture but also of the island as a whole.

Lou was also concerned about a perceived tendency for rebellion to spread quickly from one part of the island to others. He and other observers felt that the rapidity with which rebellion spread was related to the armed affrays and perhaps stemmed in part from them. The Lin Shuangwen rebellion of the 1780s, which spread swiftly from the central part of the island and resulted in the sack of Zhuqian city in 1786, was only the most notable example of the extreme contagion that unrest and revolt was felt to have in Taiwan. If the overseers and others could restrain the natural volatility of the villagers and isolate them from outside agitation, the outcome would be "amity" in the countryside.

Lou explicitly prohibited several other activities that were the more standard worries of local government officials. Violent crime, land boundary encroachment, rent and tax resistance, and lower degree holders' interference in litigation make up the other prohibitions that Lou published. One violent crime seemed particularly to have bedeviled Danshui and the rest of Taiwan for many years. Kidnapping for ransom was pointedly mentioned in Lou's third prohibition, even though this long-standing problem had been specifically addressed by a substatute on kidnapping and holding for ransom that had been added to the Qing Code in 1788 based on a precedent-setting decision in a Taiwan case.[37] To Lou Yun, the seeming ubiquity of crime and litigation reflected a society in chronic turmoil that required special measures to suppress.

Lou Yun's instructions to the incipient corps of village leaders went beyond merely preventing pernicious outside influences from inciting villagers to wrongdoing. The leadership was actively to reform and cleanse their villages from within, making them into "pure villages" (*qingzhuang*). The overseers and their subordinates were to expel known bandits from the villages and find ways for the poor, landless men most likely to turn to crime to make an honest living. Village leaders were empowered to levy 5 percent of the village's aggregate annual income and set it aside as a reserve fund to finance entry of the indigent into tenant farming, commerce, or training for handicraft production. Were they fit for none of these occupations, they could be hired as field patrollers and night watchmen.[38]

Under Subprefect Lou's plan, overseers had a number of other responsibilities as well.[39] They attempted to mediate disputes between villagers who were threatening to file litigation. When intervillage disputes arose, the overseer for the area called together the different villages' leaders for discussions to reach a settlement.[40] If mediation failed and a lawsuit was accepted by the subprefecture or county court, overseers had to be ready to carry out any court directives that arose from the case.

Overseers have a high profile in some law cases because Lou's directive, in effect, granted them police powers in their jurisdictions. To prevent crimes, they were empowered to place lawless young men who were village residents in preventive detention in an attempt to reform them. If reform proved impossible, the overseers could send them to court for prosecution. In addition, when arrest warrants had been issued for criminals thought to be in an overseer's jurisdiction, he became a deputy to the runners charged with capturing the suspect.[41]

Lou Yun's directive did not address the methods or procedures that overseers might employ. His village regulations contain no guidance, for example, on just how reform of wayward individuals might be effected. Perhaps Lou hoped that by allowing the cadre of town and village leaders freedom from excessively detailed and restrictive guidelines, their work might proceed more effectively.

An overseer's responsibility for the security of the towns and villages under his charge extended to local guard and militia organizations. Organizing winter guards (*dongfang*) to prevent off-season encroachment on land farmed by the villagers as well as field and crop patrollers to be employed during the growing season fell to overseers. Once villages had been cleansed of the lawless and made pure, overseers were to organize pure villages into larger complexes known as "linked villages" (*lianzhuang*). Linked village groups then assumed, under overseer direction, responsibility for control and apprehension of criminals and for defense against outside threats. In 1843, for example, in an area south of Zhuqian city, the market town Tunxiao and its surrounding villages united for the dual purposes of bandit suppression and protection against possible attacks by the British, whose recent Opium War (1839–42) victories had revealed them to be a potential threat to any part of maritime China. The agreement was formalized by means of a compact (*heyue*) [12203:17] drawn up by the Tunxiao overseer and the heads of the market town and the villages. The compact notes that the pure villages had been ordered by the subprefect to unite. They were "to band together and train" (*tuanlian*) the villages' able-bodied and courageous men. In this way overseers were to become instrumental in forming the local self-defense units known as *tuanlian* militia and supporting these local militias by raising funds for their equipment and training.[42]

Overseers had broad but diffuse responsibility for the management of public affairs and even supervised the rudimentary *baojia* system in compiling household registers. They worked with local gentry to collect subscriptions for local public works and then directed the actual project operations. Finally, they were responsible for ensuring that the inhabitants in the areas under their control were informed of any government proclamations issued or transmitted by the subprefect or magistrate. In short, although in the context of this study I stress the significance of overseers for local law enforcement, it is apparent that the creation of the town and village leader networks was in part an attempt to repair a systemic weakness of government at the local level. Clear-sighted administrators such as Lou Yun realized that the formal structure of local government could be enhanced and supported the creation of a semiformal or quasi-bureaucratic leadership framework of overseers and other village leaders.[43]

Lou Yun did not detail the qualities an overseer and the other leaders should have. In Dan-Xin case documents a set of rather vague, stereotypical attributes is mentioned repeatedly. The ideal overseer was honest (*chengshi*), prosperous and settled (*youshi youjia*), and careful, diligent, and knowledgeable in carrying out public matters (*jinshen bangong, anlian gongshi*) [12203:5]. Managers, village heads, and assistants apparently needed similar qualifications. In other words, Subprefect Lou expected that town and village leaders who emerged naturally from among the residents of local towns and villages would fill the new, formalized posts, but those men who had assumed leading positions by virtue of corruption or violence would be disqualified.

In the village leadership hierarchy, managers, village heads, and assistants were the overseers' subordinates. An overseer located in a market town (*jie*) might be assisted by one or more managers and sometimes a town head, and below them in the farming villages (*zhuang*) were village heads and their assistants. A history of Xinzhu compiled by Japanese researchers shortly after the island passed to Japanese control in 1895 claimed that an overseer was placed over each market town and ten or more or several tens of villages. Each market town was said to have had a number of managers, and each village had both a head and an assistant.[44] As we shall see later, although there was a fairly dense coverage of village leaders in rural Danshui/Xinzhu, with overseers in all market towns, not every farm village had a village head and assistant, nor did every overseer have managers to assist him.

One might conclude overseers and the others to be little different than the ordinary sorts of locally prominent notables that assumed leadership in rural and lineage milieux because of examination system success, wealth, wisdom and charisma acquired through age and experience, military prowess, or simply control of armed men.[45] Yet, I believe they were as a group distinct in two senses. First, they were not members of the "gentry elite." Occasionally we find references to overseers with purchased *jiansheng* degrees. As a group, however, these village officials stood below the gentry in the social hierarchy. They came from the peasantry and common people. Second, while they may have exhibited some of the characteristics of "ordinary local notables," they assumed a distinctive identity because, at least from the time of Lou Yun's proclamation on, they began also to occupy an officially legitimated niche within the bureaucratic hierarchy and to possess a privileged communications link with local government. Earlier writers have mentioned without elaborating that some village leaders were given official appointment.[46] Their official status is precisely what I wish to emphasize.

Regardless of the fact that there was nothing in the formal administrative regulations mentioning overseers or managers, these positions were created by specific order of the chief administrative officer of the local government. When an overseer position was vacant (*eque*), a nomination process that was formally and publicly conducted went into motion. Nominees were subject to the yamen head's approval, sometimes only after the subprefect or magistrate personally interrogated them. Such approval was signified by issuing an appointment edict and a seal of office (*chuoji*). Once appointed, overseers were specially burdened by a range of responsibilities beyond that of other traditional village leaders such as village elders but at the same time were set apart because of a right to bypass the usual channel of access to the local chief administrator. When reporting on matters falling within their scope of responsibility, overseers and the other village leaders were, according to the terms of Lou Yun's regulations, "authorized to stamp the report with their seals of office and are exempted from transmitting it through a scrivener."[47] When an overseer was not conscientious in carrying out his duties, he was impeached and stripped of his office. The formality of the procedure seems to have invested overseers with some of the aura and power of a position in the regular bureaucratic hierarchy.

Nomination, Appointment, and Vacating Office

The Dan-Xin cases offer several examples that may serve to illustrate the system's functioning.[48]

Vacancy. In every known case, when a subprefect or county magistrate was notified that a village leadership position was vacant, he issued an order to a runner to go and meet with local leaders and notables to select (*xuanju*) an honest and dependable nominee and then petition that he be allowed to succeed to the position [12203:2].

Nomination. In one example of the process, in 1843 a number of local notables convened in Yuanli market town's Empress of Heaven Temple (*Tianhou gong*)[49] and consulted to select a nominee to fill the Yuanli market town overseer position. Subsequently, a second meeting was held in the Benevolence Temple (*Cihe gong*) to confirm their selection. Those who conferred to select a nominee included an overseer from another market town, a manager, several town and village heads, village elders, *shengyuan* and *jiansheng* degree holders, store owners, a lineage head, the head of a group whose members were descended from Hakkas who had remained loyal to the government during the Lin Shuangwen rebellion in the previous century, and a runner representing the yamen [12203:11, 14].[50] In another instance, an overseer who wished to retire at age 60 and return to his ancestral home in the mainland had a nominee to succeed him chosen beforehand. The old overseer then submitted a petition at once asking to retire and nominating his replacement [12214:1].

Confirmation and Appointment. Once local notables had selected a nominee, at least three documents were required to be drawn up. The nominating group submitted (1) a petition to the yamen requesting that their nominee for office be confirmed and (2) a bond (*baojie zhuang*) guaranteeing that the nominee was honest, energetic, and worthy of the office and also that if he made any mistakes in his duties, they (the guarantors) themselves would be willingly responsible. The nominee himself had to file a document called an "acceptance of appointment" (*renchong zhuang*) in which he guaranteed that he would be diligent and not dare make careless errors [12203:23, 24].[51] Occasionally the nominee was summoned to be questioned by the subprefect or magistrate before his appointment was approved. The few examples [12202:20, 12203: 27] that appear in the Dan-Xin cases show the questions to be perfunctory inquiries into the nominee's background. It is not clear why some were called to the yamen, while most apparently were not. In either case, if the nominee was deemed satisfactory, the subprefect or magistrate wrote a directive (*tangyu*) approving the appointment and issued the new appointee a copy of the directive and an official seal of office.

Vacating or Removal from Office. Sometimes a village leader requested that he be allowed to resign because of age and ill health. One village head filed a petition [12201:1] saying that he had become paralyzed on one side of his body and at 73 years of age was fearful of making criminal errors in doing his job. In other cases, local leaders were removed from office because they had already been negligent. One overseer "lacked initiative in handling business" (*banshi buqian*) [12203:19]. Another had "made mistakes in public matters and was deprived of his office" (*wugong chige*) [12203:4]. A third's "administration was not good" (*banli bushan*) [12203:9]. Negligence and mistakes were, of course, not the only reason for dismissal. In 1868, an overseer, manager, and three others, probably village heads, were dismissed for extorting money in the course of carrying out their official duties [12209:13]. In impeachment cases a yamen directive so ordering was issued, and then a runner was ordered to confiscate (*diao*) the impeached leader's seal and turn it in for cancellation (*jiaoxiao*) [12203:2].

The burdens on these town and village leaders could be heavy, and they received no official salary. Errors or below par performance could lead to the humiliation of impeachment and confiscation of one's seal. It seems to have been difficult to persuade suitable candidates to serve, and for several reasons local notables who had to select a nominee were not happy when an experienced overseer was removed from office. In 1842, a group of at least 31 local leaders petitioned [12203:4] the Danshui subprefect requesting that Zheng Maguan, who had been impeached, be reinstated. An extract from their petition illustrates some of the problems that made good men hard to find.

We have publicly deliberated and together decided: It is not satisfactory to select another overseer for that place; it is suitable to retain the former one. Men are not Yao and Shun. Who is faultless? We are earnest in our findings that the area's market town and villages border on the sea to the west; whenever there are sea pirates, they come ashore and cause trouble. [The town and villages] have their backs to the mountains in the east throughout which there are fierce aborigines and robbers full of harm. The main road goes through the area from south to north making it a really vital location. The thirteen villages contain both Min and Yue in various places. People have different ideas; the strong and the weak are both present, the good and the evil are thereby differentiated. That is why it is difficult to select an overseer there and why it is difficult to serve as one. Thus, if we want to select a Min person, it is hard to get the Yue people to go along. If a Yue person is selected, it is hard to get Min people to go along.

However, Zheng Maguan served in that position for more than 40 years. He retired three times and was reselected three times. He was neither glad nor irritated, not stubborn or grasping in performing his duties. Although he is of Yue ancestry, he in no way protects only those close to him and so was acceptable to the Min people, who indeed submitted to his leadership. His disposition is firm, upright, daring, courageous, and energetic. Each time there were expenses, he used his own resources and so did good works for the locality. In repairing bridges and building roads, he took the lead in raising contributions and initiated building the Empress of Heaven Temple, renovating the Shrine to Mr. Shou [Tongchun], and establishing the Nanhe Guardpost to protect against aborigines and robbers. Whenever anyone in the town or villages had either a serious or minor dispute, he immediately stepped in to prevent it from going too far. Minor disputes were mediated and misfortune avoided. Serious disputes were reported for adjudication that inevitably led to dislike and resentment. In all there were only one or two confused accusations against him, and they are known to have been fraudulently brought by dishonest people. There were absolutely no bribes accepted. Major disputes were made less serious and minor disputes disappeared. He captured bandits several times and sent them to court, as the record will attest. As his fellow countrymen and neighbors, we know well and thoroughly apprehend that the responsibility of the area's overseer is not light.

This passage graphically illustrates the varied obligations for which overseers were responsible. For dispute mediation, arrest of criminals, local self-defense, and public works, the residents of thirteen villages all looked to the overseer for leadership. The petition also reveals the serious problems that ethnic and subethnic conflict posed for such men. Again, we are struck with the crucial legal and administrative roles of overseers and their subordinates and the extent to which the yamen was compelled to reach out to them to ensure that essential governmental services were performed.

Communication between the yamen and the overseers was often effected through yamen runners, who acted as liaison. As noted earlier, each runner section was assigned to a given township and consequently was responsible for liaison with the market town overseers of that township. The township duty runners (*duibaoyi*) dealt constantly with overseers and other village leaders. When runners were given arrest warrants or were ordered to summon witnesses, their orders invariably directed them to seek the assistance of the overseer and other rural leaders in the area concerned.[52]

The cadre of market town and village leaders not only had responsibility for assisting runners but also were actively involved in investigating crimes, collecting evidence, summoning witnesses, and arresting suspects. In this way yamen runners were able to rely on a network of auxiliary "police" intimately familiar with the local scene. The village leaders serving in this way actually were crucial, since they could reach the locale of an incident within a short time of its occurrence, while it often took days for information to reach the yamen and runners to be ordered out.

Long delays in yamen response to incidents were especially the case as tea and camphor production in the area increased in the second half of the nineteenth century. Remote upland areas in the northern part of the island's interior east of the earlier settled coastal plain were prime locations for both tea cultivation and camphor distillation. As the production of both spread, conflict and violent disputes between producers and earlier settler-farmers or the indigenous native population became more common. The boundary dispute case summarized earlier shows the importance of an overseer in investigation.[53]

As we will recall, three businessmen from Xinpu, a market town in the mountains east and a little north of Xinzhu city, had formed a partnership to recruit tenants to plant tea. The land chosen for cultivation and leased from an aborigine settlement bordered an area used to pasture cattle owned by residents of several nearby

Chinese villages. When a boundary dispute escalated into crop destruction, a fire fight between tea planters and farm village residents, who were both armed with muskets, broke out, with one man killed. The Xinpu overseer and a local constable were the first to learn of the affray. They arrived after it ended but took custody of the corpse and were able to verify that tea bushes and sweet potatoes grown and harvested by the tea cultivators had been destroyed. The dispatch of yamen runners days later with instructions from the magistrate had to await submission of an accusation by the aggrieved parties. Without the overseer and local constable, the corpse and other traces of the battle might well have been removed long before runners arrived.

Village leaders were expected to take the initiative in suspicious circumstances. In 1887, a former lijin station tax collector was kidnapped. He was taken into the mountains by a camphor smuggler and his gang, whose illegal goods he had earlier confiscated. As the gang passed through a village, the village head became suspicious, stopped the group, and freed their captive.[54] The village head acted to frustrate the kidnappers when runners and soldiers in pursuit were unlikely to catch the gang before they reached a safe haven in the mountains.

The responsibility of village leaders did not end with capturing criminals. They and village residents were sometimes obliged to deliver the captive to court. In an 1882 case, after a robbery suspect was apprehended, villagers were hired or assigned to convey the prisoner to Xinzhu. The village overseer directed other village leaders to collect money from the local residents to pay their travel expenses.[55] Once again a member of this quasi-bureaucratic network of overseers and village leaders had prevented a suspect from escaping the law's net.

Development and Scope of Overseer Networks

A detailed examination of the evolution of the village leader system is precluded by a lack of comprehensive source material. Although the appointment and duties of overseers, managers, and village heads and assistants were not formalized and made systematic in Danshui subprefecture until 1836, Dai Yanhui has shown that overseers and managers either had been appointed or were unofficially selected by residents in some villages as early as

1807.[56] The 1842 petition quoted above asserted that the impeached overseer had served for over 40 years. Although this seems an improbably long tenure, it is likely that he was an overseer well before Lou Yun proclaimed the new village regulations. The earliest list [12213:4] still extant of overseers, managers, and village heads was compiled in 1872, before the subprefecture was divided.

At the time the subprefecture was organized in territorial units called *bao* or townships. Besides the urban and suburban precincts of Zhuqian city, there were twelve rural townships. According to the subprefectural local history, published in 1871,[57] the twelve rural townships contained 295 towns and villages. These towns and villages were covered by 110 overseers, fourteen managers including only one gentry manager (*shendong*), and ten village heads, according to the 1872 list. The preponderance of overseers among the total number of town and village leaders officially recognized by the yamen indicates that the overseers were felt to be the crucial link between formal government institutions and local society. Certainly there existed in most or all villages some person, whether called village elder or village head, recognized by the inhabitants as possessing the mantle of leadership authority. In ordinary times, however, the yamen did not feel it necessary to invest the majority of these men with any formal recognition because overseers with an ability to manage affairs on a supra-village basis had already been appointed.

Overseers were located not just in market towns but also in a number of population centers designated "farm villages" (*zhuang*) by the local history. Farm villages with overseers often were either located at critical points along the subprefecture's maritime or mountain frontiers or probably had grown to become small commercial centers without their changed status being reflected in redesignation from village (*zhuang*) to market town (*jie*). An incomplete 1874 tally [12403:49] of the population covered 122 of the 295 towns and villages listed in the local history. This census shows a few examples of both kinds of villages. Sanwan, a village in Zhonggang township south of the subprefectural capital, had an overseer and was reported to have a larger population than Zhonggang market town itself, which also had an overseer. Farther south, in Houlong township, two villages, Tongluowan and

Gezishi, each had an overseer. Each was only about half the size of Houlong town, but both were larger than either Zhonggang or Yuanli, the market town centers of the townships north and south of Houlong. Sanwan, Tongluowan, and Gezishi were located in the mountains along their townships' (and subprefecture's) eastern border, beyond which were lands inhabited by unpacified aborigine tribes. In the eighteenth century each had been the headquarters for a guardpost (*ai*), an organization with hired civilian guards and a series of watch towers and outposts set up to protect Chinese settlers from attacks by the aborigines. It should not necessarily be thought that overseers in such guardpost centers were primarily concerned with defense and security-related duties. Each guardpost organization had its own commander and cadre, independent of the overseer. While I cannot conclusively demonstrate it to be the case, I believe the large size of these villages points to their commercial importance, which in turn required an overseer. In addition, the last Chinese character of Gezishi's name indicates that it was originally the site of a periodic market.

Other villages' overseers may have been concerned mostly with security or curbing ethnic feuds. Ribei village in Yuanli township and Guilunkou in Taojian township were Hakka villages whose neighboring settlements were mainly Hokkienese. Both villages had overseers. There were so many Hakkas and Hokkienese living in the Zhonggang marketing area that both a Hakka and a Hokkienese overseer had been appointed by 1857 [12205:1, 2]. In 1867, a petition to the subprefect asserted that the appointment of an overseer was necessary to mediate disputes between Hokkienese in Jiuqionglin village and Hakkas in Liuzhangli village. In short, in places where subethnic friction could not be eased by a single overseer such as the redoubtable Zheng Maguan (see above), both Hakka and Hokkien interests could be catered to by the device of dual overseer appointment.

Significance of Village Leaders

The preceding discussion leads us into the larger question of defining the role that the formally constituted and formally recognized town and village leader network played in Danshui and Xinzhu. Subbureaucratic quasi-officials were not unique to Taiwan. Philip Huang and Prasenjit Duara have found similar functionaries in north China.[58] In Baodi county, Zhili, for example, functionaries called *xiangbao* played a somewhat similar role to that of overseers in Danshui and Xinzhu. The Baodi *xiangbao,* who were responsible for tax collection, were the lowest level subcounty officials during the nineteenth century. "In [Baodi] each [*xiangbao*] oversaw an average of twenty villages. He was usually someone nominated by the supra-village and village elites, and then confirmed and formally appointed by the county yamen." *Xiangbao* in Baodi county traveled to the yamen to take an oath of office (but apparently received no seal or appointment edict) and filed a document similar to a *renchong zhuang* acknowledging their responsibilities. They seldom had duties other than collecting taxes and tended to be of middle peasant status, in these ways being distinct from *zongli* in northern Taiwan. The *zongli* and other quasi-officials of Danshui and Xinzhu seem in some ways to conform to Duara's protective brokerage model of rural intermediaries between state and society. Duara's model, however, assumes that protective brokerage organizations such as he describes were created to control predatory entrepreneurial brokers such as tax farmers, who were, from the point of view of rural society, pernicious agents of an increasingly intrusive state. The protective broker thus insulated local society from the reach of the state. In the very different circumstances of northern Taiwan, where state power remained quite weak, the *zongli* and other subbureaucrats served not to insulate state from society but rather to integrate them more fully.

As catalysts for state-society integration, these quasi-bureaucrats may appear to have been agents of the state rather than protective buffers or even neutral mediating agents between their local communities and the county government. Their function and position can be understood more clearly if we remember that they were part of a dynamic and partly contradictory process of both state building and social construction. Local social entities such as lineages, business partnerships, or villages, while sometimes defensive when faced with intrusive or even predatory state behavior, were not necessarily or at least not always hostile to it. I have argued that when society in this locality was unable to control or restrain violence, people began more and more to look to the legal system. The state cast about for ways to augment its control. The cadre of local leaders were at the core of this process, sometimes representatives of the town and villages, sometimes agents of the state, but also men whose own interests were always at stake. In this way they were not disinterested mediators, acting merely as a kind of interface between the yamen and the village. Instead they were a potent and key group of self-made, independent, and influential men who after selection to leadership roles by their local communities then attracted the attention of subprefects and magistrates hoping to coerce or entice them to assume new functions. The relationships were complex, dynamic, and reflective of the social and political transformation of the time and place.

I have tried to stress the importance overseers, managers, and village heads had in crime prevention and police work while at the same time indicating that their responsibilities also extended beyond the legal realm into many other areas of concern to the state. Three additional points may help further clarify the nature and function of the market town and village leader network.

First, overseers, who were located in virtually every market town and many large villages as well, were the means by which commercial and marketing networks were formally linked for communication and control purposes to the government's administrative hierarchy. Japanese field researchers in the late nineteenth and early twentieth centuries felt that the establishment of the village leadership system was somehow related to trade and commerce. The quasi-officials in market towns and villages acted, they thought, as a control or management mechanism for commerce.[59] Four of the five overseers whose occupations can be determined from their appointment hearings at the yamen were merchants or tradesmen [12202:7, 12203:27, 12214:8, 12218:20, 12219:2]. This is too small a sample to be more than suggestive. It is supported, however, by the numerous petitions nominating overseers that include store owner households (*puhu*) among the signatories. An 1872 petition [12214:1] impressed with the seals of 21 store owners from the town of Xinpu is the most extreme example, but many more are to be found in the Dan-Xin case files. The increasing importance to the island's economy of tea and camphor,[60] two cash crops that had world markets, implied widening commercialization and a concomitant expansion of commercial and trade networks. The one or two shops in some large farm villages and the 21 or more establishments in a market town like Xinpu were economic and social foci for the Taiwanese. Affluent store proprietors began to assume more importance for local law enforcement and local administration. Overseers were required to raise money for various uses such as public works, transport of suspected criminals, and the support of local militias. I believe the ability of a tradesman or merchant to tap into the network of his commercial associates made him an attractive candidate for an overseer's position. Skinner has suggested that "marketing had a significance for societal integration in traditional China which at once paralleled and surpassed—which both reinforced and complemented—that of administration."[61] I interpret the overseers and their assistants in the market towns of northern Taiwan to be the mechanism joining the economic network to the political hierarchy. As Skinner put it, the one "reinforced and complemented" the other to promote "societal integration" in an area of very fragmented cultural and ethnic loyalties.

The second point to be made about the significance of the town and village leader system is that the village leadership system was the critical mechanism through which subprefects and magistrates attempted to mobilize local society to help meet the foreign pressure that began to threaten the Qing government's hold on the island in the nineteenth century. We have already seen how in one instance a village compact was instituted partly to meet expected British attacks. The first manifestation of a more serious and ultimately successful challenge to Qing control of the island came in the 1870s. In 1871, some Liuqiu (Okinawan) fishermen were blown by a storm to a coastal area controlled by aborigines in southern Taiwan, where they were killed by tribesmen. Nearly three years later, in April 1874, the Japanese government, after diplomatically outmaneuvering the Qing court, sent a punitive expedition to punish the offending tribe. In a spasm of anxiety the central government appointed Shen Baozhen to be special commissioner in charge of Taiwan's maritime defense.[62] One measure ordered by Shen, perhaps drawing on his experience in Jiangxi, was the creation of local militia units. The Danshui subprefect consequently ordered a Militia Bureau (*tuanlian zongju*) established in Zhuqian with a branch (*fenju*) in Houlong township [12215:1, 3]. Another *tuanlian* bureau was created in Dajia, the large town on the subprefecture's southern edge [12216:2, 3].

Although each branch was headed by a gentry manager, he depended on overseers and village heads to recruit militiamen and to solicit money to support the militia units. The order to establish militia branches required that the village leadership system be expanded and formalized. The Houlong overseer asked the subprefect to issue official seals to 24 Houlong area village heads who until then had not had this sign of official approval [12215:2]. A few days later the subprefect received a petition from the Dajia militia bureau chief asking that the selection of two new overseers and new heads for 49 more villages be approved for the Dajia area [12216:1]. It seems that at least in this case the organization of local militia units was not an ad hoc process but was carried out largely by a system of government-appointed local leaders that had by then been developing for nearly 40 years.

The third and final point I wish to suggest is that the village cadre could point to their official or quasi-official status, symbolized by an edict of appointment and a seal of office, as legitimating their leadership positions and their right to cooperation from villagers in law enforcement, local self-defense, and certain other matters. This, though, was not a one-way street. Government, too, sought to legitimate its effort to mobilize rural society and to extend its power into the countryside.[63] When subprefects or magistrates co-opted locally prominent men by granting them quasi-official status, those central government appointees added to their own authority by augmenting it with the prestige adhering to such local men. In a symbiotic relationship, each legitimated the other.[64]

Some of the most crucial and stressful interaction between the residents of the Danshui/Xinzhu area and the legal system occurred during the process of search and summons or arrest. I have suggested that because of the relative underdevelopment of local government institutions, local administrators in this area invented or adapted quasi-formal leadership structures to accomplish the duties expected of them by higher organs of government and to extend essential government services expected by members of local society. In particular, the inadequacies of yamen runner "police" forces led to the creation of an overseer network that played a vital role in extending yamen control into rural areas and mediating between local government and society. Once an overseer had acted on yamen orders to help locate, summon, and arrest those whose presence was demanded by the court, he had fulfilled his most important responsibility to the legal system. His involvement in the legal process did not, however, always end at that time. Quite often overseers were called to give their testimony before the magistrate's bench during the course of trying a case. In the next chapter I shall explore some of the aspects of the trial and verdict that most directly affected those who found themselves kneeling before the bench to be heard and judged by the court.

9

Hearing and Verdict

THE HEARING

Wariness and skepticism guided subprefects and magistrates in evaluating petitions and investigating the circumstances of a case. In the end, however, local judges accepted cases for investigation and trial. Even though compelled by disadvantaged social status and penury to delay and dishonesty in performing their duties, runners eventually arrested suspects and summoned witnesses, and ultimately all gathered before the bench for hearing, judgment, and sentence. As with other stages of the adjudication process, much that occurred was not made part of the official record and is, therefore, largely invisible to us now. The cases do, however, allow us to gain some limited sense of the experiences of litigants, suspects, and convicted criminals as they underwent interrogation, detention, and execution of sentence.

The initial step in this final stage of the local court's judicial obligation was to bring the parties before the subprefect or magistrate. A local chief administrator acting in his judicial capacity must have often had occasion to interview prisoners or litigants privately before a formal court hearing was convened. However, since no records of such private sessions are contained in the case files—if indeed any such accounts were ever made—our discussion must exclude any such preliminary or unofficial interrogations. Thus, the first official procedure was to convene a hearing.

After a list of persons to be interrogated was drawn up, suspects, witnesses, and others it was thought necessary to interrogate were brought before the bench, questioned, and their testimony recorded. Often this transcript included a draft of the court's instructions, interim decision, or final judgment. An example [22609:17, 18] from the dispute over family property between Mrs. Zhou née Xu and her brothers-in-law may serve to illustrate.

Court Testimony

HEARING LIST (*tixun mingdan*); CASE CLERK (*cheng*): Chen Yuan; RUNNER (*chai*): Ni Feng.

LIST (*jikai*):

Original accuser (*yuangao*): Mrs. Zhou née Xu.

Proxy filer (*baogao*): Zhou Chuncao.

Accused (*beigao*): Zhou Wuniang viz. the *jiansheng* Zhou Qichang, who has filed a counterplaint.

Shengyuan continuation petitioner (*xucheng shengyuan*): Zhou Guoxiang viz. manager Zhou Liang.

[FINDINGS]: Zhou Qichang submitted to the court one contract and also one acceptance document (*lishishou*) that had been signed by the mediators. Naturally this is reliable proof. In addition Mrs. Zhou née Xu and Chuncao also acknowledged that there was this written proof. As for admitting the validity of the documents, she claims the acceptance agreement is not this document that was submitted. Concerning the mediators, except for Wei Duliu, who has died, immediately bring Chen Qianfu, Guo Tiansi, and Zhou Pankai to court for a second hearing. So directed. Zhou Qichang and the others are all to be turned over to the custody of runners.

Second MONTH 26th DAY interrogated (*xun*).

[TESTIMONY]:

MRS. ZHOU NÉE XU: My husband's registration was Anqi county [Quanzhou prefecture, Fujian]. At present I reside on Yanjiezi.[1] My son Chuncao and my other son work as laborers. My husband died in TZ 11 (1872). My husband and his brothers totaled four men in all. The second brother was Yuhang, the third Yushu, and the fourth Wuniang. My husband Dongfu was the eldest. Because at the time my husband's younger brothers, Wuniang and Yushu, who had remained on the mainland, were still children, they were raised by me to adulthood. During the Daoguang years (1821–50), my husband and my father-in-law crossed to Taiwan and proceeded to Zhuqian, where they opened the Cha-Tai store and did business. During the Xianfeng years (1851–61), my husband's three younger brothers crossed to Taiwan. My husband, Dongfu, became ill and turned the Cha-Tai store over to the brothers to manage. After that my husband died. They took the Cha-Tai store, which is family property, and arrogated its management (*baguan*) to themselves. The Cha-Yuan store that my husband had started himself had earlier already gone bankrupt. During TZ 13 (1874) I came forward to dispute for possession by going to the battalion commander and filing a petition. He invited in mediators (*gongqin*), who arbitrated a payment of 550 foreign dollars. This was turned over to me to repay the large debts I owed. A document was drawn up and turned over to him [her brother-in-law Zhou Wuniang] as proof. Moreover, at that time [when the management of the store changed hands], my husband indicated that he had been paid 180 foreign dollars. An agreement was drawn up that can serve as evidence. At present the Cha-Tai store, a family property (*jiaye*), has been illegally taken over by those three. I have not yet divided the estate with them. I am not greedy (*buyuan*). Today I have been questioned and request clear consideration and a just ruling.

ZHOU CHUNCAO: My testimony is the same as Mrs. Zhou née Xu.

ZHOU WUNIANG VIZ. *JIANSHENG* ZHOU QICHANG: My age is 42 *sui*. I am an Anqi county registrant. At present I reside on Taiye street. I opened the Cha-Tai store and am engaged in business there. I am married and have children. There were four brothers: the eldest collateral line Dongfu; the second Yuxing, the third Yushu, and me. In the Daoguang period, my brother Dongfu accompanied our father, crossed to Taiwan, and opened the Cha-Tai store in Zhuqian. Subsequently our father died. The business was then managed by my brother Dongfu for ten years. However, he had only his own welfare at heart. In XF 9 (1859), my brother Dongfu sent a letter urging the three of us brothers to come to Taiwan and live. Before long he claimed the business lacked capital. He invited in a mediator so that he could divide the family property (*fenjia*) with us. At the time the mediator [text missing] paid 150 silver dollars. We also recompensed the eldest grandson, Chuncao, 30 silver dollars. The money was turned over to our brother Dongfu, who accepted it to start a new business. All the Cha-Tai store's debts and merchandise were turned over to the three of us to manage. A document was drawn up that I hold as proof. At the time our brother Dongfu himself opened the Cha-Yuan store to do business. In TZ 11 (1872), older brother died. This evil nephew, Chuncao, took the business's money and spent it all. By TZ 13 (1874), this evil nephew, Chuncao, had incited our older sister-in-law to go to the battalion commander and falsely accuse us. At the time, mediators and lineage relatives came forward to exhort us to pay 5[5]0 silver dollars as provision for her support (*yangshan*). Once again we drew up supporting documents. At present there are mediators that can serve as witnesses. Unexpectedly, this evil nephew, Chuncao, with greed in his heart made extortionate demands on us several times with no success. Instead, I am being accused falsely by him. Today I have been questioned and request a just decision.

ZHOU GUOXIANG VIZ. MANAGER ZHOU LIANG: My testimony is the same as Zhou Qichang's.

COURT DIRECTIVE (*tangyu*): Zhou Qichang submitted to the court one contract and also one acceptance document (*lishishou*) that had been signed by the mediators. Naturally this is reliable proof. In addition Mrs. Zhou née Xu and Chuncao also acknowledged that there was this written proof. As for admitting the validity of the documents, she claims the acceptance agreement is not this document that was submitted. Concerning the mediators, except for Wei Duliu, who has died, immediately bring Chen Qianfu, Guo Tiansi, and Zhou Pankai to court for a second hearing. So directed. Zhou Qichang and the others are all to be turned over to the custody of runners.

[GX 9/]2/25 (2 April 1883)
[testimony ends]

The inquisitorial nature of court proceedings afforded the subprefect or magistrate wide discretionary powers in handling the final stage of legal proceedings when civil suits were decided or criminal guilt determined. A preliminary hearing or interrogation as a preparatory stage to a formal trial was not a procedural requirement under the traditional legal order. Once the principals and witnesses in a case had been brought before the court, their depositions taken, and physical evidence gathered, judgment could be passed immediately. Quite often, as in the case of Mrs. Zhou's suit, interrogation would reveal the need for summoning further witnesses to be heard at subsequent court sessions. An initial hearing might also, of course, reveal that additional physical evidence was needed to reach a decision. There was nothing, however, to prevent any case from being accepted, heard, and concluded in the space of a single sitting provided the magistrate (and his advisers) was satisfied that there was a sufficiency of testimony and evidence. The court's decision was communicated in the form of a "court edict" (*tangyu*), or "court directive," as we shall translate the term. Almost every transcript of court testimony ends with a court directive. It follows, therefore, that while final judgment and sentencing by the yamen administrator were given in the form of a court directive, not every court directive signaled a final decision and sentence. Most directives were simply orders that the case being heard be continued until those before the court could be questioned again, at-large suspects could be captured, further witnesses could be summoned, or additional evidence could, if possible, be gathered.

If the court could not reach a decision at the first hearing, principals and witnesses might be detained at the yamen to await further court sessions, or they might be released to be called to court at a later date. If we were to judge solely by codified law, which did not sanction imprisonment as a legal punishment, we might suppose that litigants or suspects in detention signified that a case had not yet been concluded. Such a presumption would be unwarranted, as we shall see later in this chapter.

We may infer from these observations, first, that in a traditional Chinese local court there was no sharply defined procedural sequence. A second and related point is that we must not suppose that codified law rigidly defined the outer limits of procedure. Instead, the system tolerated a range of approaches and practices depending on local conditions and the preferences of the yamen administrator in question. With these cautionary precepts in mind, we can turn to a consideration of the interaction between Dan-Xin area litigants and the yamen court, beginning with questioning of witnesses.

Interrogation

When court was in session in Xinzhu, magistrate, yamen personnel, and the parties involved may have been arrayed much like the schematic in Figure 9.1.[2] Unfortunately, the Dan-Xin case records do nothing to confirm this picture. The hearing record translated above is entirely representative. Of all the yamen personnel indicated in the figure, only the case clerk and runner or runners handling the case were consistently noted on the hearing records. The case clerk, who usually handled the paperwork of a given case until it was concluded, was present in order to provide rec-

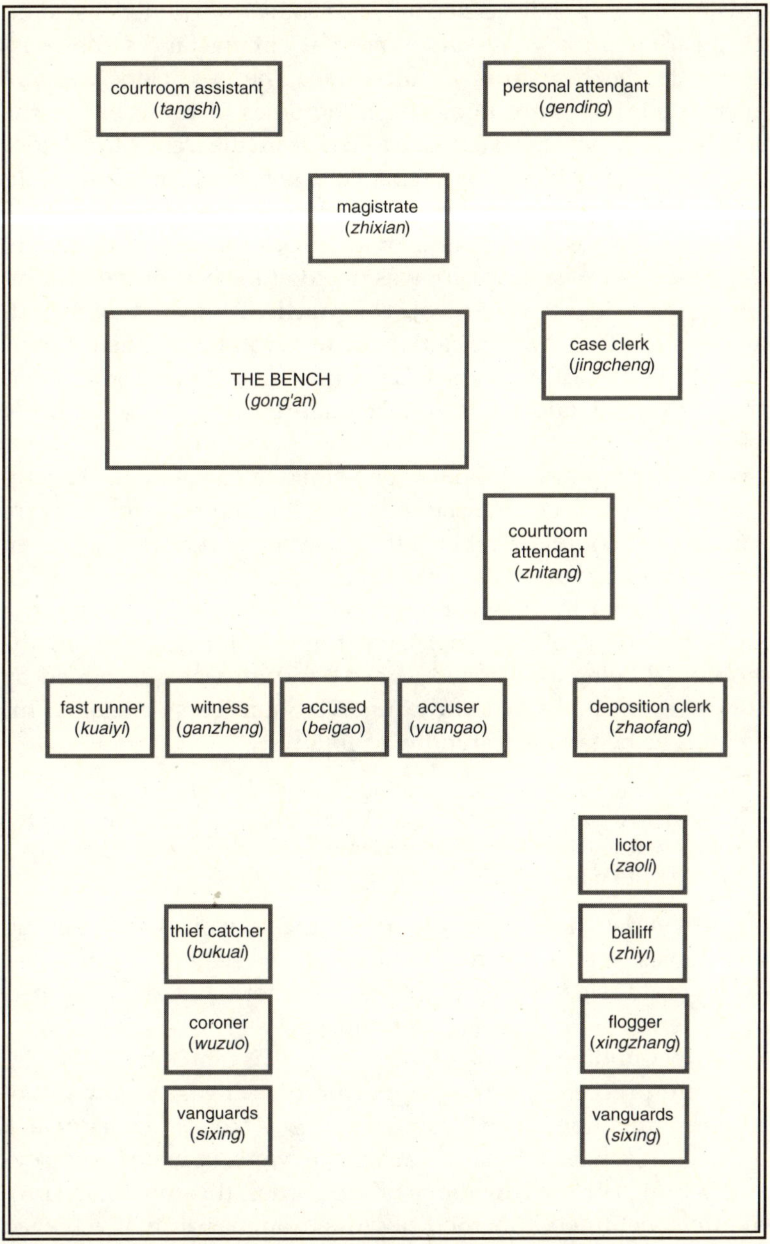

FIGURE 9.1. Arrangement of Courtroom Personnel.

ords from the case file as needed. The runner or runners listed on the hearing form were under normal circumstances those assigned to the case from its inception. The case clerk was not responsible for transcribing the testimonies of those before the bench. This task was assigned to a clerk from the Deposition Office (*tangzhaofang*), which was responsible for recording both testimony and any court order or decision (*tangyu*) that might be issued.[3] On occasion the name of the deposition clerk, referred to as the duty copyist (*zhishan*), was noted at the end of the hearing record [22415:89; 22609:85, 90]. The practice of invariably recording the names of the case clerk and runner indicates their importance to a given case. The clerk kept track of all paperwork generated by the litigation. The runner might himself be called on to testify.

The hearing records are a one-sided conversation. The responses have been transcribed, but the interrogatories were passed over completely. Since the answers are known, however, there is seldom any difficulty in reconstructing the questions. In most instances the magistrate began the hearing by eliciting a limited amount of personal background information from the individual being questioned. When Xu Awu was questioned by Subprefect Zhang Qixuan during Wu-Shun-Ji's suit against his tenants, he began his testimony as follows:

> Xu Awu; age 26 *sui*. I am a Zhenping county registrant. I was born in Taiwan. My parents are deceased. I am the fifth of eight brothers. I have a wife and children. I live in Daqiqian, Sanhu village. I farm my own land to make a living [22202:5].

Degree holders normally were spared the necessity of identifying themselves so elaborately. A woman, as we see in the translated example at the beginning of this chapter, normally identified herself in terms of her husband and oldest son.

The fact-finding process of the hearing was inquisitorial. Parties in a court proceeding had no opportunity to engage in any sort of cross-examination, since the magistrate was the sole finder of fact. It has been suggested that because there were, in most cases, several hearings or interrogations of the parties, this multistage procedure constituted a method of cross-examination that achieved somewhat the same effect as the adversarial process of the Anglo-

Saxon legal tradition.[4] Such an analogy can be drawn with much more assurance if we remember that in reality the processes of hearing a case and submissions by petitioners proceeded synchronously. The opportunity (and necessity) of presenting numerous prompting petitions following the initial complaint or counterplaint allowed parties on either side of a case to object to falsifications, errors, or distorted logic in both the written submissions and the testimony of their opponents.

An illustration of this process may be found in the armed robbery case (summarized in Chapter 3) brought before the Xinzhu court in 1882. When the testimony [33319:19] of a captured suspect, Zhan Ajian, implicated Chen Desheng in the crime, Desheng's father, Chen Bolai, quickly responded with a counterplaint and petition [33319:28, 43] to the court. Chen Bolai protested that his son had been accused because he had helped capture Zhan and because Bolai, in his role as a minor village official, had helped collect subscriptions to pay villagers to take the captive to the yamen. Subsequently in court testimony [33319: 47], one of the robbery victims, Lan Huagun, claimed a minor village functionary such as Chen Bolai could have had no responsibility for raising funds. Therefore, Lan implied, Chen was lying, and his son, Desheng, probably was involved in the robbery. Following this attack on his credibility, Chen Bolai took advantage of his own interrogation [33319:60] to explain more fully his position in the village and to demonstrate why, in those particular circumstances, he would have been (and was) called upon to collect money. Thus we see that there was at least some limited opportunity in the Chinese system to allow truth to emerge by subjecting the assertions of one party to challenge from the opposition.

Local court officials could accept or reject all or part of the written and oral testimony of those before the bench. Judges had wide discretionary powers in determining the truth in a case. This wide-ranging inquisitorial power could, as the Chinese legislators themselves were well aware, easily lead to abuses. Perhaps the practice of judicial torture (discussed below) was the most dangerous in this regard. Still, with some exceptions, the impression gained from the cases is that magistrates hearing cases normally reached their conclusions using methods and techniques not foreign or repugnant to us today.

After a case had been accepted for adjudication, the parties were questioned, often during several different court sessions. When doubtful testimony was given, each party was questioned while confronted by the other (*zhixun* or *zhishen*) in the hopes that prevarication could be exposed or contradiction resolved. The practice of confrontation presumably also was designed to lessen the incidence of false accusation by obliging the accuser to face the person he had implicated. So, for example, when, in the third lunar month of GX 8 (1882), Fan Ahai was brought before the court on suspicion of armed robbery, he testified [33319:21] by explaining the accusation against him with what appeared to the magistrate as an obvious falsehood. The magistrate ordered Fan to be again questioned once the victim of the crime, his original accuser, could be summoned to court to confront Fan during interrogation. Even more than the testimony of the principals in a given case, eyewitness testimony and real or physical evidence were given the heaviest weight.

Documentary proofs were demanded when the court heard disputes involving land, property, or indebtedness.[5] Contracts, deeds, and other documents offered in evidence were carefully inspected for signs of forgery or alteration of dates. Early in GX 12 (1886), villagers involved in a dispute with the Jin-Liu-He partnership submitted a prompting petition [22514:110] pressing their case.[6] The magistrate's endorsement caustically dismissed a reclamation deed they had previously turned over in evidence as a forgery. Although the document was supposedly over a century old, "the inking is fresh and clear; the seal has all its lines. It is a fake. There is no doubt."

In short, a magistrate ideally was skeptical of or at least reserved judgment on all evidence and testimony until the weight of one or both was sufficient for him to reach a decision confidently. Testimony or written submissions were evaluated on their internal consistency and on their agreement with other evidence available.

When a disputed document's authenticity could not be established by visual inspection, witnesses whose testimony could resolve the issue were summoned. During the course of Mrs. Zhou's unsuccessful lawsuit, two documents were introduced by the defendant, her brother-in-law Zhou Wuniang.[7] Mrs. Zhou agreed that documents had been drawn up but denied that one of the papers submitted was genuine [22609:18]. The magistrate noted that three of the four mediators who had negotiated the original settlement and then signed as witnesses to the agreements were still alive and ordered them summoned to settle the question. To this point, all the court's procedures seem rational, nonprejudicial, and capable of producing an authentic image of the facts of the case in the mind of any magistrate who was interested in achieving this end.

These methodologies were, however, used in conjunction with other techniques that may have tended to introduce more uncertainty into the results. What Conner terms "demeanor evidence," that is, the movements, posture, and facial expression of those questioned in court, were keenly observed by the subprefect or magistrate and given equal weight with other types of evidence.[8] On GX 8/6/28 (11 August 1882), Xu Xizhi encountered a tangle of contradictions and evasions when interrogating [33319:69] suspects in the armed robbery case summarized in Chapter 3. The reaction of one suspect, Fan Ahai, aroused Xu's suspicion. Xu in his court directive remarked, "Why [when accused of robbery] did Fan hang his head and not speak?" Nine months later, Magistrate Xu ordered a hearing convened at which he interrogated [22609:23] Mrs. Zhou, her son Chuncao, and others involved in the litigation she had initiated. Xu listened to the testimony of some of the former mediators and examined documentary evidence. Both inclined the magistrate to believe that Mrs. Zhou's case was groundless. His opinion was solidified when, faced with such damaging evidence, Mrs. Zhou and Zhou Chuncao "bowed their heads and had no reply."

Mrs. Zhou and her son were residents of the county seat and, given this proximity to the yamen, may well have been spectators at other hearings. If that had been the case, they might have been less in awe of the court or less nervous and apprehensive before the bench. In their case, perhaps such demeanor evidence had some validity. The same can hardly be said in the case of a suspect such as Fan Ahai, who came from a farm village and probably saw the courtroom for the first time while kneeling before the bench flanked by the threatening presence of runners bearing instruments of punishment. Did Fan avert his eyes because of guilt or simply out of fear? Although there is no evidence that cases were ever decided solely on the basis of "demeanor evidence," such evidence did play a role in court findings. Hence our earlier expressed confidence in the overall rationality of traditional Chinese trial methods must be tempered to some degree, especially when we turn to certain coercive methods of extracting testimony allowed under the imperial legal system.

Judicial Torture

The presence in the courtroom of a flogger (*xingzhang*), a runner holding instruments of punishment, inevitably leads to the one feature of the traditional legal system most remarked upon (and criticized) by foreign observers. Through the Dan-Xin cases we can catch glimpses of one of the most physically trying aspects of ordinary persons' involvement in the legal system. The ability of local courts to use judicial torture to obtain confessions from suspects and the statutory authorizations and constraints placed on the court employing such measures have been discussed by earlier writers.[9] As these authorities have pointed out, in nearly all cases, a suspect could not be convicted and sentenced unless he confessed to the crime. In light of this requirement, judicial torture was perceived to be a necessary adjudicatory technique.

What concerns us here is the light that the case materials shed on this practice. Records of actual cases seem to contain few references to judicial torture. Certainly in the five cases that we have analyzed in detail there are only one or two unambiguous references to judicial torture. In XF 2 (1852), for example, Xu Awu, who was thought to be able to lead the court to a tenant farmer who had refused to pay rent to Wu-Shun-Ji, was in detention in Zhuqian.[10] In an attempt to force him to help place the nonpaying tenant into the court's hands, the subprefect ordered [22202:12] Xu brought before the bench and slapped across the face (*zhangze*).

Although it certainly occurred, judicial torture was such an ordinary, unremarkable feature of court hearings that it was mentioned only in passing if at all. More fruitful material may be found if we turn to a magistrate's attempts to explain to his superiors certain criminal cases long on the books but as yet unsolved. It becomes evident both that Xinzhu magistrates resorted to the practice when faced with a recalcitrant suspect and that occasionally even torture could not produce a confession.[11]

In GX 9 (1883), Deng Xichuan was arrested after being accused of being part of a gang that burglarized a store. Deng, who alone among the suspects had been apprehended, was interrogated by Zhou Zhikan, the magistrate at the time, and confessed to taking part in the crime. His testimony was recorded and reported to higher authorities for review, but before adjudication was complete, Magistrate Zhou was transferred. Subsequently, Xu Xizhi, a successor to Zhou, convened a hearing at which Deng suddenly retracted his previous testimony, thus effectively preventing a conviction in the absence of corroborating evidence. Deng was interrogated several times during Xu's tenure but refused to admit guilt.[12] This history was recounted by Magistrate Peng Dasun in a report [31808:2, 3] to his prefect on prisoners currently held in Xinzhu. Peng then recounted his own efforts.

> After I assumed my office, I also brought [Deng] again before the bench. I employed judicial torture (*aoshen*), repeatedly administering severe punishment. This notwithstanding, however, once the suspect had recanted, he utterly refused to acknowledge guilt. It was as if an iron door had closed.

Female prisoners were not spared. In GX 5 (1879), Mrs. Li née Wang was accused of plotting with her lover to kill her husband. Soon after she and her paramour, Chen Ting, were arrested, Chen died of illness in the Xinzhu jail. Mrs. Li admitted to engaging in illicit sexual relations with Chen but steadfastly denied any knowledge of or participation in the killing of her husband. After taking office and reviewing the case, Magistrate Peng was outraged that the woman maintained her innocence of the murder charge.

> In my humble opinion the adulteress is a criminal guilty of the premeditated murder of her husband. Her crime is great; her evil extreme. How could I accept her lying testimony that would delay her execution? She has undergone days and nights of judicial torture. This notwithstanding, however, the adulteress has endured all punishments and will not concede [guilt].

On occasion Magistrate Peng was convinced that a prisoner's professions of innocence even under torture or the threat of it were not criminal obduracy. Cai Kun was a cashiered yamen runner accused by Liu Fu of accepting bribes and extortion. During hearings before previous magistrates, Cai insisted the charges were false and stemmed from a dispute between the two parties. Cai's denial was buttressed when Liu afterward failed to appear in court for a hearing. After taking office, Peng interrogated Cai several times, but he would not admit guilt.[13] Therefore, the magistrate attempted "to intimidate by bambooing" (*jia yi xinghe*), but Cai merely "cried out against the injustice done to him" (*jikou huyuan*). The ex-runner's persistence coupled with the suspicious failure of Liu to follow up his charges convinced the magistrate that Cai could safely be released under bond until his accuser could be brought to court for a hearing.

All the cited instances of judicial torture in Peng's report occurred during criminal rather than civil cases. This evidence supports Brockman's conclusion that torture was apparently not used in civil suits.[14] It would be going too far, however, to conclude that litigants in civil cases needed to have no fear at all of severe handling. As already shown above, Xu Awu was subjected to judicial torture, albeit in a mild form, in a civil case. But this is not the only instance that can be cited even in just the three civil cases summarized in Chapters 4–6. In early 1884, Magistrate Zhu Chenglie became exasperated as Mrs. Zhou and her son Chuncao continued to press their lawsuit even after they had accepted an earlier compromise settlement.[15] The magistrate was especially upset when Chuncao refused to reveal the name of the litigation specialist who had obviously assisted him in drawing up a prefectural appeal. After hearing testimony [22609:52] from several of the parties involved, Zhu's court directive [22609:51] concluded that some litigious rascal had incited Mrs. Zhou to reopen the case. Zhu decided to "beat him [Chuncao] with the light stick (*chize*) as a warning. After detention, I will order him to testify, giving the pettifogger's name. Then I will approve his release."

Although the beating Magistrate Zhu mentioned is the first or least severe of the five officially sanctioned punishments to which convicted criminals could be sentenced, and none of the ordinary terms indicating judicial torture are used, it is difficult to make any real distinction between the procedure employed to loosen Zhou Chuncao's tongue and the beatings administered to Deng Xichuan, Mrs. Li née Wang, or Cai Kun. It is clear that at that point in the case Chuncao would have escaped further legal sanctions were he to have revealed the identity of the pettifogger. It seems that even though employing the legal specialist was unlawful, the court was not interested in punishing Chuncao as long as he supplied the desired information. Just as judicial torture was intended to force confession in criminal cases, so was a beating with the light stick designed to force a confession not of guilt but of guilty information.

Subprefects and magistrates were, after all, under pressure from their superiors above, who evaluated their performance, and from complainants below to bring cases to satisfactory conclusion. Law courts in nearly every society draw on several kinds and sources of authority, one of the most prominent being the ability to exploit the force and coercion available through state power. Judicial torture as a feature of an otherwise enlightened legal tradition is easier to comprehend given the legal sanction granted of a certain degree of coercive interrogation coupled with the pressures on local judicial authorities to clear their case loads. To handle in some conclusive way the complaints and charges laid before the court was incumbent on officials who hoped to gain promotion or at least to avoid demotion. As we shall see, several alternative methods of disposing of a case were available.

FINAL DISPOSITION

Mediation or Adjudication; Guilt or Innocence

The people of Danshui and Xinzhu brought their disputes to court seeking relief, usually because other methods of conflict resolution had failed. Subprefects and magistrates were constrained to effect a settlement in civil actions and determine guilt and innocence in criminal cases. In China, as everywhere, out-of-court settlements in civil litigation were perceived to be socially preferable to lawsuits. There was a long history stretching back even into the pre-imperial period of attempts to institutionalize mediation.[16] The Dan-Xin cases provide an insight into the relationship between the legal system and more informal dispute resolution processes.

Mediation. As already suggested in earlier chapters, mediation was the alternative preferred by Danshui and Xinzhu yamen administrators in all noncriminal litigation. Such cases might not be accepted for adjudication if the parties did not demonstrate that they had attempted to settle their disputes through conciliation. A characteristic example is the case of Mrs. Zhou née Xu versus her brothers-in-law. Mrs. Zhou's initial petition [22609:1] was rejected partly because she had not indicated whether she had requested lineage relatives to mediate. Sometimes, after a case was accepted by the court, it was discovered that mediators had previously brought the disputants to an agreement, which subsequently was rejected by one of the parties. The aforementioned case of Mrs. Zhou née Xu again serves to illustrate this phenomenon. Under the circumstances, the court, after hearing testimony from the original mediators, decided that the settlement that had already been negotiated was authoritative and should be enforced, albeit with a small additional award to Mrs. Zhou.

Even in cases where previous mediation had failed or had seemed impossible, magistrates often directed the parties to solicit mediation from relatives or local notables. In the dispute over the boundary between a tea plot and some adjoining pasture land discussed in Chapter 5, the parties were directed to accept the settlement worked out by two locally prominent men who also owned rights to land in the same area. If private mediation was for some reason impractical, the magistrate himself or his representatives might play the role of mediator. In an example [23418] cited earlier, a widow, Mrs. Zheng née Zhuang, sued the manager of a revolving loan society for the return of money she had invested. The magistrate eventually ordered runners to mediate the dispute.

Once the local yamen accepted a case for handling, even a subsequent privately mediated settlement became part of the public record, as it were, thus receiving formal recognition from both parties and legal ratification from the court. Written instruments called "willingness bonds" (*ganjie zhuang*) were drawn up and signed by all parties to an agreement. These bonds or copies of them were placed in the case file and preserved in the yamen archives. Apposite examples from the boundary dispute case just cited are two "willingness bonds to end litigation" (*hexiganjie zhuang*) [22514:158, 159] in which the Jin-Liu-He tea land partnership and villagers opposing it in the lawsuit agreed that at the urging of mediators they would end litigation.

In civil cases the local court preferred mediation outside the legal system or mediation ratified by the system because very often these cases were intrafamily squabbles. Disputes over marriage, the family, and commonly owned lineage property arose constantly. Not only was it more appropriate, more seemly in a sense, for disputing relatives to appeal to another member of the family to mediate the issue, but also such a mediator could more easily understand the basis and ramifications of a dispute and would be more likely to be allowed to ascertain the actual facts of the case than would an outsider, even if the latter were the local magistrate. In such cases it was often difficult to make a clear-cut determination of right and wrong. When local courts decided cases by fiat, it was easy to offend both parties, thus diverting the animus of both toward the government. It is not surprising that time and again Danshui subprefects and Xinzhu magistrates handed down court directives urging litigants to ask a mediator to work out a settlement.

As the cases consistently demonstrate, however, mediation often failed. Many of the Dan-Xin cases resulted from the complex, multitiered system of land rights and especially disputes over rent between large-rent landlords (*dazuhu*) and their tenants, small-rent holders (*xiaozuhu*). In general terms, over the course of the nineteenth century small-rent holders gradually were able to wrest control of the land from the original or primary land-right holders, the large-rent landlords. Because mediation tended to reinforce the existing power structure,[17] it ran directly counter to the interests of small-rent holders, whose economic power was growing at the same time that of large-rent landlords was declining. It is probably safe to conclude that whatever the dispute, the tendency of ostensibly impartial mediation to enforce the status quo caused the failure of most attempts at compromise.

Guilt or Innocence. Complaints involving criminal offenses could not, by definition, be privately mediated. In such cases all of the responsibility for hearing, judgment, and sentence rested with the court. Normally, the majority of those persons implicated or alleged to have been somehow mixed up in the case were found to have been innocent or not directly involved in the incident being adjudicated at all. Such persons, if being detained in one of the yamen jails, were allowed to return to their homes after release. First, however, all these legally vindicated suspects were required to enter into bonds guaranteeing their good behavior even if the court had found them to have been falsely or accidentally implicated.

Many instances of this process might be cited. In 1884, for example, Fan Ahai, a carpenter who had been arrested two years earlier on suspicion of armed robbery, was finally cleared of the charge on the basis of an alibi provided by Tian Songlai. Both Fan and Tian were required to enter into bonds. Tian's document [33319:132] was termed a "receipt bond" (*ling zhuang*). In this bond, Tian agreed, in effect, to receive or accept custody of Fan in the sense of guaranteeing responsibility for his good behavior. Fan in turn signed a "precise guarantee" (*qiejie zhuang*) [33319:133] affirming his innocence and agreeing not to do any wrong later. Both bonds noted that if Fan subsequently violated his bond by committing a crime, Tian would also be called to account.

Sentencing

When a suspect did credibly confess to guilt in a criminal case, the local yamen administrator was required to pass a provisional sentence. This sentence was then reported to higher judicial levels in the form of a recommendation for final disposition of the case.[18] The two criminal cases summarized in Chapters 3 and 5 as well as the many other such cases in the Dan-Xin archives contain many "court directives" (*tangyu*), where we might hope or even expect to find definitive judgments and proposed sentences. Somewhat surprisingly, this is seldom the case. Instead, for a clear exposition of the court's findings and recommendations we must examine the report made to his superiors by the subprefect or magistrate. Unfortunately, these reports (*xiang*) are not consistently found in the case files.

In the armed robbery case just cited, we know from a record of testimony [33319:144] and a draft court directive [33319:143] that after the chief suspect, Zhan Ajian, admitted guilt, Magistrate Fang Zuyin intended to report to his superiors suggesting that Zhan merely be locked in fetters and put on public display to inculcate respect for the law among onlookers. The magistrate's stated rationale was that, even though the criminal should be harshly sentenced to the maximum allowed by law, Zhan had already been jailed for several years, understood his mistake, and was willing to reform. Unhappily for historians, Fang never made a report to his superiors on the case, or else the report was not included in the file. Consequently, we never learn, for example, the precedent or legal basis that Fang relied on in arriving at this proposed handling of the confessed criminal.

Luckily, some case file records do contain drafts of Xinzhu reports that elucidate in some detail the findings and proposed sentence in a given case and also explicate the reasoning behind the recommendations. One such report on a case in which Chen Zhenxiang had been charged with kidnapping (see Chapter 5) was addressed to Taibei Prefect Lei Qida and also the three highest Taiwan provincial officials, Governor Liu Mingchuan, Financial Commissioner Shen Xirong, and Judicial Commissioner Tang Jingsong. As in the previous example, the magistrate trying the case and issuing the GX 15/4/12 (11 May 1889) report [32611:79] was Fang Zuyin.

As we have seen, late the previous year, Chen had been arrested and questioned in court but had denied complicity in the kidnapping. Magistrate Fang, therefore, was prevented from sentencing Chen for that particular crime. Fang, however, was convinced of Chen's guilt in another aspect of the case. The incident was sensitive because it had stirred up unrest among aborigines in the southern part of the county. Chen, naturally enough, had denied any responsibility for inciting the tribe. However, as Fang explained in his report, he was convinced that that part of Chen's testimony was false. Chen earlier had gained a reputation as a lawless character and one who had incited aborigines to cause trouble. As Fang had discovered during the course of a personal investigation, since Chen's arrest, the aborigine settlements in the area had been law abiding and peaceful. In Fang's own words:

> On visiting I heard that it was because of his provocation that in the past that settlement's aborigines had gone out and caused trouble and harm to the people. At present, aborigines and the people live peacefully enjoying their occupations. This can be termed a clear proof. At this juncture when we want to soothe the aborigines and open settlement of land, why tolerate rascals who incite harm and bring about endless enmity between aborigines and the people? Naturally we should punish him most se-

verely to prevent further imitation in doing evil. However, that settler's [Chen's] evil nature is set. If we sentence him to the cangue, a beating, and then release, he certainly will hide in an aborigine settlement, and the old knowledge will again sprout to do harm that will really not be inconsequential. Is it possible or not, by analogy to the substatute on locking up the insane, for me to impeach and deprive him of his military title and permanently lock him up? [If so,] I would then wait until duties connected with aborigine settlements and land reclamation have all been completely taken care of, examine the circumstances, and thereupon again report to superiors requesting his release.

The magistrate's problem, as he saw it, was twofold. Chen could not be sentenced for the more serious kidnapping offense because he refused to confess. He could, once deprived of his military rank and honors, be summarily punished as a troublemaker with a beating and a term of wearing the cangue. If this course was chosen, Chen would have to be released and would soon resume his old bad habits. Casting about for a better solution, Fang or his legal adviser hit upon a provision in the Qing Code that allowed long-term confinement for the mentally incompetent.[19] Fang thus was able to apply the very common adjudicatory technique of sentencing for an offense not specifically mentioned in the Code by analogy to a legal provision dealing with a different offense.[20]

As it turned out, Fang was being too creative. He later received a response from the governor [32611:91] relayed through the judicial commissioner and the prefect informing him that there was no need to sentence by analogy. He was merely to impeach and deprive Chen of his rank and then imprison him. The question of the legal basis for this sentence was not addressed as far as the record shows. Nevertheless, it is important to take note of the local magistrate in his role as judge and jury as he labored to stretch a rather inelastic legal code to adjust to particular circumstances. The local bureaucracy felt itself constrained, even under the pressures of a large-scale campaign to pacify the aborigines and extend Han settlement, to work within the boundaries of the legal system.

Execution of Sentence

A magistrate in a court such as Xinzhu at the lowest level of the judicial hierarchy could, relying on his own authority, hand down and execute only sentences for minor misbehavior or infractions for which the statutory punishment was beating with the light (*chi*) or heavy stick (*zhang*).[21] Several instances of one or the other punishment appear in the case records.[22] Disputes over the nature of land sales seemed often to end in beating with the light or heavy stick for the losing party. An example is found in a case [23103] from GX 7–8 (1881–82). Jiang Tengjiao complained to Magistrate Xu that after he had bought a piece of land from Zhang Guo under terms of unconditional sale, Zhang later began to demand the right to redeem it. Zhang argued that the transaction was conditional sale (*dianmai*) and that he was legally entitled to reclaim the land after paying Jiang redemption money. The magistrate upheld Jiang's complaint and ordered Zhang beaten with the heavy stick.

Such references from the Dan-Xin cases incline us to believe that suspects and recalcitrant witnesses often suffered beating in Chinese law courts.[23] When beating as a method of juridical inquisition was such a routine occurrence, beating as a formal sentence and punishment for minor crimes must have been viewed by the court if not by the afflicted prisoner as lenient treatment.

When hearing cases of more serious crimes that would call for sentences of penal servitude, exile, or death, primary level courts could only suggest provisional sentences to higher judicial authorities, who reviewed such cases and pronounced final sentence. There is little to be learned from the Dan-Xin materials once prefectural and provincial judicial officials became responsible for final handling of a case.[24] Records of deliberations at these higher level courts were seldom included in the local yamen case files. What can be gleaned from the cases is the exceptional frequency with which the yamen resorted to long-term imprisonment for suspects and convicted criminals alike. This form of punishment seems unremarkable to us but was not legally sanctioned in imperial China.

Detention and Imprisonment

Of course short-term, temporary detention of suspects and even witnesses while awaiting trial was not forbidden. Confinement of that type, however, was meant to be for a period of only three months at the maximum, by which time local courts were constrained to have completed handling of even the most complicated and serious type of case, in which death sentences might be passed. Less serious criminal cases together with civil litigation, which naturally made up the majority of the issues before any court, were to be handled within one or two months.[25] Thus, according to law, suspects could be held in local yamen jails only three months at the most before their cases were settled or they were transferred to a higher level court for further handling. As we shall discover, in the Danshui/Xinzhu yamen, this implicit restriction was routinely ignored.

Before elaborating on long-term imprisonment, it will be useful to consider the Dan-Xin prison facilities in which those involved in legal actions might have found themselves incarcerated. By the nineteenth century, several enclosures of varying security designed to house different types of criminals or suspects had been established within the Danshui and Xinzhu yamen compound. In addition to three actual jails, the offices or rooms assigned to different runner sections often served as places of detention for suspects awaiting a hearing and especially litigants involved in civil suits. Little is known about the particulars of size, number of cells, or layout of these lockups, but some description has survived.[26]

By 1756, ten years after the city's founding, three separate jails or prison complexes had been built in the subprefectural yamen in Zhuqian. The least intimidating of the specialized houses of correction in the yamen was the Runner's Jail (*zongjia guan*), also known as the Outer Compartment (*waishi*). The Outer Compartment seems to have been a part of or an annex to the yamen runner section offices. There is some indication that there was more than one *waishi*.[27] Prisoners convicted of the least serious crimes (for example, burglary) were detained in the Outer Compartment under the supervision of runners. Convicts sentenced to the cangue (*jia*) could be jailed there for several months. Others sentenced to confinement in chains (*suodun*) could be held there for up to five years.

Those accused or convicted of slightly more serious crimes (assault, accessory to rape, or banditry) were placed in the "detention center" (*yaguan*). The detention center was also called the Main Gate Office (*toumenguan*) by reason of its location near the yamen's principal entrance. The inscription above its entrance, "The Reformatory" (*congshansuo*), announced its function in large characters.

The main prison (*jianyu*), located in the yamen's northwest quadrant, housed suspects or convicts awaiting execution of sentence for the most serious crimes (murder, robbery, piracy).[28] The main prison was also known as the Tiger Head Prison (*hutoujian*), for above the gate portal a tiger's head had been painted. Near the tiger's head the words "laggard repentance" (*fan hui chi*) had been written in a horizontal inscription.

Detainees with the higher status conferred by an examination system degree, whether earned or purchased, seem to have been held under somewhat better conditions than ordinary commoner prisoners. Gan Nanwang, a *jiansheng* detained during the armed robbery case, was held in the Tea Department Office (*Chafang guan*).[29] The term "office" (*guan*) in this context seems to have been a euphemism, since Gan's place of confinement was probably no more than one of the ordinary rooms assigned to the Tea Department. Another degree holder, the aborigine *shengyuan* Liao Qionglin, who had been arrested for his involvement in litigation between Jin-Liu-He and the villagers of rural Xinpu, was first detained in the Tax Department (*liangfang*), later moved to the Tea Department, and finally transferred into the custody of the county director of schools.[30]

The number of convicts, detained suspects or witnesses, and other jailed prisoners varied widely. According to an 1885 report [31808:3], there were at that time five prisoners (*jianfan*) charged with crimes ranging from accepting bribes (the accused had been a runner) to burglary, armed robbery, and murder. There were two persons guilty of homicide, one a woman who had murdered her husband. One prisoner was described as a detainee (*yafan*), even though on the basis of his alleged crime, homicide, it would seem he should have properly been categorized as a serious criminal to be incarcerated in the main or Tiger Head Prison.[31] He had been held since 1882. In addition to these six prisoners, two men were being held to wait for a hearing.

Three years later, if Magistrate Fang Zuyin did not exaggerate in a statement of account or memorandum (*qingzhe*) [11407:2] of 8 March 1888 submitted to the prefect, there were 12 prisoners (*qiufan*),[32] 40 detainees, and 15 inmates in fetters (*dunfan*) in the runners' outer compartment jail. The Xinzhu prisoner population had grown from 8 to 67 in the space of three years. This seems an extraordinary increase in the prison population for Xinzhu. Perhaps the outbreak of an armed affray had temporarily swollen the number of those incarcerated. The large number of detainees seems to indicate that some sort of uprising or mob violence had erupted.[33]

Prior to the early nineteenth century, imprisonment was not a recognized punishment. When prisoners were held, it was merely a matter of holding suspects during trial until acquittal or conviction. Convicted criminals sentenced to one of the statutory punishments were, of course, held in prison until execution of sentence could be carried out. In the latter decades of the century, imprisonment was becoming in at least some instances an accepted alternative punishment in cases of major crimes to which one of the statutory sentences applied.[34] In Xinzhu county, for example, Magistrate Peng Dasun's prisoner report cited earlier listed a murderer who had been imprisoned for 21 years (TZ 3 to GX 11, or 1864–85). The simple fact of such extended periods of incarceration may not be startling. Based on their study of appellate cases, Bodde and Morris note that "[w]rongdoers, of course, might be detained for considerable periods (sometimes years) in prison before final execution of sentence, but their sentence per se never included imprisonment."[35] This assertion notwithstanding, the Dan-Xin cases show that local magistrates could and did propose formal sentences to terms of imprisonment.

In the 1885 report [31808:3] already cited, Magistrate Peng Dasun's account of inmates in the Xinzhu jails cast some light on how a person convicted of a crime with a statutory punishment of penal servitude or more might instead be sentenced to long-term confinement in chains, a punishment that would seem to have had no formal, statutory basis. In 1864, Liu Ahai had mortally wounded Chen Alai by firing a bamboo mortar (*zhuchong*). Liu was arrested and admitted the act but claimed he had been incited to shoot the mortar by Huang Achang. Huang had fled and eluded capture, so Liu's story could not be confirmed. The Danshui subprefect provisionally sentenced him to life exile but also decreed that he was to be confined in jail to await confirmation of his testimony. Liu was confined for ten years with no progress in the case before another subprefect suggested that in view of the prisoner's long incarceration, his sentence be changed to confinement in chains for five years. No action was taken on his proposal, however, perhaps because of the confusion of the administrative reorganization that Taiwan began to experience in 1874–75. Liu continued to languish in what had become the Xinzhu county jail for another ten years before Peng's predecessor magistrate had resubmitted the 1874 proposal, but again without result. After reviewing this history, Peng explained that after the 1874 request for diminution of sentence had been refused or ignored, each succeeding magistrate had taken no action in the case because each considered that with the refusal, a precedent had been set (*ge yu chengli*).

Peng then made his own suggestion for bringing the case to a conclusion. Liu's sentence should be commuted to three years' confinement in chains followed by unconditional release. Peng justified his suggestion by noting that Liu should long ago have been transported into life exile. This sentence could not legally be passed without capturing Huang Achang, an exceedingly remote possibility after more than 20 years. Liu was then (1885) well over 60 *sui*. The longer he was held, the more likely he was to die under the harsh conditions of prison life. He would be over 70 by the time he had served the further three years stipulated in Peng's proposal and thus would be incapable of further evil actions.

Peng presented a somewhat analogous rationale in discussing the case of Deng Xichuan, a burglary suspect who had first confessed, then recanted. The magistrate suggested that the suspect be sentenced to five years' confinement in chains, after which release could be requested. In the meantime, yamen runners would continue to search for the prisoner's suspected confederates who, if captured, might offer testimony disproving Deng's plea of innocence. At the time of the magistrate's report, Deng had already been in custody for two years.

Thus it becomes clear that incarceration was a real sentencing option for magistrates. It appears to have been regarded as useful in circumstances where legal technicalities protected criminals whose guilt was evident from imposition of one of the statutory punishments. In both cases cited by Magistrate Peng, an obviously guilty (in the magistrate's eyes) prisoner who adamantly maintained his innocence could not be convicted because witnesses who could invalidate the denials of guilt could not be brought before the court.

Even in the absence of such a formal prison sentence, inmates, as Bodde and Morris tell us, might find themselves held for very long periods. The summarized core cases show several other examples of suspects or convicted criminals detained in jail for years at a time. Chen Zhenxiang, after his capture and conviction for kidnapping, was imprisoned in Xinzhu for more than six years (1888–95).[36] The original irregular nature of incarceration remained visible, however, in that confinement had no fixed term. As seen in the case summaries, very often long-term prisoners were released only when serious illness threatened to become terminal. Sometimes, as in the cases of Liu Dongjin and Pengxu Huoyan, prisoners expired of disease, never obtaining their parole.[37]

Conditions within the various jails were undoubtedly unhealthy and dangerous. "Prisons were filthy, dark, and sunless. Under conditions of hunger, cold, and overcrowding, disease flourished. In every [prison] many died of ill treatment. Wardens and guards, moreover, often made extortionate demands. If a prisoner did not acquiesce, he encountered bitter and poisonous treatment. In a house of darkness and silence he became a companion of ghosts."[38] The steamy heat of Taiwan's summers and the damp cold of its winters coupled with inadequate sanitation quite naturally made prisoners extremely susceptible to gastrointestinal and respiratory illness. The cases establish the above characterization of jails in Taiwan to be more than mere rhetoric. Virtually every long-term inmate encountered in the Dan-Xin case files eventually was reported to have contracted diarrhea, dysentery, cold, influenza, or other febrile disease.

Most often prisoners' illnesses were described in a phrase or two by their jailers. Entirely representative is a report [22202:80] submitted to the subprefect by Lin Yong, Head of the Six Runner Sections (*liuban touyi*). The report relayed information from a Reformatory guard that the day before, detainee Fan Ahai had "suddenly become ill with abdominal pain and was spitting up blood." Many prisoners were reported to have caught cold, influenza, or possibly typhoid fever (*ganmao, ganfeng, shanghan*) indicated by chills, fever, and stupor alternating with delirium. In 1886, Liao Qionglin became ill in detention. A runner report [22514:115] described his symptoms. "His exhalations are prolonged and inhalations short. At night he is insensible. His phlegm rises, and he becomes confused, talks wildly, or pants and coughs." There are also numerous reports of prisoners spitting or coughing up blood (*tuxue*). Illnesses marked by fever coupled with diarrhea (*louxie*) or dysentery (*liji*) seem to point to typhoid fever or cholera.[39] The sick soon lost their appetite or ability to take food and drink. Nearly all descriptions of prison maladies concluded with the phrase "he drinks and eats hardly at all" (*yinshi shaojin*).

As will be demonstrated below, the yamen was obliged to provide medical care for prisoners when necessary. In most instances, however, it was felt preferable to release prisoners to receive treatment outside the yamen, usually in the home. The usual procedure called for the detainee to be brought before the magistrate to be examined and questioned. During the course of the armed robbery case summarized earlier, Gan Nanwang was implicated and detained in the Tea Department offices pending a hearing. On 6 November 1882 (GX 8/9/26) Tea Department runners reported [33319:82] Gan was ill.

> Since the 20th day of the 5th month, when *jiansheng* Gan Lin viz. Gan Nanwang was sent to the Tea Department office for us to look after, he has been waiting to be interrogated with no problems. Unexpectedly last night the said criminal suddenly became ill with vomiting, diarrhea, and stomach pain. He can eat or drink little. It is very serious, and we really fear the unexpected. . . . Should he be sent to a doctor or brought up for examination?

A doctor was summoned to treat Gan, but with little success. On 22 November 1882 (GX 8/10/12), the runners again handed in a report [33319:87] saying that "a doctor was brought in for treatment but he was not completely cured. On the third of the tenth month he suddenly began to suffer a stomach illness worse than before. . . . Should a doctor be summoned or should he be brought up to be examined?" The following day Gan was brought before the bench, where the magistrate could see Gan's condition and hear his testimony: "I vomit and have diarrhea with severe stomach pains. I do not feel like drinking or eating and have dysentery. It is extremely difficult." With the runners' report and the distressed prisoner both before him, the magistrate determined that a different approach toward treating the illness was preferable.

Once a prisoner's illness was determined to be genuine, it was necessary for a guarantor to be found who was willing to enter into a bond that ensured the prisoner would return to the yamen once recovered. Normally the prisoner's family would recruit a socially respectable man linked to them by kinship or other ties for this purpose. For a degree holder such as Gan Nanwang it was an easy proposition. Within a few days of his testimony a stipendiary (*lingsheng*), an imperial tribute student (*gongsheng*), and another man identified only as a resident of the city had signed bonds [33319:94, 95] for Gan's release.

Prisoners of low status or with no family probably found it more difficult to locate a guarantor. By the fifth month of GX 12 (1886), Zhan Ajian had been held for four years on suspicion of robbery and had finally admitted guilt when he became so ill that he was given permission for release under bond. Zhan unfortunately had a reputation as a habitual criminal among people in his own village. Zhan's task was compounded when, as a runner report [33319:145] noted, his "wife née Xu returned to her parents and is no longer at home. So [after that] only his aged mother née Huang was there. Yesterday she died, rendering it hard to find a guarantor." The magistrate, realizing that Zhan would find it impossible to obtain a guarantor's bond without official intervention, directed [33319:147] that the local constable (*dibao*) be assigned responsibility for finding a guarantor so that Zhan could be released temporarily for medical treatment. The constable accomplished his commission with reasonable dispatch, and within eight days of the magistrate's order a local store owner had made himself accountable for Zhan's return once cured.

Zhan Ajian's release under bond for medical treatment is noteworthy beyond the unusual method utilized to find a guarantor. Zhan was a felon who (finally) had confessed to armed robbery. The magistrate had decided [33319:143] to recommend that Zhan be harshly sentenced to the maximum punishment allowed by law and while waiting for a higher court's pronouncement be locked up in fetters on public display (*sodun shizhong*). Permission was apparently given to so display the confessed felon, who was later referred to as a "criminal in fetters" (*dunfan*) in the bond

[33319:149] signed for his release. Zhan's case shows not only that the yamen was willing to forgo physical custody of detained suspects such as Gan Nanwang whose guilt or even involvement in a case was problematic but also that even persons provisionally convicted of some of the most serious crimes could be released, always providing they had responsible guarantors willing to enter into a written bond. Zhan Ajian was not the only beneficiary of this policy, which can be cited even in five core cases in this study. Chen Zhenxiang, a confessed kidnapper, was released because of illness once a Xinzhu store owner had agreed to accept culpability for any misdeeds the convict might commit once freed.

Even though they might be ill, releasing prisoners who could be dangerous criminals was not a course of action that greatly appealed to a local yamen administrator. Upon receiving a report of a sick inmate, the subprefect or magistrate normally ordered a physician (*yixue* or *yisheng*) brought in to determine the seriousness of the ailment and provide treatment if necessary. One Xinzhu medical specialist, Pan Yukun, seemed to serve almost as a prison doctor. He was summoned repeatedly over at least an eight-year period (1885–93) to treat prisoners. The earliest mention of Pan in the case files of the five cases summarized in the earlier chapters was Magistrate Peng Dasun's GX 11/5/1 (13 June 1885) order [33319:139] to a runner to summon the doctor to treat Liu Haixing for an influenza-like illness. Pan was called to the yamen as late as GX 19/5/23 (3 July 1893) to treat Chen Zhenxiang for influenza [32611:140]. In the eight years, Pan treated Liao Qionglin, Pengxu Huoyan, Lu Liu, Chen Aqi, Zhan Ajian, and undoubtedly several others.[40] Most of Pan Yukun's patients survived long enough to be released from yamen custody; several did not. Liao Qionglin and Pengxu Huoyan died of illness while in detention in spite of Pan's ministrations. The case of Liu Dongjin, another suspect who died while being held in jail, displays the inexorable course of disease despite the physician's ministrations.

Liu had been arrested after Lan Huagun and Zhan Ajing accused him of harboring men who had robbed their opium store. Sixteen months of detention had weakened the elderly Liu, who had testified [33319:9] at the time of his arrest that he was over 60 *sui*. In the seventh lunar month of GX 9 (1883), Liu became very ill. On the ninth of the month, Wang Zuo, head of the First Lictor section, relayed the information [33319:108] that the prisoner was sick again. Liu had earlier been reported ill and had, in fact, already received medical attention on two occasions in the few days before Wang Zuo's report revealed the prisoner's deteriorating condition. Liu's symptoms included chills and fever and loss of appetite. Wang Zuo hinted that Liu's condition was grave. He noted that "the unexpected is feared." Magistrate Zhou Zhikan endorsed the runner's report with instructions to have a doctor treat Liu. The physician is not identified.[41] At any rate, the medical specialist, although anonymous, did leave evidence of his expertise in the form of three diagnoses *cum* prescriptions [33319:109, 110, 111].

Each of these prescriptions / diagnoses is in the form of a list of eleven or twelve herbal materia medica in directed quantities followed by instructions for decocting a medicinal potion. The prescriptions are in each case followed by two or three lines characterizing the patient's condition and ordering administration of the decoction. The two earlier diagnoses illustrate the course of Liu's disorder.

> The illness of Liu Dongjin, the prisoner held in the first lictor's office, is serious. He has alternating sensations of chills and fever; his head aches, he is thirsty, and his mouth is hot inside. His four limbs are heavy, and he has no desire for drink or food. He is an elderly man whose configurational energy (*qi*) is depleted. Use codonopsis pilosula (*dangshen*) and perilla leaf (*suye*) drink, increased or reduced [as necessary], to treat him. [GX 9/] 7/3, examined and prescribed.[42]

The medicinal drink given to Liu consisted in large part of antifebrifuge agents. They produced little positive effect, however, and Liu was visited again three days later.

> The illness of Liu Dongjin, the prisoner in the first lictor's office, [is characterized by] internal complaints and serious external effects. Moreover, it is about to become a completely febrile ague with no chills. Its internal and external symptoms are all hot. The four limbs are heavy; bowel movement and urination are both blocked. He is thirsty but has no desire for drink or food. He is an elderly man whose *qi* is depleted. His symptoms are extremely serious and cannot be ignored. For the time being use a decoction of large hare's ear root, increased or reduced [as necessary] to treat him.
> [GX 9/] 7/6, midday, examined and prescribed.

As of the tenth of the month the prisoner's condition continued to show no improvement, and the runner Wang Zuo began to fear that Liu was in extremis. The doctor examined him again, but it seems there was little to be done.

The illness of Liu Dongjin, the prisoner in the first lictor's office, exhibits serious symptoms. Treatment has effected little improvement. Today he is again suffering from the symptoms of headache, hot sensations, and congested chest. He has no interest in drink or food and is coughing. He is an elderly man whose *qi* is depleted. His symptoms are serious. For the time being use a decoction of small hare's ear root, increased or reduced [as necessary], to treat him.
[GX 9/] 7/10, examined and prescribed.

The magistrate finally became convinced of the seriousness of Liu's illness. After he was brought before the court and his condition verified, Magistrate Zhou authorized his release under bond for treatment. On GX 9/7/15 (17 August 1883), however, the prisoner died before a guarantor could be found.

A prisoner's death could result in serious consequences for a local chief administrator if it were determined that the fatality had been due to overzealous use of judicial torture or mistreatment by runners or jailers.[43] A magistrate who ignored a report of a prisoner's illness that subsequently proved terminal could be impeached and lose his position. He might even be subject to criminal charges that called for the offender to be handled as if he had been the instigator in a premeditated homicide.[44] The statutory punishment for the latter offense was decapitation.

Runners, jail wardens, and magistrates with such undesirable possibilities in mind, therefore, certainly had strong incentive in the first place to ensure prisoners received medical attention or, failing that, to cover up any irregularity. The magistrate, however, immediately after learning of the prisoner's demise, was constrained by substatute to summon relatives of the deceased to court to view an inquest and bring charges against the runners if they so desired.[45] The day after the report of death was filed, Magistrate Zhou interrogated [33319:115] Liu Dongjin's wife, two sons, and his prison guard. The guard, of course, testified that Liu had not been mistreated. More importantly, Mrs. Liu and her sons agreed that death had eventuated from disease, not mistreatment. They had little choice, whatever their true feelings in the matter. In the first place, accusing the guard of mistreatment was a two-edged sword. Such an allegation, if found to be unproven, would under the same substatute necessarily result in an indictment for false accusation. The crucial factor in this particular situation, however, was that the yamen in effect had Mrs. Liu's sons as hostages. They themselves were still in detention on suspicion of complicity in harboring armed robbers. The leverage that the sons' incarceration provided the yamen probably was behind Mrs. Liu's entreaty, granted immediately, that her husband's body be released for burial without an inquest. The Code specifically authorized such requests when a prisoner had died from disease.[46] With all parties agreeing in writing that there had been no mistreatment, Magistrate Zhou found that there was no evidence that death had been caused by illegal cruelty (*lingnue qingbi*). Once Liu Dongjin's corpse had been released to his wife, charges of death because of cruelty could not be substantiated without an exhumation of the body. Such a step was so fraught with dangerous moral and religious implications for all involved that Liu's burial effectively ended any danger of punishment for magistrate or prison staff.

Despite the undeniably harsh and unhealthful nature of prison conditions, the availability of medical care shows it is unwarranted to assume that no thought was given to prisoners' welfare. The same conclusion is true regarding food and clothing for inmates. Indeed, adequate food, clothing, and medical treatment were mandated by law. Although prisoners were expected to rely on their families for sustenance and support, a provision in the Qing Code made the local yamen responsible for indigent inmates with no relatives to care for them.[47] Code law instituted by the central government was silent on just how far local administrations were required to go in providing the items in question. Nor was there any explicit provision for detainees as opposed to actual long-term convicts.[48] Neither, it seems, did the Fujian provincial government, which included Taiwan in its dominion for nearly the entire Qing period, ever devise any legislation covering this point.[49] Naturally, whether a local yamen complied with even the statutes on the books is a different issue. Funding for prisoner maintenance was a regular item in local budgets, however, and it does appear that by the late nineteenth century this budgetary component had grown to a substantial figure in Xinzhu. More precisely, funding for prisoners should have been substantial in view of the size of the prison population.

Magistrate Fang Zuyin's earlier cited memorandum [11407:2] that tabulated the number of prisoners held also itemized the money budgeted to support each class of inmate. Each main Tiger Head Prison inmate (*qiufan*) was allotted four *ban* (0.04 dollars) per day for provisions (*kouliang*). Detainees (*yafan*) and prisoners in fetters (*dunfan*) were each allotted three *ban* daily. The higher sum spent on a *qiufan* presumably reflected the more rigorous conditions inside the main prison. Fang highlighted his mastery of the obvious by remarking in his memorandum that "if food expenditures are not sufficient for a prisoner, he will inevitably die of starvation." Nonetheless, Fang made perfectly clear the strain that large prison populations put on the county's finances. The amount budgeted for maintenance of all prisoners was 20 taels per annum. As Fang pointed out, this figure was grossly inadequate. The 12 main prison inmates, 40 detainees, and 15 fettered prisoners would require 766.8 dollars, an amount equivalent to 552.096 taels. As Magistrate Fang's tabulations show, Xinzhu county's budget deficit for this item alone came to 532.096 taels.

Interestingly enough, the annual total for a single Tiger Head Prison inmate came to 14.6 dollars and for a detainee or fettered prisoner came to 10.95 dollars. If we accept G. L. MacKay's estimate, the family of a native preacher during the same period in northern Taiwan could be provided with food (rice and salt vegetables) and clothing for 7.38 dollars per month.[50] MacKay's account did not say how large a family such as he was discussing might be. Wolf and Huang have demonstrated that even among the poor, large families were the norm in this part of Taiwan.[51] Even if we assume families to have been somewhat smaller before the post-1895 initiation of public health programs by the Japanese, a northern Taiwanese family to G. L. MacKay would have meant five or six people at the smallest. In this light, the monthly sum budgeted for each prisoner (1.22 dollars) and detainee (0.91 dollars) would appear to have been adequate, if only barely.[52]

Guarantors and Release Under Bond

As we have seen, most yamen detainees sooner or later were released. To secure their liberty, prisoners were required to find guarantors willing to pledge in writing on penalty of being prosecuted themselves that the freed person would return home, work at his livelihood peacefully, and commit no (more) criminal acts. Not only those considered guilty of some wrongdoing, however, were required to find a guarantor willing to enter into a bond in order to obtain release. Many times, even the innocent were forced to satisfy the same condition.

We might conclude that such a procedure reflected a general presumption of at least partial guilt for all who ended up in court. Certainly presumption of suspects' guilt has been one of the features conventionally ascribed to traditional Chinese law, but it is not at all clear that "guilty until proven innocent" is an accurate description of the legal philosophy of magistrates under the imperial order.[53] The common practice of demanding guarantor bonds for even the innocent certainly lends support to the conventional view. Although the issue is probably incapable of definitive resolution, an alternative interpretation is possible. If we recall from Chapter 8 the difficulty faced by local administrators in exerting government control or extending the reach of the law beyond the yamen wall, it might be argued that the pervasive employment of guarantors for the innocent as well as the guilty was in part deemed a method for reminding the local populace of the duty to be law-abiding and to go about one's business peacefully. In this sense, guarantors (and in slightly different ways also scriveners, mediators, and even pettifoggers) were another mechanism used to strengthen the links between society and the legal system.

Limits

If we were to follow the logical progression of litigation from an initial complaint through to the end, the final step in the sequence would be appeal of sentence to a higher court. By introducing a new factor, the interplay between litigants and higher level judicial organs, a discussion of appeals would, however, take us beyond the level of local government and local society on which we have tried to focus in this study. Clearly the appeals process was significant in many cases. We have already seen in Chapter 6 how Mrs. Zhou and her son Chuncao were able to gain reconsideration of their case more than once by means of appeals to prefectural and even higher level officials. Even so, the evidence relevant to appeals in the Dan-Xin cases is sparse and cryptic. In the absence of documentation from higher judicial authorities, any discussion based on data from the Dan-Xin cases alone would be excessively speculative. This being the case, it is appropriate to terminate this discussion of specific issues of litigation and litigants with a short overview before proceeding to the concluding chapter.

OVERVIEW

If we were to single out the one most striking attribute of the legal system and the trial process in Danshui subprefecture and Xinzhu county, it might be its diversity. Many and varied were the complaints brought before the yamen court for resolution, as another glance at Appendix 1 will confirm. As Chapter 7 has attempted to demonstrate, also very diverse were not only criminal suspects but litigants who voluntarily initiated cases as well. Men and women, Han Chinese and aborigines, gentry landlords and day laborers, individuals and corporate groups all sought satisfaction through legal redress. Cases might be decided quite expeditiously. However, litigation could through obstruction, delay, or continued appeal be prolonged for years or decades. As discussed in Chapter 8, overburdened local administrators groping for ways to enforce legal norms and judicial verdicts utilized authorized and quasi-official personnel and exploited various indigenous structures of local governance to forge new and stronger links between the yamen and the society it was charged to control. Finally, in spite of seemingly rigid strictures governing trial, judgment, and sentence that were spelled out in codified law, administrative regulations, and precedent, local judicial officers could be creative and flexible in responding to particular circumstances, litigants, and criminals. In another sense, the legal system at this lowest level played a variety of functional roles in its relationship to society and social change. These topics will be the focus of the concluding chapter, which follows.

10

Conclusion: Law and Society

THIS study was initiated in part because any hope of understanding the socioeconomic as well as the political order of traditional China requires that we take the imperial legal system seriously. By building on a centuries-long tradition of continuity leavened by periodic amendment and renewal, the legal code and its attendant machinery accumulated enormous authority. A new code was an important symbol of legitimization promulgated without fail by each successive dynasty.

It has been argued that the importance of law in traditional China may be traced in large part to its ability to operate in the symbolic realm. The ruler turned to law and, by punishing those who through criminal violence or moral and ritual impropriety had violated social harmony, was able to restore the unity of the human and natural realms. Law, in other words, was seen as a way to restore cosmic harmony.[1] Traditional law in this sense is viewed as an analog to the codes of ritual behavior and customary practices that so thoroughly ordered social life. Without downplaying the importance of the symbolic, it seems nonetheless clear that law, the courts, and the legal bureaucracy possessed utilitarian virtues that have not been fully appreciated. Any such misunderstanding must not be attributed to the Chinese themselves. Both rulers and ruled clearly comprehended and respected the role of law in society.

This is not to deny that in specific historical circumstances the laws were accorded high regard only in proportion to the efficiency and honesty of those administering them. The conventional view of nineteenth-century China, for example, holds that under conditions of severe underdevelopment of the institutions of local governmental and reliance on nonrational methods of financing local administration, local officials, deprived of legitimate sources of income, concentrated on irregular and illegal methods of squeezing funds from the populace.[2] Moreover, as the century progressed, internal rebellion and external foreign pressure contributed to the decline of state authority, including that of local magistrates. Under these circumstances, many local officials viewed their posts merely as opportunities for self-enrichment. Obviously, manipulation of the outcome of litigation would have been a prime method of revenue enhancement, whether for government use or personal gain. Naturally, respect for law and the courts would have declined.

Even though, as we have seen, it is undeniable that in reality those charged with upholding and enforcing the laws might have fallen far short, such an observation is in an important sense irrelevant. We might note in passing that China's bureaucracy in its late traditional form, which included legal administration among its functions, was sufficiently rationalized, efficient, and honestly managed to maintain itself for nearly five centuries. Even in periods of decline and corruption, however, there existed a perception of the courts as a mechanism for dispensing just resolution of disputes and for restoring the balance when criminal activity had disturbed the moral equilibrium of society.

The tone for the entire bureaucracy was set by the emperor, and the best and the most conscientious of them took the responsibilities of their roles as supreme judge and legislator seriously. Officials staffing the provincial, prefectural, and local judicial organizations of the empire were expected to model their administrations accordingly. Even under less than exemplary rulers, officialdom was expected to carry out the duties of office ethically. The ethical indoctrination of Confucian education that nearly all officials underwent as a prerequisite for acceptance into the cadre of government was designed to force the internalization of these norms of administrative honesty and diligence.[3]

In view of such expectations—no matter how idealized—on the part of officialdom and thus government itself, we should expect ordinary people to have viewed the legal system as an integral facet and function of the government and to have demanded that the part, like the whole, be responsive to their needs in return for their continued fealty and support. Indeed, our materials reveal just this. Virtually every petition submitted to the Dan-Xin court calls on the magistrate to hold to the law and act benevolently, to hear the case and pass judgment fairly and in accordance with the law, or some variant of these phrases. Even if we consider this kind of language to be merely formulaic, such clichés defined the moral parameters that were expected to guide the courts.[4] Even in bad times, when the yamen and its courtroom were havens for corrupt officials and rapacious underlings preying on litigants, such a situation was perceived as a deviation from higher standards that should have been the norm.

Even a cursory reading of this study will, I hope, demonstrate that the inhabitants of the Danshui and Xinzhu administrative areas regarded adjudication of litigation as they did other functions (such as tax collection, military protection, and public works) of the state machinery. Dealings with the government were approached warily and handled cautiously with an awareness that few transactions were cost free. Nonetheless, as the Dan-Xin cases almost by their very existence demonstrate, area residents were far from timid about initiating legal actions. The enormous variety of disputes that were brought before the court, the wide range of social status observable among litigants from day laborers to degree-holding gentry elite, the ability of litigants to press their cases, persisting in their demands for satisfaction over months and years, all demonstrate a society that, while not litigious, was not backward in insisting on enforcement of customary and legal norms in the family, in social intercourse, and in economic practices. With surprising frequency, consumers of local government legal services demonstrated a high level of sophistication.

Supplying a corrective to skewed perception is useful. Insisting on a serious consideration of traditional Chinese law, however, has more significant implications for understanding economic, political, and social change, particularly in nineteenth-century northern Taiwan. Most sociologists of law hold that in the relationship between social change and legal change the former is primary and the latter takes place in response. The theory goes even further to assert that old laws, once rendered dysfunctional by social change, are inevitably discarded.[5] Such a formulation goes too far. It has been shown, for example, that a number of rules of Roman private law that were taken into English law and enforced by the courts were "in large measure out of step with the needs and desires of society and even of its ruling elite."[6] When we examine the relationship between law and local society in Danshui and Xinzhu, it is easy to find instances of law and legal institutions attempting to cope with an evolving society and economy. At the same time, it seems possible to discern a process in which changes in society may be traced to the influence of codified law and the action of the courts. The Taiwan case shows how the legal system and its tenets could be a positive force in directing social evolution. Therefore, after first examining two manifestations in nineteenth-century Taiwan of legal change in response to a new socioeconomic reality, we will by way of contrast conclude with a consideration of society transforming itself in important ways in response to legal norms.

LAW AND SOCIAL CHANGE

Subbureaucratic Administration

A significant dynamic in late imperial Chinese history is the escalating tension between private and public at the local level. The proliferation of guilds, temple associations and sectarian assemblies, and poetry and literary societies, secret societies, militia and self-defense organizations and the like were manifestations of a trend toward the creation of interest groups whose operation was largely outside local government. As Philip Kuhn has argued, the local gentry were probably the most important of these local special interest groups. Very often the local gentry, despite their long tradition of cooperation with the authorities, acted largely outside the old formal structures of government.[7]

In response, during the nineteenth century some local governments made strenuous efforts to increase the articulation and sophistication of their administrative control by utilizing town and village leaders a step below the gentry elite in status. Building on emergent or already existing subbureaucratic mechanisms, local yamen administrators attempted to attack a number of social problems without relying on the local gentry, at least as we have come to understand the term. We have already seen how this was accomplished in Danshui subprefecture and Xinzhu county.

The most convenient and most useful way to exploit the market town and village leadership was to delegate to them some of the yamen's law enforcement authority. As I have suggested earlier, by incorporating the overseers and their subordinates in a quasi-formal manner into the bureaucratic hierarchy, the yamen gained a cadre of auxiliary police while at the same time tapping a new source of funding for the expenses of investigation, search and arrest, and dispatch of suspects to court. The subbureaucratic leaders were invested with some of the legitimacy of the imperial government but at the same time strengthened the authority of the yamen through its association with them and their own community prestige. Any attempt to explain the structure and dynamics of government-society interaction and integration must take such local subgentry elites and the diverse roles they played into account.

As for the paradigm of law and social change, legal institutions, specifically the mechanisms of local law enforcement, had proved inadequate to contend with a multifarious and contentious social structure situated in a physical environment that allowed alleged criminals and others wishing to elude the reach of the law to do so easily. In response, as already described, the legal system significantly modified or expanded its enforcement arm to deal with local circumstances. This kind of innovation may be linked to a long tradition in Chinese statecraft of relying on certain parts of society to assist in controlling others. In a more fundamental sense, the Dan-Xin cases also reveal that legal doctrine as expressed in local practice could evolve new concepts in reaction to the increasing importance of collective social and economic entities.

Legal Personae

Time and again, litigants petitioning the Dan-Xin court presented themselves not as individuals or natural persons but as representatives acting for a collective or corporate entity. Of these legal persons, one type, the corporate lineage, is very familiar in the literature. During the quarter-century-long course of the rent resistance case, the Wu-Shun-Ji lineage acted to seek enforcement of rent collection and later itself became the focus of tax collection efforts. Several different natural persons submitted petitions or were interrogated on behalf of the lineage, but Wu-Shun-Ji as a collective body was central. Lineages, however, are only one variety of legal person. In the case summaries we may note partnerships such as the tea enterprise, Jin-Liu-He, commercial firms such as Cha-Tai *hao* and He-Xing *hao*, and perhaps even entire villages or groups of villages such as were represented by the farmers opposing Jin-Liu-He.[8]

The de facto recognition by the court of legal as well as natural persons has certain implications for our understanding of social structure and political action in this locality (see below). In a different context, the very ubiquity of these collective personae suggests their relevance for understanding the nature of the economy and the course of economic growth in northern Taiwan. A thorough investigation of this topic lies outside the scope of this study; however, the evidence presented so far permits some preliminary observations.

As the court's handling of contractual relations entered into by such entities indicates, and here we might particularly remember the Jin-Liu-He partnership, duties and rights conferred by contract accrued and were retained or alienated by the partnership as a legal person, not the individual natural persons comprising it. The four villages as collective entities that were Jin-Liu-He's antagonists in the litigation, even though losing the case, were found to possess rights to adjoining land that had been established by contract decades before the birth of any individual villager alive at the time of the lawsuit. Even the fact that the villages had been renamed sometime in the years between their acquisition of the land and the beginning of the dispute did not affect their land rights. The same kind of legal attitude is evident in the rent resistance case involving the Wu-Shun-Ji lineage, although the rights and obligations involved were different.

That such legal precedents seemed to be well established in this locality has powerful implications for the rationality and predictability of economic transactions. An earlier chapter focused on the potential for litigation and crime that was generated by the explosive growth in northern Taiwan of an international export trade in tea and camphor. Here the emphasis may be shifted to suggest that the precedents from earlier litigation had already established the nature of the contractual standing of legal persons. This legal status provided a degree of stability, rationality, and predictability so necessary to the firms, partnerships, and other commercial organizations engaged in the trade of these two commodities. The study of commercial law and regulation and the effect of law on the economy in imperial China are not well developed. The Dan-Xin cases suggest that, although the statutes of codified law may appear indifferent at best,[9] precedents established through the findings of local courts were far from inimical to economic growth.[10]

The discussion so far has been centered around the reaction of legal institutions to changed conditions. As suggested earlier, however, the Dan-Xin cases also allow us to see how the law itself sometimes served as a transformative agent, operating on individuals and groups to promote alterations in the nature of local society.

Law and Societal Integration

The problem of social integration, especially in frontier regions, was faced time and again by Chinese governments. The problem was not merely to find ways to compel a heterogeneous frontier population to acknowledge Chinese overlordship. Even more important was the necessity of bringing social groups, some of which were often non-Han, to a shared conception of state and society, shared assumptions about the ways villages, tribes, or other congeries should interact. Societal integration in this sense meant persuading, educating, or forcing these groups to internalize a worldview that placed them all within a common framework that accepted the political strictures of the imperial state and acceded to Chinese norms and customs, at least when engaged in intergroup transactions.

Nongovernment community and kinship organizations were extremely important, but government, too, through explicit policy measures and through its everyday operation, was a highly effective transformative agent working to change the social structure from a fragmented collection of antagonistic groups toward a society in which even competing individuals or groups acknowledged the mediating authority of the state in dispute resolution. In this sense, the role of the state was not to impose an artificial consensus. Rather, the state recognized the inevitability of conflict and sought to define and sanction the framework and mechanisms through which individuals and collective bodies were to resolve it. In a quite different but contemporary social setting, the huge Yangtze River port city of Hankou, conflict itself may have played a socially integrative role. William T. Rowe, building on the theoretical insight of Georg Simmel, suggests the positive nature of conflict in creating a sense of shared community among the heterogeneous social groups making up Hankou's population. Rowe finds Hankou to have been "a near perfect example of the sort of pluralist local society" in which "[c]onflict is the necessary complement to cooperation, providing a safety valve for routine tensions, as well as establishing and maintaining impersonal norms and rules of behavior by system participants." In northern Taiwan as in Hankou, it is possible to see conflict as a sign of emerging community interdependence. However, in northern Taiwan before the late nineteenth century, in contrast to Hankou, the still incomplete development of commercial, kinship, or other corporate structures that could mediate conflict and make it socially integrative rather than violently destructive made the role of government crucial.[11] One of the implicit themes running throughout this study has been the importance of the legal system and the local court in Danshui and Xinzhu as instruments of a type of social change that induced a population divided by language, customs, and ethnicity to see common ground.

By the middle decades of the nineteenth century, Taiwan had undergone two centuries of slow transformation from an island sparsely inhabited by non-Chinese tribal peoples to a full-fledged if somewhat backward province of the empire populated overwhelmingly by Han Chinese. The change was slow. This Chinese frontier expansion was not explosive, probably because of the constraints of terrain and technology. But by 1895, except in the inner mountain fastness still held by resistant unpacified tribes, a Chinese society and culture had emerged that were as representative of the whole as any other region of the vast, diverse empire. Many social, economic, and governmental institutions played a part in transforming a fragmented and violent, even rebellious, frontier into a part of the Chinese cultural sphere. The Dan-Xin cases permit us to understand why the local court was one of the more effective institutions in the transmutation.

As suggested in Chapter 3, the vestiges of an atomized and antagonistic frontier society were still visible in the latter stages of Qing rule. Incompletely sinified aborigine tribes continued to be perceived as a significant threat to the Han. The memories of turmoil arising from a patchwork social fabric consisting of unstable clusters of native place associations, sworn brotherhoods, secret societies, and unabashed bandit gangs were vivid in the minds of Han Chinese themselves. However, the futility of attempts to fashion grievances against the Qing state into a unifying vehicle for throwing off imperial rule were evident. Divisions among the populace that prompted Hakka and aborigine to ally themselves with the state against Hokkienese rebels had permitted the government to crush even large-scale revolts such as those of Lin Shuangwen. In the Dai Chaoqing uprising, even the tie of Zhangzhou Hokkienese commonality was broken because of previous local feuds, causing Qing government forces to gain important allies from among the local elite against the rebels. On the frontier, more parochial disputes had often been settled by violent armed affrays. Yet even to the victor in a pitched battle, this method of resolution was neither cheap, efficient, nor even final. For the vanquished, defeat was merely temporary until they could regroup, recruit new allies, and wait for a pretext to reignite the conflict.

In these circumstances, even if we ignore the interest of the state in repressing violent strife, it cannot surprise us that more rational methods of conflict resolution appealed to many. For reasons suggested in Chapter 4, both the large-rent and small-rent strata in Taiwan's multitiered system of land holding found themselves in need of an outside mediating authority. Large-rent landlords were forced to seek a champion in the yamen court in order to compel rent payments from an increasingly powerful small-rent landlord stratum, whose proximity to the land and control of its use might have allowed them to ignore demands not backed by legal sanctions.

However, a long history of concealing land reclamation in order to lessen tax liability also left large-rent landlords vulnerable to counterattacking litigation. In this way, both groups, who formerly might have resorted to private violence and intimidation to resolve disputes, began more and more to appeal to state power.

The cases also reveal that the state represented by the local court stood as perhaps the only institution that might peacefully resolve disputes crossing ethnic lines. Sinicized aborigine landlords who lacked any ability for self-help in disputes with Han Chinese tenants turned to the court to protect their rent collection rights.[12] Hokkienese whose subethnic Zhangzhou-Quanzhou rivalries left them divided in disputes with the more cohesive Hakka settlers turned to litigation as armed affrays became more and more inconclusive as a means for settling grievances.

The process just outlined was one in which the state established its authority. The Dan-Xin cases show a separate but related pattern in which the courts acted to foster the growth of characteristic Chinese social organizations. In Taiwan, the main principle of social organization changed from native place links to lineage ties. It was a slow process that only became visible around 1860 and after.[13] As the case summaries have shown, a guiding principle of subprefects and magistrates, especially in minor family and property-related disputes, was to force mediation by lineage relatives when at all possible. By reinforcing the authority and prestige of the extended lineage, the court was a conservative force for change from frontier norms to the standard, traditional societal structures of China.

Thus, law and the courts operated to integrate disparate groups within society, to link government and society, and to promote the formation of traditional social institutions.

Reference Matter

Appendix 1

The Dan-Xin Archives as Classified and Numbered by Dai Yanhui

HOW CASES ARE NUMBERED AND CITED

Each of the Dan-Xin cases was assigned a five-digit number by Dai when he organized and classified them. I use these numbers throughout this study for citation purposes. In each five-digit number, the first digit indicates in which of the three major categories the case was classified: 1, administrative; 2, civil; and 3, criminal. The second digit indicates the relevant secondary classification within each of these major categories, for example, "real property" under "civil." The third digit shows the heading under that secondary division, as for example "rent resistance" under "real property" cases. Thus the first three digits in any citation assign the case to a discrete position within a three-level hierarchy of categorization. Cases having to do with rent resistance will always be coded "[222xx]."

The last two digits identify the specific case within the particular category assigned by the first three digits, e.g. "02, 18, 44" (44 is the highest number of cases within any third-level category).

Within each case file, individual documents were ordered chronologically and numbered sequentially. Citations to individual documents follow a colon after the five-digit case number. So, for example, the first document in the rent resistance case discussed in Chapter 4 would be cited as [22202:1].

TABLE OF CONTENTS OF THE DAN-XIN ARCHIVES, WITH NUMBER OF CASES IN EACH CATEGORY

A. Administrative cases (*xingzheng*)[1xxxx], 574
- I. General matters (*zongwu*)[11xxx], 100
  1. Sacrifices and ceremonies (*siyi*), 7
  2. Clerks and other personnel (*liwu*), 17
  3. Yamen staff crimes (*liji*), 27
  4. Stipends and subsidies (*xinjin*), 11
  5. External affairs (*waishi*), 11
  6. Turning over office (*yijiao*), 10
  7. Miscellaneous (*zashi*), 17

- II. Civil administration (*minzheng*)[12xxx], 91
  1. Educational affairs (*xuewu*), 4
  2. Rural townships (*xiangbao*), 44
  3. Linked villages (*lianzhuang*), 4
  4. Census and surveillance (*baojia*), 6
  5. Improving customs (*housu*), 22
  6. Charity granaries (*yicang*), 6
  7. Relief and charity (*jiuxu*), 5
- III. Financial administration (*caizheng*)[13xxx], 100
  1. Land tax (*tianfu*), 11
  2. Cadastral surveys (*qingfu*), 24
  3. Property deed tax (*shuiqi*), 16
  4. Issuance of permits (*jizhao*), 7
  5. Transit tax (*lijin*), 8
  6. Coinage and currency (*qianbi*), 4
  7. Tax collection (*zhengshou*), 10
  8. Dispatch to storehouses (*jieku*), 14
  9. Miscellaneous, 6
- IV. Industry and public works (*jianshe*)[14xxx], 72
  1. Private businesses (*minye*), 6
  2. Salt monopoly affairs (*yanwu*), 35
  3. Camphor (*zhangnao*), 14
  4. Mining (*kuangchan*), 10
  5. Public works (*gongcheng*), 7
- V. Transport and posts (*jiaotong*)[15xxx], 47
  1. Postal stations (*yizhan*), 14
  2. Shipping administration (*chuanzheng*), 18
  3. Railroads (*tielu*), 2
  4. Public ferries (*yidu*), 13
- VI. Military affairs (*junshi*)[16xxx], 61
  1. Military administration (*junzheng*), 8
  2. Troop provisions (*bingxiang*), 16
  3. Wall construction (*chenggong*), 7
  4. Income from land rent (*xizhuang*), 18
  5. Illegal weapons manufacture (*sihuo*), 12
- VII. Pacification and settlement (*fuken*)[17xxx], 103
  1. Aborigine settlement affairs (*shewu*), 15
  2. Aborigine settlement rents (*shezu*), 13
  3. Guardpost affairs (*aiwu*), 41
  4. Military settlement affairs (*tunwu*), 34

B. Civil cases (*minshi*)[2xxxx], 222

- I. Persons (*renshi*)[21xxx], 13
  1. Missing persons (*shizong*), 1
  2. Marriage (*jiehun*), 7

3. Divorce (*lihun*), 2
4. Adoption (*shouyang*), 2
5. Guardianship (*jianhu*), 1

II. Real property (*tianfang*)[22xxx], 137
1. Rent and lease (*zujie*), 7
2. Rent resistance (*kangzu*), 27
3. Compelled payment (*bashou*), 3
4. Forcible occupation (*bazhan*), 42*
5. Boundary disputes (*zhengjie*), 27
6. Disputes over wealth (*zhengcai*), 15
7. Common property (*gongye*), 10
8. Water rights (*yongshui*), 4
9. Foreclosure (*chaoya*), 2

III. Monetary obligations (*qianzhai*)[23xxx], 67*
1. Sale of goods (*maimai*), 3*
2. Conditional sales (*diandang*), 10
3. Title deposit loans (*taijie*), 13
4. Loans (*jiedai*), 24
5. Consignment (*weiji*), 3
6. Payment (*taowu*), 4
7. Encroachment (*kangtun*), 6
8. Accounting disputes (*kangsuan*), 3
9. Contract concealment (*niqi*), 1

IV. Commercial affairs (*shangshi*)[24xxx], 5
1. Guilds (*jiaohang*), 1
2. Partnerships (*hegu*), 1
3. Bankruptcy (*daobi*), 1
4. Infringement of rights (*qinquan*), 2

C. Criminal cases (*xingshi*)[3xxxx], 365

I. General matters [31xxx], 120
1. Laws and regulations (*faling*), 6
2. Case list reports (*cebao*), 18
3. Directives (*zhihui*), 7
4. Reciprocal aid and delivery to court (*huzhu yijie*), 22
5. General searches (*tongqi*), 42
6. Inquests (*yanshi*), 6
7. Decision and sentence (*dingyan*), 3
8. Execution of sentence (*zhixing*), 14
9. Other (*qita*), 2

II. Personal security (*renshen ziyou*)[32xxx], 61
1. Homicide (*renming*), 7
2. Assault (*oushang*), 17
3. Ransom (*leshu*), 1
4. Abduction by enticement (*youguai*), 10

5. Seizure and sale of persons (*luemai*), 7
6. Abduction and illegal detention (*lujin*), 12
7. Abduction by force (*qianglu*), 7

III. Forcible seizure of property (*caichan qinduo*)[33xxx], 123

1. Theft (*qiedao*), 39
2. Unarmed robbery (*qiangduo*), 19
3. Armed robbery (*qiangdao*), 30
4. Armed robbery with personal injury (*qiangdao shashang*), 10
5. Piracy (*haidao*), 5
6. Intimidation and threats (*konghe*), 3
7. Fraud (*zhaqi*), 6
8. Sale of stolen property (*daomai*), 7
9. Destruction and abandonment (*huiqi*), 4

IV. Public order (*gonggong zhixu*)[34xxx], 19

1. Banditry (*feitu*), 9
2. Infringement on water rights (*qinhai shuiyuan*), 2
3. Disturbing the peace (*saorao*), 7
4. Rumors (*yaoyan*), 1

V. Public morals (*fenghua*)[35xxx], 42

1. Unfiliality (*wuni*), 5
2. Destruction of graves (*huifen*), 13
3. Adultery (*tongjian*), 6
4. Luring into adultery (*guaijian*), 5
5. Gambling (*dubo*), 13

TOTAL, 1,161

NOTE: An asterisk by a number indicates that I disagree with the total given by Dai Yanhui in his table of contents heading *Dan-Xin dang'an xuanlu xingzheng bian chuji*. Two cases [22443, 23102] do not appear on the film and, insofar as I was able to determine from personal inspection, are not now among the originals. One criminal case [34109] was inadvertently omitted during the filming but is still among the original case files.

Appendix 2

Measures of Land and Grain

The *jia* unit of land measurement may have originated during the period of Dutch control of the island in the seventeenth century.[1] As with most weights and measures, there were significant local variations. One Japanese investigation concluded that the *jia* was equivalent to 0.978 Japanese *chō* or 0.970 hectares (2.39 acres).[2] The commission for the investigation of old Taiwan customs, however, concluded that the *jia* ranged from 1.01 *chō* (1.002 hectares) to 1.53 *chō* (1.518 hectares).[3]

As noted in Chapter 4, the *jia* was thought to be equivalent to 11.3 *mou*.[4] If we accept the more conservative finding of Japanese field investigators that a *jia* equaled 2.39 acres, the standard *mou* would have equaled 0.212 acres (0.086 hectares). Lian Heng, the preeminent Taiwanese historian of this century, claims the *jia* was equal to just over 13.3 *mou*.[5] This figure would make the *mou* equivalent to 0.1802 acres (0.073 hectares). Both figures are considerably larger than the 0.1518 acres (0.061 hectares) usually considered to be the size of the standard *mou* during the Qing period.[6] In view of local variations in the sizes of *jia* and *mou*, no definitive solution to the equivalency problem seems possible.

The *shi* grain measure, according to the first Japanese source cited above, equaled the Japanese equivalent of 2.95 U.S. bushels or 103.95 liters.[7] As with other measures, there seemed to be no standard. In central Taiwan the Japanese found a *shi* of polished rice to be 36 percent smaller than in northern Taiwan. Around Tainan, at the other extreme, a *shi* of grain other than rice was 11 percent larger than in the Taibei area.

Appendix 3

Tea and Camphor Export Figures

TABLE 1

Annual Exports of Oolong Tea

	Exports[a]		Total	Average	Total
	to U.S.	to Europe	exports[a]	price[b]	value[b]
1866	—	—	180,826	10.00	13,596
1867	—	—	270,790	15.00	30,540
1868	—	—	528,210	20.00	79,430
1869	—	—	729,243	18.00	98,693
1870	—	—	1,405,348	34.00	359,261
1871	—	—	1,982,410	30.00	447,195
1872	2,032,220	75,153	2,601,801	41.00	802,058
1873	1,261,361	57,360	2,081,324	25.00	396,225
1874	2,891,959	283,742	3,338,846	34.00[c]	853,536
1875	4,869,345	400,679	5,543,140	28.00	1,167,040
1876	6,487,840	1,102,369	7,854,020	32.25	1,904,459
1877	7,704,693	608,844	9,230,754	28.00	1,943,312
1878	8,152,168	1,287,360	10,701,524	35.33	2,842,793
1879	9,783,513	1,056,034	11,337,710	46.83	3,992,070
1880	10,884,127	636,225	12,063,450	39.50	3,582,754
1881	11,978,605	614,151	12,854,355	35.65	3,445,547
1882	10,406,260	752,473	12,040,446	34.04	3,081,630
1883	11,202,569	1,018,480	13,206,726	36.13	3,587,662
1884	11,779,448	726,293	13,155,437	34.85	3,447,120
1885	14,601,082	931,270	16,364,041	23.51	4,412,091
1886	13,797,879	920,470	16,171,605	37.72	4,586,413
1887	14,534,015	1,199,950	16,816,736	34.46	4,375,178
1888	14,961,048	947,514	18,053,553	36.95	5,015,630
1889	14,539,894	1,007,646	17,384,164	34.99	4,573,473
1890	14,212,326	925,264	17,107,257	37.34	4,802,895
1891	15,029,535	746,229	18,055,149	31.81	4,318,303
1892	15,211,076	735,368	18,230,000	36.64	5,022,159
1893	18,479,927	744,181	21,908,530	38.52	6,345,237
1894	16,748,236	754,444	20,533,733	44.74	6,907,363
1895	15,912,426	784,891	19,556,116	41.14	6,049,163

[a]In pounds.
[b]Per picul (=133 lbs.) in silver dollars.
[c]In May.
SOURCE: Davidson, 395–96.

TABLE 2

Annual Exports of Baozhong Tea

Year	Total exports[a]	Average price[b]	Total value[b]
1881	40,666	26.25	8,026
1883	152,000	30.00	34,284
1885	769,230	33.00	190,886
1889	1,367,583	—	—
1893	1,966,833	—	—
1894	2,290,266	—	—
1895	2,700,000	—	—

[a]In pounds.
[b]Per picul (=133 lbs.) in silver dollars.
SOURCE: Davidson, 396.

TABLE 3

Danshui Camphor Exports
(pounds)

Year	Amount	Year	Amount
1864	1,171,464	1880	1,640,555
1865	1,035,405	1881	1,239,028
1866	1,123,474	1882	656,089
1867	674,310	1883	410,438
1868	1,485,477	1884	58,919
1869	1,835,001	1885	399
1870	1,925,973	1886	128,212
1871	1,288,903	1887	335,160
1872	1,367,373	1888	382,109
1873	1,430,415	1889	476,273
1874	1,606,507	1890	983,186
1875	946,487	1891	2,511,173
1876	1,169,602	1892	2,332,820
1877	1,752,408	1893	4,431,560
1878	1,795,766	1894	5,260,416
1879	1,469,384	1895	5,586,000

SOURCE: Davidson, 442.

Appendix 4

Yamen Organization and Personnel in Xinzhu County[1]

Magistrate (*zhixian*), civil service rank 7B
- Private secretaries
  - Law (*xingming*)
  - Taxation (*qianliang*)
  - Correspondence (*shuqi*)
  - Bookkeeping (*zhangfang*)
  - Essay examination (*yuejuan*)
  - Enforcement of tax collection (*zhengshou*)
  - Red and black brushes (*zhumo*)
- Magistrate's personal servants
  - Bodyguards (*huyong*), 20
  - Tea infusers (*paoding*), 4
  - Water and fire boys (*shuihuofu*), 4
  - Extra hired guards (*tiangu zhuangyong*), 20
  - Personal servants (*qinding*), 20
  - Retinue (*gending*), 20

Jail warden (*dianshi*), unranked

Yamen departments
- Personnel (*lifang*)
- Revenue (*hufang*)
- Taxes (*liangshuifang*)
- Rites (*lifang*)
- Military (*bingfang*)
- Legal (*xingfang*)
- Public works (*gongfang*)
- Document receipt and distribution (*chengfafang*)
- Court depositions (*tangzhaofang*)

General yamen runners and servants
- Section heads (*zhangban*), 4
- Tea section runners (*chafang*), 4
- Messengers (*tingchai*), 4
- Yamen managers (*baya*), 2

Inner and outer night watchmen (*nei wai gengfu*), 4
Sweepers (*dasaofu*), 2
Lictors (*zaoli*), 16
Horsemen (*makuai*), 8
Sedan chair, parasol, & fan bearers (*jiao san shanfu*), 9
Jailers (*jinzu*), 8
Treasury janitor (*kuzi*)
Grain measurers (*douji*), 4
Commoner guards (*minzhuang*), 28

Subdirector of schools (*xundao*), civil service rank 8B
Library servant (*zhaifu*)
Messenger (of an educational official) (*mendou*)
Stipendiaries (*lingshansheng*), 4
Stipendiaries' servant (*shanfu*)

NOTE: This list does not include the staff of the county director of schools (*ruxue zhaifu*), runners of the warden (*xundian yi*), or the clerical staff. Each of the yamen departments was staffed with several clerks (*shu*), with the revenue department usually employing the greatest number.[2] For example, the tax department, the only one for which a detailed listing is available, was staffed by seven clerks and five assistant clerks. In addition, this department enjoyed the services of a doorman and a cook [11407:4].

APPENDIX 5

Danshui Subprefects and Xinzhu Magistrates

This appendix lists, in double-column tabular form, the chief administrators of Danshui Subprefecture and Xinzhu County from 1841 to 1895 (Daoguang 21–Guangxu 21), with dates of tenure in office, if known. Information on known civil and military officials in Taiwan has been conveniently aggregated in Taiwan sheng wenxian weiyuanhui, comp., *Taiwan dili ji lishi, juan* 9, *Guanshi zhi*. Unless otherwise noted, all information has been taken from this source.

SUBPREFECTS

Cao Jin; DG 21/7/26.
Shi Mi; ca. DG 25/5.
Huang Kaiji; DG 25/10.
Shi Mi; DG 27/3/12–27/3/18.
Cao Shigui; DG 27/3/18–27/12/24.
Huang Kaiji; DG 28.
Shi Mi; DG 30/3/8–XF 2/1/17.
Zhu Caizhe; before XF 1/4.
Zhang Qixuan; XF 1–XF 4/12/22.
Zhu Caizhe; XF 4.
Ding Yuejian; XF 4.
Tang Jun; XF 6.
Ma Qingzhao; XF 7.
Qiu Yuejin; XF 7.
En Yu; XF 8.
Ning Changjing; XF 9.
Zhang Chuanjing; XF 10.
Qiu Yuejin; XF 11–TZ 1/3/19.
Zhang Shiying; after TZ 1/4–before TZ 1/7.
Zheng Yuanjie; TZ 1–ca. TZ 3/10.
Wang Yong; TZ 4.
Yan Jinqing; TZ 5–possibly TZ 8.
Fu Lehe; TZ 7–possibly TZ 9/1.
Chen Peigui; TZ 8.
Zhou Shilian; TZ 10/5/13–TZ 11.
Xiang Tao; TZ 11.
He Enqi; TZ 12.
Chen Xingju; TZ 12.
Lin Daquan; dates unknown.
Zheng Yuanjie; unknown–GX 3/2/6.
Chen Xingju; GX 4.

MAGISTRATES

Xiang Tao; GX 3.[a]
Lin Daquan; GX 4.[a]
Chen Xingju; GX 4.[a]
Liu Yuanbi; GX 5/i3–8.
Li Yujie; GX 5/9 or 6/3–6/9.
Shi Xiwei; GX 6/4.
Xu Xizhi; GX 7/9/4–9/6/6.
Zhou Zhikan; GX 9/6/6–after 9/10.
Zhu Chenglie; GX 9/11.
Xu Xizhi; GX 10/3–after 10/9.
Peng Dasun; GX 10/12.

Fang Zuyin; GX 11/11–after GX 15/4.
Zhang Tinggan; GX 15/11–16/4.
Shen Maoyin; GX 16/4–17/9.
Shen Jiceng; GX 17/8.
Ye Yishen; GX 18/12–20/2.
Liu Wei; GX 20/2/24.
Fan Kecheng; GX 20/3/25.
Wang Guorui; GX 21/1/26.
Li Quan; GX 21.
Liang Chengnan; dates unknown.

[a]Xiang Tao, Lin Daquan, and Chen Xingju all served as magistrates of Xinzhu county during their terms as Taibei prefects. Even though Chen is not on the Xinzhu magistrate list given in the source mentioned above, documents [for example, 32101:1 dated GX 4/12/26] found in the *Dan-Xin dang'an* show that he also had jurisdiction in Xinzhu county in GX 4.

Appendix 6

Lou Yun's "Four Village Regulations"

Below is a translation of the "Four Village Regulations" (*Zhuanggui size*) promulgated by Danshui Subprefect Lou Yun in 1836.

[1.] Each village is to establish overseers (*zongli*), managers (*dongshi*), village heads (*zhuangzheng*), and assistant village heads (*zhuangfu*). The government will issue an edict of appointment and a seal of office. Villagers will not be permitted to fight, cause trouble, or kidnap people as bandits do. Those who disobey are to be reported to the government for prosecution. Or, if an official discovers one of these matters and sends a directive to the village, the overseer and manager are to report on it in reply. They are authorized to stamp it with their seals of office and are exempted from transmitting it through a scrivener in order that the details of the case can be made known to the court. The established law basically is thorough and detailed. But after a time abuses will occur such as the overseers, managers, village heads, and assistants in carrying out their duties showing bias toward one party. Moreover, they may protect their sons and younger brothers or form cliques to cause trouble. If there are not clear and definite regulations, there will be no way to make them respect the law. From now on when villagers feel they have been unfairly treated in a matter within their own village, then they are to report it to their village overseer, manager, and other officials to handle. If the incident occurred in another village, they are to report it to the overseers, managers, and other officials of both villages to handle. If the matter is not rectified, then they should request that a neighboring village's overseer, manager, and other leaders hold discussions to resolve the problem. If finally there is still no resolution, they are then to make an accusation to the court for it to investigate and decide. If anyone does not first file suit but goes ahead and starts a fight, no matter what the circumstances of the case, the instigator will be arrested and punished. If an overseer, manager, village head, or assistant protects a son or younger brother or forms a clique to cause trouble, he will be given an additional degree of punishment as provided by substatute.

[2.] It is proper that overseers, managers, village heads, and assistants vigorously implement the pure village (*qingzhuang*) law in order to expel bandit types. There are both large and small lineages, poor and rich villages; certainly not everyone as yet has sufficient clothing and food.

Nourish and later instruct was the constant maxim in ancient times. It is a certainty that the destitute will turn to banditry. A village's overseer, manager, head, and assistant are to calculate the village's yearly income and take half of about 10 percent, which will revert to the public coffers. Then they are to determine who among the village's able-bodied adult males are poor and landless and record their names in their lineage temples. Those without a temple are to be recorded in the earth god temple (*shemiao*). Hold a meeting and public discussion to decide whether to allocate dry fields for them to farm as tenants, to loan them funds for commerce, to order them to serve as field patrollers and night watchmen, or to train them in a handicraft. These young men must be made to have a steady occupation and not permitted to be roving vagrants idly stirring up trouble. Naturally, in this way they will not be forced into banditry. Violent criminals who are robbers, kidnappers, or murderers are to be captured and sent to court for trial. If it is feared that a powerful criminal will take revenge, immediately submit a detailed petition to the court, which will then supervise his capture and prevent any repercussions against our rural areas. For every bandit that is gotten rid of, there is one less person to commit robberies or violent acts. The benefit received by villages throughout the area will not be superficial. Let this be implemented immediately with no excuses.

[3.] Any lawless young man in a village is to be detained preventively by the overseer, manager, village head, and assistant. If there are any that are obdurate in crime and do not reform, send them to court immediately for trial. By analogy to the punishment for those who voluntarily come forward and confess to a crime, their punishment can be reduced. If there are criminals who have not yet been accused and sent to court and the court learns of them on inquiry, or there are criminals for whom an arrest warrant has been issued, the relevant village overseer, manager, village head, and assistant are to take charge of some men in the village to help runners arrest and send them to court. It is not permitted to protect or hide them. In cases where a person is charged in civil litigation or in a capital case, whether or not the charge is true or false, the village leaders must also summon or order them to go to court. If they feel that is an injustice, there is no objection to inviting a witness along with the accused and lodging an accusation. If they remain obstinately fixed on a delusion and intend to conceal a criminal or are persuaded to release one, then the village overseer, manager, head, and assistant will be the ones punished.

[4.] In essence the responsibility of each village overseer, manager, head, and assistant is to restrain the village people and bring amity to the countryside. If they are skillful in restraining the people, there will be no incidents of violence, theft, robbery, kidnapping, illegally occupying land, rent resistance, or arson. If this situation obtains for one year, a badge of merit will be issued; if for three years, then a plaque will be issued.

Notes

The following abbreviations are used in the notes and bibliography:

JAS *Journal of Asian Studies.*
TKK *Taiwan kanshu kiji* (Notes on Taiwan customs).
TW *Taiwan wenxian* (Documents on Taiwan).
TWC *Taiwan wenxian congkan* (Taiwan documentary collectanea). 309 titles. Taibei: Bank of Taiwan, Economic Research Office, 1957–72.

CHAPTER 1

1. For a consideration of the problems of doing social history, see Duara, 261–65.

2. Zhuqian, founded in 1733, was the Danshui subprefectural seat. In 1875, the city's name was changed to Xinzhu when it became the administrative center of the newly created county of the same name. Lamley, "The Formation of Cities," 158.

3. In the interests of economy of expression, subprefectural chief administrators (*tongzhi*) will be termed "subprefects" rather than "subprefectural magistrates," as suggested by Hucker, nos. 6748 and 7471.

4. Susan Naquin's works on sectarian groups are certainly the prime examples. See her *Millenarian Rebellion in China: The Eight Trigrams Uprising of 1813* (New Haven, Conn.: Yale University Press, 1976) and *Shantung Rebellion: The Wang Lun Uprising of 1774* (New Haven, Conn.: Yale University Press, 1981). On the use of confessions, see Naquin, "True Con-

fessions: Criminal Interrogations as Sources for Ch'ing History," *National Palace Museum Bulletin* [Taiwan] 11, no. 1 (1976).

5. Here, of course, I refer to Bodde and Morris.

6. See, for example, Robert J. Antony, "The Social Meaning of Larceny in the Mid-Qing," unpublished paper delivered at the 1992 annual meeting of the Association for Asian Studies, Washington, D.C., April 2–5, 1992.

7. Of course, criminal cases often have their origins in "civil" disputes and can therefore also be extremely revealing. For an example, see Thomas Buoye, "Property Rights Disputes in Guangdong During the Qianlong Period," paper presented at the 38th Annual Midwest Conference on Asian Affairs, Oct. 28–29, 1989, Michigan State University, East Lansing.

8. There is also a brief description of the archives in Chang Bin Liu, Appendix A, 309–13.

9. *Xinzhu xian zhidu kao.*

10. See Suzuki Sōgen, especially his introductory remarks on the first page of the first installment of his three-part series. Chang Bin Liu, 309, is mistaken in asserting that "there is no evidence that [the Japanese] ever used these archival materials."

11. Dai, "Qingdai Dan-Xin dang'an," 1.

12. See Guoli Taiwan daxue, Falü xuexi, preface by Sa Mengwu, vii–viii; Dai, "Qingdai Dan-Xin dang'an," 2-5; Dai and Shi; and *Dan-Xin dang'an xuanlu xingzheng bian chuji.*

13. This may soon change if, as reported, a Taiwan publishing company is in the process of preparing the cases for publication. See Yin, *Taiwan jindaishi lun*, 183.

14. In 1968, the cases were microfilmed in Taiwan, and a copy of the film sent to the University of Washington. Beginning in 1977, it became possible to purchase copies from the university, and various institutions have done so.

15. See Dai, *Qingdai Taiwan zhi xiangzhi.*

16. Shi, "Qingdai Zhuqian."

17. Jonathan Ocko has also utilized some of the civil cases in his study of family conflict.

18. Shiga Shūzō, "Tan-Shin tōan."

19. See Bodde and Morris and the works cited therein. Most of the contributors to Cohen, Edwards, and Chen, a notable recent publication focusing on law, rely mainly on dynastic legal codes.

20. This translation, confined to the text of the Code's statutes, is the work of William Jones of the School of Law, Washington University, St. Louis. It will replace the first English translation of the Qing Code by Staunton, published in the early nineteenth century.

21. See McLeod and Yates, Johnson, and P. H-C. Chen. Hulsewé's

study of Han (206 B.C.–A.D. 220) law is based on references to statutes quoted or alluded to in the dynastic histories (Anton F. P. Hulsewé, "'Contracts' of the Han Period," in Lionello Lanciotti, ed., *Il Diritto in Cina: Teoria e Applicazioni durante le Dinaste Imperiali e Problematica del Diritto Cinese Contemporaneo*, pp. 11–38 [Venice: Leo S. Olschki, 1978]). The Han Code has not survived. A project to translate the Ming (1368–1644) code seems to have become moribund.

22. An earlier treatment of Han contracts is found in Hulsewé.

23. Brian E. McKnight, *The Quality of Mercy: Amnesties and Traditional Chinese Justice* (Honolulu: University Press of Hawaii, 1981); and McKnight, translated, Sung Tz'u, *The Washing Away of Wrongs* (Ann Arbor: Center for Chinese Studies, University of Michigan [Science, Medicine, and Technology in East Asia, vol. 1], 1981).

24. See, for example, Zhang, Zhang, and Zeng and also the appropriate sections (pt. 1, chap. 2, sec. 5) of Zhang Deze. Some short discussions of various aspects of China's legal history may be found in *Falüshi luncong* (Treatises on legal history) (Beijing: Shehui kexue chubanshe). I have been able to inspect the 1981 and 1982 issues.

25. The concept and acceptance of macroregions in China are, of course, most directly traceable to the work of G. William Skinner, especially his contributions to Skinner, *The City in Late Imperial China*.

26. Two outstanding examples are Shepherd, and Wolf and Huang.

27. Here I am thinking of studies such as Ng and also Gardella, "The Maritime History of Late Imperial China." See also the publications of John E. Wills, Jr., such as *Pepper, Guns, and Parleys: The Dutch East India Company and China, 1622–1681* (Cambridge, Mass.: Harvard University Press, 1974).

28. See the case summaries in Chapters 3 and 4 and the first part of Chapter 5.

29. See *Dan-Xin dang'an xuanlu*.

30. Only 1,160 cases were microfilmed. See Appendix 1.

31. Buxbaum, 256.

32. There was a well-defined body of administrative law governing the agencies and personnel of the government. It was compiled in such works as Wen.

33. Shiga, "Criminal Procedure," 2.

34. Buxbaum, 261–63. Buxbaum also points out that while the covers of some cases were explicitly labeled "criminal" (*xing*), the others did not bear any notation corresponding to the concept of a civil case. Ibid., 256, n. 2. It may be that the label signified that the Legal Section (*xingfang*) or the magistrate's legal secretary (*xingming muyou*) was to deal with the case.

35. Xue, 334:01 (vol. 4, 991–92). This is the most convenient compilation of the Qing Code. Xue's work was based on the 1863 edition of the Code, which was in use until 1905, and includes annotations appended to nearly

every statute and substatute. Xue's notes point out ambiguities and inconsistencies in Code provisions along with the date of origin and any subsequent revision of each item. Bodde and Morris, 67–68.

36. The Qing Code as a whole contained 436 statutes in six major sections. The section containing "civil" statutes was titled Household Laws (*hulü*). Xue, 075:00–157:00 (vol. 2, 229–vol. 3, 413).

37. This was the procedural rule for appeals, but as Ocko demonstrates in "I'll Take It All the Way," in practice appeals of minor matters often went beyond the provincial authorities "all the way" to the highest level judicial authorities in the capital.

38. Buxbaum, 265–66, Table I.

39. This period, perhaps coincidentally, almost exactly corresponds to the years between the establishment of an independent county magistracy in Xinzhu and the splitting off of Xinzhu's southern half to form Miaoli county in 1889.

40. Buxbaum, 266.

41. Cole, 151, cites a comparable incident in 1912 after the fall of the Qing dynasty, in which the Zhuji county (Shaoxing prefecture, Zhejiang) archives, reportedly extending back "several hundred years," were intentionally burned in order to destroy evidence of tax fraud.

42. See Chapter 2 for a discussion of Mengjia.

43. See TWC.

44. For a description, see Huang Youxing, 100–119.

45. See, for example, TW in the Bibliography.

CHAPTER 2

1. In terms of present-day administrative divisions, the area included a small sliver of northern Taizhong county, the western portions (i.e., the coastal plains and foothills) of Miaoli and Xinzhu counties, much of Taoyuan and Taibei counties, again excepting the mountain regions, as well as the municipalities of Taibei and Jilong.

2. By 1895, at the end of the period studied here, Xinzhu county looked very similar to the modern county except that to the north it included much of present-day southern Taoyuan county.

3. The clearest and most succinct accounts of the subprefecture, county, and city that served as administrative seat for both are Bi, 278–86; and Lamley, "Formation of Cities," 158–64. Unless otherwise noted, the following summary is based upon them. For the evolution of administrative centers in Taiwan as a whole, see Shi, "Qingdai Taiwan."

4. Skinner, "Cities," 308, 321.

5. Zhanghua county had also been established in 1723.

6. The name of the city literally meant "bamboo moat," and its derivation is often traced to the protective bamboo hedge that was not replaced

by more substantial fortifications until early in the nineteenth century. See, for example, Lamley, "Formation of Cities," 158. It seems more likely that the name was taken from the Zhuqian aborigine tribe who lived there long before the arrival of the Chinese. The tribe's name in their own language was rendered as Zhuqian by early Chinese visitors. For several citations of the name Zhuqian from works written years or decades before 1733, see Chen Chaolong, 11–12.

7. Chen Peigui, 46. Yin, "Xinzhuang xunjian," 360.

8. Chen Peigui, 46. Yin, "Xinzhuang xunjian," 361. One source asserts that Danshui subprefects began to spend half the year away from Zhuqian only after the creation of the Mengjia vice subprefect post, which is said to have taken place not until 1809. Abe, 95.

9. On the growth of Mengjia and the other towns, see Lamley, "Formation of Cities," 168–72.

10. Shinchiku chō somuka, 298.

11. Cases from this area had long been tried in Mengjia in any event.

12. As explained below, central government concern over the anomalous status of tribal peoples and tribal land was significant in prompting an island-wide reorganization.

13. The spread of Han settlers into the Zhuqian region and areas north and south of it have been detailed in Sheng. My account here will rely heavily on Sheng's work.

14. Hsu, "From Aboriginal Island," 10. Chinese had inhabited the Penghu (Pescadores) islands situated in the Taiwan Straits between Taiwan and the Chinese mainland as early as the eleventh century. Ibid, 6.

15. Ibid., 17.

16. The Spanish also established a presence in northern Taiwan between 1626 and 1642 but confined their activities to proselytization of the native tribes. The Dutch finally drove these rivals out of Taiwan back to the Spanish colony in the Philippines. Ibid., 12–14.

17. Ibid., 17–18.

18. Ibid., 23–25.

19. As we shall see, after 1683 immigrants continued to be predominantly male but for other reasons.

20. Hsu, "From Aboriginal Island," 17.

21. Sheng, 159–60. Shi, "Taiwan lishi," concludes that Wang Shijie's group arrived circa 1705–15.

22. Sheng, 160. Wang Qichu, who had a different surname, was not related to Wang Shijie. For a thorough discussion of the area settled by Wang Qichu, see Shi, "Qingdai Zhuqian."

23. The system of land rights in the area is discussed in Chapter 4.

24. Corporate entities will be discussed in more detail in later chapters.

25. Sheng, 161.

26. Ibid., 169.

27. See Shepherd, *Statecraft*, especially chaps. 7 and 9.
28. Sheng, 168.
29. On Hakka settlement in the area, see Lian Wenxi.
30. Sheng, 143.
31. See the discussion of overseers in Chapter 8.
32. On restrictive immigration and border policies in Taiwan, see Shepherd, *Statecraft*, chap. 7; also Yang Xi, 73–99.
33. Sheng, 139.
34. Ibid., 143. For more on Jin-Guang-Fu, see Chapter 4.
35. Ibid., 143.
36. Ibid., 149–150.
37. A recent account and evaluation of the attempt to open the mountains for settlement by pacifying the tribes may be found in Zhang Shixian, 129–50, 286–92.

CHAPTER 3

1. On the innovations in policing, see Chapter 8.
2. See Lee for Manchuria and Waley-Cohen for Xinjiang.
3. Perdue explores these issues for Hunan province; for Sichuan, see Entenmann.
4. Shepherd, *Statecraft*, 7.
5. Harry Lamley has studied these armed affrays extensively. See his "Subethnic Rivalry," and also "*Hsiehtou*."
6. Most immigrants in Taiwan came from four prefectures in Fujian: Quanzhou and Zhangzhou primarily but also Tingzhou and Xinghua. Ino, vol. 3, 382.
7. Besides Jiaying department, Hakkas came from Huizhou and Chaozhou prefectures in Guangdong. Fujian's Tingzhou prefecture was also the point of origin for some Hakka immigrants to Taiwan. Chen Yundong, 97. In 1926, descendants of Guangdong immigrants who were, it is presumed, mostly Hakkas made up 60.7 percent of Xinzhu county's Chinese population. Lian Wenxi, 16, citing Taiwan Sōtokufu, *Taiwan zaiseki Kan minzoku kyōkanbetsu chōsa* (An investigation of the native places of Taiwan's Han population), a Japanese colonial government census published in 1928. Taking the island as a whole, Lian (p. 19) estimates that Hakkas made up 15 percent of the total population during the late Qing and Japanese periods.
8. Ng, 101.
9. Dai, *Qingdai Taiwan zhi xiangzhi*, 296–98.
10. Many claimed Guangdong's Lufeng county as their native place.
11. Dai, *Qingdai Taiwan zhi xiangzhi*, 304–09.
12. Of 87 rebellions or uprisings in Qing Taiwan, 78 began in the southern or central part of the island. See Liu Niling, 258–59. In a few

instances, such as the 1862 Dai Chaochun uprising that began in Zhanghua, rebel activity spread northward into Danshui subprefecture.

13. Zheng and Zeng, 211–12.

14. Lamley, "Subethnic Rivalry," 304.

15. Ibid., 294–95. As the Wu family (to be discussed in Chapter 4) demonstrates, however, some strong, unified lineages did develop in the Dan-Xin area.

16. Ibid., 309–12.

17. For the text, see Chen Peigui, 180.

18. Zhang Gucheng, 84.

19. On immigration policy, its fluctuation, and results, see Shepherd, *Statecraft*, 142–46.

20. Ibid., 143.

21. Hsu, "Frontier Social Organization," 88, citing Lan Dingyuan, *Dongzheng ji*.

22. Ibid., 90–93. There is a voluminous literature on Chinese secret societies. For an introduction, see Chesneaux.

23. Liu Niling, 300, 304.

24. Ibid., 303.

25. Ibid., 304–5.

26. In this case summary and those to follow, citations of documents from the Dan-Xin archives are indicated by bracketed numbers that specify the case and document. See Appendix 1 for a fuller explanation.

27. Legally the term "armed robbery" meant robbery by force (or the threat thereof) committed openly. For the statute and its 49 substatutes, see Xue, 266:00–49 (vol. 3, 589–622).

28. A manager was a person selected to oversee the operations of public organizations, particularly those with religious or ritual purposes. See "Kyūkan mondo roku" TKK 1, no. 6 (June 1901): 36–44. The town and village leadership system will be discussed in Chapter 8.

29. It is not clear what *dianqi*, which has been translated as "shop bills," were. Because Zhan listed them among the stolen goods, they probably were assets such as IOUs whose theft would mean financial loss to the store or possibly documents such as negotiable financial instruments that could be sold by the robbers.

30. The guardpost in question was probably the Jin-Guang-Fu Large Guardpost. See the discussion of guardpost rent in Chapter 4.

31. Harboring robbers or thieves, a crime that included receiving stolen goods, was a serious accusation, since punishment for it could be as severe as decapitation, depending on the circumstances of the case. Xue, 278:00 (vol. 4, 752–53), "Harborers of Robbers" (*daozei wozhu*).

32. Identical to a petition (*cheng*) in every way, the term *su* was a purely formal indicator that the document had been filed by someone already accused in a case. As Chapter 7 will make clear, normally a woman was

legally required to file complaints through a proxy filer (*baogao*), a close relative whose name was to be listed on the complaint. No proxy is listed for Mrs. Liu. This may have been a clerical error, or it may indicate that the magistrate accepted her plaint in spite of its technical legal flaw. A subsequent plaint [33319:96] filed by Mrs. Liu also failed to list a proxy.

33. It was probably not an oversight that Mrs. Liu's plaint did not state whether her sons had actually collected the money or not.

34. It is unclear whether or not this project was the work referred to by Mrs. Liu in her counterplaint.

35. The implication, of course, was that only landlords were subject to such a levy.

36. *Dabi* was an archaic legal term used during the predynastic period to indicate the death penalty. The *locus classicus* of the term seems to be the *Lüxing* section, which is regarded as authentic, of the *Documents* (*Shangshu*) classic. See James Legge, trans., *The Chinese Classics* (5 vols. Hong Kong: Hong Kong University Press, 1961 [1893–95]), vol. 3, *The Shoo King*, 605.

37. Xinpu was a market town about six kilometers north of Jiuqionglin (modern Qionglin), the location of the He-Xing store, while Shuqilin (modern Zhudong) was about 2.4 kilometers south and slightly east of Jiuqionglin. See Map 5.

38. Only in certain parts of the Xinzhu area where Hakka numbers were concentrated could they shed their usual minority status vis-à-vis Hokkienese.

39. This *jiashou* identified himself as being responsible for irrigation matters in the locality [33319:30]. See also Kobayashi (2), 83, where the term is defined as a person selected to manage irrigation canals. The terminology had no apparent connection to the *baojia* system, which was not implemented in the Xinzhu area until 1871. Even then it seemed to function only as a census mechanism. Dai Yanhui, *Qingdai Taiwan zhi xiangzhi*, 81.

40. Linked villages (*lianzhuang*) seemed to have security and defense functions similar to the *baojia* system. The *lianzhuang* system differed from the more familiar *baojia* in that persons within the former unit were not saddled with collective responsibility for crimes committed by their fellow villagers. As will be shown in Chapter 8, *lianzhuang* were similar to *tuanlian* militias described by Wakeman and also Kuhn.

41. In the early days of settlement, settlers sometimes organized themselves in groups called *jie*. The head of such a group was called a *jieshou*. Kobayashi (7), 85. Later, in areas where an attempt was made to organize the *baojia*, a unit of ten households seems originally to have been called a *jie*. Each *jie* was headed by a *jieshou*. Later, the more conventional terms *pai* and *paishou* came into use. Dai Yanhui, *Qingdai Taiwan zhi xiangzhi*, 67, citing case 12403:3 dated 1872 (TZ 11).

42. Gan Nanwang and Fan Ahai both contracted cases of diarrhea or perhaps dysentery and appear to have been seen by a physician [33319:89, 91, 99, 100]. It is not clear whether the doctor came to their cells or runners took the prisoners to be treated. In the case of Liu Dongjin, the physician was summoned to examine him at the yamen. The doctor treated Liu with antipyretics. The diagnoses and prescriptions [33319:109, 110, 111] were copied into the case file, possibly in order to absolve the authorities of any liability for his death. See Chapter 9 for a discussion of prisoners and disease.

43. On the significance of bonds and guarantors, see Chapter 9.

44. The details are obscure. Regarding this incident only three pieces of evidence, each with the same viewpoint, remain in the case file. Lan Huagun's father, Lan Tong, and Zhan Ajing, the other partner in the store, filed a report [33319:104] on 8 July 1883 (GX 9/6/5) and also a petition [33319:122] on 20 February 1884 (GX 10/1/24). Information contained in these records is augmented by a report [33319:105] from Lan Huagun himself on 25 February 1883 (GX 9/6/10). Both of the documents filed by Lan Tong and Zhan Ajing have appended several earlier court directives and, in the case of the petition, a transcription of testimony taken earlier.

45. Lan Huagun's original complaint [33319:4] named one Huang Azan but no one else surnamed Huang.

46. His release had been justified on the grounds that if he were eventually found not to have instigated the death of Huang Wang, then at most he could be punished only by beating with the heavy stick (*zhang*). This brief summary of the charges against Wen and Lan did not specify the legal basis for the possible sentence of beating.

47. Zhu followed Zhou Zhikan as chief administrator in Xinzhu.

48. In addition to the allegations made against Zhan Pengcai in this case, in GX 13 (1887), he was implicated in a different incident for allegedly helping abduct a married woman. See case 35404.

CHAPTER 4

1. See the discussion of settlement in the Danshui/Xinzhu area in Chapter 2. Settlement and reclamation practices in this area were characteristic of those of most of the northern half of the island. The same cannot be said of southern Taiwan because of the distinctive nature of land settlement during the Dutch and Zheng periods.

2. The reference here is to the famous "one-field, two- (or three-) owners" (*yitian liang (san) zhu*) customary practice of land tenure. See Niida, "Fukken no ichi-den ryōshu oyobi sanshu kanshū" (Fujian's custom of one field, two owners or three owners) in his *Chūgoku hōsei-shi kenkyū*, vol. 2, 198–215. For a short comparison of similar practices in southeast China and Taiwan, see Yang Guozhen.

3. The following discussion is based on Lian Yatang, 201–32.

4. See the summary of the boundary dispute case in Chapter 5.

5. Sheng, Wang, and Gao, 461.

6. One example can be seen in a lease reproduced in *Qingdai Taiwan dazu diaocha shu*, 64.

7. Ino, vol. 2, 541. But see Appendix 2, "Measures of Land and Grain."

8. See Appendix 2, "Measures of Land and Grain."

9. Taxes were assessed at the following rates. Paddy fields: upper grade—0.08534 taels of silver and 0.00695 *shi* of autumn rice per *mou*; middle grade—0.065884 taels and 0.00387 *shi* of autumn rice; lower grade—0.05755 taels with no rice levy. Dry fields: upper grade—same as middle grade paddy fields; middle grade—same as lower grade paddy fields; lower grade—0.05618 taels and no rice. The commutation rate was 0.36 taels per *shi* of ordinary grain and 10 *shi* of autumn rice per every 2 *shi* of ordinary grain. Thus in terms of *jia* (with 1 *jia* defined for tax purposes to be equal to 11 *mou*) and ordinary grain, the tax burden for the three grades of paddy was 2.74, 2.08, and 1.75 *shi* per *jia*; for dry fields it was 2.08, 1.75, and 1.71. These figures are taken from Zheng and Zeng, 49–50. One *shi* equaled 2.95 U.S. bushels or 103.95 liters. See Appendix 2.

10. New tax rates were also published, with paddy being assessed at 3.08561, 2.52351, and 2.08054 taels per *jia*. Dry fields were discounted as before, with lower grade dry fields assessed at 8 / 10 of low grade paddy, or 1.66 taels. Zheng and Zeng, 53–54.

11. Sheng, 165–66. Ibid., 167, n. 1, reproduces part of an estate division agreement dated QL 9 (1744) that discusses land reclamation around Daqiqian.

12. As many other examples in the Dan-Xin cases show, land rights could also be mortgaged or used to repay debts.

13. Rinji Taiwan kyūkan chōsa kai, *Taiwan shihō furoku sankōsho* (1910. Reprint, 13 vols. Taipei: Southern Materials Center, 1983), *ken* 1, *jō*, 195, (hereafter cited as *Shihō* or *Shihō sankōsho* when referring respectively to the main text or to the supplemental volumes).

14. Ch'iu-k'un Ch'en, "Landlord and Tenant," 186, n. 2.

15. The text may be found in Chen Chaolong, 226–28.

16. It is nearly an invariable rule that the area of the plot in question was not given in any land transaction documents. Plots were specified by describing the boundaries. This being the case, it is difficult to obtain enough data on rent rates to reach statistically significant findings.

17. "Technically, the meltage fee was a charge added to regular tax remittances to compensate for the inevitable loss of silver that resulted when taxes were melted down into large ingots for transporting to the central government. . . . At the same time, the term *huo-hao* [meltage fee] came to describe almost any general percentage surcharge for which no other special term existed." See Zelin, *The Magistrate's Tael*, 88. In the

documents under consideration here, the meltage fee is denoted by the term *haoxian*, a synonym for *huo-hao*.

18. The aboriginal rent had been abolished or more properly speaking transformed after the creation of the military settlement system following the Lin Shuangwen rebellion. See the discussion below.

19. The 1786 rebellion was that of Lin Shuangwen. See below.

20. Irrevocable sale should be contrasted with conditional sale (*dian*), for which see Xue, 95:00–11 (vol. 2, 280–84).

21. A petition [22202:128] seems to imply that Wu and ten other lineages owned the large-rent rights to most of the land in the entire Daqiqian area.

22. See also the discussion of collective legal personae in Chapter 7.

23. See Chapter 5, boundary dispute case.

24. The reconquest of the rebel-held parts of the island was one of the so-called ten completions (*shi quan*) or military achievements claimed by the Qianlong emperor. See Xiao, vol. 2, 129–35. On the Lin Shuangwen rebellion, see Lian Yatang, 913–22, and Ino, vol. 1, 819–42.

25. Fukang'an has a biography in Hummel, 253–55. For his memorial, see Ino, vol. 1, 366. The imperial edict approving his proposal can be found in *Qingdai Taiwan dazu diaocha shu*, 1023–29.

26. Setting up *tun* was a common practice on other Chinese frontiers. According to Danshui's local history, the establishment of *tun* in Taiwan followed the precedent set in Sichuan province, where tribal settlements became the nuclei of military settlements. See Chen Peigui, 64–65. The best secondary account of the military settlement system in Taiwan and its role in transforming some aborigines into rent-collecting landlords is Shepherd, *Statecraft*, 332–52. See also Dai, *Qingdai Taiwan zhi xiangzhi*, 465–530.

27. Chen Peigui, 64–65.

28. Dai, *Qingdai Taiwan zhi xiangzhi*, 496–97.

29. Ibid., 511–12, citing Rinji Taiwan kyūkan chōsa kai, *Taiwan shihō*, 399.

30. Chen Peigui, 64.

31. Ibid., 45.

32. Dai, *Qingdai Taiwan zhi xiangzhi*, 544–46.

33. Ibid., 548–49.

34. Chen Peigui, 46.

35. Ibid., 44–47. One additional post was classified as civilian, but it was financed by military settlement rent rather than guardpost rent.

36. On Jin-Guang-Fu, see Guo Zhiting, 1–6; Dai Yanhui, *Qingdai Taiwan zhi xiangzhi*, 561–62, n. 2; Moser, 2–9.

37. This is an unusual case of collaboration between Hakka and Hokkienese. One partner, Jiang Xiuzuan, was a Hakka descended from Guangdong settlers. The other partner was of Fujianese stock. Jiang's

original partner, Lin Dexiu, was subsequently replaced by Zhou Bangzheng, also descended from Fujian settlers. Their firm's name reflected their differing backgrounds: Guang for Guangdong and Fu for Fujian. Jin, the first component of the organization's name, meant "gold" or "money" and because of its auspicious connotation was a common initial element in partnership and commercial names. Various accounts of the origin of the partnership are summarized in Sheng, 144. See also Zhuang and Chen, 15–16.

38. Reprinted in Dai Yanhui, *Qingdai Taiwan zhi xiangzhi*, 607–9.

39. At least one instance of an even higher figure, twenty *shi* is on record in Houdong village in Zhubei second township. See 17305:5.

40. Danshui county, the other administrative unit created from the old subprefecture, reported much lower rates, with a maximum of only three *shi* and an average of two *shi* per *jia* of paddy land. Unfortunately, there seem to be no more precise figures. Even the ranges given by Xinzhu county were based on "questioning some county people" rather than documentation that the county admitted it did not have. It also seems impossible to determine how much cultivated land was subject to guardpost rent. An 1886 report [17333:1] concluded that overall the 45 guardposts in Xinzhu county collected 23,380.92 *shi* plus 259 silver dollars in rent. No mention of cultivated land area was made, however. Neither report addressed the question of different rates for paddy and dry fields in Xinzhu county. It was disclosed in the circa 1888 document [13212:1] that nearby Yilan county on Taiwan's east coast reported that dry field guardpost rent was half that of paddy fields.

41. Chen Peigui, 63.

42. When landlords who had taken out interest-bearing loans from the prefectural government treasury defaulted and their land rent rights were taken over, such lands were termed *shengxi*. Such cases appear to have been confined to southern Taiwan. Lian Yatang, 219–20. The practice of investing public funds at interest seems to have been an innovation developed during the fiscal reform movement initiated by the Yongzheng emperor. The first recorded instance of such a loan was in Jiangxi in 1735. Zelin, *The Magistrate's Tael*, 281.

43. Chen Peigui, 65. The Dai Chaochun uprising can be traced to a mixture of local feuds and anti-Qing secret society activities. See Meskill, 117–28. For a biography of Dai Chaochun (courtesy name: Wansheng) and an account of his rebellion, see Lian Yatang, 983–94. See also the biographies of Lin Zhanmei and Luo Guanying, 1003–8 in the same work.

44. On *banbing*, see Li Ruhe.

45. For Azuma on the economy, see 239–88, "Shinchō jika Taiwan no chidai kankei" (Land rent relationships in Taiwan under Qing rule). Azuma relied primarily on Taiwan Government-General surveys and

reports, principally Rinji Taiwan kyūkan chōsakai dai ichi bu (first section), and Rinji Taiwan kyūkan chōsa kai.

46. Lian Yatang, 207.

47. Such at least was the belief of Japanese investigators in 1901. See Kinashi, TKK 1, no. 8 (Aug. 1901): 62.

48. See, for example, leasing agreement between landlord Li Chaoying and four tenants reproduced in *Qingdai Taiwan dazu diaocha shu*, 60–61.

49. Kinashi, TKK 1, no. 8 (Aug. 1901): 62.

50. The lease is reproduced in *Qingdai Taiwan dazu diaocha shu*, 64.

51. Rinji Taiwan kyūkan chōsa kai, 217–18.

52. Azuma, 270.

53. As before, rents are in terms of the 10 percent oversized *shi* used by the large-rent householders, and price, tax, and income amounts are in foreign silver dollars.

54. Wang Yitao, 309–10. For a treatment of Liu's reform program as a whole, see Speidel; also Chu.

55. Wang Yitao, 310.

56. The 125 *shi* figure is misleading since land was not evenly distributed. Depending on the rent register, either 58 percent or 64 percent of the tenants rented less than five *jia* of land.

57. Chen Chaolong, 67.

58. "Taisoken ni kansuru ken" (Concerning the large-rent right), 44–47 in "Kyūkan mondo roku" (Record of questions and answers about old customs). TKK 1, no. 6 (June 1901): 36–47.

59. It seems likely that these statements about "damaging" the land or "digging holes" in it refer to mining operations. Coal and sulfur were important minerals found in northern Taiwan, and tenants may have preferred to shift to nonagricultural pursuits.

60. Shepherd, "Rethinking Tenancy," 424.

61. Dai Yanhui, "Qingdai Taiwan zhi daxiaozu ye," 26; Azuma Yoshio, 262–64.

62. Chen Peigui, 60.

63. As we will recall, Liu Dongjin was an innkeeper who, after being jailed on suspicion of harboring robbers, died of disease in the Xinzhu jail.

64. The term transliterated as *bak* is a Taiwanese word that as far as I have been able to discover has no Mandarin Chinese pronunciation. By itself it means "to arrange" or "to tie up." I am grateful to Fu-mei Chen for this information. In the Dan-Xin documents I have seen it indicates a small-rent arrangement.

65. Dadu was located between Jiuqionglin and Shuqilin. See Map 5, Chapter 3.

66. As Azuma made clear, these were estimates only. For his sources, see n. 45 above.

67. *Qidiyin*, literally "gravel land money," has been translated as "caution money" by Ch'en Ch'iu-k'un, 110, n. 7; Zhuang and Chen, 27, citing Rinji Taiwan kyūkan chōsa kai 1: 581, explain the term as originating from the landlords' desire to be compensated for the labor and expense entailed in transforming wasteland into productive fields.

68. In an XF 5/2/3 (20 March 1855) petition [22202:29], Wu Shifen stated his family had five collateral lines. Wu Jiqing, in testimony [22202:151] during XF 11, confirmed that there were five collateral branches. However, an even later (1862) petition [22202:178] makes reference to copies of a notice of certain supplementary tax surcharges. Only four names—Wu Youji, Wu Yuanji, and Wu Liji as well as Wu Shunji—were listed. The common final character of the four names indicates that each may have been a collateral line (*fang*) of a parent lineage. Another petition [22202:165] had been filed by "Wu Shunji viz. Wu Yuanji viz. Wu Zhixiang." However, that was the sole appearance in the files of anyone named Wu who identified himself with other than the Wu Shunji appellation by itself.

69. In the case files the Chinese word *ji*, when it appears between two different appellations of the same person, is intended to indicate that the second name is a more formal one such as a cognomen (*zi*) or is used to show that the second name marks the individual who is acting or is identified as the representative of a group. In the first case *ji* means "namely" or "also known as." In the second it means something like "in the person of." In all instances *ji* is translated as "viz."

70. Other Wu lineage members joined the case leader in filing on occasion. See, for example, 22202:128, where, in addition to Wu Jiqing, Wu Shiren, Wu Shijing, and Wu Rongsheng joined Wu Guoying in filing.

71. Sheng, 166, locates Daqiqian near the modern town of Xinwu, that is, in the eastern part of the area between the modern city of Yangmei in Taoyuan county and the sea coast. The territory so identified is bounded on the north and south by the Daku and Shezi Rivers (*qi*), respectively. The Danshui subprefecture local gazetteer placed Daqiqian *zhuang* only 25 *li* (approximately 13.5 kilometers) from the yamen. Chen Peigui, 49.

72. Although the lineage employed managers to assist them in the struggle against their tenants, the bursary (*zuzhan*), an institution so important at about the same time for landlords in the Suzhou area of the lower Yangzi region, apparently did not exist in northern Taiwan. On bursaries, see the two works by Muramatsu; also Lojewski.

73. Large sections of this document have been damaged.

74. Xue, 090:00 (vol. 2, 267), "Fraudulently concealing land taxes" (*qiyin tianliang*).

75. First Lictor Section head runner, Gao Sheng, who was the township duty runner (*duibao*) [22202:19], XF 3/12/22 (20 Jan. 1854).

76. As noted in Appendix 2, one *shi* equaled 103.95 liters.

77. In 1792, not long after the Lin Shuangwen rebellion had shaken Qing control over the island, Hadang'a, commanding general of the Taiwan brigade, proposed a substatute, which was approved for inclusion under the Code's statute on rebellion, specifically targeted against secret societies in Fujian, to which Taiwan was administratively subordinate, and Guangdong. Xue, 255:07 (vol. 3, 565), "Secret society bandits in the two provinces of Min [Fujian] and Yue [Guangdong] who plunder and resist arrest" (*Min Yue liangsheng huifei qiangjie jubu*). Xue mistakenly refers to Hadang'a as Hashang'a.

78. Their petition lists ages of 21 and 18 for the brothers. This would have made them 11 and 8 in 1845.

79. The petition from Wu is not in the file.

80. There was some confusion about Luo's given name. Here and in one or two other documents he was referred to as Luo Ase.

81. Fan Linxiang was one of the principal rent-resisting tenants named in Wu-Shun-Ji's first petition in the case file.

82. Yamen runners and their organization are discussed in Chapter 8.

83. On overseers and other quasi-bureaucratic village leaders, see Chapter 8.

84. Danshui subprefects spent half of each year in Mengjia.

85. Here Fan acknowledged the close connection between large rent and land taxes.

86. Jiang Dianbang, two years earlier the mediator between the Wu lineage and the brothers, Jiang Shuangnian and Jiang Shuangquan, was the son of Jin-Guang-Fu Large Guardpost founder Jiang Xiuzuan. See Zhuang and Chen, 10, chart 2. Jiang Dianbang's son, Jiang Ronghua, also became involved in the case. See the discussion of events in late XF 11.

87. At least one tax receipt [22202:70] was returned to the yamen because the tenant did not pay the full amount.

88. In the documents money amounts were expressed in dollars per ten *shi*. Thus the grain market price reported by Jiang et al. was 6.5 dollars per ten *shi*. Transport costs were given in the same fashion. In truth, the figure reported by the three men on XF 6/10/25 (22 November 1856) may have been lower than the actual or final sale price. Four months later, Chief Tax Clerks Zhang Wen and Zhu Ying reported [22202:75] that grain could be sold for 0.74 dollars per *shi*. If the latter figure was accurate, we may assume that the overseer and his associates, including the miller, made a handsome commission on the transaction.

89. My summary of the tenants' allegations against Wu draws also on four subsequent complaints [22202:92, 98, 119, 133], the last of which was filed on XF 10/i3/25 (15 May 1860).

90. A *jia* was very nearly equivalent to one hectare. See Appendix 2, "Measures of Land and Grain."

91. The "1-9-8" method was unusual. In areas where variable rates

remained customary in the nineteenth century, the normal administrative fee was 5 percent, and the system was termed "1-9-5." See the discussion earlier in this chapter.

92. If substandard harvests occurred with significant frequency or if crop yields on the land were declining, the landlord would be expected to prefer a fixed rent rather than a percentage share of the harvest. In such circumstances tenants would have been better off with share rents. Since Wu Guoying argued for share rents, crop yields must have been constant or increasing, in which case tenants would have favored fixed rents.

93. Although it is not apparent from the text of the court directive, later documents [22202:160] make clear that 25 tenants were liable for back rent. Xu and the three others arrested were in a sense their surrogates.

94. Interestingly, although termed military settlement rent, the money was to be used to supplement the flood damage allotment (*shuizhong zhi'e*) item in the yamen accounts.

95. It is not clear whom the subprefect was threatening with impeachment. Wu Zhixiang, who filed the petition in question, did not indicate that he possessed a degree. Other members of the lineage, however, had acquired the *shengyuan* or *jiansheng* degrees. Wu Guoying, who seems to have been the most senior member of the lineage to file petitions during the case, called himself a "dignitary" (*zhiyuan*), a word often used in the Dan-Xin area to refer to notables serving in some local, non-bureaucratic leadership position such as head of a reclamation and settlement organization or guardpost. Such men often added to their prestige by purchasing the *jiansheng* degree.

96. In China's interior at the time of this petition, XF 11/12/20 (19 Jan. 1862), the Taiping Rebellion had, of course, not yet been quelled.

97. Fan Atian, who had been in the yamen jail earlier, was released on XF 7/11/30 (14 Jan. 1858) after his grandfather agreed to pay back rent claimed by Wu [22202:90].

98. These other tenants were probably secondary tenants, the so-called primary cultivators, who, as we have seen, were responsible for actually remitting both large- and small-rent payments.

99. After 1862 (TZ 1), Danshui subprefects were undoubtedly prudent in their reluctance to move as vigorously as Qiu Yuejin had done. In the third month of that year, Qiu was killed while helping lead government troops against rebel forces in Zhanghua county just south of the Danshui subprefecture during the Dai Chaochun (Dai Wansheng) uprising. Although the uprising was engendered in an immediate sense by subethnic feuding rather than disputes over rent, it seems likely that Qiu's successors took his death as a signal for even greater caution in dealing with local problems. See Qiu's biography in Chen Peigui, 119–20.

100. See, e.g., 22202:183, 219, and 223 dated TZ 1/11/29, GX 2/7/7, and GX 4/10/24 (18 Jan. 1863, 25 Aug. 1876, and 18 Nov. 1878), respectively.

101. Until construction of the new prefectural offices at Taibei was completed, the prefect made his headquarters in Xinzhu, the old Danshui subprefectural seat, and administered both of the new counties, Xinzhu and Danshui, formed from the old subprefecture.

102. Some villagers seemed to be unaware of or perhaps unhappy with the new administrative boundaries. On GX 10/2/1 Daqiqian *zhuang* landlord Zeng Guoxing and others submitted a petition [12225:1] to Xinzhu magistrate Zhu Chenglie asking that the seal of an already impeached overseer be confiscated. See also petition [12226:1, GX 10/2/8] from Daqiqian residents and copy of a mutual aid covenant [12226:2, GX 9/9] submitted by Daqiqian residents in an attempt to avoid compulsory salt purchases from Mengjia.

103. See the lawsuit [23402] filed in 1858 by Wu Jiqing against a delinquent borrower.

CHAPTER 5

1. Because of resistance to the new regime, Ming loyalism, and the Rebellion of the Three Feudatories (1673–81), China's southern maritime regions were of intense concern to the Qing court from the founding of the dynasty until the conquest of Taiwan in 1683. As an offshore base for Zheng Chenggong (Koxinga) and his successors, who were the last group to pose a serious threat to Manchu control, Taiwan was particularly a focus of political and military policy. See Wills.

2. As early as the late seventeenth century, Quanzhou and Zhangzhou prefectures in southern Fujian relied on rice imports from Taiwan to offset local production shortfalls. Ng, 99.

3. In fact, because of the explosion in tea and camphor production as signaled by exports of those products from the port of Danshui, the economic center of the island had moved from the south to the north by the latter third of the nineteenth century. Lin Manhong, 87–90; also Daniels, 66.

4. Davidson, 394.

5. By 1899, of the 3,057 registered camphor stills on the island, 2,270 (74 percent) were located in Miaoli and Xinzhu counties. Ibid., 415, n. 1.

6. Head-hunting continued to be practiced by "raw" aborigines into the twentieth century. Ibid., 428–29.

7. Chen was the principal suspect in the kidnapping case summarized in this chapter.

8. *Lijin* was a mercantile tax first developed and controlled by provincial and local officials in the mid-nineteenth century. It was most often collected as a transit duty on goods but sometimes also took the form of "a production tax at the point of origin or as a sales tax at the destination." Feuerwerker, 61–62. For an extended discussion of *lijin*, see Mann, chapters 6 and 7.

9. Sheng, Wang, and Gao, 470–71, citing Chen and Zhou, *Zhuluo xianzhi* (Gazetteer of Zhuluo county), and Huang Shujing, *Taihai shicha lu* (A tour of duty in the Taiwan sea).

10. Sheng, Wang, and Gao, 471; Lian Yatang, 735. The tea was planted in the area of modern Ruifang *zhen*, Taibei county.

11. "[Taiwan] tea is green, not black. It is exported in great quantities to China, where it is used as a medicine. Generally the Chinese drink very little green tea." Julius H. Klaproth, *Mémoires relatifs à l'Asie, contenant des recherches historiques, geographiques et philologiques sur les peuples de l'Orient* (Paris: Librarie orientale de Dondey-Dupre, 1826–28), cited in Davidson, 373, n. 1.

12. Chen Peigui, 71.

13. Davidson, 395–96; Zhou Xianwen, 86.

14. Li Guoqi, *Zhongguo xiandaihua*, 349–50.

15. Ibid., 350.

16. Ibid., 350–51.

17. Ibid., 352.

18. Lin Manhong, 17, Table 9.

19. Unless otherwise noted, the following discussion is based on Shinchiku chō somuka, 513–15.

20. The land in question was near Dahukou.

21. For more details of the cultivation and harvest cycle see Shinchiku, chō somuka, 514–15, and Davidson, 380–82.

22. Rinji Taiwan kyūkan chōsa kai, *Sankōsho, ken* 1, *chu*, 369–70.

23. For example, when the partnership filed its first petition in the litigation, Lan Bin's younger brother, the Stipendiary (*lingsheng*) Lan Zhang, was the chief complainant. The other five partners listed in this first document were Liu Weiyan, Liu Bukui, Lai Xinkai, Liu Meilin, and Lu Xinfu. In subsequent documents filed by Jin-Liu-He, Liu Shangda replaced Liu Weiyan and became the partnership's chief representative. Similarly, Lan Bin replaced his brother (Lan Zhang), and Lu Zhangquan's name replaced that of Lu Xinfu.

24. When land was in the process of being cleared for planting tea, after trees were cut down, their roots removed, and sometimes the land burned over, "a crop of indigo or sweet potatoes is planted to be replaced, the following season, with young tea plants." Davidson, 380.

25. By the time of this case, the names of three of the four villages (*zhuang*)—Fangliao, Shangmayuan, Xiamayuan, and Miaoerding—named in the deed had changed.

26. Xu Xizhi, who had held office when the case was first opened, left the Xinzhu magistracy in GX 9/6 (ca. July 1883) but resumed the post from GX 10/3 (ca. Apr. 1884) to around GX 10/11 (Dec. 1884–Jan. 1885).

27. As suggested earlier, French military actions in northern Taiwan may have disrupted local administrative routine even as far south as Xinzhu. The French blockade was in effect until early April 1885. The French did not finally withdraw from the northern port of Jilong until June 22 (GX 11/5/10). Zheng and Zeng, 216. At any rate, there is a gap.

The documentary record is anomalous in another way. Documents up to the report of Fan Jisheng's death are in file number 22510, but the remainder of the case record is in file number 22514. Because no other records or references to this case have come to light, it seems likely that some relevant materials are missing from the Dan-Xin files.

28. From later comments by the magistrate following an interrogation [22514:35], it appears the court directive was an order to make a survey of the field boundaries.

29. Liu Afa's losses were representative: 1 thatched hut and all household articles burned, 3 large and small red cattle, 3 pigs, over 70,000 tea shrubs, over 4,000 catties of sweet potatoes, 6 piculs of early rice, over 50 piculs of dry field grain, 10 quilts and mosquito nets, over 80 catties of ready tea, 7 foreign dollars, 500 Qing cash, and men's and women's clothing stolen [22514:9].

30. Liao is recorded as the author of an inscription dated GX 4/6/6 commemorating the renovation of the Zhuqian aborigine settlement's public hall in Xinshe. Chen Chaolong, 234–35.

31. Apart from the contract and the grant [22510:5, 8] already copied into the case file two years before, Zhou Sunwei submitted a reclamation deed (*kenzi*) at the GX 11/8/29 (7 Oct. 1885) hearing.

32. The magistrate characterized Liao as daring "not to obey the horizontal tablet." The so-called horizontal tablet (*wobei*) referred to a list of eight exhortations and prohibitions directed at *shengyuan*. They were originally issued by the imperial court in 1651. The fifth of the eight articles enjoined *shengyuan* from involvement in lawsuits even as a witness. A *wobei* was required to be erected in each government school as a warning to students. Ch'ü, *Local Government*, 189, 321, n. 33. For the text of the horizontal tablet, see Chen Chaolong, 167–69.

33. Liu Bukui in his petition [22514:2] for the partners mentioned without being specific that the armed intruders had claimed to have a court order.

34. Chen Chaolong, 113, 116. Lin Hengmao was a member of the same lineage as Lin Zhanmei, who helped defend Zhuqian during the Dai Chaochun uprising. See Zhuang and Chen, 33.

35. This seems to be the first reference to a contract (*heyue*).

36. The gang member's double surname is very unusual. Confirmation that it was a two-character surname may be found in two case file documents [22514:133, 134], where his wife was referred to as Mrs. Pengxu née Cai (*Pengxu Cai shi*).

37. See 22514:103.

38. Fang appears later to have softened his view somewhat, as indicated in his endorsement of a report [22514:146] filed on GX 12/7/14 (13 Aug. 1886) by the aborigine landlord Qian Ronghe. See the discussion near the end of this case summary.

39. The absence of the petition of Zheng and Liu from the case file

regrettably deprives us of an opportunity to understand more clearly how they influenced this case.

40. A somewhat contrary position was taken three months later in comments appended to a petition accepted at the yamen. On GX 12/7/14 (13 Aug. 1886), the Zhuqian aborigine who had inherited the ultimate rights to the land granted to Jin-Liu-He and Jin-Jian-Mao proffered a report [22514:146] supporting the latter partnership's charges against the marauding Luo gang from Fenjiwo village. To this Fang replied: "I find that upland fields at Fengshanqiding were first sold to the four villages for cattle pasture. The deed records that Qingshan is the boundary to the east. There is conclusive proof of it. After this, you also sold the eastern boundary area to Jin-Liu-He to be agricultural land. This produced one property being divided among several parties thus causing conflict and stubbornness and resulting in the taking of human life."

These comments are very surprising, for it appears that the magistrate very nearly reversed himself. In response to other petitions, he several times rejected the villagers' contention, supported by their supposedly forged deed, that their land extended east to Qingshan. In fact, Fang's endorsement here contradicts both his earlier findings [22514:118] and the final boundary settlement [22514:160] that conformed to those findings.

41. Fang had earlier, on GX 12/2/12 (17 Mar. 1886), ordered [22514:100, 101] runners to transfer Liao from detention in the Tea Department to the supervision of Director of Schools Shi Tianjun.

42. Actually, this provision is contained in a statute entitled "Remaining at home to care for parents or to perpetuate the ancestral sacrifices" (*fanzui cunliu yangqin*). Xue, 018:00 (vol. 2, 61). See also Bodde and Morris, 139.

43. The accusers were the six partners (Liu Shangda, Liu Chunlian, Lan Bin, Liu Meilin, Lai Xinkai, and Lu Zhangquan) plus their tenant Zhong Haigu. The accused villagers were represented by Yang Chun, Zhou Sunwei, Wang Qiantai, Luo Axie, and Lo Tingchun. Mediators were Zhang Dexuan, Zhu Yuming, Huang Longxiang, Zhuang Jiangsheng, Lin Shouqi, and Huang Yanhe.

44. Davidson, 407, 405. Presumably the British intended to market the camphor in India.

45. Lian Yatang, 575.

46. Ibid., 575, says this was the British merchant firm *Deji yanghang*, identified as Tait & Co. in Sheng, Wang, and Gao, 427. Davidson, 400, points to an American, W. M. Robinet, as the first foreigner to trade in camphor. Azuma, 331, and Li Guoqi, *Zhongguo xiandaihua*, 353, both follow Davidson.

47. Lian Yatang, 575. If this is correct, between 3,458,000 and 3,990,000 lbs. were sold in total, with between 1,596,000 and 1,729,000 lbs. exported through Mengjia. Davidson, 442, indicates that in 1864, 1,171,464 lbs. were shipped from Danshui, that is, the Mengjia camphor office.

48. The camphor bureau paid six dollars a picul for the camphor and sold it to foreigners at sixteen dollars a picul. Li Guoqi, *Zhongguo xiandaihua*, 335.

49. Davidson, 402–4.

50. Ibid., 404–5; Li Guoqi, *Zhongguo xiandaihua*, 355.

51. Davidson, 405; Li Guoqi, *Zhongguo xiandaihua*, 355.

52. Lian Yatang, 578; Davidson, 406–7; Li Guoqi, *Zhongguo xiandaihua*, 356. The bureau overseeing the camphor monopoly also regulated the trade in sulfur.

53. The official determination of the facts of the earlier (GX 9) phase of the case was summarized by the Xinzhu magistrate in a report [32611:16] to both the Taibei prefect and the Taiwan provincial governor.

54. Xue, 336:05 (vol. 4, 998–99): "False Accusation: Accusers who do not appear in court for the hearing or who flee" (*yuangao bu daoan tingshen ji tuotao*).

55. On Chen, see Zhang Gucheng, 86.

56. Honorary ranks awarded for meritorious action during military campaigns were instituted during the Taiping Rebellion. Oda, 691–92. See also Brunnert and Hagelstrom, no. 974.

57. Chen's entry into camphor distillation was outlined in a message from the manager of the arsenal to the battalion commander who eventually captured Chen. See 32611:66.

58. Bi, 285.

59. Riaguai was head of the southern branch of the Shilixing tribal group. Its settlement was located in the mountains about fifteen kilometers east of modern Miaoli city in the area of Penglai village, Nanzhuang district (*xiang*). Sheng, 154.

60. Riaguai as well as headmen of several other aborigine tribes had begun to lease tribal lands to Han farmers in 1885. Zhang Gucheng, 87. These tenants would have been at risk in any tribal belligerency. As of the early 1850s, the Shilixing tribe was still counted among the "raw" or uncivilized tribes that carried out attacks on Chinese and pacified tribes. Ibid., 82. The Chinese administration was wise to be wary of Riaguai. In 1902, he led his tribe in an uprising against the Japanese. Taiwan Sōtokufu kambō bunshoka, 34.

61. Shinchiku chō somuka, 525–26; Zhang Gucheng, 89.

62. Although this report was sent during the fourth month, a runner report [32611:59] and separate surety bonds from the headmen of Danwenhu, Shuiliutan, and Malintan villages denying that the aborigines had been taken captive do not appear in the file until GX 14/7/16 (23 Aug. 1888).

63. The overseer did not explain whether the temple was merely to be a convenient meeting place for discussions or if persons associated with the temple would serve as arbitrators.

64. Cen was governor of Fujian for just over a year in 1881–82 (GX

7/4/8–8/5/7). Qian, 198–99. The policy, referred to as *kaishan fufan*, had been prompted by the Japanese punitive expedition of 1874, and the first steps had been taken by Shen Baozhen, who was a specially appointed imperial commissioner in charge of maritime defense at the time. Zhang Shixian, 129–50. For the date of Cen's edict, see ibid., 148, n. 37.

65. Magistrate Fang's decision is appended to the interrogation name list [32611:73].

66. Xue, 273:14 (vol. 4, 715): "Extorting Money by Threats: Kidnapping for ransom." The substatute's actual language is *zhuoren leshu*.

67. One source translates this term as "The Soldier's Medal." It was "an oblong plate of thin silver, having the character *Shang* (reward) embossed upon it, which is bestowed at reviews and inspections upon meritorious soldiers." Mayers, no. 466. See also Oda, 184.

68. Xue, 292:15 (vol. 4, 859): "Killing or wounding a person during play, by mistake, or by accident: Reporting insane persons to the authorities for confinement . . ." (*fengren baoguan suojin*).

69. Chen Jixun had joined Chen Zhenxiang in applying to the superintendent of the Taiwan arsenal for a permit to distill camphor. See 32611:66.

70. As a province Taiwan remained under the jurisdiction of the Fujian/Zhejiang governor-general, who at this point was Bian Baodi. Although the report was also addressed to the provincial governor, no name was given since Liu Mingchuan had retired and his replacement, Shao Youlian, had not yet arrived.

71. Peng, described as "an office termite well versed in litigation" (*ji'an yadu*), had been jailed by magistrate Zhang Tinggan sometime before he left office in GX 16/4 (May–June 1890). Magistrate Shen's report was dated GX 17/4/25 (1 June 1891).

72. "Prisoners under sentence of death or charged with transportable offenses are required to wear prison dress (a reddish brown suit)." Alabaster, 74.

73. Peng Ying and another prisoner who had been sentenced to transportation to the Penghu Islands were also returned.

74. The imperial amnesty had actually been announced a year earlier on the first day of GX 20 (6 Feb. 1894). It was promulgated in honor of Empress Dowager Cixi's sixtieth birthday. Liu Jincao, vol. 3, 10012 (*juan* 256, *Xingkao; youshe*). *Da Qing Dezong Jing (Guangxu) huangdi shilu*, vol. 12, part 5, 2963 (*juan* 332).

75. Davidson, 268.

CHAPTER 6

1. The literature on lineage and family in south China and Taiwan is quite voluminous. Most treatments take the work of Maurice Freedman, particularly his *Lineage Organization in Southeastern China* (London: Athlone Press, 1958) and *Chinese Lineage and Society: Fukien and Kwangtung*

(London: Athlone Press, 1966), as a point of departure. For discussions mainly of contemporary Taiwan, see Arthur P. Wolf, "Domestic Organization"; Lung-sheng Sung, "Property and Family Division"; and the works cited in both in Emily Martin Ahern and Hill Gates, eds., *The Anthropology of Taiwanese Society* (Stanford, Calif.: Stanford University Press, 1981), 342–60, 361–78. The best historical study of a Taiwanese lineage is Meskill. A controversial understanding of lineage formation in Taiwan is Burton Pasternak, "The Role of the Frontier in Chinese Lineage Development," *Journal of Asian Studies* 28 (1969): 551–61. The most important work on lineages in China as a whole is Ebrey and Watson. See also Brook, 465–99.

2. Evelyn Rawski has shown us that descent groups in Northwest China's Shaanxi province were able to maintain continuity without resorting to lineage organization at all. See "The Ma Landlords of Yang-chia-kou in Late Ch'ing and Republican China," in Ebrey and Watson, 245–73.

3. Watson, "Chinese Kinship Reconsidered," 594. See also the more extended definition proposed in Ebrey and Watson, 5.

4. Ebrey and Watson, 5.

5. Okamatsu, Appendix, p. xxiii. Okamatsu's work is a condensed summary of some of the material that was later published in Rinji Taiwan kyūkan chōsa kai. His treatment of succession and inheritance is elaborated in idem, *Shihō, ken* 2, *ka*, "Zaisan shōkei" (Succession to property), 546–93. See also Shiga, "Family Property," and Cohen.

6. Okamatsu, Appendix, xxiv.

7. In the Dan-Xin archives see, among others, cases 22706 and 21501.

8. Okamatsu, Appendix, xxiv.

9. Ibid., Appendix, xxiv–xxv.

10. For example, see 21501:2. See also Okamatsu, Reference No. 88.

11. Complications could arise if a son adopted from agnates became or claimed to be joint heir of more than one collateral line. See, for example, cases 22606 and 22707.

12. Wolf and Huang, 110–11, discuss *minglingzi*. They quote from a Lu Xun story to explain the etymology of this term. Briefly, the *mingling* is a small green caterpillar found on mulberry trees. Its young are said to be carried away by the sphex (diggerwasp) to be changed into wasps. Waltner, 26–27, 74–75, demonstrates that the origin of the sphex legend is to be found in the *Shijing* (Book of songs), one of the most ancient surviving Chinese literary works. See also Ino, vol. 2, 380–84.

13. Okamatsu, Appendix, xvi. A Taiwanese folk proverb suggests that the estate share going to a *minglingzi* was only one-fourth that of a natural son. See Rinji Taiwan kyūkan chōsa kai, *Shihō, ken* 2, *ka*, 566. The editors of this section, however, discount this bit of folklore, and Okamatsu, as noted, follows them.

14. The facts of the case are taken from testimony [22601:39] of those involved.

15. Pasternak, 122. I retain Pasternak's "co-wife" terminology here even though it is not technically appropriate. As Patricia Ebrey points out (p. 7) in her introduction to Ebrey and Watson, from early imperial times on China was monogamous: a man could legally have only one wife. Other consorts or companions are best referred to as concubines.

16. Zhou Qichang will be referred to as Zhou Wuniang throughout.

17. The background information and summaries of points of agreement and disagreement found in the following paragraphs are extracted from the parties' testimony [22609:18, 23] under interrogation in court as well as their petitions and counterplaints cited in the text.

18. When Zhou Wuniang filed a counterplaint [22609:5] in GX 8 (1882), he was 41 *sui*. Thus, he would have been born around DG 21 (1841).

19. There is a single reference to a second son, Zhou Fengchun, but he played no role in the litigation. See [22609:7].

20. The unit, the Northern Right Battalion (*bei you ying*), was one of three battalions making up the Taiwan Northern Route Regiment (*Taiwan beilu xiebiao*), a Green Standard unit. The battalion commander at the time was Major Huang Tiancheng. See Lin Hengdao, *Taiwan dili*, fascicle 2, 256. Mrs. Zhou complained to Major Huang because Zhou Yushu was a soldier in his battalion at the time. See 22609:52.

21. By TZ 13, Zhou Yuhang, the second of the four brothers, apparently had died, since the second collateral line was represented by the *shengyuan* Zhou Guoxiang, whom Wuniang termed his nephew in his initial counterplaint. Guoxiang had also filed a petition [22609:8] that in substance repeated Wuniang's contentions.

22. See 22609:71.

23. See the bond (*ganjie zhuang*) [22609:15] entered into by Mrs. Zhou and Zhou Chuncao affirming that their account of the facts is accurate.

24. See note 19.

25. See particularly 22609:3 and 16. The latter lists 20 parcels of irrigated paddy fields from which the firm was receiving rental income or income in the form of loan interest payments.

26. False accusation (*wugao*) was a crime punishable by sentencing the accuser to a penalty two or three degrees more severe than that the (falsely) accused would have received for the alleged crime. See Xue, 336:00–27 (vol. 4, 995–1010), for the basic statute and its 27 substatutes.

27. Several magistrates made court awards to the Mingzhi Academy. See, for example, cases 23411, 22419, 22506, and 22513. These court awards seemed to be a method chosen in this county to subsidize education.

28. No copy of this appeal is in the case file, but an order (*zha*) [22609: 38] dated GX 9/9/18 (18 Oct. 1883) from the prefect to Xinzhu county quotes from it.

29. Brockman, 93, suggests that part of the function of the scrivener

was to screen out pettifoggers, or presumably petitioners who employed them. This may explain the prefect's use of the scrivener when a runner might seem more appropriate.

30. The Taibei prefectural seat was a new city constructed on a site adjoining the older towns of Mengjia and Dadaocheng on the Danshui River.

31. See the draft of the court's directive written at the end of an interrogation list [22609:51] dated GX 9/12/17 (14 Jan. 1884). In the draft of his court directive the magistrate did not state the number of blows that were to be administered during Zhou Chuncao's punishment. A prompting petition [22609:68] filed two years later by Zhou Wuniang said Chuncao had received 500 blows with a length of split bamboo (*banzi*). The split bamboo had come to be used in place of both the light (*chi*) and heavy (*zhang*) sticks. Sun, nos. 1724, 1811.

32. Mrs. Zhou's appeal was summarized in Prefect Liu's order and quoted in full in Magistrate Fang's report in response [22609:78] dated GX 12/2/25 (30 Mar. 1888).

33. The tenures of Xizhen, a Mongol bannerman, and Wei are noted in Qian, 89, 200. The two had been ordered to Taiwan to investigate the case of the impeached Taiwan intendant, Liu Ao. See Wei's biography in Zhao et al., vol. 16, 12498. Submitting litigation by proxy is discussed in Chapter 7.

34. See the coroner's testimony [22609:90] and bond attesting to injuries [22609:91], both written on the same day as Mrs. Zhou's prompting petition.

35. A sampling may be found in Sprenkel, 135–36, app. 3, "Proverbial Sayings." Two characteristic examples: "Let householders avoid litigation; for once go to law and there is nothing but trouble." "Win your lawsuit and lose your money."

36. Further discussions of legal specialists and yamen personnel may be found in Chapters 7 and 8.

37. An analogy might be made to the situation in late twentieth-century America, where widely held attitudes of hostility, contempt, and even fear of the judiciary and lawyers certainly do not indicate any hesitancy to initiate litigation.

CHAPTER 7

1. Besides Dan-Xin case documents, this discussion of petition forms used in Danshui and Xinzhu draws on Shinchiku chō somuka, 270, and Suzuki, 10.

2. Suzuki, 1, no. 2, 9.

3. Shinchiku chō somuka, 270. On the Receipt and Distribution Office, see Ch'ü, *Local Government*, 40, 78. On the handling of litigants' petitions

within the yamen, see Shinchiku chō somuka, 271. The procedure described there conforms to that outlined by Ch'ü in the above citation.

4. As we shall see presently, this type of petition was not technically legitimate.

5. Suzuki, 1, no. 2, 10.

6. Chapter 6.

7. As noted earlier in the case summary in Chapter 6, when Mrs. Zhou and her son had not gotten favorable results in their lawsuit at the Xinzhu yamen, she "stopped the sedan chair" of two imperially deputed officials on an inspection tour to submit an appeal.

8. The format of the document was typical of traditional Chinese written material, with entries ordered from right to left and top to bottom.

9. These initial entries are those found on all county forms, which are by far the most numerous in the collection. Some subprefectural forms were more elaborate, with entries for certain local subbureaucrats, neighbors, landlord or tenant, and so on. These forms also allowed more space for the body of the petition. A schematic example [22402:1] may be found in Lin Hengdao, *Taiwan sheng tongzhi, juan 3, zhengshi zhi, sifa bian*, fascicle 1, 31b–33a.

10. This notation was handwritten in the upper margin. Zhubei is a reference to the residence of the petitioners.

11. This warning was printed horizontally in large characters above the text of the petition.

12. Reciprocal punishment meant that when an accusation was false, the accuser was sentenced to the punishment for the crime of which he had accused the innocent party.

13. The procedural rules printed at the end of the petition form were usually not included on the microfilm edition of the cases. They can be seen on 22609:33 as well as a few other petitions. Numbers in brackets in the translation have been added. Subprefectural petition forms had the first ten of the regulations translated here, albeit in different order, plus an eleventh, which has been taken from 22402:1 and appended to the translation.

14. Ch'ü, *Local Government*, 118.

15. Rule 3.

16. The cases contain few if any references to inns in Zhuqian / Xinzhu. In the litigation summarized in Chapter 6, Zhou Chuncao testified [22609: 41] that while at Taibei prefecture to file an appeal, he stayed in a guest house (*kedian*) in Mengjia.

17. Huang Liuhong, *Fuhui quanshu*, 127. This passage is translated in Huang Liu-hung, *A Complete Book Concerning Happiness and Benevolence*, 262–63. According to the translator's introduction, "Huang's book served as a manual for local administrators and their legal and fiscal advisors"

throughout the dynasty. Ibid., 1. Presumably it or other similar works would have been known to officials posted to Danshui and Xinzhu.

18. Chang Wejen, personal communication. In China a seal was (and still is) more official than a written signature. Scriveners will be further discussed below.

19. Ch'ü, *Local Government*, 3–4; Hsiao, *Rural China*, 64–66; Watt, 190–91.

20. This topic will be examined in more detail in Chapter 8.

21. Of course, in a very long case clerks or runners might leave or be removed from their positions.

22. One's mainland native place remains significant today in Taiwan. In funeral services, a ritual pronouncement asking pardon for the wrongs of the deceased includes a statement of his place of origin on the mainland. Ahern, 22.

23. Shinchiku chō somuka, 270.

24. Some further discussion of proxy filers is to be found below.

25. Suzuki, 1, no. 3, 14; Ch'ü, *Local Government*, 98.

26. See Chapter 6.

27. See 33319:1, 2, 3, and the summary in Chapter 3.

28. Ch'ü, *Local Government*, 98–101.

29. W. Gregory, dispatch to Foreign Office, 25 Sept. 1869; Public Record Office, Foreign Office (microfilm) FO 17/536.

30. G. L. MacKay, a missionary in northern Taiwan in the 1870s and 1880s, estimated that a Chinese lay preacher and his family could be supported on less than $120 annually. MacKay, 286.

31. *Qing Dezong (Guangxu) shilu xuanji*—GX 3/2/17 (21 Mar. 1877) (*juan* 48 in the original *Da Qing Dezong Jing* [*Guangxu*] *huangdi shilu*), 34. Zheng was subprefect in 1862–64 and again circa 1874–77.

32. Buxbaum, 271.

33. See Chapter 6.

34. See citation in Chapter 5, n. 54.

35. One such case [22431] occurred in 1887, when the Dajia police chief accused a farmer of illegally occupying land that had earlier been confiscated by the government and then leased out with the rent going toward support of the local Water God Temple (*Shuishen miao*).

36. Contrast the situation during the Sung dynasty when the "authorities prohibited private individuals both from printing or copying any laws and from possessing any code provisions." Miyazaki, 58.

37. See Mair, especially 351.

38. Keightley, 51, suggests that "an emphasis on the group rather than the individual" has been a characteristic of Chinese civilization since the Neolithic period.

39. I am grateful to Jonathan Ocko for suggesting this point.

40. Bodde and Morris, 170–71.

41. See the section called "Women Should Not be Summoned to Court without Good Reason" in Wang Huizu's *Zuozhi yaoyan* (Precepts for local administrative officials), translated in Sprenkel, 146–47.

42. The potential to abuse the privilege by making false accusations to cause trouble and then exploiting the Code's provision to redeem punishment for the wrongful charge was probably negated by the knowledge that the courts seldom allowed women to take advantage of monetary redemption.

43. Xue Yunsheng was puzzled that the provision found in Ming law allowing women and also children under ten *sui* to use proxy filers had been excised from the Qing Code. Xue, 339:01 (vol. 4, 1018–19): "Prisoners May Not Bring Charges in a Separate Case—Elderly and incapacitated are allowed proxy filers" (*nian lao duji xu ren daigao*).

44. In title deposit (*tai*) transactions, deeds to land were used as security for loans. The lender obtained possession of the deeds themselves but gained no other rights to the land. Okamatsu, 150–55.

45. Chapter 6.

46. See Chapter 3.

47. Chapter 5.

48. In a 1670 case from Tancheng county, Shandong, that may have been well known to magistrates because of its inclusion in Huang Liuhong's famous handbook, the court accepted without comment the assertion that an "unofficially adopted [adopted through purchase (*mingling*)] brother, being an outsider, could not ask for a share of the inheritance." Huang, *A Complete Book Concerning Happiness and Benevolence*, 295. Jonathan Spence made this case the core of Chapter Three, "The Widow," in his *The Death of Woman Wang* (New York: The Viking Press, 1978).

49. There were, to be sure, many more criminal (365) than civil (224) cases.

50. Xue, 342:00 (vol. 4, 1025): "For Officials Involved in Litigation, Household Members Deliver the Plaint" (*guanli cisong jiaren su*); 339:01 (vol. 4, 1018–19): "Prisoners May Not Bring Charges in a Separate Case—Elderly and incapacitated allowed proxy filers."

51. Ch'ü, *Local Government*, 174, uses the phrase "official-gentry or scholar-gentry" to denote the group afforded the proxy filer privilege. Although the statute in question specifies "officials" (*guanli*), as we shall see, the Dan-Xin cases confirm the assumption of Ch'ü and others that in practice the language of the statute was interpreted to include degree holders whether or not they held or had held office. In a note (322, n. 46) Ch'ü presents evidence suggesting that in some jurisdictions the proxy filer privilege was not absolute for lower degree holders and low-ranking officials.

52. Yao and Hu, vol. 4, 2923, cited in Na, 82. This rule was not part of

the Code itself but was printed in the commentary section of the page above the statutes and substatutes.

53. Zhang Weiren (Chang Wejen), vol. 1, 156–57.

54. Ibid., 157, citing two nineteenth-century officials: Liu Heng, "Lisong shitiao" (Ten articles on handling litigation), no. 1; also Yuqian, "Yu ge daishu bei" (Stele with an edict to scriveners), "Zai yu ge daishu bei" (Another stele with an edict for scriveners).

55. Zhang Weiren (Chang Wejen), vol. 1, 157.

56. See also Brockman, 92–93, 95–96.

57. Shinchiku chō somuka, 270.

58. Xue, 340:04 (vol. 4, 1020), "Instigating Litigation—Local officials who are unable to search out and prohibit pettifoggers from causing disturbances" (*difang guan buneng chajin songshi raohai*).

59. Huang, *A Complete Book Concerning Happiness and Benevolence*, 135–36, 259–62.

60. Xue, 061:00 (vol. 2, 207), "Lecturing on and reading the laws" (*jiangdu lüling*).

61. Zhang Weiren (Chang Wejen), vol. 1, 224, n. 104. See also Na, 54, and Xue, 340:07 (vol. 4, 1021), "Printing, selling, or concealing pettifoggers: secret books are forbidden" (*weijin zhuanyin fanmai ji zangni songshi miben*).

62. Zhang Weiren (Chang Wejen), vol. 1, 157.

63. Ibid., vol. 1, 157.

64. Chapter 6.

65. Chapter 5.

66. See Chapter 5.

67. Gan, who was also know as Gan Tinghan, had been implicated in the armed robbery case summarized in Chapter 3.

CHAPTER 8

1. Ch'ü, *Local Government*, 242, n. 123, calls this type of warrant a *tangqian*. Other terms, especially in Taiwan, were *huoqian* and *leiqian*. Rinji Taiwan kyūkan chōsa kai, *Taiwan shihō, ken* 3, *ka*, 464. Because the Dan-Xin archives contain only drafts of *qian*, details of nomenclature and form of *qian* warrants in this jurisdiction are unknown.

2. Rinji Taiwan kyūkan chōsa kai, *Taiwan shihō, ken* 3 *ka*, 465.

3. Runner organization is discussed later in this chapter.

4. Ch'ü, *Local Government*, 72. There seems to have been no formal regulation governing runner deadlines. The time limits were set by the individual magistrate at his own discretion.

5. These runner reports were probably transcribed by yamen clerks on the basis of oral statements.

6. Ch'ü, *Local Government*, 72.

7. See Chapter 4.

8. As well as certain other social groups, notably actors, prostitutes,

and slaves, "mean people" status was a legal category that among yamen personnel included most runners, commoner guards, jailors, coroners, and doormen. Such persons and their offspring were denied the opportunity to compete in the civil service examinations. Ch'ü, *Local Government*, 62; also idem, *Law and Society*, 129–32.

9. Magistrate Fang Zuyin report [11407:2] to Taibei Prefect Lei Qida, GX 14/1/26 (8 Mar. 1888).

10. Ch'ü T'ung-tsu contends that most local governments organized their runners into four distinct groups: lictors (*zaoli*), swift-hands (*kuaishou*) divided into horsemen and foot messengers, commoner guards (*minzhuang*), and policemen (*buyi* or *bukuai*). Each group had different functions. Ch'ü, *Local Government*, 57, 60–61. Huang Liuhong mentions the "runners of the three groups (*sanban*)," explained by his translator as lictors, messengers (*kuaishou*), and constables (*bukuai*). Huang Liuhong, *Fuhui quanshu*, 41c; *A Complete Book Concerning Happiness and Benevolence*, 122, n. 10.

11. Shinchiku chō somuka, 82. A third subordinate of the subprefect, the Mengjia vice subprefect (*xiancheng*), although higher in rank than the police chief, employed only four lictors and four commoner guards. I have not found any information in the Dan-Xin cases on the total number of runners employed by Danshui subprefecture.

12. An 1888 report [11407:2] on Xinzhu's income and expenditures listing many of the yamen employees by type gives these figures. Shinchiku chō somuka, 98. *Xinzhu xian zhidu kao*, 3–4. The latter source notes that the appellation "horsemen" included fast runners as well.

13. Shinchiku chō somuka, 98; *Xinzhu xian zhidu kao*, 4.

14. Dan-Xin archives, 11409:8, GX 15/1/6 (5 Feb. 1889).

15. Ch'ü, *Local Government*, 58–60. Li Rongzhong, 97–98.

16. See Shinchiku chō somuka, 297–304, on runners.

17. The discussion of runner sections found in Shinchiku chō somuka, 304, seems to imply the contrary.

18. Runner reports or warrants are the sources locating runner activities. See 22514:15, GX 11/8/26 (4 Oct. 1885); 32103:6, GX 9/1/24 (3 Mar. 1883); 32104:7, GX 9/5/28 (2 July 1883).

19. Shinchiku chō somuka, 299–300.

20. See the rent resistance case summary in Chapter 4.

21. See the various documents in case 11325.

22. Shinchiku chō somuka, 303. Zhang Weiren (Chang Wejen), vol. 1, 229, n. 146.

23. Magistrate Fang Zuyin report [11407:2] to Taibei Prefect Lei Qida, GX 14/1/26 (8 Mar. 1888).

24. Myers, "The Commercialization of Agriculture," 178.

25. The Mexican or Spanish silver dollar commonly used in Taiwan was equivalent to 0.72 taels (*liang*). Zhou Xianwen, 115.

26. Mackay, 286. Mackay itemized these expenses as follows: rice per month, $3.00; salt vegetables, $4.00; coal or wood, $1.50; carrying water and cleaning rice, $.65; shaving heads, $.30; shoes, stockings, and clothes, $.38.

27. Zelin, *Magistrate's Tael,* explains the difficulties of financing local government and the strategies developed by yamen employees to supplement their meager salaries in an earlier period.

28. Shinchiku chō somuka, 303. For Zhan Ajian's false implication of the villagers, see the armed robbery case summary in Chapter 3.

29. Na, 43–44; Ch'ü, *Local Government,* 67–70; Zelin, *Magistrate's Tael,* 20–21, 237–41. Na, for example, lists nineteen customary fees that runners expected to collect in the course of yamen business.

30. The clearest statement of this viewpoint is Kuhn, 215–23.

31. Dai Yanhui, *Qingdai Taiwan zhi xiangzhi,* 81.

32. Sheng. For a map showing gross concentrations of Quanzhou, Zhangzhou, and Hakka populations during the late Qing, see Chen Qilu, 14.

33. See Chapters 2 and 3.

34. See the studies by Lamley cited in Chapter 3, n. 5.

35. For Lou Yun's proclamations, *Zhuanggui jinyue, Zhuanggui size,* and *Jinyue batiao,* see Chen Peigui, 169–70. Appendix Six, "Lou Yun's 'Four Village Regulations,'" contains a translation of *Zhuanggui size.*

36. *Jinyue batiao.*

37. Xue, 273:09 (vol. 4, 713): "Extorting Property by Threats: Unregistered vagrants in Taiwan who with wanton and savage ferocity break the law" (*Taiwan wuji youmin kuanghan xionge sixing bufa*).

38. *Zhuanggui size,* no. 2.

39. Shinchiku chō somuka, 115.

40. *Zhuanggui size,* no. 1.

41. Ibid., no. 3.

42. In their self-defense aspect, Linked Village networks in Danshui subprefecture seem to resemble the lowest level militias organized in Guangdong in response to the British threat at about this same period. Wakeman, 36–38. Wakeman calls these low-level militias "genuine *tuanlian.*" The definitive work on the growth of *tuanlian* militias as well as the general militarization of society as a response to rebellion in nineteenth-century China is Kuhn.

43. Lou Yun's village regulations are the most striking illustration but not the only example of efforts to enhance local security and local government in Taiwan. In 1838, two years after Lou's initiative, the Jiayi county magistrate, Fan Xueheng, promulgated a similar directive in response to an order from Taiwan Circuit Intendant Yao Ying. Yang Xi, 159.

44. Shinchiku chō somuka, 114–15.

45. Meskill, 93, referring to northern Zhanghua county in the 1840s, suggests, in fact, that in some instances the office of *zongli* may have been utilized by local strongmen to justify maintaining private armies. She

asserts without adducing any evidence that this was also often the case in Danshui subprefecture.

46. Hsiao, *Rural China*, 267, 271.

47. *Zhuanggui size*, no. 1. Scriveners, as discussed in Chapter Seven, were yamen-appointed scribes. Most documents submitted to the yamen's chief administrator had to be given to a scrivener for retranscription and were not accepted by the yamen unless impressed with a scrivener's seal.

48. See also Dai Yanhui, *Qingdai Taiwan zhi xiangzhi*, 112–14.

49. Tianhou was the officially approved name for the goddess worshipped throughout the southern maritime regions of China and popularly known in Taiwan as Mazu. See Watson, "Standardizing the Gods."

50. The participation of several distinct groups and especially the use of two temples hint that factional or perhaps subethnic competition was at play in the selection process.

51. Bonds and acceptances of appointment were simply written out on blank paper, not on preprinted forms.

52. One reader has suggested that it must have diminished the standing of the overseers to deal with the yamen through runners rather than directly. Such may well have been the case. We might speculate that magistrates and subprefects attempted to prevent the bridging of the sociopolitical gulf that separated the overseers as a subelite group from the official and elite strata in traditional society.

53. See the summary of the boundary case [22510:9, 21] in Chapter 5.

54. See the kidnapping case summary [32611:33] in Chapter 5.

55. See the armed robbery case summary [33319:47] in Chapter 3.

56. Dai Yanhui, *Qingdai Taiwan zhi xiangzhi*, 14.

57. Chen Peigui, 48–51.

58. P. C. C. Huang, 50, 224–31; Duara, 52–57. See also Thompson.

59. Shinchiku chō somuka, 115.

60. On the mushrooming exports of tea and camphor, see Chapter 5 and Appendix 3.

61. Skinner, "Marketing and Social Structure," pt. 1, 31.

62. Shen Baozhen had earlier achieved national renown while governor of Jiangxi (1862–65) for his success against Taiping armies and later during the years 1867–74 as head of the Fuzhou Navy Yard. Shen's biography may be found in Hummel, 642–44.

63. The Chinese state in late imperial times and in the twentieth century has frequently attempted with at best mixed results to extend its reach directly or through utilizing nonbureaucratic personnel. See Mann on the state's legitimation of the "liturgical" leadership of local merchants in tax collection; MacKinnon, chap. V, on Yuan Shikai's new government policies promoting local reforms; and Shue on the post-1949 period.

64. Compare the upward flow of political power and legitimacy in the classical Balinese state as described by Geertz, 62–63.

CHAPTER 9

1. Yanjiezi, a street in Xinzhu city, is called Anjiezi in most sources.

2. This diagram is taken largely from Suzuki, pt. 3, 2. For a somewhat different rendering of the functional titles of the courtroom personnel, see Myers, "Taiwan Under Ch'ing Imperial Rule, 1684–1895: The Traditional Order," 512, Chart IV.

3. *Xinzhu xian zhihdu kao*, 3.

4. Zelin, "The Rights of Tenants," 522.

5. On the overall rationality of the adjudication process, see Conner. On the categories of evidence, see ibid., 29.

6. See the boundary dispute case summarized in Chapter 5.

7. See the litigation over lineage property summarized in Chapter 6.

8. Conner, 29.

9. The most thoughtful discussion of the legal significance of torture is in Conner, especially 132–43. See also Bodde and Morris, 97–98. For the regulations on judicial torture, see Xue, 396:00, and its seven substatutes (vol. 5, 1202–06): "Deliberate imprisonment or deliberate examination [under torture] of unimplicated persons" (*gujin gukan pingren*).

10. See Chapter 4.

11. A confession was highly desirable but not absolutely necessary for a conviction.

12. This was actually Xu's second tour of duty in the Xinzhu yamen. There was a rapid turnover of county magistrates during the years 1883–84. See Appendix 5, "Danshui Subprefects and Xinzhu Magistrates." Xu Xizhi had been magistrate for nearly two years, 1881–82. He was followed by Zhou Zhikan and Zhu Chenglie, both of whom were in office only four months each. Xu then returned as magistrate in 1884, but for only six months. Peng Dasun, the author of the report on which this account is based, then succeeded Xu.

13. Magistrate Peng's report [31808:2, 3] cited earlier also contains the information about the interrogations of Mrs. Li née Wang and Cai Kun.

14. Brockman, 93, citing Rinji Taiwan kyūkan chōsa kai, *Shihō, ken 3 ka*, 471.

15. See Chapter 6.

16. Hsiao's short study *Compromise in Imperial China* concentrates on arbitration mechanisms in Qing China; see also Sprenkel, 116–23.

17. For this insight and remarks on other social effects of mediation, see Upham, 12.

18. In capital cases, for example, a final sentence of death could be passed only by the Three High Courts (*san fasi*) in the capital. It was then

required that the emperor ratify the sentence. For a concise explanation of the system of judicial review and appeal in Qing China, see Bodde and Morris, 113–22, especially the table on p. 116.

19. The provision may be found in Xue, 292:13 (vol. 4, 859).

20. On the use of analogy in sentencing, see Bodde and Morris, 175–79, 517–33; Na, 141.

21. As noted earlier, by the nineteenth century, all sentences involving blows of the light or heavy stick were said to have been changed to flogging with a length of split bamboo. See Chapter 6, n. 31.

22. In the rent resistance case summarized in Chapter 4, for example, Fan Atian, who had been jailed for refusing to pay large rent, was sentenced to beating with the heavy stick [22202:56].

23. The case evidence is persuasively reinforced by the reminiscences of Gong Debo (b. 1891), who as a child witnessed many sessions of a late Qing local court in Luqi county, Zhenzhou prefecture, Hunan. Gong vividly depicts a sight he saw many times, the beating of an alleged criminal who had tried the patience of the Luqi magistrate too far. Gong, 74–75.

24. Legal documents from higher levels do exist and have been studied for legal procedure farther up the hierarchy. See Zhang Weiren (Chang Wejen).

25. Na, 156–57, citing statute number 394 in the Qing Code. For the relevant provision, see Xue, 394:01 (vol. 5, 1181).

26. The following characterization of the Dan-Xin yamen jails and the prisoners assigned to each is drawn from Shinchiku chō somuka, 277–79.

27. References to the First Lictor's Outer Compartment (*yizao waishi*) [33319:99] and Second Fast Runner's Outer Compartment (*erkuai waishi*) [22514:123] make it appear possible that each runner section's headquarters included a cell or cells called the "outer compartment."

28. A sketch map of the yamen showing the *jianyu* and some of the other offices may be found in Chen Peigui, 13.

29. See 33319:82.

30. See 22514:43, 67, 100.

31. This was Wen Fengyun who had been accused of knifing a man at the instigation of Lan Huagun, one of the principal complainants in the armed robbery case. See Chapter 3.

32. *Qiufan* and *jianfan* were synonyms for prisoners held in the main Tiger Head Prison because of being under suspicion for major crimes.

33. The only outbreak of relatively large-scale violence in the year or two before Fang's memorandum was an uprising by aborigines in the Dakekan area near the Danshui-Xinzhu county line in 1886. Zhang Gucheng, 142.

34. Alabaster, 72–73; Staunton, 431, note accompanying text.

35. Bodde and Morris, 79. See also Bodde, 311–33, in which virtually

the only first-person account of prison life during the Qing written by a Chinese is translated and discussed.

36. See the kidnapping case summary in Chapter 5.

37. For Liu, see the rent resistance case in Chapter 4; for Pengxu, the boundary dispute case in Chapter 5.

38. Lian Yatang, 326.

39. During the first six years of Japanese rule in Xinzhu, most deaths from disease were attributed to dysentery. Of 103 reported cases, 61 were fatal. Only about half as many cases of bubonic plague, the second leading killer, were reported, but the mortality rate was much higher. Forty-two of 54 reported cases were fatal. Typhoid fever, with 9 deaths among 25 cases, was the third most serious disease reported. Shinchiku chō somuka, 341. Bubonic plague was probably not present in Taiwan before 1894. Wong and Wu, 514–15.

40. See 22514:116, 123, 140, 142, 145, 149; 33319:146; 32611:107, 131, 134.

41. It probably was not Pan Yukun since another practitioner, Zhang Yongqing, was employed by the yamen in GX 10 (1884), a year after Liu Dongjin was treated and nearly a year before Pan's name appears in the cases.

42. For the identity of these medicines, see Jiangsu xin yixueyuan, no. 3764, vol. 2, 1837–39; no. 4877, vol. 2, 2356–58. Perilla leaf *suye* is the leaf of the plant *zisu* perilla frutescens.

43. Both criminal and administrative sanctions might be applied against officials guilty of cruelty to prisoners. See Ch'ü, *Local Government*, 34–35. For the criminal penalties, see Xue, 398:00 (vol. 5, 1208): "Mistreating prisoners" (*lingnue zuiqiu*). For administrative punishments, see Wen Fu, *juan* 49:2b–3b (vol. 2, 1028–30), "Imprisonment" (*jinyu*), "Mistreating prisoners."

44. This provision is found in the fourth substatute under the article on mistreatment of prisoners cited in the previous note. See Xue, 398:04 (vol. 5, 1210), "Officials who without authorization confiscate a report of illness thus bringing about a prisoner's death." For the statute on premeditated homicide, see ibid., 282:00 (vol. 4, 775), "Premeditated homicide" (*mousharen*).

45. Xue, 412:20 (vol. 5, 1274), "Death of detainees in runners' custody . . ." (*chaiyi kanya renfan shensi . . .*).

46. Ibid., 412:02 (vol. 5, 1268), "In cases of suicide by hanging or drowning, when there are no other causes, approval may be granted to requests to waive the inquest" (*ziyi nishui shensi bie wu ta gu zhun gao mien jian*). Death from disease is mentioned in the body of the substatute.

47. Ibid., 401:00 (vol. 5, 1215), "Food and clothing for prisoners" (*Yuqiu yishi*).

48. Xue singled out this omission as one of his "remaining doubts." See his comment after substatute 401:01 (vol. 5, 1216), "Clothing and food for

criminals sent to the Board of Punishment or sent to higher jurisdictions in the provinces" (*jiebu ji tijie waisheng fanren jiyu yiliang*).

49. I have been unable to find any relevant provision in the Fujian provincial regulations (*Fujian shengli*). According to Chang Bin Liu, 86, these regulations remained in force in Taiwan after the island became a province in its own right in 1885.

50. See Chapter 8, n. 26.

51. In Haishan, a part of the former subprefecture just north of the Xinzhu county line, "families . . . were large and complex before [1895]." In 1935–36, the average family size in the area corresponding to Danshui county during the late Qing was 7.6 persons. This was well above the largest average family size (7.0) found in mainland China during the same period. Wolf and Huang, 68, 131, 328.

52. Xinzhu county spent more to maintain a prisoner or detainee than it did to compensate a runner for his services. Compare the prisoner maintenance allocation to the 8.61 dollar (6.2 tael) annual salary for yamen runners, and it works out that the yamen spent an amount equal to 1.7 times a runner's salary to support a prisoner guilty of one of the more serious crimes. Even detainees and others kept under more benign conditions were entitled to 27 percent more than an ordinary runner. Of course, prison guards and other runners undoubtedly skimmed off a portion of the prisoner maintenance allowance.

53. For the presumption of guilt thesis, "the assumption (nowhere explicitly stated but everywhere implied in the treatment of defendants) that a suspect must be guilty unless and until he is proven innocent," see Bodde and Morris, 28. But Buxbaum, 270, concludes that "the presumption of guilt in ordinary civil or criminal cases does not seem to exist." Conner, 26, also finds that magistrates attempted at least to evaluate evidence objectively without any assumption of guilt or innocence.

CHAPTER 10

1. Bodde and Morris, 4, 43–48, 561–62. The supposed connection between crime and cosmic harmony has been strongly questioned in Hsu Dau-Lin, 111–25.

2. For the general thesis of increasing misgovernment at the local level, see Hsiao, *Rural China*, passim. On the problem of funding local administration in the nineteenth century, see Zelin, *The Magistrate's Tael*, 300. The explosive growth of local militia organizations is also thought to have increased pressure on revenue sources and further degraded local fiscal and administrative systems. Kuhn, 211–15.

3. On this internalization of ethical norms, see the discussion of the so-called probationary ethic of late imperial officials in Metzger, 170–76.

4. Metzger, 13, has shown us the importance of taking seriously the

"clichés" of Chinese political culture. See the second of his methodological points.

5. The view that legal change inevitably follows social change relies strongly on examples drawn from the history of American law. "Some of the old is preserved among the mass of the new. But what is kept of old law is highly selective. Society in change may be slow, but it is ruthless. Neither evolution nor revolution is sentimental. Old rules of law and old legal institutions stay alive when they still have a purpose—or at least, when they do not interfere with the demands of current life." Friedman, 14.

6. Alan Watson, ix.

7. Bays, 5–6.

8. For Wu-Shun-Ji, see the rent resistance case summary in Chapter 4. Jin-Liu-He and the villagers are in the boundary dispute case in Chapter 5 and the Cha-Tai and He-Xing stores in the dispute over property in Chapter 6 and the armed robbery case in Chapter 3, respectively.

9. The Qing Code, for example, made no mention at all of contracts. Bodde and Morris, 4. If we shift our focus away from legislation sanctioned by the central government, the law might be found less aloof from commerce. Compendia of provincial government regulations are one source of law that bear further examination in this regard. Those for Fujian include samples or models for various types of contracts as well as numerous provisions regulating commercial transactions. For two sample contracts, see *Fujian shengli*, vol. 3, 442–43.

10. On the importance of customary law for economic development, see Chen and Myers.

11. See Rowe, 216.

12. Case 22212 and others show some tribal landlords possessed a sophisticated understanding of the importance of land deeds and rental contracts in establishing one's legal claims in court.

13. Chen Qinan, 115–47.

APPENDIX 2

1. Zheng and Zeng, *Chugao, juan* 2, *Fuyi zhi, tianfu*, 50.

2. See TKK 5, no. 1 (Jan. 1905), table of weights and measures following page 94. One *chō* equals 0.992 hectares (2.45 acres).

3. Rinji Taiwan kyūkan chōsa kai, *Shihō, ken* 1, *jō*, 102.

4. Ino, *Bunka shi*, vol. 2, 541.

5. Lian Heng, 31.

6. Perkins, Table B.2, 220, conveniently lists the variations in size of the standard *mou* since very early times. Perkins also notes in the text accompanying the table that there were wide regional variations in the *mou* even during the same period.

7. This is in close agreement with John Shepherd's note on measures of land and grain. See his *Statecraft*, 425.

APPENDIX 4

1. The information in this appendix is based on a report [11407:2] from Magistrate Fang Zuyin to Taibei Prefect Lei, GX 14/1/26 (8 Mar. 1888); also *Xinzhu xian zhidu kao*, 1–4.

2. Taiwan Sōtokufu, *Taiwan Sōtokufu kōbun ruisan*, Meiji 28 (1905), kōshu eikyū (Grade one, permanent storage) 3 (unpaginated bound volume), item 2, "Taiwan ni okeru kyū Shinkoku kaku gamon kansei: Taihoku chihū ni kaizaiseshi kyū Shinkoku kaku gamon no meishō oyobi soshiki no ippan" (Bureaucratic organization of each yamen in Taiwan under the old Qing state: A general list of the office titles and organization of all yamen existing in Northern Taiwan under the old Qing state) (2b–7b in unpaginated material). Taiwan sheng wenxian weiyuanhui Archives, Taizhong, Taiwan.

Bibliography

Abe Akiyoshi. *Taiwan chimei kenkyū* (Studies on Taiwan place-names). Taihoku (Taibei): Bango kenkyūkai, 1938.

Ahern, Emily Martin. *Chinese Ritual and Politics*. Cambridge, Eng.: Cambridge University Press, 1981.

Alabaster, Ernest. *Notes and Commentaries on Chinese Criminal Law*. Taibei: Ch'eng Wen, 1968 [1899].

Alford, William P. "Of Arsenic and Old Laws: Looking Anew at Criminal Justice in Late Imperial China." *California Law Review* 72, no. 6 (Dec. 1984): 1180–1256.

Andō Shizuka. "Hokubu Taiwan ni okeru kyōyū ni kansuru kyūkan" (The old custom of joint ownership in northern Taiwan). TKK 4, no. 6 (June 1904): 19–29.

Azuma Yoshio. *Taiwan keizai shi kenkyū* (Research on Taiwan's economic history). Taihoku: Toto shoseki k.k., Taihoku shiten, 1944.

Bays, Daniel H. *China Enters the Twentieth Century: Chang Chih-tung and the Issues of a New Age, 1895–1909*. Ann Arbor: The University of Michigan Press, 1978.

Bi Qingchang, ed. *Xinzhu xinzhi* (New gazetteer of Xinzhu). Taibei: Zhonghua congshu weiyuanhui, 1958.

Bodde, Derk. "Prison Life in Eighteenth Century Peking." *Journal of the American Oriental Society* 89, no. 2 (1969): 311–33.

Bodde, Derk, and Clarence Morris. *Law in Imperial China Exemplified by 190 Ch'ing Dynasty Cases (Translated from the Hsing-an hui-lan) with Histor-*

ical, Social, and Juridical Commentaries. Cambridge, Mass.: Harvard University Press, 1967.

Brockman, Rosser H. "Commercial Contract Law in Late Nineteenth-Century Taiwan." In Jerome Alan Cohen, R. Randle Edwards, and Fu-mei Chang Chen, eds., *Essays on China's Legal Tradition*, pp. 76–136. Princeton, N.J.: Princeton University Press, 1980.

Brook, Timothy. "Funerary Ritual and the Building of Lineages in Late Imperial China," *Harvard Journal of Asiatic Studies* 49, no. 2 (Dec. 1989): 465–99.

Brunnert, H. S., and V. V. Hagelstrom. *Present Day Political Organization of China*, rev. N. Th. Kolessoff, trans. A. Beltchenko and E. E. Moran. Taibei: Ch'eng Wen, 1971 [1911].

Buxbaum, David C. "Some Aspects of Civil Procedure and Practice at the Trial Level in Tanshui and Hsinchu from 1789 to 1895." JAS 30, no. 2 (Feb. 1971): 255–79.

Cai Yuanjie. "Qingdai Taiwan de yiken shehui" (Settler society in Qing period Taiwan). In *Taiwan shehui yu wenhua bianqian (shangce)* (Social and cultural change in Taiwan, vol. 1), edited by Qu Haiyuan and Zhang Yinghua, 45–67. Taibei: Zhongyang yanjiuyuan, Minzuxue yanjiusuo; Monograph Series B, No. 16, 1986.

——. "Qingdai Taiwan jiceng zhengzhi tixi zhong feizhengshi jiegou zhi fazhan" (The development of unofficial structures in the hierarchical governmental system of Qing period Taiwan). *Guoli Taiwan shifan daxue lishi xuexi/yanjiusuo Lishi xuebao* (National Taiwan Normal University Department/Research Institute of History, Journal of Historical Studies) 11 (1983): 97–111.

Cen Yuying. "Cen Xiangqin gong zougao xuanlu" (Selections from the draft memorials of Cen Yuying). In *Taiwan guanxi wenxian jiling* (Miscellaneous documents related to Taiwan), 103–36. TWC no. 309, 1972 [1881].

Chen Chaolong (attributed). *Xinzhu xian caifangce* (Record of visits to Xinzhu county). TWC no. 145, 1962 [1894].

Ch'en, Ch'iu-k'un. "Landlord and Tenant: Varieties of Land Tenure in Frontier Taiwan, 1680–1900." Ph.D. dissertation, Stanford University, 1987.

Chen, Fu-mei Chang, and Ramon H. Myers. "Customary Law and the Economic Growth of China During the Ch'ing Period." *Ch'ing-shih wen-t'i* 3, no. 5 (Nov. 1976): 1–32; 3, no. 10 (Dec. 1978): 4–27.

Chen, Han-seng. *Landlord and Peasant in China: A Study of the Agrarian Crisis in South China*. New York: International Publishers, 1936.

Chen Huifen. "Qingdai Taiwan de yiken yu minjian jieshe de fazhan" (Settlement and the development of associations among the people in Qing period Taiwan). *Jiaoxue yu yanjiu* (Teaching and research) 4 (June 1982): 105–30.

Chen Menglin and Zhou Zhongxuan. *Zhuluo xianzhi* (Gazetteer of Zhuluo county). TWC no. 141, 1958 [1717].

Chen, Paul Heng-Chao. *Chinese Legal Tradition Under the Mongols: The Code of 1291 as Reconstructed*. Princeton, N.J.: Princeton University Press, 1979.

Chen Peigui. *Danshui tingzhi* (Danshui subprefecture gazetteer). Taiwan yanjiu congkan (Taiwan research collectanea), no. 46; Taiwan fangzhi huikan (Taiwan gazetteer collection), vol. 1. Taibei: Taiwan yinhang, Jingji yanjiusuo, 1956 [1871].

Chen Qilu. *Minzu yu wenhua* (Race and culture). Taibei: Liming, 1981.

Chen Qinan. "Qingdai Taiwan shehui de jiegou bianqian" (Change in the social structure of Qing period Taiwan). *Zhongyang yanjiuyuan, Minzuxue yanjiusuo jikan* (Academia Sinica, Institute of Ethnology Quarterly) 49 (1980): 115–47.

Chen Xiang. "Qingdai Taiwan gongshu Fujian de bingliang yu juangu" (Qing period Taiwan's supply of military rations and grain allowances to Fujian). *Shihuo yuekan* (Economic monthly) n.s. 1, no. 6 (Sept. 1971): 308–18.

Chen Yundong. *Kejia ren* (Hakkas). Taibei: Lianjing, 1978.

Chen Yuqing and Cai Zhaoji. "Xinpu de kaifa yange yu zongjiao xinyang" (Religion and the opening up of Xinpu). TW 32, no. 2 (June 1981): 171–83.

Chen Zhengxiang. *Taiwan dizhi* (A geography of Taiwan). 3 vols. Taibei: Fuming chanye dili yanjiusuo, 1959–61.

Chesneaux, Jean. "Secret Societies in China's Historical Evolution." In Jean Chesneaux, ed., *Popular Movements and Secret Societies in China, 1840–1950*, pp. 1–22. Stanford, Calif.: Stanford University Press, 1972.

Chu, Samuel C. "Liu Ming-ch'uan and the Modernization of Taiwan." JAS 23, no. 1 (Nov. 1963): 37–53.

Ch'ü, T'ung-tsu. *Law and Society in Traditional China*. Paris: Mouton, 1961.

——. *Local Government in China Under the Ch'ing*. Cambridge, Mass.: Harvard University Press, 1962.

Cohen, Myron L. "Family Partition as Contractual Procedure in Taiwan: A Case Study from South Taiwan." In David C. Buxbaum, ed., *Chinese Family Law and Social Change in Historical Perspective*, pp. 176–204. Seattle: University of Washington Press, 1978.

Cole, James H. *Shaohsing: Competition and Cooperation in Nineteenth-Century China*. The Association for Asian Studies Monograph No. 44. Tucson: University of Arizona Press, 1986.

Conner, Alison Wayne. "The Law of Evidence During the Ch'ing Dynasty." Ph.D. dissertation, Cornell University, 1979.

Dai Baocun. "Xinzhu jiancheng zhi yanjiu" (Research on the construction of Xinzhu's city wall). *Jiaoxue yu yanjiu* (Teaching and research) 4 (June 1982): 87–103.

Dai Yanhui. "Qingdai Dan-Xin dang'an zhengli xushuo" (Preliminary remarks on putting in order the Qing period Dan-Xin archives). *Taibei wenwu* (Taibei cultural relics) 2, no. 3 (Aug. 1953): 2–7.

——. "Qingdai Taiwan zhi da- xiaozu ye" (The large- and small-rent landlords of Qing period Taiwan). *Taibei wenxian* (Taibei documents) 4 (June 1963): 1–45.

——. *Qingdai Taiwan zhi xiangzhi* (Rural government in Qing period Taiwan). Taibei: Lianjing, 1979.

Dai Yanhui and Shi Qiyun. "Dan-Xin dang'an ziliao" (Materials from the Dan-Xin archives). *Taibei wenwu* (Taibei cultural relics) 4, no. 3 (Nov. 1955): 15–37.

Daniels, Christian. "Shinmatsu Taiwan nambu seitōgyō to shōnin shihon" (The southern Taiwan sugar industry and mercantile capital in the late Qing). *Tōhōgakuhō* (Oriental studies journal) 64, nos. 3–4 (March 1983): 65–102.

Dan-Xin dang'an xuanlu xingzheng bian chuji (First collection of selections from the administrative cases of the Dan-Xin archives). TWC no. 195, 1971.

Da Qing Dezong Jing (Guangxu) huangdi shilu (Veritable records of the Dezong Jing [Guangxu] emperor of the Great Qing). Taibei: Taiwan Huawen, 1964.

Davidson, James W. *The Island of Formosa: Historical View from 1430 to 1900.* New York: Macmillan, 1903.

Duara, Prasenjit. *Culture, Power, and the State: Rural North China, 1900–1942.* Stanford, Calif.: Stanford University Press, 1988.

Ebrey, Patricia Buckley, and James L. Watson, eds. *Kinship Organization in Late Imperial China, 1000–1940.* Berkeley: University of California Press, 1986.

Entenmann, Robert Eric. "Migration and Settlement in Sichuan, 1644–1796." Ph.D. dissertation, Harvard University, 1982.

Fang Hao. "Taiwan hangjiao yanjiu daoyan yu Taibei zhi 'jiao'" (Introductory remarks concerning research on Taiwan guilds and the guilds of Taibei). *Dongfang zazhi fukan* (Far Eastern Magazine supplemental publications) 5, no. 12 (June 1972): 36–50.

——. "Xinzhu zhi 'jiao'" (Xinzhu guilds). *Zhongguo lishi xuehui shixue jikan* (Chinese historical studies society, historical studies quarterly) 4 (May 1972): 309–23.

Feuerwerker, Albert. "Economic Trends in the Late Ch'ing Empire, 1870–1911." In John K. Fairbank and Kwang-ching Liu, eds., *The Cambridge History of China*, vol. 11, *Late Ch'ing, 1800–1911, Part 2*, pp. 1–69. Cambridge, Eng.: Cambridge University Press, 1980.

Friedman, Lawrence M. *History of American Law.* New York: Simon and Schuster, 1973.

Fujian shengli (Fujian provincial regulations). 8 fascicles. TWC no. 199, 1964 [ca. 1874].

Fujii Hiroshi. "Shoki ichiden ryōshu sei no shin kenkyū" (New research on the early period of the one-field, two-lords system). *Tōhōgaku* (Oriental studies) 69 (Jan. 1985): 89–104.

Gardella, Robert P. "The Boom Years of the Fukien Tea Trade, 1842–1888." In Ernest R. May and John K. Fairbank, eds., *America's China Trade in Historical Perspective*, pp. 33–75. Cambridge, Mass.: Harvard University Press for The Committee on American-East Asian Relations of the Department of History in collaboration with The Council on East Asian Studies / Harvard University, 1986.

——. "The Maritime History of Late Imperial China: Observations on Current Concerns and Recent Research." *Late Imperial China* 6, no. 2 (Dec. 1985): 48–66.

Geertz, Clifford. *Negara: The Theatre State in Nineteenth-Century Bali*. Princeton, N.J.: Princeton University Press, 1980.

Gong Debo. "Xian Taiye" (The county magistrate). In Gong, *Ye shi yuhua* (It's also foolishness), 53–84. Taibei: Zhuanji, 1969.

Guoli Taiwan daxue, Falü xuexi, ed. *Guyou fazhi yu xiandai faxue* (The traditional legal system and modern legal studies). Taibei: Ch'eng Wen, 1978.

Guo Zhiting. "Ji Jin-Guang-Fu daai xingken Zhuqian dongnan xiang" (Recording Jin-Guang-Fu large guardpost's settlement of the area southeast of Zhuqian). *Xinzhu wenxianhui tongxun* (Xinzhu historical documents committee newsletter) 13 (Apr. 1954): 1–6.

Hayes, James. *The Hong Kong Region, 1850–1911: Institutions and Leadership in Town and Countryside*. Hamdon, Conn.: Archon Books, 1977.

Hsiao, Kung-chuan. *Compromise in Imperial China*. Seattle: University of Washington, School of International Studies, 1979.

——. *Rural China: Imperial Control in the Nineteenth Century*. Seattle: University of Washington Press, 1960.

Hsu, Dau-Lin. "Crime and Cosmic Order." *Harvard Journal of Asiatic Studies* 30 (1970): 111–25.

Hsu, Wen-hsiung. "From Aboriginal Island to Chinese Frontier: The Development of Taiwan Before 1683." In Ronald G. Knapp, ed., *China's Island Frontier: Studies in the Historical Geography of Taiwan*, pp. 3–29. Honolulu: The University Press of Hawaii and The Research Corporation of the University of Hawaii, 1980.

——. "Frontier Social Organization and Social Disorder in Ch'ing Taiwan." In Ronald G. Knapp, ed., *China's Island Frontier: Studies in the Historical Geography of Taiwan*, pp. 87–105. Honolulu: The University Press of Hawaii and The Research Corporation of the University of Hawaii, 1980.

Hu, Shiu-ying, with editorial assistance from Y. C. Kong and Paul P. H. But. *An Enumeration of Chinese Materia Medica*. Hong Kong: The Chinese University Press, 1980.

Huang Liuhong. *Fuhui quanshu* (A complete book concerning happiness and benevolence). Jiusi series, no. 53. Reprint of 1850 Japanese edition annotated by Obata Yukihiro, republished 1974 with an introduction by Yamane Yukio; Taibei: Jiusi, 1978 [1699]. Translated by Djang Chu as *A Complete Book Concerning Happiness and Benevolence: A Manual for Local Magistrates in Seventeenth-Century China*. Tucson: The University of Arizona Press, 1984.

Huang, Philip C. C. *The Peasant Economy and Social Change in North China*. Stanford, Calif.: Stanford University Press, 1985.

Huang Shujing. *Taihai shichalu* (A tour of duty in the Taiwan sea). TWC no. 4, 1957 [1736].

Huang Youxing. "Tan bensheng Wenxianhui shouzang de Riben tushu" (A discussion of the provincial historical commission's collection of Japanese books). TW 32, no. 3 (Sept. 1981): 100–119.

Huang Zhongsheng. *Xinzhu fengwu zhi* (A record of Xinzhu folkways). Lianhe, Xinzhu branch, 1960.

Hucker, Charles O. *A Dictionary of Official Titles in Imperial China*. Stanford, Calif.: Stanford University Press, 1985.

Hui Cun. "Qingdai Taiwan zhi zufu" (Rent and taxes in Qing period Taiwan). TW 10, no. 2 (June 1959): 91–147.

Huixinshi zang Dan-Xin dang'an (Dan-Xin archives documents stored in the Huixin household). Extract from *Chenshi zupu* (Chen lineage genealogy). N.p., n.d.

Hulsewé, Anton F. P. "'Contracts' of the Han Period." In Lionella Lanciotti, ed., *Il Diritto in cina: Teoria e Applicazioni durante le Dinastie Imperiali e Problematica del Diritto Cinese Contemporaneo*, pp. 11–38 (Venice: Leo S. Olschki, 1978).

——. *Remnants of Han Law*, vol. 1. Leiden: E. J. Brill, 1955.

Hummel, Arthur W. *Eminent Chinese of the Ch'ing Period*. One-volume reprint ed. Taibei: Ch'eng Wen, 1970 [1943].

Ino Kanori. *Taiwan bunka shi* (Cultural history of Taiwan). 3 vols. Tokyo: Tōkōshoin, 1965 [1928].

Jiang Daozhang. "Taiwan Danshui zhi lishi yu maoyi" (History and trade of Danshui, Taiwan). *Taiwan yinhang jikan* (Bank of Taiwan quarterly) 14, no. 3 (Sept. 1963): 264–78.

Jiangsu xin yixueyuan, comp. *Zhongyao dazidian* (A large dictionary of Chinese medicine). Shanghai: Shanghai kexue jishu, 1977.

Johnson, Wallace S., translated with an introduction. *The T'ang Code*. Vol. 1, *General Principles*. Princeton, N.J.: Princeton University Press, 1979.

Ke Fangzhi. "Qingdai Taiwan zhi fangwu zulin" (House rents in Qing period Taiwan). In Guoli Taiwan daxue, Falü xuexi, ed., *Guyou fazhi yu xiandai faxue* (The traditional legal system and modern legal studies), 231–45. Taibei: Ch'eng Wen, 1978.

Keightley, David N. "Early Civilization in China: Reflections on How It Became Chinese." In Paul S. Ropp, ed., *Heritage of China: Contemporary Perspectives on Chinese Civilization*, 15–54. Berkeley: University of California Press, 1990.

Kinashi Ryōzōrō. "Shinchiku oyobi Toshien chihō ni okeru tochi kyūkan" (Old customs of the locality from Xinzhu to Taoyuan). TKK 1, no. 8 (Aug. 1901): 58–67; 1, no. 11 (Nov. 1901): 67–72; 1, no. 12 (Dec. 1901): 42–46.

Knapp, Ronald G. "Land Tenure in Eighteenth Century Taiwan." *China Geographer* 2 (1975): 39–48.

Kobayashi Rihei. "Taiwan jii" (A collection of Taiwanese words) (1–16). TKK 3, no. 8; 4, no. 4 (Aug. 1903–Apr. 1904); 4, nos. 6–9 (June–Sept. 1904); 4, no. 11; 5, no. 1 (Nov. 1904–Jan. 1905).

Kuhn, Philip A. *Rebellion and Its Enemies in Late Imperial China: Militarization and Social Structure, 1796–1854*. Paperback ed. with a new preface by the author. Cambridge, Mass.: Harvard University Press, 1980 [1970].

Kurihara Jun. "Shindai chūbu Taiwan no ichi kōsatsu: Shōka chihō ni okeru ichiten ryōshū sei o meguru shomondai" (An examination of central Taiwan during the Qing period: Some questions concerning the one-field, two-lords system in the Zhanghua area). *Tōyō gakuhō* (Oriental journal) 64, nos. 3–4 (Mar. 1983): 33–64.

Lamley, Harry J. "The Formation of Cities: Initiative and Motivation in Building Three Walled Cities in Taiwan." In G. William Skinner, ed., *The City in Late Imperial China*, pp. 155–209. Stanford, Calif.: Stanford University Press, 1977.

——. "*Hsiehtou*: The Pathology of Violence in Southeastern China." *Ch'ing-shih wen-t'i* 3, no. 7 (1977): 1–39.

——. "Subethnic Rivalry in the Ch'ing Period." In Emily Ahern and Hill Gates, eds., *The Anthropology of Taiwanese Society*, pp. 282–318. Stanford, Calif.: Stanford University Press, 1981.

Lan Dingyuan. *Dongzhengji* (Record of the eastern campaign). TWC no. 12, 1958 [1732].

Lattimore, Owen D. "The Frontier in History." In Robert A. Manners and David Kaplan, eds., *Theory in Anthropology: A Sourcebook*, pp. 374–86. Chicago: Aldine, 1968.

Lee, Robert H. G. *The Manchurian Frontier in Ch'ing History*. Cambridge, Mass.: Harvard University Press, 1970.

Lian Heng (Yatang). *Taiwan yudian* (Taiwanese dictionary). Jindai Zhongguo shiliao congkan xubian di wushiyi ji (Collectanea of modern Chinese historical materials, supplement, no. 51), Shen Yunlong, ed., vol. 507. Taibei: Wenhai, 1978.

Lian Wenxi. "Kejia ruken Taiwan diqu kaolue" (A brief study of Hakka settlement in Taiwan). TW 22, no. 3 (Sept. 1971): 1–25.

Lian Yatang. *Taiwan tongshi* (A comprehensive history of Taiwan). Taibei: Zhongwen, 1979 [1918].

Li Guoqi. "Qingji Taiwan neidihua zhengce chuangshizhe: gongzhong tiguo de Shen Baozhen" (The initiator of the policy of transforming Taiwan into Chinese territory during the Qing period: Shen Baozhen "the loyal"). *Youshi yuekan* (Young lion monthly) 44, no. 5 (Nov. 1976): 39–45.

——. *Zhongguo xiandaihua de quyu yanjiu: Min-Zhe-Tai diqu, 1860–1916* (Regional studies of China's modernization: The Fujian-Zhejiang-Taiwan area). Taibei: Zhongyang yanjiuyuan, Jindaishisuo, 1982.

Lin Hengdao, chief ed. *Taiwan dili ji lishi* (Taiwan geography and history). Vol. 9, *Guanshi zhi* (Records of government officials). 3 fascicles. Taizhong: Taiwan Provincial Historical Commission, 1980.

——, chief ed. *Taiwan sheng tongzhi* (A comprehensive history of the province of Taiwan). Taibei: Taiwan Provincial Historical Commission, 1968.

Lin Manhong. *Cha, tang, zhangnao ye yu wan Qing Taiwan* (The tea, sugar, and camphor industries and late Qing Taiwan). Taibei: Taiwan yinhang, jingji yanjiusuo, Taiwan yanjiu congkan (Taiwan research collectanea), no. 115, 1978.

Lin Renchuan and Wang Puhua. "Qingdai Fujian renkou xiang Taiwan de liudong" (Population flows from Fujian to Taiwan during the Qing period). *Lishi yanjiu* (Historical research) 2 (1983): 130–41.

Li Rongzhong. "Qingdai Ba xian yamen shuli yu chaiyi" (Clerks and runners in the Ba county yamen during the Qing period). *Lishi dang'an* (History archives), no. 1 (1989): 95–102.

Li Ruhe. "Qingdai zhu Tai banbing fangshu kao" (A study of the defense system of rotational stationing of troops in Qing period Taiwan). TW 21, no. 3 (Sept. 1970): 1–21.

Liu, Chang Bin. "Chinese Commercial Law in the Late Ch'ing (1842–1911): Jurisprudence and the Dispute Resolution Process in Taiwan." Ph.D. dissertation, University of Washington, 1983.

Liu Jincao, comp. *Qingchao xu wenxian tongkao* (Supplement to the comprehensive study of documents of the Qing dynasty). Shanghai: Shangwu, 1936 [1921].

Liu Niling. *Qingdai Taiwan minbian yanjiu* (Research on popular uprisings in Qing period Taiwan). *Guoli Taiwan shifan daxue lishi yanjiusuo zhuankan* (National Taiwan Normal University Historical Research Institute monographs), no. 9; Taibei: Guoli Taiwan shifan daxue, 1983.

Lojewski, Frank A. "The Soochow Bursaries: Rent Management During the Late Ch'ing." *Ch'ing-shih wen-t'i* 4, no. 3 (June 1980): 43–65.

MacKay, George Leslie. *From Far Formosa: The Island, Its People and Missions.* J. A. MacDonald, ed. Taibei: Ch'eng Wen, 1972 [1896].

MacKinnon, Stephen R. *Power and Politics in Late Imperial China: Yuan Shikai in Beijing and Tianjin, 1901–1908*. Berkeley: University of California Press, 1980.

McLeod, Katrina C. D., and Robin D. S. Yates, "Forms of Ch'in law: An Annotated Translation of the *Feng-chen shih*." *Harvard Journal of Asiatic Studies* 41, no. 1 (1981): 111–63.

Mair, Victor H. "Language and Ideology in the Written Popularizations of the *Sacred Edict*." In David Johnson, Andrew J. Nathan, and Evelyn S. Rawski, eds., *Popular Culture in Late Imperial China*, pp. 325–59. Berkeley: University of California Press, 1985.

Mann, Susan. *Local Merchants and the Chinese Bureaucracy, 1750–1950*. Stanford, Calif.: Stanford University Press, 1987.

Mayers, William F. *The Chinese Government: A Manual of Chinese Titles, Categorically Arranged and Explained, with an Appendix*. G. M. H. Playfair, rev. Taibei: Ch'eng Wen, 1970 [1897].

Meskill, Johanna Menzel. *A Chinese Pioneer Family: The Lins of Wu-feng, Taiwan, 1729–1895*. Princeton, N.J.: Princeton University Press, 1979.

Metzger, Thomas A. *Escape from Predicament: Neo-Confucianism and China's Evolving Political Culture*. New York: Columbia University Press, 1977.

Min Tu-ki. *National Polity and Local Power: The Transformation of Late Imperial China*. Philip A. Kuhn and Timothy Brooks, eds. Cambridge, Mass.: The Council on East Asian Studies/Harvard University and the Harvard-Yenching Institute; distributed by the Harvard University Press, 1989.

Miyazaki, Ichisada. "The Administration of Justice During the Sung Dynasty." In Jerome Alan Cohen, R. Randle Edwards, and Fu-mei Chang Chen, eds., *Essays on China's Legal Tradition*, pp. 56–75. Princeton, N.J.: Princeton University Press, 1980.

Moser, Michael. *Law and Social Change in a Chinese Community*. Dobbs Ferry, N.Y.: Oceana Publications, 1982.

Muramatsu, Yuji. "A Documentary Study of Chinese Landlordism in Late Ch'ing and Early Republican Kiangnan." *Bulletin of the School of Oriental and African Studies* 29, no. 3 (1966): 566–99.

——. *Kindai Kōnan no sosan: Chūgoku jinushi seido no kenkyū* (Rent bursaries in modern Jiangnan: Studies of the Chinese landlord system). Tokyo: Tōkyō daigaku shuppankai, 1970.

Murray, Laura May Kaplan. "New World Food Crops in China: Farms, Food, and Families in the Wei River Valley, 1650–1910." Ph.D. dissertation, University of Pennsylvania, 1985.

Myers, Ramon H. "The Commercialization of Agriculture in Modern China." In W. E. Willmott, ed, *Economic Organization in Chinese Society*, pp. 173–91. Stanford, Calif.: Stanford University Press, 1972.

——. "Taiwan Under Ch'ing Imperial Rule, 1684–1895: The Traditional Order; The Traditional Economy; The Traditional Society." *The Journal of the Institute of Chinese Studies of The Chinese University of Hong Kong* 4, no. 2 (Dec. 1971): 495–520; 5, no. 2 (Dec. 1972): 373–409, 413–51.

Na Silu. *Qingdai zhou xian yamen shenpan zhidu* (The judicial system in department and county courts during the Qing period). *Wenshizhexue jicheng* (Collected studies on literature, history and philosophy), no. 77. Taibei: Wenshizhe, 1982.

Ng, Chin-keong. *Trade and Society: The Amoy Network on the China Coast, 1683–1735*. Singapore: Singapore University Press, 1983.

Niida Noboru. *Chūgoku hōseishi kenkyū* (Studies in Chinese legal history). 3 vols. Tokyo: Tōkyō daigaku shuppankai, 1959.

Ocko, Jonathan K. "Hierarchy and Harmony: Family Conflict as Seen in Ch'ing Legal Cases." In Kwang-Ching Liu, ed., *Orthodoxy in Late Imperial China*, pp. 212–30. Berkeley: University of California Press, 1990.

——. "I'll Take It All the Way to Beijing: Capital Appeals in the Qing." JAS 47, no. 2 (May 1988): 291–315.

Oda Yorozu. *Qingguo xingzhengfa fanlun* (Outline of the administrative law of the Qing state). Taibei: Huashi, 1979 [1909].

Okamatsu, Santaro. *Provisional Report on Investigations of Laws and Customs in the Island of Formosa*. Taibei: Ch'eng Wen, 1971 [1902].

Pan Chaoyang. "Xinzhu xian diqu tongsu zongjiao de fenbu" (The distribution of popular religions in the Xinzhu county area). *Taiwan fengwu* (Taiwan folkways) 31, no. 4 (Dec. 1981): 27–50.

Pasternak, Burton. *Guests in the Dragon: Social Demography of a Chinese District, 1895–1946*. New York: Columbia University Press, 1983.

Perdue, Peter C. *Exhausting the Earth: State and Peasant in Hunan, 1500–1850*. Cambridge, Mass.: Harvard University Press, 1987.

Perkins, Dwight. *Agricultural Development in China, 1368–1968*. Chicago: Aldine, 1969.

Qian Shifu. *Qingji zhongyao zhiguan nianbiao* (Chronological tables of important officials of the Qing era). Beijing: Zhonghua, 1959.

Qingdai Taiwan dazu diaocha shu (Qing period Taiwan large-rent investigation documents). Originally published as Rinji Taiwan tochi chōsakyoku, *Taiso torishirabe sho fuzoku sankōsho* (Large-rent investigation documents with appended reference volumes). Taihoku (Taibei): Taiwan sōtokufu. TWC no. 152, 1963 [1904].

Qing Dezong (Guangxu) shilu xuanji (Selections from the veritable record of Qing Dezong [Guangxu]). TWC no. 193, 1964 [1875–1907].

Qi Sihe. *Huang Juezi zoushu, Xu Naiji zouyi, hekan* (Memorials of Huang Juezi, Memorials of Xu Naiji, published together). Beijing: Zhonghua, 1959.

Rinji Taiwan kyūkan chōsa kai. *Taiwan shihō furoku sankōsho* (Taiwan private law with appended reference volumes). 13 vols. Taipei: Southern Materials Center, 1983 [1910].

Rinji Taiwan kyūkan chōsakai dai ichi bu. *Chōsa dai ichi kai hōkokusho furoku sankōsho* (Report of the first investigation with appended reference volumes). Kyoto: Rinji Taiwan kyūkan chōsa kai, 1903.

Rinji Taiwan tochi chōsakyoku. *Taiso torishirabe sho fuzoku sankōsho*. See *Qingdai Taiwan dazu diaocha shu*.

——. *Taiwan tochi kankō ippan* (General discussion of usual practices regarding land in Taiwan). 3 vols. Taihoku: Taiwan sōtokufu, 1905.

Rowe, William T. *Hankow: Conflict and Community in a Chinese City, 1796–1895*. Stanford, Calif.: Stanford University Press, 1989.

Saeki Tomi. "Shindai no kyōyaku, chiho ni tsuite: Shindai chihō gyōsei no hitokusari" (On rural compacts and local constables in the Qing period: One aspect of Qing local administration). *Tōhōgaku* (Oriental studies) 28 (July 1964): 91–100.

Sangren, Steven P. "Traditional Chinese Corporations: Beyond Kinship." JAS 43, no. 3 (May 1984): 391–415.

Schipper, Kristofer M. "The Written Memorial in Taoist Ceremonies." In Arthur P. Wolf, ed., *Religion and Ritual in Chinese Society*, pp. 309–24. Stanford, Calif.: Stanford University Press, 1974.

Scogin, Hugh T., Jr. "Between Heaven and Man: Contract and the State in Han Dynasty China." *Southern California Law Review* 63, no. 5 (July 1990): 1325–1404.

Sheng Qingyi. "Xinzhu, Taoyuan, Miaoli san xian diqu kaibi shi (shang), (xia)" (The history of the opening of the three-county region of Xinzhu, Taoyuan, and Miaoli, parts one and two). TW 31, no. 4 (Dec. 1980): 154–76; 32, no. 1 (Mar. 1981): 136–57.

Sheng Qingyi, Wang Shilang, and Gao Shupan, comp. *Taiwan shi* (A history of Taiwan). Taibei: Zhongwen, 1977.

Shepherd, John. "Rethinking Tenancy: Explaining Spatial and Temporal Variation in Late Imperial and Republican China." *Comparative Studies in Society and History* 30, no. 3 (July 1988): 403–31.

——. *Statecraft and Political Economy on the Taiwan Frontier, 1600–1800*. Stanford, Calif.: Stanford University Press, 1993.

Shiga, Shūzō. "Criminal Procedure in the Ch'ing Dynasty: With Emphasis on Its Administrative Character and Some Allusion to Its Historical Antecedents," parts I and II. *Memoirs of the Research Department of the Tōyō Bunko* 32 (1974): 1–45; 33 (1975): 115–38.

——. "Family Property and the Law of Inheritance in Traditional China." In David C. Buxbaum, ed., *Chinese Family Law and Social Change in Historical Perspective*, pp. 109–50. Seattle: University of Washington Press, 1978.

——. "Shindai shuken gamon ni okeru soshō anken o meguru jakkan no shoken: Tan-Shin tōan o shiryō to shite" (Certain observations regarding litigation in Qing period departments and counties: The Dan-Xin archives as historical material). *Hōseishi kenkyu* (Legal history research) 37, no. 1 (1987): 37–61.

——. "Tan-Shin tōan no shohoteki chishiki: soshō anken ni arawareru bunsho no ruikei" (A first step in understanding the Dan-Xin archives: Types of documents found in litigation case files). In Shimada Masao Hakushi Shōju Kinen Ronshū Kankō I-inkai, ed., *Tōyōhōshi no Tankyū: Shimada Masao Hakushi Shōju kinen ronshū* (Inquiries into East Asian legal history: Commemorative symposium in honor of Dr. Shimada Masao), pp. 253–86. Tokyo: Kyūko Shoin, 1987.

Shinchiku chō somuka, ed. *Shinchiku chōshi* (Xinzhu county gazetteer). Taihoku: Taiwan nichinichi shinpo sha, 1907.

Shi Tianfu. "Qingdai Taiwan shijie de fenhua yu chengzhang: xingzheng, junshi he guimo de xiangguan fenxi (shang), (zhong)" (Distribution and growth of cities and market towns in Qing period Taiwan: An interrelated analysis of administration, military affairs, and size, parts one and two). *Taiwan fengwu* (Taiwan folkways) 39, no. 2 (June 1989): 1–41; 40, no. 1 (Mar. 1990): 37–65.

——. "Qingdai Zhuqian diqu de 'kenqu zhuang': Cuifeng zhuang de sheli he yanbian" ("Settlement villages" in the Zhuqian area during the Qing period: The establishment and evolution of Cuifeng village). *Taiwan fengwu* (Taiwan folkways) 39, no. 4 (Dec. 1989): 33–69.

——. "Taiwan lishi dili yanjiu zhaji (er): Zhuqian, Zhuqian pu he 'luchang ban bei liumin kai'" (Miscellaneous notes concerning research on the history and geography of Taiwan [2]: Zhuqian, the Zhuqian plain and "half the deer hunting grounds have been settled by refugees"). *Taiwan fengwu* (Taiwan folkways) 39, no. 3 (Sept. 1989): 73–82.

Shue, Vivienne. *The Reach of the State: Sketches of the Chinese Body Politic.* Stanford, Calif.: Stanford University Press, 1988.

Shuqilin zhi (Shuqilin gazetteer). TWC no. 63, 1960 [1898].

Skinner, G. William. "Cities and the Hierarchy of Local Systems." In G. William Skinner, ed., *The City in Late Imperial China*, pp. 275–351. Stanford, Calif.: Stanford University Press, 1977.

——. "Marketing and Social Structure in Rural China." 3 parts. JAS 24, no. 1 (Nov. 1964): 3–44; 24, no. 2 (Feb. 1965): 195–228; 24, no. 3 (May 1965): 363–99.

Speidel, William M. "The Administrative and Fiscal Reforms of Liu Ming-ch'uan in Taiwan, 1884–1891: Foundation for Self-strengthening." JAS 35, no. 3 (May 1976): 441–59.

Sprenkel, Sybille van der. *Legal Institutions in Manchu China: A Sociological Analysis*. New York: Humanities Press, 1966.

Staunton, George Thomas, trans. *Ta Tsing Leu Lee; Being the Fundamental Laws, and a Selection from the Supplementary Statutes, of the Penal Code of China*. Taibei: Ch'eng Wen, 1966 [1810].

Strauch, Judith. "Community and Kinship in Southeastern China: The View from the Multilineage Villages of Hong Kong." JAS 43, no. 1 (Nov. 1983): 21–50.

Stuart, G. A. *Chinese Materia Medica: Vegetable Kingdom.* 2nd revised edition by Ph. Daven Wei. Taibei: Ku T'ing Book House, 1969 [1911].

Sun, E-tu Zen. *Ch'ing Administrative Terms.* Cambridge, Mass.: Harvard University Press, 1961.

Sung, Kwang-yu. "Religion and Society in Ch'ing and Japanese Colonial Taipei (1644–1945)." Ph.D. dissertation, University of Pennsylvania, 1990.

Suzuki Sōgen. "Taiwan no kyūsoshōhō" (Taiwan's former litigation rules). TKK 1, no. 2 (Feb. 1901): 1–17; 1, no. 3 (Mar. 1901): 14–23; 1, no. 4 (Apr. 1901): 1–25.

Taiwan sōtokufu kambō bunshoka, comp. *Taiwan shashinjō* (A collection of photographs of Taiwan). Tokyo: Tayama Sōgyo, 1908.

Taizhong, Taiwan. Taiwan Provincial Historical Commission Archives. Taiwan Sōtokufu. *Taiwan Sōtokufu kōbun ruisan* (Classified collection of Taiwan government-general documents).

Tang Zangun. *Taiyang jianwen lu* (A record of things seen and heard in Taiwan). TWC no. 30, 1958 [1891].

Tao Xisheng. *Qingdai zhou xian yamen xingshi shenpan zhidu ji chengxu* (The system and procedures of criminal case adjudication in Qing period department and county courts). Taibei: Jingji yuekan, 1972.

Thompson, Roger R. "Visions of the Future, Realities of the Day: Local Administrative Reform, Electoral Politics, and Traditional Chinese Society on the Eve of the 1911 Revolution." Ph.D. dissertation, Yale University, 1985.

Tōen chō, comp. *Tōen chōshi* (Taoyuan county gazetteer). Taoyuan: Taoyuan District Government, 1906.

Tomita Yoshirō. "Taiwan shuraku no kenkyū" (Research on Taiwan's villages). In Wang Rende, ed., *Taiwan bunka ronsō dai ichi shū* (Treatises on Taiwan's culture, first collection), pp. 149–221. Taihoku: Shimizu Bookstore, 1943.

Upham, Frank K. *Law and Social Change in Postwar Japan.* Cambridge, Mass.: Harvard University Press, 1987.

VanderMeer, Canute, and Paul VanderMeer. "Land Property Data on Taiwan." JAS 28, no. 1 (Nov. 1968): 144–50.

Wakeman, Frederic, Jr. *Strangers at the Gate: Social Disorder in South China, 1839–1861.* Berkeley: University of California Press, 1966.

Waley-Cohen, Joanna. *Exile in Mid-Qing China: Banishment to Xinjiang, 1758–1820.* New Haven, Conn.: Yale University Press, 1991.

Waltner, Ann. *Getting an Heir: Adoption and the Construction of Kinship in Late Imperial China.* Honolulu: University of Hawaii Press, 1990.

Wang Shiqing. "Haishan shihua (shang)" (Haishan historical anecdotes, part one). *Taibei wenxian* (Taibei documents) 37 (Sept. 1976): 49–131.

——. "Minjian xinyang zai bu tong zuji yimin de xiangcun zhi lishi" (A history of popular beliefs in a village of settlers of different places of origin). TW 23, no. 3 (Sept. 1972): 1–33.

——. "Qingdai Taiwan de michan yu wai xiao" (Rice production and export sales in Qing period Taiwan). TW 9, no. 1 (Mar. 1958): 15–32.

——. "Qingmo jiansheng qianhou Taiwan junzheng shouzhang yu difang tushen zhi guanxi" (The relationship between local elites and the commanders of Taiwan's military government around the time of the establishment of provincial status in the late Qing). *Youshi yuekan* (Young lion monthly) 44, no. 5 (Nov. 1976): 46–57.

Wang Yitao. "Guangfu qian Taiwan zhi tudi zhidu yu tudi zhengce" (The land system and land policies in preretrocession Taiwan). *Taiwan yinhang jikan* (Bank of Taiwan quarterly) 15, no. 2 (June 1964): 295–329.

Watson, Alan. *Society and Legal Change*. Edinburgh: Scottish Academic Press, 1977.

Watson, James L. "Chinese Kinship Reconsidered: Anthropological Perspectives on Historical Research." *China Quarterly* 92 (Dec. 1982): 589–622.

——. "Standardizing the Gods: The Promotion of T'ien Hou ('Empress of Heaven') Along the South China Coast, 960–1960." In David Johnson, Andrew J. Nathan, and Evelyn S. Rawski, eds., *Popular Culture in Late Imperial China*, pp. 292–324. Berkeley: University of California Press, 1985.

Watt, John R. *The District Magistrate in Late Imperial China*. New York: Columbia University Press, 1972.

Wei Shuizhu. "Shen Baozhen dui Taiwan maixiang xiandaihua de yingxiang" (The influence of Shen Baozhen on Taiwan's march toward modernization). TW 33, no. 2 (June 1982): 103–9.

Wen Fu, comp. *(Qinding chongxiu) Liubu chufen zeli* ([Imperially directed, revised reprint] of regulations on administrative sanctions of the Six Boards]). 2 vols. Taibei: Wenhai, 1974 [1887].

Wills, John E. Jr. "Maritime China from Wang Chih to Shih Lang: Themes in Peripheral History." In Jonathan D. Spence and John E. Wills, Jr., eds., *From Ming to Ch'ing: Conquest, Region, and Continuity in Seventeenth-Century China*, pp. 201–38. New Haven, Conn.: Yale University Press, 1979.

Wolf, Arthur P., and Chieh-shan Huang. *Marriage and Adoption in China, 1845–1945*. Stanford, Calif.: Stanford University Press, 1980.

Wong, K. Chimin, and Wu Lien-teh. *History of Chinese Medicine*. New York: AMS Press, 1973 [1936].

Wu Xueming. *Jin-Guang-Fu ken'ai yu Xinzhu dongnan shanqu de kaifa* (The Jin-Guang-Fu settler guardpost and the opening of the mountain region southeast of Xinzhu). Taibei: Guoli Taiwan Shifan Daxue, Lishi Yanjiusuo zhuankan 14 (National Taiwan Normal University, Historical Research Institute Special Publication, No. 14), 1986.

Wu Ziguang. *Taiwan jishi* (Records of Taiwan incidents). TWC no. 36, 1959 [1875].

Xiao Yishan. *Qingdai tongshi* (Comprehensive history of the Qing period). 5 vols. Taibei: Taiwan shangwu, 1962 [1923].

Xinzhu xian zhidu kao (A study of Xinzhu county's institutions). TWC no. 101, 1961 [ca. 1898].

Xue Yunsheng. *Duli cunyi* (Concentration on doubtful matters while perusing the substatutes). Punctuated and edited by Huang Jingjia. 5 vols. Taibei: Chinese Materials and Research Aids Service Center, 1970 [1905].

Yang Guozhen. "Taiwan yu dalu da-xiaozu qiyue guanxi de bijiao yanjiu" (Comparative research on large- and-small rent contractual relations in Taiwan and the mainland). *Lishi yanjiu* (Historical research), no. 4 (1983): 121–35.

Yang Xi. *Qingdai Taiwan: zhengce yu shehui bianqian* (Qing period Taiwan: Government policy and social change). Taibei: Tiangong, 1983.

Yao Yuxiang and Hu Yangshan, eds. *Da Qing lüli huitong xinzuan* (Comprehensive new edition of the statutes and substatutes of the Great Qing). 5 vols. with consecutive pagination. Taibei: Wenhai, 1964 [1873].

Yin Zhangyi. *Taiwan jindaishi lun* (Essays on Taiwan's modern history). Zili congshu no. 30. Taibei: Zili wanbao, 1986.

——. "Xinzhuang xunjian zhi shezhi ji qi zhiquan, gongneng: Qingdai fenshou xunjian zhi yige an yanjiu (shang), (xia)" (The establishment of the Xinzhuang police chief and his authority and function: Research on one example of a Qing period police chief). *Shihuo yuekan* (Economic monthly) n.s. 11, no. 8 (Nov. 1981): 351–70; 11, no. 9 (Dec. 1981): 389–404.

Zelin, Madeleine. *The Magistrate's Tael: Rationalizing Fiscal Reform in Eighteenth-Century Ch'ing China*. Berkeley: University of California Press, 1984.

——. "The Rights of Tenants in Mid-Qing Sichuan: A Study of Land-Related Lawsuits in the Baxian Archives." JAS 45, no. 3 (May 1986): 499–526.

Zeng Wangyang. *Taiwan jiaotong shi* (History of Taiwan's transportation and communications). Taibei: Taiwan yinhang, 1953.

Zhang Deze. *Qingdai guojia jiguan kaolue* (Summary study of the nation's organizations during the Qing period). Beijing: Zhongguo renmin daxue, 1981.

Zhang Gucheng. *Xinzhu congzhi* (General gazetteer of Xinzhu). Xinzhu: Xinzhu congzhi bianzheng weiyuanhui, 1954.

Zhang Guohua, ed. *Zhongguo falü sixiang shi* (History of Chinese legal thought). Beijing: Falü chubanshe, 1982.

Zhang Jinfan, Zhang Xipo, and Zeng Xianyi, eds. *Zhongguo fazhi shi* (History of Chinese law), vol. 1. Beijing: Zhongguo renmin daxue, 1981.

Zhang Shengyan. "Qingdai Taiwan Hanren tudi suoyou xingtai zhi yanjiu" (Research on the forms of landownership among Han Chinese in Qing period Taiwan). TW 34, no. 2 (June 1983): 15–42.

Zhang Shixian. *Wan Qing zhi Tai zhengce (Tongzhi shisan nian zhi Guangxu ershiyi nian)* (Late Qing policies for ruling Taiwan [1874–1895]). Taibei: Dongwu daxue chubanshe, 1978.

Zhang Weiren (Chang Wejen). *Qingdai fazhi yanjiu* (Research on the legal system of the Qing period). 3 vols. Zhongyang yanjiuyuan, Lishi yuyan yanjiusuo Special Publications series, no. 76. Taibei: Zhongyang yanjiuyuan, Lishi yuyan yanjiusuo, 1983.

Zhang Yongwu. "Qingji Taiwan zhi huobi liutong kao" (A study of the circulation of money in Qing Taiwan). *Taiwan yinhang jikan* 1, no. 2 (Sept. 1947): 78–96.

Zhao Erxun et al. *Qing shi gao* (Draft standard history of the Qing). 18 vols. Punctuated and indexed by Yang Jialuo et al. Taibei: Dingwen shuju, 1981 [1928].

Zheng Pengyun and Zeng Fengzhen. *Xinzhu xianzhi chugao* (First draft of a gazetteer of Xinzhu county). TWC no. 61, 1959 [1898].

Zhou Shengren. "Qingdai Taiwan mijia zhi" (A record of rice prices in Qing period Taiwan). *Taiwan yinhang jikan* (Bank of Taiwan quarterly) 15, no. 4 (1964): 291–310.

Zhou Xianwen. *Qingdai Taiwan jingji shi* (The economic history of Qing period Taiwan). Taibei: Taiwan yinhang, jingji yanjiusuo; Taiwan yanjiu congkan [Taiwan research collectanea, no. 45], 1957.

Zhou Zongxian. "Qingdai Taiwan minjian de diyuan zuzhi" (Geographically based organizations among the people of Taiwan during the Qing period). TW 34, no. 2 (June 1983): 1–13.

Zhuang Jinde. "Taiwan tunzheng zhi xingfei" (The rise and decline of military settlement government in Taiwan). TW 11, no. 4 (Dec. 1960): 33–107.

Zhuang Shunyuan. "Dajia qi xunjian xiaokao" (A small study of the Dajia River police chief). *Shiji kankao* (Investigation of historic events) (June 1979): 120–22.

Zhuang Yingzhang and Chen Yundong. "Wan Qing Taiwan beibu Hanren tuoken xingtai de yanbian: yi Beipu Jiangjia de kenbi shiye weili" (The evolution of forms of Han Chinese expansion and settlement in late Qing northern Taiwan: Based on the example of the Beipu Jiang family's settlement activities). In Qu Haiyuan and Zhang Yinghua, eds., *Taiwan shehui yu wenhua bianqian (shangce)* (Social and cultural change in Taiwan, vol. 1), pp. 1–43. Taibei, Nangang: Zhongyang yanjiuyuan, Minzuxue yanjiusuo; Monograph Series B, No. 16, 1986.

Zhuo Kehua. "Xinzhu hangjiao chutan" (Preliminary remarks on Xinzhu guilds). *Taibei wenxian* 63/64 (June 1983): 213–42.

Character List

ai 隘
aiding 隘丁
aishou 隘首
aiwu 隘務
andu 案蠹
aoshen 熬審
bachi baolan baihui mengzhu 把持包攬拜會盟主
Baguahui 八卦會
baguan 覇管
baiyi 白役
ban 班
ban 瓣
banbing 班兵
banli bushan 辦理不善
banshi buqian 辦事不前
banzi 板子
bao 堡
baoan 包案
baogao 抱告
baojia 保甲
baojie zhuang 保結狀
baozhang 堡長
baozheng 保正
baozhong 包種
bashou 覇收
baya 快衙
bazhan 覇佔
bei you ying 北右營
beigao 被告
benyi 本役
bing 稟
bingfang 兵房
bingxiang 兵餉
bingxu 兵糈
bugu 補谷
bukuai 捕快
buyi 捕役
buyuan 不愿
caichan qinduo 財產侵奪

caizheng 財政
canbo kulei dianren 殘剝苦累佃人
caoshu 草書
cebao 册報
chafang 茶房
Chafang guan 茶房舘
chai 差
chaiyi kanya renfan shensi. . . . 差役看押人犯身死
chaofeng 抄封
chaoya 抄押
cheng 呈
cheng 承
cheng bak shuitian zi 承墣水田字
chengfa fang 承發房
chenggong 城工
chenghu 城虎
chengshi 誠實
chengzhuang ren 呈狀人
chi 笞
chige 斥革
chize 笞責
chize guanya 笞責管押
chō 町
chuancheng 傳呈
chuanxiao 傳銷
chuanzheng 船政
chuoji 戳記
Cihe gong 慈和宮
congshansuo 從善所
cuicheng 催呈
da'ai 大隘
dabi 大辟
daishu 代書
dan 担
dan 單
Dan-Xin dang'an 淡新檔案
dancui 單催
dangshen 黨參
daobi 倒閉
daomai 盜賣
daozei wozhu 盜賊窩主
dasaofu 打掃夫
dasun yin 大孫銀
dazu 大租
dazuhu 大租戶
dian 典
dian 佃
diandang 典當
dianhu 佃戶
dianmai 典賣
dianqi 店契
dianshi 典史
dianshou 佃首
diao 吊
dibao 地保
difang guan buneng chajin songshi raohai 地方官不能查禁訟師擾害
dingyan 定讞
dongfang 冬防
dongshi 董事
dou 斗
douji 斗級
du'an 蠹案
dubo 賭博
duibao 對堡
duibaoyi 對堡役
dunfan 磡犯
enzhao 恩照
eque 額缺
erkuai waishi 二快外室
ewai 額外

faling 法令
fan hui chi 反悔遲
fan shengyuan 番生員
fandazu 番大租
fang 房
fanzui cunliu yangqin 犯罪存留養親
fawai zhi en 法外之恩
feitu 匪徒
fencuan jiushu 分爨鬮書
fenghua 風化
fengren baoguan suojin 瘋人報官鎖禁
fenjia 分家
fenju 分局
fugongsheng 附貢生
fuken 撫墾
Fumu hui 父母會
ganfeng 感風
ganguo dian 乾菓店
ganjie zhuang 甘結狀
ganmao 感冒
ganzheng 干證
ge yu chengli 格于成例
gending 跟丁
gong'an 公案
gongbing 弓兵
gongcheng 工程
gongfang 工房
gonggong zhixu 公共秩序
gongguan 公舘
gonghao 公號
gongpai 功牌
gongqin 公親
gongsheng 貢生
gongxiang 公項
gongye 公業
guaijian 拐姦
guan 舘
guan'ai 官隘
guanli 官吏
guanli cisong jiaren su 官吏詞訟家人訴
guanshi 管事
guanzhuang 官莊
guilu cheng 跪路呈
gujin gukan pingren 故禁故勘平人
gunjin 棍緍
guofangzi 過房子
guoke bingxu 國課兵糈
haidao 海盗
Han dazu 漢大租
hancheng 喊呈
hao 號
haoxian 耗羨
hegu 合股
hexi cheng 和息呈
hexi ganjie zhuang 和息甘結狀
heyue 合約
heyuezi 合約字
housu 厚俗
huanbing 患病
huangmiu taishen 荒謬太甚
huaya 花押
hubu 戶部
hufang 戶房
huhun tiantu deng xishi 戶婚田土等細事
hui 會
huifen 毀墳
huikang 會抗
huiqi 毀棄
huizhong kangna 會衆抗納
hulü 戶律
huohao 火耗

huoqian 火籤
hutoujian 虎頭監
huyong 護勇
huzhu yijie 互助移解
ji 即
ji'an yadu 積案衙蠹
jia 甲
jia 枷
jia yi xinghe 加以刑嚇
jiancheng 僉呈
jianfan 監犯
jiangdu lüling 講讀律令
jianhu 監護
jianjin chakan 監禁察看
jianmin 賤民
jianshe 建設
jiansheng 監生
jiantiao 肩挑
jianwen 簡文
jianyu 監獄
jiao 醮
jiao 角
jiao san shanfu 轎傘扇夫
jiaohang 郊行
jiaosuo 轎所
jiaotong 交通
jiaoxiao 繳銷
jiaoyin zhuang 繳銀狀
jiaren 家人
jiashou 甲首
jiaye 家業
jie 街
jiebu ji tijie waisheng fanren jiyu yiliang 解部及提解外省犯人給與衣糧
jiedai 借貸
jiehun 結婚
jieku 解庫
jieshou 結首
jikai 計開
jikou huyuan 極口呼冤
Jin-Guang-Fu da'ai 金廣福大隘
Jin-Liu-He 金六和
jingcheng 經承
jinmai qi 盡賣契
jinshen bangong, anlian gongshi 勤慎辦公諳練公事
jinshi 進士
jinyu 禁獄
Jinyue batiao 禁約八條
jinzu 禁卒
jiu 鬮
jiufen 鬮分
jiushu 鬮書
jiuxu 救恤
jizhao 給照
juan 卷
juanshu 捐輸
jucheng ren 具呈人
juemai 絕賣
junshi 軍事
junzheng 軍政
kaishan fufan 開山撫番
kaishu 楷書
kangsuan 抗算
kangtun 抗吞
kangzu 抗租
kedian 客店
kendan 墾單
kenhu 墾戶
kenpi 墾批
kenzhao 墾照
kenzi 墾字
kezu 課租
konghe 恐嚇

kouliang 口糧
kuaishou 快手
kuaiyi 快役
kuangchan 鑛產
kuzi 庫子
lanyu 攔輿
Leigonghui 雷公會
leiqian 雷籤
leshu 勒贖
li 例
liang 兩
liangfang 糧房
liangshuifang 糧稅房
liangzongshu 糧總書
lianhuan qiejiebing 連環切結禀
lianzhuang 聯庄
lifang 吏房
lifang 禮房
ligongsheng 例貢生
lihun 離婚
liji 痢疾
lijin 釐金
ling zhuang 領狀
lingnue zuiqiu 凌虐罪囚
lingnue qingbi 凌虐情弊
lingshansheng 廩膳生
lingsheng 廩生
lingyin zhuang 領銀狀
lishishou 立實收
liuban touyi 六班頭役
liwu 吏務
longen zhuang 隆恩莊
longpu 礱舖
lougui 陋規
louxie 漏瀉
luemai 略賣
lujin 擄禁
Lüxing 呂刑
maimai 買賣
makuai 馬快
makuai zong 馬快總
maoshu 卯書
mendou 門斗
Min Yue liangsheng huifei qiangjie jubu 閩粵兩省會匪搶劫拒捕
min'ai 民隘
minci 民詞
mingling 螟蛉
minglingzi 螟蛉子
mingzi 螟子
minshi 民事
minye 民業
minzheng 民政
minzhuang 民壯
mou 畝
mousharen 謀殺人
muyou 幕友
naren leshu 拿人勒贖
nei wai gengfu 內外更夫
neilai suanming xiansheng 內來算命先生
nianlao duji xu ren daigao 年老篤疾許人代告
niaoqiangshou 鳥鎗手
nike fouchou 匿課浮抽
niqi 匿契
niupu qi 牛埔契
oushang 毆傷
pai 派
pai 牌
paishou 牌首
panchan 叛產
paoding 庖丁
Pengxu Cai shi 彭許蔡氏
pi 批

piao 票
piaocui 票催
ping 評
pinglun 評論
pu 埔
puhu 鋪戶
qi 氣
qian 錢
qian 籤
qianbi 錢幣
qiangdao 強盜
qiangdao shashang 強盜殺傷
qiangduo 搶奪
qianglu 搶擄
qianliang 錢糧
qianzhai 錢債
qicheng 期呈
qidiyin 磧地銀
qiedao 竊盜
qiejie zhuang 切結狀
qigeng 起耕
qinding 親丁
qingfu 淸賦
qingxin 靑心
qingzhe 淸摺
qingzhuang 淸庄
qinhai shuiyuan 侵害水源
qinquan 侵權
qita 其他
qiu zuo mulong zhe yiku 囚坐木籠赭衣褲
qiufan 囚犯
qiyin tianliang 欺隱田糧
Quanhe lun 勸和論
renchong zhuang 認充狀
renchuo 認戳
renming 人命
renshen ziyou 人身自由
renshi 人事
ruxue zhaifu 儒學齋夫
san fasi 三法司
sanban 三班
saorao 騷擾
shanfu 膳夫
shang heqi 傷和氣
shang 賞
shanghan 傷寒
shangshi 商事
Shangshu 尙書
she 社
shemiao 社廟
shenchi 申斥
shendong 紳董
shengfan 生番
shengxi 生息
shengyuan 生員
shewu 社務
shezu 社租
shi 石
shidou 市斗
shidui 石堆
shifu 恃符
shiquan 十全
shishou bangzhu yin zi 實收幫助銀字
shizong 失踪
shoubi lingyu zhi chu 瘦斃囹圄之處
shouyang 收養
shu 書
shufan 熟番
shuihuofu 水火夫
shuiqi 稅契
Shuishen miao 水神廟
shuizhong zhi'e 水沖之額
shuqi 書啟

sihuo 私火
sixing 四行
siyi 祀儀
songgun 訟棍
songshi 訟師
Sōtokufu 總督府
su 訴
suanming 算命
sui 歲
suodun 鎖礅
suodun shi zhong 鎖礅示衆
suye 蘇葉
tai 胎
taijie 胎借
Taiwan bei lu xiebiao 臺灣北路協標
Taiwan bunsho 臺灣文書
Taiwan wenxian weiyuanhui 臺灣文獻委員會
Taiwan wuji youmin kuanghan xionge sixing bufa 臺灣無籍遊民獷悍凶惡肆行不法
tangqian 堂籤
tangshi 堂事
tangyu 堂諭
tangzhaofang 堂招房
taowu 討物
tian 田
Tiandi hui 天地會
tianfang 田房
tianfu 田賦
tiangu zhuangyong 添僱壯勇
Tianhou gong 天后宮
tiaofan 挑販
tibi 提比
tielu 鐵路
ting 廳
tingchai 聽差
tixun mingdan 提訊名單
tongjian 通姦
tongqi 通緝
tongshi 通事
tongzhi 同知
toumenguan 頭門舘
tuanlian 團練
tuanlian zongju 團練總局
tuirang 退讓
tumu 土目
tun 屯
tunding jia 屯丁甲
tuntian 屯田
tunwu 屯務
tunzu 屯租
tuxue 吐血
waiguan 外舘
waishi 外室
weiji 委寄
weijin zhuanyin fanmai ji zangni songshi miben 違禁撰印販賣及藏匿訟師祕本
wen 文
wobei 卧碑
wojia 窩家
wugao 誣告
wugong chige 誤公斥革
wulai zhi tu 無賴之徒
wulong 烏龍
wuni 忤逆
wupin jungong 五品軍功
wusheng 武生
wusheng [yuan] 武生員
wuyi 武彝
wuzuo 仵作
xian 縣
xiancheng 縣丞
xiang 鄉

xiang 詳
xiangbao 鄉保
xiangcheng 鄉呈
xiangge 詳革
xiangshi 鄉試
xiao 銷
Xiaodaohui 小刀會
xiaozu 小租
xiaozuhu 小租戶
xiaze 下則
xiedou 械鬪
xiejia 歇家
xing 刑
xingbu zhengtang 刑部正堂
xingfang 刑房
Xingkao 刑考
xingke tiben 刑科題本
xingming 刑名
xingming muyou 刑名幕友
xingming qianliang 刑名錢糧
xingshi 刑事
xingshu 行書
xingzhang 刑杖
xingzheng 行政
xinjin 薪津
xinpiao 信票
xinzhong bugan 心中不甘
xizhuang 息庄
xuanju 選舉
xucheng 續呈
xucheng shengyuan 續呈生員
xuewu 學務
xun 訊
xundao 訓導
xundian yi 巡典役
xunjian 巡檢
xusuo 需索
yafan 押犯
yaguan 押舘
yangshan 養贍
yangshan yin 養贍銀
yanshi 驗屍
yanwu 鹽務
yaoyan 謠言
yehu 業戶
yezhu 業主
yicang 義倉
yidu 義渡
yijiao 移交
yinchuan 印串
yinshen 殷紳
yinshi shaojin 飲食少進
yisheng 醫生
yitian liang (san) zhu
一田兩(三)主
yixue 醫學
yizao waishi 一皂外室
yizhan 驛站
yongshui 用水
yongyuan jianjin 永遠監禁
youguai 誘拐
youshe 宥赦
youshi youjia 有室有家
yu 諭
yuanchai 原差
yuangao 原告
yuangao bu daoan tingshen ji tuotao
原告不到案聽審及脫逃
yucheng 輿呈
yuejuan 閱卷
Yuqiu yishi 獄囚衣食
yuzhi 諭止
zaoli 皂隸
zaoli zong 皂隸總
zashi 雜事

zha 札
zhaifu 齋夫
zhang 杖
zhangban 長班
zhangdan 丈單
zhangfang 帳房
zhangnao 樟腦
zhangsun yin 長孫銀
zhangze 掌責
zhangze 杖責
zhaofang 招房
zhaoxi qi 找洗契
zhaoze shengke 照則陞科
zhaqi 詐欺
zhengcai 爭財
zhenggong bugu qianliang 正供補谷錢糧
zhenggong 正供
zhengjie 爭界
zhengke 正課
zhengshou 徵收
zhihui 指揮
zhishan 值繕
zhishen 質審
zhitang 值堂
zhixian 知縣
zhixing 執行
zhixun 質訊
zhiyi 直役
zhizhao 執照
zhou 州
zhuang 庄
zhuangding 壯丁
zhuangfu 庄副
Zhuanggui jinyue 莊規禁約
Zhuanggui size 莊規四則
zhuangzheng 庄正
zhuchong 竹銃
zhumo 硃墨
zhuoren leshu 捉人勒贖
zi 字
zibei gongben 自備工本
zigao zishan 自稿自繕
zisu 紫蘇
zixing pudie shensi 自行撲跌身死
ziyi nishui shensi bie wu ta gu zhun gao mien jian 自縊溺水身死別無他故准告免檢
zong kenhu 總墾戶
zongjia guan 總甲舘
zongli 總理
zongwu 總務
zuguan 租舘
zujie 租借
zunyi jiezhuang 遵依結狀
zuozhuang 做狀
zuzhan 租棧

Index

In this index an "f" after a number indicates a separate reference on the next page, and an "ff" indicates separate references on the next two pages. A continuous discussion over two or more pages is indicated by a span of page numbers, e.g., "pp. 57–58." *Passim* is used for a cluster of references in close but not consecutive sequence.

Library of Congress Cataloging-in-Publication Data

Allee, Mark A. (Mark Anton)

Law and local society in late imperial China : northern Taiwan in the nineteenth century / Mark A. Allee.

p. cm.

Includes bibliographical references and index.

ISBN 0-8047-2272-2 (acid-free) :

1. Justice, Administration of—Taiwan—Tan-shui chen—History—19th century. 2. Justice, Administration of—Taiwan—Hsin-chu hsien—History—19th century. 3. Sociological jurisprudence—History—19th century. 4. Tan-shui chen (Taiwan)—Social conditions. 5. Hsin-chu hsien (Taiwan)—Social conditions. I. Title.

KNP490.T383A46 1994

340'.115'095124909034—dc20 94-30283

CIP